THE
MONSTER
SHOW

Also by David J. Skal

Hollywood Gothic:
The Tangled Web of Dracula *from Novel to Stage to Screen*

THE
MONSTER
SHOW

A Cultural History of Horror

DAVID J. SKAL

W. W. NORTON & COMPANY
NEW YORK   LONDON

Copyright © 1993 by David J. Skal

"The Spine Chillers" by Norman Jaffray Copyright © 1933
by the *Saturday Evening Post*. Reprinted by permission of
the Saturday Evening Post Society.

The text of this book is composed in 11/13 Bembo
with the display set in Latin Elongated and Mistral
Composition by the Maple-Vail Composition Services
Manufacturing by Courier Companies
Book design by Jo Anne Metsch

Library of Congress Cataloging-in-Publication Data

Skal, David J.
The monster show : a cultural history of horror / by David J. Skal.
p.   cm.
Includes bibliographical references (p.   ) and index.
1. Horror films—History and criticism.   2. Social Problems in motion
pictures.   I. Title.
PN1995.9.H6S57   1993
791.43'616—dc20   92-19242

ISBN 0-393-03419-4

W. W. Norton & Company, Inc., 500 Fifth Avenue, New York, N.Y. 10110
W. W. Norton & Company Ltd., 10 Coptic Street, London WC1A 1PU

1 2 3 4 5 6 7 8 9 0

For Hilary, Malaga, and Scott

Contents

Introduction
A SIDESHOW IN CAMELOT
15

Chapter One
TOD BROWNING'S AMERCIA
25

Chapter Two
"YOU WILL BECOME CALIGARI":
MONSTERS, MOUNTEBANKS, AND MODERNISM
37

Chapter Three
DREAD AND CIRCUSES
63

Chapter Four
THE MONSTERS AND MR. LIVERIGHT
81

Chapter Five
1931: THE AMERICAN ABYSS
113

Chapter Six
ANGRY VILLAGERS
161

Chapter Seven
"I USED TO KNOW YOUR DADDY":
THE HORRORS OF WAR, PART TWO
211

Chapter Eight
DRIVE-INS ARE A GHOUL'S BEST FRIEND:
HORROR IN THE FIFTIES
229

Chapter Nine
THE GRAVEYARD BASH
263

Chapter Ten
IT'S ALIVE, I'M AFRAID
287

Chapter Eleven
SCAR WARS
307

Chapter Twelve
"ROTTEN BLOOD"
333

Chapter Thirteen
THE DANCE OF DEARTH
353

Chapter Fourteen
THE MONSTER MILLENNIUM
381

Acknowledgments
389

Notes
391

Index
419

"I'll show you what horror means."

Fredric March in
Dr. Jekyll and Mr. Hyde
(1932)

THE
MONSTER
SHOW

A SIDESHOW IN CAMELOT

———

"It is hard to laugh at the need for beauty and romance, no matter
how tasteless, even horrible, the results of that are.
But it is easy to sigh. Few things are sadder
than the truly monstrous."

Nathanael West
The Day of the Locust
(1939)

IN OCTOBER 1961, while much of America was in an optimistic
mood, buoyant as Jackie Kennedy's trademark bouffant, Diane
Arbus had some ideas of her own.

She was holed up at the New Yorker Theatre at the corner of
Broadway and West 88th Street in Manhattan, watching for the
third time in as many nights the starkly magnified images of women
who had no need for hairdressers of any kind. Pinheads, after all,
didn't have hair to dress. And even a pillbox hat was an impossible
fashion statement if your cranium was the size of a softball.

Arbus took a drag on her marijuana cigarette. She exhaled and
the sweet cloud of smoke wafted before the projected shadows.
She knew about fashion; she was a fashion photographer, and a
respected one—the work she did with her husband Alan regularly

---

**An unsettling "family portrait" from Tod Browning's *Freaks* (1932). Thirty
years later, Diane Arbus would create a similar mood with her own disturbing photographs. (*Courtesy of Elias Savada*)**

appeared in *Harper's Bazaar, Glamour,* and *Vogue.* But there was another part of her that would not be fed by the world of commercial gloss; she felt a growing need to find and create images that were the pointed antithesis of glamour. The pinheads were great. And beyond the pinheads were big-headed dwarves, Siamese twins, a man without arms or legs who wriggled on the ground like a worm, a "half-boy" who ran on his hands, a human skeleton, and more.

She learned about the film from a friend of hers, an art promoter named Emile de Antonio, known familiarly as "De." He sometimes referred to himself, jokingly, as "a middle-aged vampire," probably in reference to his self-cultivated bad-boy image and legendary alcoholism. "Drink," De once said, "is my meat." He was also a filmmaker, about to begin work on a documentary drawn from kinescopes of the McCarthy hearings. Years later, due to another political documentary, *Millhouse,* he would end up, proudly, on the Nixon White House "enemies list."

The vérité aspects of the sideshow picture at the New Yorker interested him, and he knew that Arbus would like it, too. *Freaks* had been filmed by Metro-Goldwyn-Mayer in 1931 and released the following year to capitalize on the enormous box-office successes of Universal's *Dracula* and *Frankenstein.* The director of *Freaks,* Tod Browning, had in fact directed *Dracula* and a slew of other money-spinning pictures dealing with morbid obsessions, deformity, and mutilation. *Freaks* was considered so horrible, however, that it had been disowned by the studio and suppressed by censors overseas for almost thirty years. The original negative, one legend had it, had been dumped unceremoniously into San Francisco Bay.

The film's story was set in a circus, and had a darkly compelling, fairy-tale simplicity. A beautiful trapeze artist, played by Olga Baclanova, marries a midget for his money. At their wedding banquet in the big top, she is feted by the sideshow freaks and ritually accepted as "one of us." But the drunken bride reacts with revulsion, and is not forgiven. The freaks watch and wait while she attempts to kill her husband with slow poison. One night, at the height of a raging thunderstorm, they take their revenge. Deep in a rain-swept woods, they swarm over her. In a shocking epilogue, we see that their crude surgery and clownish costuming have transformed her into a mute, squawking amalgam of a woman and a bird, a pathetic exhibit in a shabby pit.

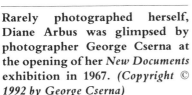

Rarely photographed herself, Diane Arbus was glimpsed by photographer George Cserna at the opening of her *New Documents* exhibition in 1967. *(Copyright © 1992 by George Cserna)*

A favorite Arbus haunt: Hubert's Museum, New York's longest-surviving flea circus and freak emporium.

In her 1984 biography *Diane Arbus,* author Patricia Bosworth paints the photographer's discovery of *Freaks* as a distinct epiphany. "She was enthralled because the freaks in the film were not imaginary monsters, but *real."* Human anomalies "had always excited, challenged and terrified her because they defied so many conventions. Sometimes she thought her terror was linked to something deep in her subconscious. Gazing at the human skeleton or the bearded lady, she was reminded of a dark, unnatural, hidden self."

Arbus had already taken some photos of twins and midgets but her discovery of the Browning film emboldened her. She began to frequent one of the last remaining freak shows in North America, Hubert's Museum on 42nd Street. In the flesh, the freaks were even more disturbing and attractive than the ones in the film had been. According to Bosworth, Arbus' reaction to the fat lady, the seal-boy, and the three-legged man was an anxious visceral excitement, accompanied by perspiration and a pounding heart. At first the freaks were aloof, but gradually they accepted the constant presence of the intense, dark-haired woman, and consented to the scrutiny of her camera. An echo of the most famous line from *Freaks* could not have escaped her, and no doubt she relished it: *We accept her—one of us!* Arbus shot her subjects with a square-format Rollei and fine-grain black-and-white film, striving for and achieving an unflinching catalog of images previously forbidden or deliberately overlooked in modern photography. The deformed. The retarded. The sexually ambiguous. The dying and the dead. All the things people wanted to look at, but had been taught they must not. She told her mentor Lisette Model that she wanted to photograph "what is evil." Evil, to Arbus' mind, evidently was synonymous with that which was taboo. And while few would contend that Arbus photographed anything that was genuinely, destructively evil, she certainly created a bad-girl niche that would go unrivaled until the rise of bad-boy Robert Mapplethorpe in the 1980s. Mapplethorpe would also use a square black-and-white format, juxtaposing forbidden imagery with the artifice of the classical still life. Arbus avoided studied compositions but had her own, recognizable mannerisms that evoked the dead-alive faces of daguerreotypes and the embalmed formalism of the wax museum.

If she had read the obituaries, Arbus would have known of the 1962 death of Tod Browning, a long-retired recluse in California. But the obituary would have told her nothing she hadn't already known or intuited. Arbus understood Tod Browning's America better than anyone. She saw that "monsters" were everywhere, that the whole of modern life could be viewed as a tawdry side-show, driven by dreams and terrors of alienation, mutilation, actual death and its everyday variations. Working-class families, through Arbus' unforgiving lens, emerged as denizens of an existential suburban sideshow. Society dowagers were close cousins to Times Square transvestites. Caught at the right moment, almost anyone could look retarded. America, it seemed, was nothing but a monster show. It was a revelation, a cause, and a creed.

The year after Arbus discovered *Freaks,* she stumbled across Tod Browning's Dracula, not in a movie theatre, but tattooed instead on the midsection of a man who called himself Jack Dracula. The word DRACULA was tattooed on his inside underlip as well. The Frankenstein monster occupied prime space, just over his navel, and nearby lurked the Phantom of the Opera, along with assorted bats, snakes, werewolves, devils, ghouls, winged dragons, and birds of prey. All in all, he had over 300 tattoos, the first of which, Arbus reported, was the image of a steel hinge, implanted in the crook of his arm. The names BORIS KARLOFF, BELA LUGOSI, and LON CHANEY were permanently engraved into his skin. Jack began being tattooed about the same time the classic Hollywood horror movies had been revived on television in the late fifties. Now he was a walking horror festival all by himself, a harbinger of the growing "monster craze" that was catching the imagination of American children, tens of thousands of whom had become devoted readers of magazines with titles like *Famous Monsters of Filmland* and *Castle of Frankenstein*. Unlike Jack Dracula, the majority of the monster-boomers decorated their bedroom walls instead of their skin; their physical experiments went no further than removable makeup effects in highly diluted, though recognizable, rites of adolescent passage and initiation. But Jack had taken one step beyond the armchair fans, using monsters as a vehicle for a true physical transformation. Like his namesake vampire, Jack had to avoid prolonged sun exposure; the light-sensitive designs contained permanently embedded dyes that could turn poisonous.

Jack Dracula was a lightning rod for the energies of the dark gods which are the subject of this book: shape-changing entities that move in the modern imagination like dream-carvings on a dark carousel. With each revolution they mutate and evolve, the better to hold our attention. There are four primary icons on this carousel, which turns to a calliope dirge: Dracula, the human vampire; the composite, walking-dead creation of Frankenstein; the werewolfish duality of Dr. Jekyll and Mr. Hyde; and, perhaps most disturbing, the freak from a nightmare sideshow—armless, legless, twisted or truncated, now shrunken, now immense—it changes each time we look, a violation of our deepest sense of the human shape and its natural boundaries. The carousel turns slowly, but steadily; if one looks long enough, one monster eventually blurs into another.

Diane Arbus' 1961 photo essay on Jack Dracula appeared in the November issue of *Harper's Bazaar,* the same publication that had previously showcased her fashion work. In a retrospective assessment, art critic Hilton Kramer noted this blurring of grotesqueries, quoting Baudelaire's dictum that, to the extent fashion represents "a sublime deformity of nature," Arbus' range as an artist presented no paradox. The fashion world, Kramer wrote, "is a world of self-conscious artifice, of cosmetic and sartorial invention, a world

Signet Classic

451-CE2363 • (CANADA $5.95) • U.S. $4.95

FRANKENSTEIN
BY MARY SHELLEY

DRACULA
BY BRAM STOKER

DR. JEKYLL AND MR. HYDE
BY ROBERT LOUIS STEVENSON

WITH AN INTRODUCTION BY
STEPHEN KING

. . . where standards of normality are under continuous revision and embellishment. . . . I can think of no better 'school' for the study of human oddities than the world in which fashion rules."

Inevitably, Arbus sought bigger prey than Times Square sideshows could offer. Dan Talbot, who ran the New Yorker Film Society, was vaguely aware of Arbus' presence in his theatre during the week-long revival of *Freaks*. "She was so attracted to the grotesque, that it didn't surprise me," he recalled. Talbot would later act as a go-between when Arbus wanted to photograph the aging Mae West for *Show* magazine. "I did it with a certain amount of trepidation," Talbot remembered. He had gained the notoriously reclusive star's trust through a correspondence that developed in the course of his reviving certain of her films. Despite Arbus' reputation as a respected fashion photographer—her most unsettling images had not yet been widely seen—Talbot was uneasy about her motives. When the spread ran, his worst fears were confirmed. Arbus' harsh images (one had the star snuggling in bed with a monkey, whose feces, the reader learned from the photographer's accompanying deadpan text, were liberally ground into the boudoir's white carpet) had turned the fading sex queen into a ghoulish sideshow. Talbot received a blistering postcard from West, whose lawyers threatened the magazine's publisher. But Arbus continued to pursue her macabre new aesthetic with a zealot's passion.

By 1967, both Diane Arbus and *Freaks* had made it to the Museum of Modern Art. They got there independently, but each no doubt helped the other. The Browning film had been rediscovered and canonized by the influential European film journals of the sixties, the decade, according to Susan Sontag, in which "freaks went public, and became a safe, approved subject of art." To Sontag, Arbus represented the "aesthetes' subversion," a peculiarly sixties phenomenon advancing "life as a horror show as an antidote to life as a bore."

The Warholian sixties marked the beginning of a tendency toward unprecedented extremes in media images. *Freaks* in its resurrection was a central driving artifact in this process, which included Warhol films (an oeuvre which would culminate in bizarre versions of

---

The interdependent natures of the major horror icons are vividly illustrated on the cover of this 1979 omnibus edition of *Frankenstein, Dracula,* and *Dr. Jekyll and Mr. Hyde. (Courtesy of New American Library)*

Dracula and *Frankenstein*), *Fellini Satyricon,* monster magazines, and Diane Arbus. As Sontag elaborates:

> Arbus's work is a good instance of a leading tendency of high art in capitalist countries: to suppress, or at least reduce, moral and sensory queasiness. Much of modern art is devoted to lowering the threshold of what is terrible. . . . Our ability to stomach this rising grotesqueness in images (moving and still) and in print has a stiff price. . . . A pseudo-familiarity with the horrible reinforces alienation, making one less able to react in real life.

Sontag's argument is one echoed time and again in discussions of extreme forms of media, be they horror movies, pornography, or the photography of Diane Arbus. Unarticulated in these arguments is a paradox: while *some* people are desensitized, others— the critics themselves—become acutely, self-righteously sensitized, the last living arbiters of exactly what is or is not "horrible." These criticisms do not take into account that there may be more to monstrous images than cultural degeneracy, or that they may contain a rich, if hidden, culture of their own. Arbus' last years were blighted by instability and depression, and certainly give the facile impression of a woman drained and destroyed by the images she beheld. But Arbus' personal history does not easily explain why the images resonated in the culture in the first place, or why so much of our imaginative life in the twentieth century has been devoted to peeling back the masks and scabs of civilization, to finding, cultivating, and projecting nightmare images of the secret self.

On July 26, 1972, Diane Arbus created her final image. After scrawling the words "The last supper" in her journal, she helped herself to a deadly banquet of barbiturates. There were no dwarves to fete her. She was found a few days later, beginning to decompose at the bottom of a drained bathtub, like Olga Baclanova in the ultimate sideshow pit. (It was rumored that she had set up a camera to record her death, though this was never proved.) By the end of her life, at the height of the Vietnam War, Diane Arbus had made a lasting mark on the world of photojournalism, which by then had few qualms about images of unprecedented frankness and brutality: napalmed children, street executions, the massacre at My Lai.

Most histories of the horror genre begin with mythological and literary antecedents—horrors and monsters of antiquity find a nineteenth-century expression in popular fiction that is borrowed and "improved" upon by the mass media of the twentieth century, leading to bigger and better monsters, more expensive movies, louder screams, spectacular new technologies of dread. In short, the story is presented as a simplistic and self-referential chronicle of "progress."

Progress is not the issue. Very little about the underlying structure of horror images really changes, though our cultural uses for them are as shape-changing as Dracula himself. Over thirty years ago, in *Love and Death in the American Novel*, Leslie Fiedler identified certain archetypal patterns of American dream-life. "Our fiction," he wrote, "is not merely a flight from the physical data of the actual world . . . It is, bewilderingly and embarrassingly, a gothic fiction, non-realistic and negative, sadist and melodramatic—a literature of darkness and the grotesque . . . a literature of horror for boys."

Fiedler's study was published in 1960, on the cusp of Kennedy's Camelot. The preoccupations he then identified as implicit in nineteenth-century fiction have become the explicit obsessions of popular culture today. Diane Arbus, in 1960, was just starting to get interested in freaks (the topic of another book by Fiedler) and the remainder of her career can be viewed, in part, as a cultural kamikaze dive into the themes and images that drive the extreme forms of media expression we categorize and marginalize as "horror." Like Tod Browning before, her, Arbus' personal obsessions had, and continue to have, a larger public significance. But in order to understand her, we first must accept her. As "one of us"—a fully participating citizen in Tod Browning's America.

Chapter One

TOD BROWNING'S AMERICA

"It's just a plain old carnival," said Will.
"Like heck," said Jim.

Ray Bradbury
Something Wicked This Way Comes
(1962)

TOD BROWNING lay in his grave, eating malted milk balls. Just twenty-one, he had already died many times, though he usually stayed dead for only a day at a stretch. But today was different; he was going for forty-eight hours underground, the better to amaze the topside rubes.

Since running away from home five years earlier, Browning had worked every job in the carnival from barker to contortionist. But his ongoing role of "The Hypnotic Living Corpse" was without question the lowest high point of his vagabond career.

He had played the part from the head of the Ohio to the mouth of the Mississippi as one of the lead attractions of a traveling "rivershow." This type of show provided a steady turnover of variety entertainment for the local amusement parks that dotted the banks of the great waterways of the American heartland. And the kind of entertainments that drew the surest crowds in the years that

Tod Browning at the height of his career. *(Courtesy of Elias Savada)*

opened the twentieth century were sensational, bizarre, and otherworldly, as if anticipating the wonders and terrors of a dawning era. Traveling families of midgets. "The Wild Man of Borneo." Fantastic patent medicines. Living corpses, resurrected before your eyes. For an admission price of twenty-five cents, you could witness the burial of Mr. Tod Browning (who had unexpectedly "died" the previous day) and receive a return ticket for his exhumation and resurrection by trumpeted nostrum the following evening. A one-day stunt was standard; the two-day burial was trickier, if more spectacular—a freak-show travesty of Easter weekend, and a guaranteed crowd-pleaser.

The first time had been the worst. "When I heard the dirt come crashing down on that coffin, I actually shivered," Browning told a reporter many years later. In time, he almost came to enjoy the confinement. The long hours underground were especially conducive to thought, he said, and he made the most of the opportunity. In the estimation of his interviewer, "That period of intensive thought did much to shape Tod's destiny and was the cause of awakening the spark of genius lying dormant within him."

What exactly does one think about in the stifling confines of a wooden casket, pinned six feet underground by a ton of earth? Browning was no master of yogic breathing (the box contained a hidden ventilation system, in addition to a sliding panel that concealed his stash of life-sustaining malted milk pellets), so it can be assumed that he remained in a more or less unaltered state of consciousness during the ordeal. But there had certainly been large changes in his life during the five years he had taken to the road. He was no longer Charles Browning, Jr., the Louisville choirboy whose angelic voice had amazed the congregation. He was Tod Browning now, his own person of no fixed address, living by his wits and energized by the excitement of easy money. There were yokels to be bilked everywhere. It was America's greatest resource, this hunger for a spectacle or a miracle, no matter how tawdry or transparent. And it sure beat working.

Charles Browning, Jr., was born in a two-story house at 1433 West Jefferson Street in Louisville, Kentucky, on July 12, 1880, the second son of Charles and Lydia Browning. He was not the only member of his family attuned to the pulse of popular obsessions and pastimes, his uncle, Pete "The Gladiator" Browning (1861–1905), was a celebrated baseball player, a legendary hitter for whom the bat later called the Louisville Slugger was originally

Tod Browning as a young man. *(Courtesy of Elias Savada)*

Pete "The Gladiator" Browning, Tod's uncle, was a flamboyant showman of the baseball field. *(Courtesy of Bret Wood)*

designed. Pete Browning was a talkative, flamboyant, superstitious sportsman who enjoyed his celebrity. He was also an alcoholic who quipped that "I can't hit the ball until I hit the bottle." His team, the Louisville Baseball Club, once left him stranded after a game when he was too drunk to find the train. Nothing is known about Charles' relationship with his uncle, but a similar admixture of showmanship and drinking would color the nephew's fortunes. Browning had an older brother, Avery, who eventually became a successful coal merchant.

The boy demonstrated an early aptitude for performance, and began mounting amateur theatricals in a backyard shed during school vacations, sometimes as many as five during a summer "season." "A sprightly boy," a Louisville journalist would later recall him, "bright as a new dime and keenly alert to the main chance." As a youngster he sang in the choir of Louisville's historic Christ Church Cathedral, where the public could hear his remarkable voice (some went so far as to declare him an "infant phenomenon" in the Victorian sense) for free. In his backyard, however, the admission price was collected, at first in pins and later in pennies. Ten cents was a good profit. He wrote, directed, and acted in productions that ranged from musicals to melodramas, and his attractions consistently drew better crowds than the neighbor children's rival penny shows. "He knew his public and he studied their wants," the *Louisville Herald-Post* reported in 1928. "He discovered that if you give the public a run for its money, the public is yours, body, soul and breeches—and this embraces both sexes of said public, for both sexes are now wearing breeches."

Browning enrolled in the Boys' High School at Eighth and Chestnut streets, but he never graduated. The seductive lure of the big show was too strong for a boy with a yen for putting on an act, and Louisville abounded in temptations. It was a central port of call for the great showboats, as well as the carnivals and theatrical stock companies that traveled from town to town by rail and wagon. Growing up in the hometown of the Kentucky Derby also fostered a lifelong love of a related pastime—the racetrack. The Derby attracted hordes of gypsies, for whom the boy felt a powerful attraction and affinity. Despite his parents' warnings, he visited their encampments and to some extent won their trust. Like amusement people, the gypsies were clannish and disdainful of outsiders. The larger culture existed only to be tricked, bilked, exploited, and scorned.

When he was sixteen years old, Charles became infatuated with a dancer, a so-called sideshow queen in the Manhattan Fair & Carnival Company, then visiting Louisville. Sexual attraction provided the crucial impetus to the break that had been building for years. In the summer of 1896, he fulfilled an archetypal American fantasy: he ran away with the traveling show.

The flight from conventional life and responsibility is one of the great transforming motifs of American art and culture; Browning marked his own transformation by rechristening himself Tod, and set off on a baptismal journey up and down the Ohio and Mississippi rivers. The waters must have contained an unusually high proportion of river silt, for the boy gravitated, quickly and with relish, to the lowest strata of carnival life: "barking" for a phony "Wild Man of Borneo." Fake wild men were only one rung removed from the absolute nadir of sideshow attractions: the geek. Frequently a wet-brained alcoholic, the geek bit off the heads of rats and chickens for often no more than his next bottle. Browning's "Wild Man" was actually a black man from Mississippi in outlandish makeup; Browning would similarly embellish his spiels with multisyllabic modifiers of the kind popularized by R. F. "Tody" Hamilton, the legendary press agent for the Barnum and Bailey Circus during the 1880s and 90s. ("Tall and towering Tody!" one of Hamilton's colleagues recalled, imitating the inimitable. " 'Tis his transmutation transmitted and translated into tens of thousands of tongues that tell thrilling titillating tales to towns that teem with thousands and that transform things trite and thin into tremendously thick and telling truths." According to Hamilton himself, "To state a fact in ordinary language is to permit a doubt concerning the statement.") Browning dug up Hamilton's compilations of bombastic adjectives, and used them whether they were appropriate or not. To the rubes, one big word was just like another.

For some boys, the lure of the show world is romantic and idealized, as epitomized in James Otis' perennially popular children's novel *Toby Tyler, or Ten Weeks with the Circus,* first published in 1881. But for every wide-eyed Toby Tyler with dreams of big-top glamour, there is also a Tod Browning, instantly at home in the shadows of the freak pit. The great American fantasist Ray Bradbury, who grew up enamored of the films created by Tod Browning and Lon Chaney in the 1920s, would later make images of "the dark carnival" central to his work: black Ferris wheels, starkly silhouetted against lowering skies; nameless, shapeless things displayed in jars of formaldehyde; and the intuition of young boys that the glittering amusements of childhood somehow arrive in the dead of night on crepe-bedraped funeral trains. Leslie Fiedler, discussing the similarly dark undercurrents of *Huckleberry Finn* and other American classics, notes that "our literature as a whole at times seems a chamber of horrors disguised as an amusement park 'fun house,' where we pay to play at terror and are confronted in the innermost chamber with a series of inter-reflecting mirrors which present us with a thousand versions of our own face."

Carnivals and circuses have included close encounters with the macabre almost since their inception. Sergeant-Major Philip Astley (born 1742), the English inventor of the modern circus ring, also ushered in the sideshow, presenting both animal and human freaks and other bizarre exhibits. According to circus historian Peter Verney, "Astley, and the showmen who succeeded him, were always ready to exploit the extra attraction. The guillotine, 'as used in France,' brought the curious flocking to his amphitheater, while the wax heads he had brought back from his Paris excursions proved an even greater draw." P. T. Barnum's American Museum, founded in New York in 1841, was an all-purpose entertainment center that featured human oddities at its core. According to freak-show historian Robert Bogdan, Barnum's cabinet of curiosities "was not a sleazy operation on the fringe of Victorian America; it was, rather, quite fashionable and most legitimate." The American Museum, rather than the circus, was Barnum's major interest. "The enterprise was more than a success," wrote Bogdan. "It was a national force." Dwarves, pinheads, Siamese twins, albinos, giants of height and girth—all became staples of American diversion. The quest for bizarre attractions was almost bottomless, but reached an arguable low point with the Sells-Floto Circus' attempt, in the 1870s, to hire the notorious wilderness-survival cannibal, Al Packer, as a sideshow performer. Packer saw fit to decline the lucrative offer, an early stab at infotainment tendered by circus owners Frederick G. Bonfils and Harry H. Tammen (who were also cofounders of the *Denver Post.*)

Popular "amusements" have a flip side that is often less than sunny, and the very word "recreation" has some usually overlooked connotations. Any process of re-creation or rebirth necessarily entails a death of one sort or another. This may explain the prevalence of sugar-coated intimations of mortality in carnivals and fun parks—spook shows, wild rides involving heart-stopping plunges and near-collisions, and the omnipresent, endlessly cycling wheels and whirligigs of chance, fate, and destiny. Freak shows similarly offer a glimpse of ourselves, re-created along strange physical or behavioral lines. Nothing is fixed, and everything is possible.

Tod Browning's early career was a playground of possibilities; the number of professional hats he wore is dizzying, and it is difficult to recall another individual whose activities so completely permeated American popular entertainment at the turn of the century. His resumé amounted to a crazy quilt. After his initial stint ballyhooing the ersatz Wild Man throughout Kentucky, Virginia, and West Virginia, he learned how to free himself from manacles, Houdini-style, without the benefit of a key. He spent a season as a clown with the Ringling Brothers Circus, followed by a turn as a rider and stable boy for Virginia Carroll, a prominent Southern turfwoman. He went to Chicago to become a spieler for a travel-

ing spectacle known as "The Deep Sea Divers." Joining the afore-
mentioned river show, he performed his macabre "Living Corpse"
act for two years, until authorities in Madison, Indiana, busted the
show for violating the Sabbath and perpetrating a fraud. The show
was fined $14.07—the total combined assets of all the company
members.

Browning turned to vaudeville, where he resurrected his skills
as a singer, and added to his repertoire slapstick and burlesque,
"buck-and-wing" performances of fast solo tap-dancing, and a
blackface minstrel routine in a show called "The Whirl of Mirth."
He claimed to have been performing in San Francisco on the day
of the 1906 earthquake. As a member of the Willard & King Company, he learned a contortionist act, pleasing audiences in Europe,
the Far East, and Africa. Other credits in his clippings include
references to work as an acrobat, aerialist, and illusionist. Although every credential cannot be verified—one must presume that
Browning knew how to give reporters, as well as audiences, exactly
what they wanted—the range of his experience is remarkable by
almost any standard. And if his cluttered resumé makes anything
clear, it is that he had not yet found the best medium in which to
utilize his diverse talents.

Like Tod Browning, the motion picture itself had begun its career
as a sideshow attraction, a curiosity at the fringes of mainstream
entertainment. In a few short years, the technology of cinema had
progressed from nickelodeons to two-reel narrative "features."
Cinema evolved more rapidly than a vocabulary for thinking about
it. Maxim Gorky, writing at about the time that Tod Browning
ran away with the carnival, found cinema to be less an entertainment than a technological nightmare, an invention that threatened
to debase the senses and confer a kind of living death on the
beholder, "a life without color and without sound . . . the life of
ghosts." Nightmare or not, never before had it been possible for
human beings to create, reproduce, and share such an evocative
simulacrum of the dream state. In Paris, Georges Méliès instinctively grasped the essentially fantastic possibilities of the motion
picture, and his studio was foremost a laboratory of the special
effect as cinematic raison d'être. In America, more direct and visceral means were favored to hold and startle an audience—loco-
motives hurtling toward the screen, for instance, or a bandit firing
his gun directly into the camera's eye (both effects were employed

Two of Browning's early makeup experiments. *(The Library of Congress)*

in 1903 by Edwin S. Porter in *The Great Train Robbery*. Quaint though these techniques may seem today, they once had the power to make audience members faint.

In 1913, nearing his thirty-first birthday, Tod Browning was introduced to a fellow Kentuckian in New York, David Wark Griffith, who offered him an acting role in a two-reel comedy, *Scenting a Terrible Crime,* he was producing at the Bronx-based Biograph-studio. Although the role was small, it had a certain significance, both for Browning's career to date and his success to come: the part Browning undertook was that of an undertaker.

Griffith took Browning to Hollywood when he became production chief for the Reliance and Majestic companies, where Browning worked as a comedian in one-reel comedies that were cranked out on a weekly basis. By the spring of 1915 he had branched out into directing. His fortunes seemed guaranteed in the movie colony, even as the world was slipping into war. But Tod Browning's sunny side was about to be permanently eclipsed. He had a fondness for drink, and for recklessness. One who grows up according to the outsider's code of the carnival does not always

Rehearsal for a death ride: Browning, cranking his auto, circa 1914. *(The Library of Congress)*

develop a respect for propriety, or laws. He enjoyed a good time. "He had a liking for flashy cars," recalled director Raoul Walsh. "I guess that went with the whiskey." Cars were getting faster every day, despite the petty new "speed limits" that were popping up everywhere. Driver's licenses had barely been invented.

Mutual's film magazine, *Reel Life,* ran a profile of Browning in 1914, suggesting humorously that his knowledge of handcuff tricks might come in handy in case the performer's "speeding mania" were to get him into trouble. The joke proved unpleasantly prescient. A few weeks before his thirty-fifth birthday, the climax of the first reel of Tod Browning's life occurred. The date was June 16, 1915.

Another Vernon Tragedy

INVESTIGATING RIDE TO DEATH

WERE ANY WOMEN IN MOTOR CAR
WHEN ACTOR WAS KILLED?

Until Two Other Film People
Who Were Injured, are Able to
Talk, Mystery Cannot Be Cleared.

"Until Todd [*sic*] A. Browning and George A. Seigmann improve sufficiently to be questioned," reported the *Los Angeles Times* on June 17, "investigation of the tragic early morning motor ride which brought death to Elmer Booth, prominent film actor, and injured his two companions so dangerously their lives are still a matter of doubt, will pend." The thirty-two-year-old Booth★ was a rising

★Booth's untimely death resulted in the birth of a distinguished Hollywood career. D. W. Griffith hired Booth's younger sister Margaret as a negative cutter in order to provide income to the Booth family. Margaret Booth eventually became one of the industry's most respected film editors, and headed the editing department at MGM from 1937 to 1968. In 1990 she was honored with a lifetime achievement award from the American Cinema Editors. She evidently never forgave Browning for the accident. Writer Elias Savada, who attempted to interview her on the subject in the 1970s, recalled her icy response: "You expect me to talk about that man who killed my brother?"

comic actor on stage and in film, and had recently appeared in the Broadway hit *Stop Thief.* Seigmann was another highly regarded performer who had just achieved notoriety for the role of the mulatto in Griffith's *The Clansman,* later known as *The Birth of a Nation.*

The accident, according to the *Times,* "takes its place in the long list of tragedies that have visited parties returning from the Vernon Country Club, a roadhouse. Reticence on the part of the survivors to reveal the number of passengers in the car has led to an investigation by the police to determine whether two women were members of the merry party returning from the roadhouse revels." Booth was killed instantly when the car, driven by Browning, collided with a railway flatcar loaded with steel rails. The train conductor had waved a lantern as a danger signal, but to no avail. The car hit the flatcar at full speed, and Elmer Booth was thrown headfirst into the jutting rails. "The impresses in his skull," the *Times* reported, "were as even and regular as the design of a waffle off the grill." Seigmann suffered four broken ribs, a deeply lacerated thigh, and internal injuries. Browning's condition was considerably worse; the *San Francisco Chronicle* predicted outright that he would "probably die." His right leg was shattered, his body "painfully cut and bruised" with both arm and face lacerations, and grave, unspecified internal injuries "[made] doubtful his recovery."

Browning was taken to the California Hospital, presumably to perish. He had made a career of Houdini-like stunts and scams, but the container that now confined him was his own battered and violated body. Part of him was indeed dead; the side-splitting clown of the two-reelers, unlike the Living Corpse, would never make a comeback.

A great war, meanwhile, raged in Europe, destroying and recreating human order. Picture shows and carnivals would, of course, survive the carnage, but they would evolve new, shell-shocked forms in response to a landscape of mass death. For Tod Browning, too, the vision of a dark new spectacle would begin to slowly take shape, one that would attract him as powerfully as had any traveling show: a cinematic circus of fear and shadow, drawn deeply from the sarcophagus of the self.

Chapter Two

"You Will Become Caligari":
Monsters, Mountebanks, and Modernism

"In time of war the devil makes
more room in hell."

An old German saying

Tod Browning was not the only carnival shill with a "Living Corpse" routine to make his way into the cinema. Fairgrounds and carnivals were the original laboratories for entertainment that thrilled and frightened, from the freak show to the roller coaster to the ghost-train, and even the nickelodeon prototypes of the motion picture itself. Browning's turn-of-the-century riverboat scam occasionally evoked the petty ire of local authorities, but, by 1921, there was a vastly more disruptive fraud in town.

On May 15, 1921, some 2,000 people marched on Miller's Theatre, Los Angeles, in a demonstration that lasted from noon to 8:30 P.M. The core protestors were members of the Hollywood post of the American Legion; many carried permanent and disfiguring evidence of their recent service. The crippled ex-soldiers brandished angry placards: WHY PAY WAR TAX TO SEE GERMAN-MADE PICTURES? The "tax" was the perceived flow into German coffers of hard-earned American entertainment dollars; a small but

Conrad Veidt and Lil Dagover in *The Cabinet of Dr. Caligari* (1919).
(The Museum of Modern Art / Film Stills Collection)

increasingly visible number of German and other foreign films were popping up in American theatres, often with more elaborate production values than the typical homegrown product. And although military engagement between the countries had ended, a formal peace had not yet been forged. A technical state of war still existed.

In addition to wounded veterans, the mob at Miller's Theatre included hundreds of sailors from the Pacific fleet, local members of the Motion Picture Directors Association, and throngs of ordinary, outraged citizens. As the day wore on, the crowd's energy gained momentum; what was at first described in the press as a "spectacular demonstration" would escalate into "wild rioting" by nightfall. The crowd achieved such proportions that police reserves were called out to quell the locals, and the naval provost guard tried unsuccessfully to subdue the protesting sailors. In time-honored theatrical tradition, the clashes were punctuated by an unending fusillade of rotten eggs.

The object of the crowd's fury was the opening of *The Cabinet of Dr. Caligari,* which had been produced in Berlin two years earlier and had its American premiere in New York the previous month, to considerable critical acclaim. The criticism, however, rubbed two ways: the perceived freshness of *Caligari* was in inverse proportion to what many considered the staleness of American motion pictures. The New York critic Kenneth MacGowan called it "the most extraordinary production yet seen . . . its narrative far more exciting and gripping than any but a very few of our native products." He saw *Caligari* as a "danger signal" to the American film industry, which showed signs of artistic inertia. "American producers have got to shake themselves out of the ruts of machine production and mere money-squandering and try to see the full possibilities of their art."

The author and art critic Willard Huntington Wright offered a similar argument. *"The Cabinet of Doctor Caligari* represents the inevitable line along which the cinema must evolve," Wright told *Variety,* "and the first American producer who has the insight and intelligence and courage to turn in that direction . . . will not only succeed financially, but will go down in the moving picture history of America as the truly great man of the industry." Motion pictures, according to Wright, "have reached an impasse—every producer who is honest with himself will admit this. A change is necessary, and the only possible change lies along the lines of the Caligari picture."

The shock and surprise of *Caligari* was its break with the established conventions of cinematography. The film was a fantastic mystery story, told in an equally fantastic visual manner. The settings were angular and distorted, their shadows created with paint instead of light. Everything was artificial and stylized. The exterior world existed to illuminate an inner landscape; there was no pretense of "realism." A similar break with established visual conventions had been underway in the worlds of painting and sculpture for decades, while the popular medium of film was hardly born.

It is difficult to overstate the kind of revelation *Caligari* represented to much of its audience, which felt it was witnessing an evolutionary leap in the cinema, one comparable to the coming of sound, or, decades later, to the overwhelming experience of *2001: A Space Odyssey* (1968), a film that similarly reconfigured the possibilities of cinematic space and form for the general public. "Space has been given a voice," wrote one early viewer of *Caligari,* Hermann George Scheffauer, whose comments in the New York periodical *The Freeman* were considered significant enough to be reprinted in *The New York Times* months in advance of the film's American premiere. Scheffauer saw the screen world of 1920 as a celluloid wasteland filled with "smirking dolls with bared teeth and oxlike eyes, creased cavaliers, prettified puppies." With *Caligari,* he wrote, "the artist has slipped into this crude phantasmagoria and begun to create."

In contrast, rabble-rousing papers like the Hearst-owned *Los Angeles Examiner,* which embroidered the slogan AMERICA FIRST into its masthead, had little use for artistic breakthroughs. (It is interesting, in retrospect, that the Hearst empire would try to suppress not one, but two of the most influential films of all time—*Caligari* in 1921 and *Citizen Kane* in 1941.) Jingoism made better copy than film criticism, and the *Examiner* and its ilk gave the impression of a clear and present challenge to the preeminence of the American film industry, and advocated an outright ban on German pictures. It sold papers, but was an irrational position. L. Auerbach, vice president of the Export & Import Film Company, Inc., made the point succinctly: "Perhaps the agitators do not know that ninety-five percent of pictures shown throughout the world are American," he said, adding that twenty American pictures were being shown in Germany for every one foreign film exhibited in the United States (only two had been shown before *Caligari*). As the major exporter of films, America would be the big loser if it instituted import restrictions that generated an international backlash.

The New York theatre impresario S. L. "Roxy" Rothafel saw the tremendous audience potential of *Caligari* when it was offered to him by Goldwyn, the American distributor, and spared no effort in promotion or performance. The premiere was held April 3, 1921, at Rothafel's Capitol Theatre at Fifty-first and Broadway. The theatre was the forerunner of the legendary Roxy, and gave its photoplays sumptuous presentations; *Caligari* received a full orchestral accompaniment with a live stage tableaux opening and closing the screenings. Brilliantly colored art posters executed in a so-called "cubist" style by designer Lionel Reiss were given prominent display. (They "fairly shriek from their stands," commented *Moving Picture World*.)

Though the word "cubist" was used almost universally to describe *Caligari* in the popular press, the film's style had very little to do with the art movement pioneered by Georges Braque, Pablo Picasso, and perhaps epitomized for the public by Marcel Duchamp's *Nude Descending a Staircase* (1912), a canvas memorably described as "an explosion in a shingle factory" by an unsympathetic critic. True cubism involved angular stylization, but was essentially about simultaneous, overlapping perspectives. *Caligari* was more properly inspired by expressionism, especially expressionism in the theatre, which forced conventional visual perspective into emotionally charged configurations. Cubism, by contrast, was more analytical and scientific. *Caligari* had plenty of angles, though, and for much of the press and public further analysis was beside the point. The film had "something to do with modern art," and that was explanation enough.

Because of its indelible imagery, a photograph from *The Cabinet of Dr. Caligari* simply cannot be mistaken for one from any other picture. As the film is known to vast numbers of people who have never actually seen it, the story warrants recounting.

A fair is in progress in the town of Holstenwall, and we immediately realize that this is no ordinary town, and no ordinary film. For while the actors have conventional bodies and faces, the world they inhabit is one of jagged shadows and angles like something out of a dream. The milieu of the carnival, with its crazily off-kilter merry-go-round, is the establishing image. Into this world hobbles a strange bespectacled figure cloaked in black, a hypnotist named Dr. Caligari (Werner Krauss) who seeks a permit from the town clerk to exhibit his somnambulist at the fair. The clerk issues the license, but only after insulting the mountebank. That night, the clerk is murdered in his room.

The following night, two students, Francis (Friedrich Feher) and Alan (Hans Heinz von Twardowski), who are both in love with the same girl, Jane (Lil Dagover), escort her to the fair. They enter Caligari's tent and are fascinated when the hypnotist introduces the sleepwalker Cesare (Conrad Veidt), a cadaverous man who sleeps upright in a wooden box. Caligari announces that Cesare has been asleep for twenty years, but while in his wakened state will be able to answer the audience's questions about the future. Alan blurts out his anxious query: "How long will I live?" The answer is straightforward: "Until tomorrow's dawn."

The next morning Francis learns that his friend has indeed been stabbed to death. He suspects Caligari and Cesare, and enlists the help of Jane's father to investigate. One night, while Francis spies on Caligari and what he takes to be Cesare in his box, the actual sleepwalker enters Jane's bedroom on Caligari's orders and raises a knife to stab her. She wakes, struggles, swoons. Cesare, as if from panic or in pity, does not kill but abducts Jane instead, carrying her through the famous zigzag maze of expressionist settings. He drops her at the foot of a bridge when a mob headed by Jane's father threatens to overtake him, and he dies of exhaustion. Francis finds that Caligari is in reality the head of a local asylum, a man so obsessed by an ancient legend of a hypnotist and his murderous sleepwalker that he cannot resist acting out the story himself. Confronted with the corpse of Cesare, Caligari flies into a lunatic rage and is placed in a straitjacket.

That is the story as it was originally conceived by writers Carl Mayer and Hans Janowitz, a political parable of unchecked authoritarianism following the cataclysm of the war. Caligari stood for the state, while Cesare represented the sleepwalking masses who had been sent by the millions to kill and be killed. The story also had more than metaphorical significances for both men. Janowitz had been persecuted by a military psychiatrist, and forced to undergo various mental tests against his will; the experience had embittered him. And together with Janowitz, Mayer had attended an actual sideshow called "Man or Machine," featuring "a strong

A 1921 Goldwyn poster for *The Cabinet of Dr. Caligari. (Courtesy of Ronald V. Borst / Hollywood Movie Posters)*

man who achieved miracles of strength in an apparent stupor. He acted as if he were hypnotized. The strangest thing was that he accompanied his feats with utterances which affected the spellbound spectators as pregnant forebodings."

Both writers favored commissioning the Czech painter Alfred Kubin to execute the sets. Kubin, a proto-surrealist who could effortlessly conjure the nightmarish image from the everyday object (his paintings included a Bosch-like canvas called *The Maw,* depicting an anonymous mass of humanity marching into an enormous, crushing mouth), was ruled out by the film's producers, who gave the assignment to designer Hermann Warm, and requested the now-classic sets. The authors may have been disappointed over losing Kubin, but they were horrified at the change in their script that producer Erich Pommer and director Robert Wiene dictated. The whole story would now be framed by a prologue and epilogue revealing the narrative to be nothing but the ravings of a madman (an earlier version of the screenplay had Francis, now a prosperous doctor, recounting the story to his friends). Caligari himself was presented as a tragic figure, the victim of mental illness. In a single stroke, the film's political back was broken, at least in the opinion of the writers. As film historian Siegfried Kracauer would later comment, "A revolutionary film was thus turned into a conformist one—following the much-used pattern of declaring some normal but troublesome individual insane and sending him to a lunatic asylum." Then as always, the producers suspected that they challenged conventional taste at their economic peril. The man in the street would regard the themes and images of *Caligari* as crazy, and therefore needed to be reassured that his opinion was the correct one.

Das Cabinet des Dr. Caligari, completed in late 1919, was released by Decla-Bioscop in February 1920. DU MUSST CALIGARI WERDEN, posters declared—"You will become Caligari," both an injunction and a prophecy. Berlin audiences were appreciative—the film was an immediate commercial hit, not just a *succès d'estime*—even if they misunderstood the film's expressionist intentions. Many believed the sets to be literal representations of the subjective visual aspects of being insane. War-oriented interpretations would come much later, despite the almost transparent evocation of war as a divisive, controlling, supernatural force evident in the film's first intertitle: *"Everywhere there are spirits . . . They are all around us . . . They have driven me from hearth and home, from my wife and children."*

Carefully promoted by the Goldwyn Company for its American release the following year, *Caligari* built up a pretentious head of steam, capitalizing on postwar xenophobia and traditional American self-doubts in matters artistic. *Caligari* was a kind of cultural sputnik launched out of nowhere by Europe, a gauntlet not thrown down, but projected up on the shivering screen of America's insecurities. And it didn't come alone—it was surrounded by all those puzzling new European composers the public was still trying to assimilate. The live orchestral complement provided by Roxy Rothafel was well calculated and well received.

"The musical setting for the production is superb," wrote one critic, "for in this art, too, the work of the moderns has been employed. Rich, weird, beautiful themes from Strauss, Debussy, Schoenberg and Stravinsky all add vitally beautiful atmosphere . . . In some portions . . . one feels that Wagner's long dreamt-of trilogy of music, drama and color has been achieved." Oddly, there is no record of this ambitious musical accompaniment ever having been reconstructed—most revivals of *Caligari* go no further than a melodramatic piano or organ accompaniment in generic "silent movie" style. The reference to the film's "color" is a probable allusion to the then-common practice of tinting films. *Caligari* is often considered an archetype of stark black-and-white photography; the originally intended effect, however, included tints of green, brown, and steel-blue.

The National Board of Review Magazine noted

> an evidence in this picture, for the first time in America, at least of something of the point of view of the 'Dadaist' to whom everything in the world is equally important—a sort of reflection in the world of plastic representation of the conceptions of relativity which are agitating mathematicians and astronomers. Thus the picture stands in the current of living thought. . . . [It] makes sanity relative as insanity is relative—and constitutes a valuable offset to the American tendency to oversureness of intellectual values.

Variety was intrigued, if skeptical. "It may catch the popular fancy," the paper conceded, comparing it to a well-paced story by Poe. "But it is morbid. Continental creations usually are." *Moving Picture World,* betraying a cultural bias, politely praised technical elements while calling it a "degenerate German invention," adding that the postwar years required "sane and helpful fiction, not allopathic doses of the morbid and grotesque." As a coda to its review, the publication offered "exploitation angles," the most quotable being "Play on the novelty of the picture and keep quiet about the German origin of the work."

The Hearst papers, aimed at a general rather than industry readership, ignored this last suggestion entirely, the result being the Los Angeles melee at Miller's Theatre on May 15. Upton Sinclair used the incident as a framing device for his 1922 novel *They Call Me Carpenter.* The narrator, Billy, is persuaded to take in *Caligari* ("a strange, weird freak of the cinema art") by a visiting German literary critic, Dr. Henner, who has already seen the film several times. "You may not know much about these cultured foreigners," Billy relates to the reader. "Their manners are like softest velvet, so that when you talk to them, you feel as a Persian cat must feel while being stroked. They have read everything in the world; they speak with quiet certainty; and they are so old—old with memories of racial griefs stored up in their souls." Henner, teasing, tells him, "This picture could not possibly have been produced in America. For one thing, nearly all the characters are thin. . . . One does not find American screen actors in that condition. Do your people care enough about the life of art to take a risk of starving for it?"

The protesting mob deters the German doctor from entering the theatre, but Billy manages to get a ticket. Suitably impressed by the bizarre photoplay, "I walked towards the exit of the theatre, and a swinging door gave way—and upon my ear broke a clamor that might have come direct from the inside of Dr. Caligari's asylum. 'Ya, ya. Boo, boo! For shame on you! Leave your own people to starve, and send your cash to the enemy.' "

> During all the time—an hour or more—that I had been away on the wings of imagination, these poor boobs had been howling and whooping outside the theatre, keeping the crowds away, and incidentally working themselves into a fury! For a moment I thought I would go out and reason with them; they were mistaken in the idea that there was anything about the war, anything against America in the picture. But I realized that they were beyond reason.

The mob attacks Billy, who takes refuge in a church. There follows a fanciful tale of the Second Coming, which is revealed at the end to be all a dream, like the *Caligari* story itself.

As it turned out, Billy's delirium-inducing blows were probably the worst injuries that resulted from the fracas at Miller's. The *Examiner* reported that a "seething mob of nearly 2000 persons turned into an orderly gathering in the twinkling of an eye when Roy H. Marshall, adjutant of the Hollywood Post of the American Legion, mounted a ladder and announced on behalf of Fred Miller, proprietor, that the film would immediately be taken from the program." To demonstrate their sense of fairness, as well as their eagerness to "buy American," the crowd swarmed into Miller's to view the replacement attraction. Interesting enough, that photoplay was Benjamin Hampton's production of *The Money Changers*—based on the novel by Upton Sinclair.

The following day, a face-saving ad appeared in the local papers:

"Raus
Mitt
Im!"

We announced that we would show a picture that would create a sensation in Los Angeles.

IT DID!

But Not in the Way We Expected

We believed that Los Angeles, the Home of our Film Industry, wanted to see what New York acclaimed a masterwork.

However, General Sherman said, "War is Hell," and General Grant said, "Let us have Peace," and we agree with both and offer for your approval

BENJ. B. HAMPTON'S
Stirring Human Drama

"The Money Changers"
By
UPTON SINCLAIR

It Gleams With Varied Life, Thrills With Action and Throbs With Romance
A Made-in-Los Angeles Production
(Signed) Fred A. Miller,
MILLER'S THEATER.

Critical controversy over *Caligari,* however, did not subside, and not all commentators agreed with the widely held view stated in the film magazine *Shadowland* that *Caligari* "has the authentic thrills and shocks of art." Two years later, Ezra Pound was still complaining about *Caligari*. He argued that film should be "essentially cinematographic, and not a mere travesty and degradation of some other art" and regarded the film as more evidence of "the progressive weakening of the popular mind." Pound wrote that *Caligari* "cribbed its visual effects, with craven impertinences, and then flashed up a notice, 'This film isn't cubism; it represents the ravings et cetera.' Precisely, ravings the inventors couldn't have thought of without the anterior work of new artists."

   Caligari was derivative, no doubt, but it shared one honest source of inspiration with the new art movements, namely the Great War just past. The war had a tremendous influence on the expressionist, dadaist, and emerging surrealist artists during the 1920s. In her

Death Aids the Dying Young Soldier, **an illustration by Hanz Witzig for** *Eine Totentanz: 1914–1918.*

recent book *Anxious Visions,* art historian Sidra Stich links the surrealist preoccupation with deformed and disfigured bodies to the
sudden presence, following the war, of a sizable population of the
crippled and mutilated. Modern warfare had introduced new and
previously unimaginable approaches to destroying or brutally
reordering the human body. Parallel advances in modern medicine
made it possible for soldiers to survive injuries that earlier would
have been fatal. "The invasion of death into the world of the living
and the representation of the human body as utterly violated are
predominant in Surrealist configurations," writes Stich. "With their
missing, dislocated, and disproportioned body parts, Surrealist
figures call attention to the body as a disunified entity in which
absence and deficiency prevail." Surrealist images, Stich notes, also
blur evolutionary and zoological distinctions. "Indeed their degraded
figures and distended flesh collapse the usual boundaries that separate humans from other species."

In 1921 there appeared in Germany a startling new horror icon
which, for the first time in the cinema, bluntly superimposed the
human and the animal to create an image of overwhelming dread.
F. W. Murnau, in *Nosferatu: Eine Symphonie des Grauens (Nosferatu: A Symphony of Horror),* presented a rat-faced vampire named
Count Orlock whose padded costume and prosthetic makeup would
later influence countless other movie monsters—though, oddly
enough, very few vampires.

Albin Grau, a German painter and architect (and, according to
film historian Lotte H. Eisner, a dedicated occultist), seems to have
had more to do with the overall conception of *Nosferatu* than did
Murnau, though his screen credit is only for décor. Grau published an essay called "Vampires" in the German publication *Bühne
und Film* around the time of the film's release; rather than discuss
the production of the film, he presented his recollections—quite
possibly embellished—of a wartime incident in Serbia. In the story,
Grau and four other companions, in need of a delousing, take up
a war against potential typhoid, hair clippers replacing more conventional weapons. One of the group, a Romanian, relates a true
story of vampirism. His own father, who died of a heart attack
while cutting trees in the Balkans, was buried without the bene-
diction of a priest. The grave was subsequently found to be empty
at night, its inhabitant an "undead," or vampire. The teller pro-
duces a yellowing official document attesting to the incident, and

Max Schreck faces the daylight in *Nosferatu* (1921).

Max Schreck, the first screen Dracula, in and out of makeup. *(Left: Courtesy of Ronald V. Borst/Hollywood Movie Posters; Right: Courtesy of Forrest J Ackerman)*

describing the destruction of the father-monster by staking and incineration. "That night," Grau wrote, "we didn't sleep a wink! Years have passed since the war. One no longer sees the terror of battle in men's eyes. . . . Suffering and grief have shaken men's hearts and have little by little, suspended their desire to understand the cause of the monstrous events that depleted the world like a cosmic vampire, drinking the blood of millions."

Nosferatu was an unauthorized adaptation of Bram Stoker's 1897 vampire novel *Dracula,* and it may not have been the first. A now-obscure film with the title *Drakula* was produced in Hungary the previous year, directed by Karoly Lajthay and photographed by Lajos Gasser, and could well have inspired Prana-Film, the producers of *Nosferatu,* to pursue their own act of piracy. *Nosferatu,* however, was a high-profile affair, a self-conscious "art" film that rapidly drew the attention of Stoker's combative widow Florence, who spent the better part of a decade trying to suppress and destroy it.★ The previous year, Murnau had cut his teeth on horror themes

★For a detailed account of Florence Stoker's obsessive battle over *Nosferatu,* see this author's *Hollywood Gothic: The Tangled Web of* Dracula *from Novel to Stage to Screen* (W. W. Norton & Company, 1990).

with a similarly unauthorized version of *Dr. Jekyll and Mr. Hyde.* Called *Der Januskopf (The Head of Janus),* the now-lost film starred Conrad Veidt, and, in a supporting role, a Hungarian actor named Bela Lugosi. Although at least one account of *Der Januskopf* suggests that the film was suppressed by the Robert Louis Stevenson estate, an examination by this author of the British Society of Authors archives dealing with dramatic rights for *Jekyll and Hyde* revealed no mention of a German controversy. The Society of Authors did, however, vigorously pursue Florence Stoker's case against *Nosferatu.*

Nosferatu, like *Caligari,* was given an elaborate premiere in Berlin with an original orchestral score by Hans Erdmann. Artistically tinted in shades of yellow, blue, rose, and sepia—and, for a brief moment before the vampire's climactic attack, in blood-red—*Nosferatu* unabashedly sought the approbation of the postwar intelligentsia, and its pestilential images were widely considered to be a reflection of the war and its wrenching aftermath. Lotte Eisner commented on the German predisposition toward morbid expressionism in *The Haunted Screen*: "Mysticism and magic, the dark forces to which Germans have always been more than willing to commit themselves, had flourished in the face of death on the battlefields. The hecatombs of young men fallen in the flower of their youth seemed to nourish the grim nostalgia of the survivors. And the ghosts which had haunted the German Romantics revived, like the shades of Hades after draughts of blood."

Other significant films of the time dealing with doubles, doppelgangers, and the fantastic included Paul Wegener's *Der Golem,* based on the Frankenstein-like creature of Jewish legend. Wegener filmed *Der Golem* twice, just before and after the war in 1914 and 1920. In 1924 *Caligari*'s director Robert Wiene reunited with actor Conrad Veidt for *Orlac Händes (The Hands of Orlac),* in which the hands of a murderer are grafted onto an accident victim, and continue to pursue their old interest. Edgar Allan Poe's memorable tale of a human double, "William Wilson," was the inspiration for 1926's *Der Student von Prag (The Student of Prague). Der Student* had originally been produced in 1913; the 1926 version was directed by Henrik Galeen, the scenarist of *Nosferatu.*

Although these films are today ranked as classics, it would be a mistake to think that Europeans of the twenties were uniformly mesmerized by the likes of *Nosferatu.* In France, André Gide called the Murnau picture "a rather nondescript German film, but of a

Paul Wegener *(center)* in *The Golem* (1920). *(Photofest)*

nondescript quality that forces one to reflect and to imagine something better." Gide then went on to anticipate perfectly the direction in which stage and cinema vampires would evolve over time:

> If I were to make over the film, I should depict Nosferatu . . .
> not as terrible and fantastic but on the contrary in the guise of
> an inoffensive young man, charming and most obliging. I should
> like it to be only on the basis of very mild indications, in the
> beginning, that any anxiety should be aroused, and in the spec-
> tator's mind before being aroused in the hero's. Likewise,
> wouldn't it be much more frightening if he were first presented
> to the woman in such a charming aspect? It is a kiss that is to be
> transformed into a bite. . . . It might be rather startling, fur-
> thermore, for the vampire to yield to the woman's charms, for-
> get the hour. . . . I can easily see him appearing a hideous monster
> to everyone, and charming only in the eyes of the young woman,
> a voluntary, fascinated victim . . . He should become less and
> less horrible until he really *becomes* the delightful person whose

mere appearance he only took on at first. And it is this delightful person that the cock's crow must kill.

In Gide's opinion, *Nosferatu* was "completely spoiled." Given the French writer's insights into the complicated Dorian Gray–like dynamics of the vampire image, it is a pity he never elaborated directly upon the theme himself.

One night in 1922, a young American composer living in Paris went to the movies with an aspiring writer friend. The evening's offering was *Nosferatu*. The twenty-two-year-old Aaron Copland was looking for a narrative structure for a ballet he was composing under the tutelage and encouragement of the celebrated teacher Nadia Boulanger. His friend, Harold Clurman, remembered that "in the first days of our friendship, Aaron asked me if I had read Freud. I had not, I said, but I knew something of his theories; he was just coming into vogue among literary folk. 'Have you ever tried to psychoanalyze yourself?' he asked. 'No,' I replied, 'it would

Conrad Veidt in *Orlac Händes* (*The Hands of Orlac*): a guilty postwar dream of murder, mutilation, and madness.

be indiscreet.' Aaron already knew himself; I didn't know myself at all. He knew that he was a composer. I had no idea what I was."

Clurman was about to discover whether he would be the first adaptor of *Nosferatu* to another medium. "By the time we reached home that night," Copland recalled, "I decided that this bizarre tale would be the basis for my ballet. Harold had never written a scenario, but he was eager to try. At first we called it *Le Nécromancien.*"

Despite his having no dance company upon which to set the work, and little prospect of finding one, Copland threw himself into the creation of an elaborate and ambitious work, a one-act ballet with a running time of thirty-five minutes. The piece was a distinctly free adaptation, with Orlock/Nosferatu transformed into a magician named Grogh—the ballet itself was eventually retitled *Grogh*—who has the power to bring corpses to life. Each corpse— an adolescent boy, an opium addict, and a prostitute—provided a pretext for sequential *danses macabres* as they rise from their coffin-boxes, one by one. "There was a taste for the bizarre at the time," wrote Copland, "and if *Grogh* sounds morbid and excessive, the music was meant to be fantastic rather than ghastly. Also, the need for gruesome effects gave me an excuse for using 'modern' rhythms and dissonances." The polyrhythmic, jazz-derived techniques foreshadowed Copland's later works. He rearranged the introductory section, "Cortège Macabre," as a self-contained work for full orchestra, two harps, and piano. It was among seven pieces chosen for the first of the American Composers Concerts, and was premiered by the Eastman Philharmonia in Rochester to considerable acclaim in 1925. Other portions of *Grogh* were incorporated into Copland's *Dance Symphony*. The original ballet itself has never been staged.

While Copland's immediate inspiration may have been *Nosferatu,* his description of the ballet's action, particularly of a magician who raises performers from coffin-boxes, evokes a central image from *The Cabinet of Dr. Caligari,* a work that would inspire or cross-fertilize an astounding number of works in film or other media. It is a bit surprising that *Caligari* never inspired an opera.

Terror films were much admired by the surrealists, who loved their disorienting effect, whether or not the filmmakers themselves had surrealist intentions. Claques of surrealists were fond of disrupting films like *Nosferatu* with shouted litanies of the kind that decades later would attend *The Rocky Horror Picture Show.*

Surrealists, of course, were by doctrine at odds with the intentional effects of expressionist films; their admiration was unabashedly out of context. And just as *Caligari* cannibalized "cubism," so would countless surrealist effects find their way, willy-nilly, into the emerging cinema of fantasy and fear. Horror has always had a certain affinity for modern art movements and has often quoted their mannerisms, possibly because, at a root level, they are inspired by similar cultural anxieties.

The visual arts were not alone in their ability to feed the burgeoning horror industry. Modernism in literature and the theatre, particularly the movement toward naturalism, had an overwhelming influence on horror entertainment as we know it today. Naturalism, as propounded by Émile Zola and others, regarded man as a victim of social and economic forces that the individual could barely comprehend, much less control. The artist's role, in this new, Darwinian world, was that of a clinician or pathologist, cold and reductionistic. "Clinical detachment," of course, has always been a good cover for morbidity and sadism, and the most unsavory aspects of naturalism were carried to their furthest and most influential expression in a deceptively modest venue.

By the mid-1920s, the Théâtre du Grand Guignol of Paris had achieved a worldwide reputation for its repertory of short, horrific plays that subjected human characters to the same kind of exaggerated violence that was formerly the province of the little *guignol,* or Punch-and-Judy show. The difference was that the "big puppets" bled, or convincingly seemed to. The Grand Guignol was founded in 1897 (a benchmark year for horror, with the publication of *Dracula,* the exhibition of Philip Burne-Jones' painting *The Vampire,* and—incidentally—the coining of the term "psychoanalysis") by Oscar Méténier, a playwright and former police clerk. Méténier had cofounded an earlier avant-garde venture, Théâtre-Libre, which had produced some of his sensational and sordid playlets. The brief sketches presented life at its most squalid, utilizing the language of the streets and the most unsavory situations and characters possible. (These *histoires des apaches,* of course, find a parallel in another art form deriving from the Parisian underground—the apache dance.) Since naturalism was deemed to be "scientific," Méténier's excursions into the lower and criminal classes were permissible for bourgeois audiences, who could vicariously contemplate base humanity—and their own baser selves— from a fashionable remove. The Grand Guignol intensified the

Le Théâtre du Grand Guignol, the Parisian playhouse of horrors.

emotional impact of its programs through a deliberate strategy of the *douche écossaise*—a "Scotch" shower of alternating emotional temperatures, i.e., rapid shifts between humor and horror.

It was appropriate that the theatre sat in a cul-de-sac, a position of no escape. The Grand Guignol was housed in the chapel of a former convent that dated to 1786, when Montmartre was still a suburban refuge. The convent subsequently served as a blacksmith's workshop and the studio of an academic painter, and by the end of the nineteenth century was hemmed in by narrow cobblestone streets, only a few short blocks from the Place Pigalle, where streetwalkers strolled and trolled. The only remaining traces of the Jansenist nuns, the building's first inhabitants, were the carved angels in the theatre's rafters, and the persistent rumor that the nuns' whispered prayers could still occasionally be heard in the silences between screams. The former chapel made a snug, extremely intimate theatre with a twenty-by-twenty-foot stage.★

Méténier had more serious artistic purposes than his successor, Max Maurey, who took over the following year and aggressively commercialized the Méténier formula, intensifying the aspect of physical horror. During Maurey's tenure, a playwright emerged whose name would become almost synonymous with that of the playhouse.

André de Lorde, by day a mild-mannered librarian of the Bibliothèque de l'Arsenal, enjoyed a nocturnal reputation as Paris' "Prince of Terror" through more than a hundred horrific and sensational plays written between 1901 and 1906. Although de Lorde's dramas were produced at numerous Paris theatres, including the Odeon and the Sarah Bernhardt, the Grand Guignol became the major venue for his oeuvre. De Lorde was a conscious technician of terror, who enjoyed extravagant comparisons to Poe in the popular press, and who, in many respects, prefigured the methods of Alfred Hitchcock. He frequently worked with collaborators, most notably the psychologist Alfred Binet, director of the Psychological-Physiological Laboratory of the Sorbonne. (It seems that de Lorde and Binet had a therapeutic as well as a literary relationship.) To the extent that their collaborations reveal a continuing, obsessive fear of insanity, they are a depressing reminder of primitive attitudes toward mental illness, even among medical professionals. But grotesque scenes of madness and passion, set in asylums

---

★Contrary to one recently published account, the Grand Guignol was not demolished after its closing in 1964, but still stands, now operating as a theatre school. In October 1989, this author was given a tour of the facility and allowed to walk its stage and examine the original architectural details and somber painted figures which still glowered down from the vaulted ceiling.

and clinics, made for riveting spectacle. One of their most infamous plays, regularly revived throughout the Grand Guignol's history, was *A Crime in the Madhouse* (1925), in which a young woman, on the eve of her release from a mental hospital, is set upon by three gargoylish crones. The trio decide there is a bird hiding behind her eyes that must be released, and so they use a knitting needle to help it escape. Following the *Lear*-like atrocity, the most violent of the patients is mutilated herself—her face is pressed against a glowing hot plate and reduced to a bubbling ooze.

Realistic stage violence was the Grand Guignol's signature, and it was a rare evening in the rue Chaptal that transpired without a stabbing, garroting, or throat-slitting. The theatre had its own formula for artificial blood: it was applied hot and coagulated as it cooled. Murky lighting often added to the horror, with the audience left to imagine even more grisly details than were actually staged.

Under the stewardship of Camille Choisy from World War I through the twenties, the Grand Guignol had its golden age, attracting fashionable audiences and even visiting royalty. Theatre historian Mel Gordon writes that Choisy—a diminutive, dandified impresario—took direct inspiration from the newfangled horrors of the Great War: "For Choisy, the technology of death helped enlarge his hideous vocabulary of torture and death: poison gas, explosive devices, electrical cables, surgical instruments and drills replaced the old pistol, dagger and primitive sword." Choisy also began taking inspiration from the cinema, and one of the theatre's most popular repertory pieces was a free adaptation of *The Cabinet of Dr. Caligari,* first presented in 1925.

Camillo Antona-Traversi, who wrote the first history of the Grand Guignol in 1933, described the uniquely theatrical ambience of an evening in the rue Chaptal:

> Entering the small playhouse in the Chaptal cul-de-sac for the first time, the spectator is seized with a vague uneasiness. For it is strange, this theatre, a long narrow chamber, its walls hung with dark material, its paneling severe, with two mysterious doors, always closed, on either side of the stage, and two unexpected angels, which, from high on the ceiling, address us with their enigmatic smiles.
>
> At the sound of three knocks, all the lights go out abruptly;

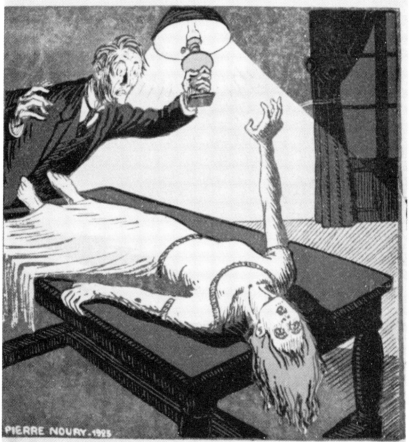

The Grand Guignol's *chef d'horreur,* André de Lorde, reached a wide audience offstage through paperback editions of his bloodcurdling plays.

and during these few moments before the curtain rises, we cannot help but shudder.

The nerves are on edge, stretched to the breaking point. One anxiously awaits the first shock, the emotional dart aimed at the target of the brain. In this atmosphere of sudden darkness, faces become ghostly white blotches, the imposing silence broken at times by the laughter of a nervous woman trying to hide her discomfort. The air is heavy with a tension that weighs heavily on sweaty brows. All the cries of pain, the screams of terror, the death rattles which are so often contained by this stage, seem to come out of the walls. . . . The curtain rises. The spectator is ready.

In October of 1923, the Grand Guignol company crossed the Atlantic and took up the unlikely venue of the Frolic Theatre in New York, a gaily lit rooftop playhouse. For several weeks they presented, in French, a repertoire consisting of their greatest hits, including *A Horrible Experience* and *The Laboratory of Hallucinations*. The mystique, evidently, did not travel well, and critics found the offerings easy to resist. "We leave it to others to say whether such scenes ought to belong to the art of the theatre," wrote *The New York Times,* "but it may be said here that MM. de Lorde and Binet, the authors, have traveled a long way from the Greeks, who would not allow any scene of violence on their stage, and who made the faithful messenger recount things too horrible to be seen." *Variety* was particularly harsh: "De Lorde is the bird Paris calls 'The Prince of Horrors' and likens to our Poe. However, the French also thought Carpentier could lick Dempsey." The sole aspects of the performance the trade paper found effective were those that were "unqualified dirt, unsubtle, coarse, vulgar, obscene and foul," its only success being that "it had at least saved the smell of the French stable and breathed it forth to the American stalls."

Whether Americans liked it or not, an enormous westward expansion of horrors was taking shape, a manifest destiny of the macabre. The dark beings that had used the European avant-garde to find a modern expression would soon begin crossing the Atlantic, in film canisters instead of coffins, waiting to be animated in darkened rooms through the application of artificial light. Their secrets had everything to do with light and shadow, projections, reflections, and doubles. The dark gods knew that the republic founded on principles of rational enlightenment would have a more than ample shadow-side, where monsters might flourish and be free. Shaken out of their ancient crypts and castles by the modern concussions of war, they began seeking a new resting place, slouching inexorably toward Hollywood to be born anew.

Chapter Three

DREAD AND CIRCUSES

"Look! You want to see! See!
Feast your eyes, glut your soul
on my cursed ugliness!"

Gaston Leroux
The Phantom of the Opera
(1911)

THE LIVING CORPSE, of course, would not stay dead.

The wonder of the river show did not die in the bone-crushing collision that followed the Vernon Road House revels. It was an old trick, the secret of which would have been welcome in 1915 to the untold thousands of combatants who were dying in the trenches and field hospitals of Europe. Browning received his wartime wounds at home, but his own creative output would thematically parallel that of writers and artists who survived actual combat, and whose works began to be appreciated in the late twenties.

Browning's artistic focus sharpened gradually. He returned to active film work the year following his accident (his interim credits are for stories only), played a bit part as a car owner in the "mod-

---

Shared obsessions: Tod Browning directing Lon Chaney in *The Unknown* (1927). *(Courtesy of Elias Savada)*

---

ern" sequence of D. W. Griffith's *Intolerance,* and in 1917 directed his first feature-length film, *Jim Bludso,* a riverboat drama based on the popular stage play of the same name. His emphasis drifted increasingly toward melodrama and crime; his early flair for the farcical was now as much a thing of the past as was his singing in the choir. In June of 1917 he married the actress Alice Wilson, with whom he had worked in vaudeville and in films.

Browning's first major commercial hit was *The Virgin of Stamboul* (1920), an elaborately produced desert adventure for Universal starring Priscilla Dean, a popular ingenue who played both melodrama and comedy. *The Virgin of Stamboul* anticipated the public's interest in exotic locations, which would reach a benchmark the following year when Rudolph Valentino played *The Sheik.* *Virgin* established Browning firmly as a specialist in thrills and action, and he directed several pictures featuring Dean for Universal, including the gangster film *Outside the Law* (1921), featuring a rising young character actor named Lon Chaney. Browning had directed Chaney once previously, in *The Wicked Darling* (1919).

Browning's career and marriage were threatened by a deepening alcoholism that left him effectively blacklisted in 1923 and 1924. Recalling the early Hollywood days when he worked with Browning, director Raoul Walsh once said, "I knew he was from Kentucky because he was always talking about Kentucky whiskey, and I remember he always had a bottle of laughing water with him.

"He never got drunk though," Walsh said, presumably meaning that Browning never lost control. "He'd stay up half the night, drinkin' and playin' cards, and then come to the studio in the morning looking as fresh as a daisy." After a time the sham no longer worked; he lost his contract with Universal and his wife separated from him for a period of several months. Interviewer Joan Dickey reported five years later that "the story of Tod Browning's two sick, inactive years from the screen is too well known to need detailed repetition. He is quite frank in admitting that he could not get a job because he was otherwise occupied in trying to drink up 'all the bad liquor in the world.' " Browning's wife reconciled with him during his recovery, and was instrumental in negotiating his comeback assignment with Irving Thalberg at MGM. The film was *The Unholy Three* (1925), based on a best-selling thriller by Clarence Aaron "Tod" Robbins concerning a crime spree perpetrated by three circus performers—a ventriloquist (Chaney), a midget (Harry Earles), and a strong man (Victor McLaglen). The ventriloquist disguises himself as an old lady, and the midget (Earles) assumes the guise of a baby. The film was an astonishing hit. *The New York Times* called it one of 1925's ten best pictures, in the company of such blockbusters as *Ben Hur*. *Times* critic Mordaunt Hall called it "a startlingly original achievement which takes its place with the very best productions that have been made."

With *The Unholy Three* Browning struck upon two winning elements that would shape the remainder of his career. The first was the circus sideshow, his own nurturing milieu, but one that he had never before explored in a film. The second was Lon Chaney himself, by now the world-famous "Man of a Thousand Faces," an actor sufficiently protean to give convincing shape to Browning's dark visions of physical limitation and disfigurement.

Chaney's parents could neither speak nor hear, and so he had become adept at pantomime in early life. He spent years in vaudeville, as a comedian, hoofer, and stage manager, before establishing himself in Hollywood just before the war. His gift for physical contortion was first given prominent display in *The Miracle Man* (1919), in which he played a phony cripple. The following year he perfected the basic formula for later mutilation-revenge melodramas with *The Penalty*. The story concerned a child whose legs are mistakenly amputated, and who grows up to become a vengeful king of the underworld. As Blizzard, the criminal kingpin, Chaney plots an insane, grisly revenge on the daughter of the doctor who mutilated him: he plans to have her fiancé's legs cut off and grafted to his own stumps. The actor wore a painful leg harness that enabled him to walk on his knees, aided by a pair of short crutches. Against the advice of doctors, he insisted on wearing the torturous appliance long enough to dangerously inhibit circulation, and is said to have collapsed on the set repeatedly.

The Penalty firmly established Chaney as a star of the first magnitude, his fame enhanced immeasurably by the martyr-like spectacle of his punishing disguises. His physical ordeals were no doubt exaggerated to some extent for press purposes, but it would be a mistake to believe that Chaney did not willingly undergo a perverse amount of discomfort in pursuit of his art.

Though its theme was veiled, *The Penalty* also spoke suggestively of the impotent rage of maimed war veterans who were being assimilated back into society in unprecedented numbers. In

Lon Chaney being fitted with a harness to simulate amputation for *The Penalty* **(1920).** *(Courtesy of Ronald V. Borst / Hollywood Movie Posters)*

A Blind Bargain (1922) Chaney varied the cripple formula by trans-forming himself into an apelike hunchback, the assistant to a mad scientist (whom he also played). The makeup for Chaney's two most celebrated characterizations, *The Hunchback of Notre Dame* (1923) and *The Phantom of the Opera* (1925), both bore more than a passing resemblance to the faces of the *mutilés de guerre* that haunted Europe and America, with smashed features, missing noses, and mouths full of broken teeth. For *The Hunchback,* the actor wore a fifty-pound rubber cast, another masochistic test of endurance.

As Quasimodo, Chaney's fictional deformity was presumably congenital; as Erik, the Opera Ghost, the cause of the ruined face was never made clear, and the Phantom of Paris could easily have taken his place in the Union des Gueules Cassées—the French brotherhood of bashed faces (or, more literally, "broken mugs"), a group of more than 5,000 disfigured veterans, members of which traditionally led the Armistice parades.

The Hunchback of Notre Dame and *The Phantom of the Opera,* two

Lon Chaney in *The Penalty*.

of the mid-twenties' most elaborate spectacles (and both produced at Universal by Carl Laemmle, Sr.), each juxtaposed stories of physical deformity with obsessively detailed physical reconstructions of European landmarks—the Cathedral of Notre Dame, the Paris Opera, etc. (As *Life* magazine quipped: "If Carl Laemmle had only expended his vast resources on the devastated areas in France itself instead of in southern California, there would be no traces of the Great War left.") In Europe, spectacles of mutilation and reconstruction were approached less metaphorically: Jacques W. Maliniak, M.D., an army plastic surgeon, recalled in 1934 that "Val-de-Grasse, the well-known military hospital in Paris, has an unusually large collection of casts taken from the wounded during the war. The Charité Hospital in Berlin also has such a museum. In London there is a collection in wax, showing the different stages of repair. . . . Thousands of people visit on holidays, to look with awed horror on the authentic reproduction of the suffering and mutilation of war."

War wasn't mentioned explicitly in *The Phantom of the Opera,* but since no explanation of any kind was given for the Opera Ghost's hideous appearance, Chaney's skull-like face could pluck at the culture's rawest nerves, unbridled by rationale. Later, and less

The postwar reconstruction of Europe at Universal City: studio executives stand before Carl Laemmle's recreation of Notre Dame. *(Courtesy of Lupita Tovar Kohner)*

effective, adaptations of the Gaston Leroux novel would add an explanation for the Phantom's deformity—usually acid thrown in his face—but Chaney's opera ghost was primally, congenitally horrible; birth itself was the monstrosity. Chaney used a contoured wire appliance to flare and pull back his nose (the guide wires were hidden under putty). "He suffered, you know," said the film's cinematographer, Charles Van Enger, recalling the nasal contraption, which would sometimes cause Chaney to "bleed like hell." The famous scene in which actress Mary Philbin rips the mask from Erik's face as he pumps his subterranean organ is an assault on the audience verging on visual rape. Erik's bulging bald head and stiff carriage give him the aspect of a ruined penis that can no longer seduce, only repulse the beloved. (Murnau's Nosferatu had this same "phallambulist" quality, which has been examined in detail by French critic Roger Dadoun.)

There was more to the Chaney mystique than morbid mutilation anxiety, however. In an America still very much in the thrall

Otto Dix, *Transplantation* (Skin graft), 1924 (Plate 10 of *Der Krieg IV*). *(The Robert Gore Rifkind Center for German Expressionist Studies, Los Angeles County Museum of Art)*

Lon Chaney as Quasimodo in *The Hunchback of Notre Dame*. *(Courtesy of Philip J. Riley)*

Les mutilés de guerre: maimed French war veterans as depicted in *L'Illustration*, June 11, 1927. *(The Library of Congress)*

of Horatio Alger, with aspirations further energized by the boom-
ing, speculative 1920s, Lon Chaney was an almost inevitable
development. Film historian David Thomson summed up Chaney's appeal: "There is not a screen performer who so illustrates
the fascination for audiences of the idea, promise and threat of
metamorphosis. . : . Chaney's fluctuating appearance seethed with
the audience's lust for vicariousness." The protean spirit of Lon
Chaney so permeated the American consciousness that a familiar
saying of the time, referring to spiders, lizards, or other crawling
things, was "Don't step on it—it might be Lon Chaney." Another
popular myth about the actor was that he was fond of using his
natural appearance as yet another disguise, one that enabled him
to mix unrecognized with the public. You might be rubbing
shoulders with him, and never know it. The idea of Lon Chaney
was everywhere.

In addition to providing vicariousness and wish fulfillment,
Chaney served as a link between popular culture and modernist
developments in the arts and sciences. With no fixed reality or

The prospect of a new Lon Chaney picture always created tremendous
public anticipation. Here, actress Mary Philbin and young fans gather
before billboard heralding *The Phantom of the Opera*. *(Courtesy of Lupita
Tovar Kohner)*

nature, he was the fragmented, relativistic Everyman created by the war, existentialism, and modern physics. Chaney's plastic experiments on his own body shadowed the concurrent efforts of cubist, dadaist, and emerging surrealist painters to stretch the human form into increasingly bizarre configurations. In one sense, he was the prototype of our contemporary image of the Hollywood star—he was the first actor in the film colony to affect dark glasses in public, and the first to deliberately cultivate an inaccessible persona. "There is no Lon Chaney," he, or his press agent, was fond of saying. "I am the character I am creating. That is all." And if it was permissible for a big star like Lon Chaney to lack identity, then what a relief and validation this provided to the anonymous mass of his fans, many of whom already suspected they might be nobody themselves. A glimpse at the back pages of the fan magazines that published studio-canned features on the Man of a Thousand Faces is revealing; up front, you could discover Chaney's latest grueling disguise, and the agony he was enduring, Christ-like, on your behalf; and when you finished reading about the actor's latest hunchback harness, you could peruse innumerable back-of-the-book advertisements for products to straighten your own spine, reduce or enlarge your body, or give yourself a "round, pretty" face instead of "unsightly hollows." Women especially would be expected, more and more, to become wizards of makeup in order to withstand the looming sexual rigors of the twentieth century. Lon Chaney undoubtedly did his part to make a segment of the public acutely aware of "unsightly hollows" it had previously never noticed.

Browning and Chaney followed *The Unholy Three* with *The Blackbird* (1926) and *The Road to Mandalay* (1926), in which Chaney again was crippled and hideously scarred. "When we're getting ready to discuss a new story," Browning told an interviewer in 1928, Chaney would "amble into my office and say, 'Well, what's it going to be, boss?' I'll say 'This time a leg comes off, or an arm, or a nose'—whatever it may be."

Their dovetailing obsessions reached their pinnacle with *The Unknown* (1927), a wildly Freudian circus melodrama that would be a signature piece for both men. An appraisal by the *New York Herald Tribune* encapsulated the mood of Browning's fixations:

> The case of Mr. Tod Browning is rapidly approaching the pathological. After a series of minor horrors that featured such

Disfigurement anxiety was a constant presence in both the front and back of movie magazines of the 1920s. Here are samples of advertisements that appeared in fan magazines around the time of *The Phantom of the Opera*.

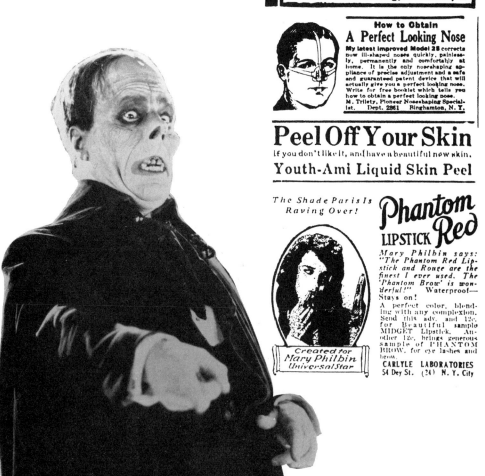

comparatively respectable creations as murderous midgets, crippled thieves, and poisonous reptiles, all sinister and deadly in a murky atmosphere of blackness and unholy doom, the director presents us now with a melodrama that might have been made from a scenario dashed off by the Messrs. Leopold and Loeb.

The Unknown was a kind of upper-torso version of *The Penalty,* featuring Chaney as Alonzo the Armless, a man masquerading as a sideshow attraction to avoid detection by the police. Alonzo is a fake freak who binds his arms, eating, smoking, and even throwing knives with his feet. He is in love with Estrellita (Joan Crawford), a beautiful circus performer with a peculiar sexual phobia: she is repulsed by the idea of being held in a man's arms. Ironically, he must keep his love at a distance—not only would she discover his "repulsive" appendages, but she might also recognize the double thumb on his right hand, the unique imprint of which was left on the throat of Estrellita's father when Alonzo, unbound, killed him because of his cruelty to his daughter. The convoluted story (which nonetheless still plays surprisingly well, like a lurid, forbidden fairy tale) reaches a dark crescendo when Alonzo blackmails a doctor into actually amputating his arms. He returns for Estrellita, only to find that she has overcome her phobia, thanks to the patient attentions of the resident strong man. Alonzo sabotages the strong man's act and nearly succeeds in having wild horses rip off the performer's arms in revenge, but the plot fails when Alonzo is trampled by the horses during a fatal moment of remorse.

Joan Crawford never mentioned Browning in print, but in a career interview called working with Chaney in *The Unknown* "both traumatic and delightful." Although her impressions of Browning were less distinct—she remembered the director in an unpublished letter as "soft-spoken," "sensitive," and "knowledgeable," but provided no anecdotes—Crawford found Chaney the actor to be "the most tense, exciting individual I'd ever met, a man mesmerized into his part. Between pictures when you met him on the lot you saw a grave, mild-mannered man with laughing black eyes who seldom laughed, but when he did, his laughter was irresistible." When Chaney acted, Crawford remembered, "it was as if God were working, he had such profound concentration. It was then I became aware for the first time of the difference between standing in front of a camera, and acting."

The actress described the excruciating lengths to which the performer would go to achieve his effects: "Mr. Chaney could have unstrapped his arms between scenes. He did not. He kept them strapped one day for five hours, enduring such numbness, such torture, that when we got to this scene, he was able to convey not just realism but such emotional agony that it was shocking . . . and fascinating."★

The movies weren't the only place where the public was agonizing over mutilation allegories in the late twenties. The previous year, Ernest Hemingway had published his novel *The Sun Also Rises,* and had set the literary world buzzing with his anguished story of Jake Barnes and his emasculating war wound. The critics accepted Hemingway's explanation of why he wrote the story in the first place: that while convalescing from his own war injuries in Milan, he had the occasion to visit a genitourinary ward in a different hospital. As recounted by his biographer Kenneth S. Lynn, "There he had talked to a number of soldiers who had suffered genital injuries, and as a result of wondering about their plight he had come to imagine Jake Barnes's . . . [But] missing from this plausible-sounding story was a convincing explanation of why Hemingway had been so interested in the wounded in that particular ward."

Hemingway's fiction is, of course, full of challenges to manhood, some more literal than others. In one very short and grisly story, "God Rest Ye Merry, Gentlemen," Hemingway writes of a sixteen-year-old boy, maddened by sexual desire and religious guilt, who comes to an emergency room on Christmas Day and begs the doctors on call to castrate him. When they refuse, he goes home and lops off his penis with a straight razor. ("On Christmas Day, too," one of the doctors mutters, recounting the tale.)

Hemingway may or may not have been bedeviled by conscious fears or fantasies of phallic loss; the theme, however, indisputably recurs in his work. Working simultaneously in another medium, Tod Browning, with or without Lon Chaney, was turning castration symbolism into a cottage industry. The image of human beings paralyzed, mutilated, or otherwise "cut off" below the waist occurs

★Crawford biographer Alexander Walker noted that the actress' future stardom would also "be sanctified by this kind of self-sought Calvary. Working on a Crawford film set was seldom without its pains. Even her insistence on keeping the temperature down to a frigid 58 Fahrenheit was a way of 'concentrating people's minds on the work.' "

Nothing below the waist: a typical Browning image from *The Show* (1927).

repeatedly in Browning films; it is a virtual leitmotif of the Browning oeuvre. *The Blackbird, The Show* (1927), *The Unknown* (where "legs" become "arms"), *West of Zanzibar* (1928), and, later, *Freaks* (1932) and *Miracles for Sale* (1939) all presented images of literal or figurative truncations. A variation on the theme occurs in a recurring use of stolen, dangling "jewels" as a plot element in several films, or, as in *The Show,* a whole story revolving around the attempted beheading of a lead character named Cock (Robin, played by John Gilbert), set in a sideshow full of bottomless people, disembodied heads, and the like. *The Mystic* (1925) featured a pointed scene in which a knife-thrower slices off the end of a sausage sandwich which a character has just inserted into her mouth.

In his essay "The 'Uncanny,' " published at the end of the first world war, Sigmund Freud first discussed the relationship of the castration complex to macabre fantasy stories. In Freud's view, the doppelganger (the basis of all monster images) is a defense mechanism; the unconscious mind, sensing a mortal danger to the ego, eye, limb, or genital, creates an imaginative stand-in for the threatened part. (The double-thumb motif in *The Unknown* is such a pure demonstration of Freud's thesis that one must wonder if Tod Browning himself had been directly influenced by reading "The 'Uncanny,' " "Dismembered limbs, a severed head, a hand cut off at the wrist . . . all of these have something peculiarly uncanny about them," Freud wrote, adding that "this kind of uncanniness springs from its proximity to the castration complex." In the same discussion, Freud unintentionally touched on the deeper associations of Browning's "Living Corpse" routine: "To some people the idea of being buried alive is the most uncanny thing of all. And yet psycho-analysis has taught us that this terrifying phantasy is only a transformation of another phantasy which had originally nothing terrifying about it at all . . . the phantasy, I mean, of intra-uterine existence."

It is tempting to look for a "smoking wound" in Browning's life to explain his extraordinary career focus on castration images. Public documents concerning the extent of his injuries in the 1915 crash contain insufficient detail to ascertain whether he did or did not sustain pelvic trauma. At some point, however, he suffered a considerable injury to the mouth, and was reported to have worn a set of upper and lower dentures at a relatively early age. Before being blacklisted for drinking, he was said to have responded to a San Francisco hotel manager's request to party a bit less rambunctiously by handing over his false teeth and telling the man to "Go bite yourself!" Whether or not he lost the teeth in the 1915 crash is a matter of speculation; but he does seem to have told acquaintances in later life that he had been "kicked by a horse" in his carnival/racetrack days.

Whatever their cause, dentofacial injuries or disfigurement can have profound psychological effects. Frances Cooke Macgregor, a leading authority on facial trauma and reconstruction, notes that "the area in and around the mouth is both emotionally charged and strongly connected with one's self-image. As an instrument of speech, eating and kissing, as well as a mirror of emotions, it also has unique social and psychological implications and symbolic meaning." Browning and Chaney created a particularly anxious image of a human mouth in *London After Midnight* (1927), wherein Chaney played a fake vampire with a shark-like set of dentures. The primitive razor-mouth, superimposed on a human face, is a clear evocation of a Freudian concept: the devouring,

Lon Chaney in *London After Midnight* (1927). *(The Stephen Jochsberger Collection)*

castrating *vagina dentata*. *London After Midnight* marked Browning's first foray into the world of vampirism, a bottomless realm of sexual displacements and orality that would continue to fascinate him.

Browning's universe of castration anxiety and relentless sexual frustration would seem to be at odds with a jazz-age public that was otherwise and everywhere being exhorted to sally forth and screw. As Frederick Lewis Allan recalled the era in *Only Yesterday,* "The first requirement of mental health was to have an uninhibited sex life. If you would be well and happy, you must obey your libido. Such was the Freudian gospel as it imbedded itself in the American mind . . . Clergymen who preached about the virtue of self-control were reminded by outspoken critics that self-control was out-of-date and really dangerous."

Nonetheless, part of America wanted to hear what Browning wanted to say—and a fairly good part, from the box-office receipts. Neither his nor Chaney's audience was to be found among the sophisticates of Manhattan or the film colony. Both men, in fact, were loners who rarely socialized with the Hollywood set. The Chaney/Browning appeal was to the working masses, even though Browning's salary at Metro-Goldwyn-Mayer was hardly blue-collar; it was reported to be $150,000 in the late twenties, twice that earned by the president of the United States. It was probably an inflated figure—an internal memo at another studio on the industry salaries of directors in 1926 estimated Browning's annual compensation at $78,000—but even the lower figure places Browning near the top of the scale for contract directors. The comparison of Browning to a political figure is apt, however, for movies amounted to a kind of populist politics, with Tod Browning playing the role of Mutilation T. Cornpone, as it were, appealing to America's most visceral fears, though perhaps not allaying them.

Both Lon Chaney and Tod Browning remain enigmas: Browning would die childless and reclusive; Chaney's surviving family has never cooperated with a biographer. Curt Siodmak, the writer-director who worked on numerous occasions with Chaney's son Creighton (known professionally as Lon, Jr.), recalled that Chaney, Sr., "seemed to have been a sadistic character, the way he treated Lon as a child and young man." Lon, Jr., in Siodmak's recollection, emerged from his father's domination "a tortured person." The Man of a Thousand Faces may have had good reasons for keeping his true face private. Browning's obsession to depict barely concealed genital traumas is likewise an impenetrable conundrum. To mainline Freudians, castration fear makes the world go round; real castration is hardly required. Does Browning reveal a purely personal psychology, or merely his facility for accessing shared primal terror?

It is somehow appropriate that these two shadowy men, both driven by their own demons to project indelible images of self-fragmentation, somehow found completion in each other. And, like some recombinant sideshow monstrosity, it was something the public wanted to see, or see itself in. Just as burlesque was becoming ever more racy, Tod Browning and Lon Chaney seemed intent on revealing yet concealing themselves through a crazy new kind of striptease, one that didn't stop at the skin, the bone, or even the brain.

Or, as Diane Arbus would define "identity" to a class of students three decades later: it's the thing that's left when you take everything else away.

Chapter Four

THE MONSTERS AND MR. LIVERIGHT

"Drama—what literature does at night."

George Jean Nathan
(1931)

LIKE A DARK, binary star system, fixed in the twilight of our cultural horizons, the twin images of Dracula and Frankenstein's monster present a dynamic, if demonic mythology for modern times. Each figure conjures the other by contrast: Dracula is suave, sinister, supernaturally masterful, an aristocratic wraith slipping through a keyhole as a mist, transforming himself from man to bat to wolf and back again, with never a hair out of place. The Frankenstein creature, by contrast, is relentlessly downscale, a proletarian clod. Like a parody of the scientific method, he moves slowly, deliberately, one heavy step at a time. Dracula flaps ahead effortlessly, shape-shifting at will. The vampire's manner is seamless. Frankenstein's monster shows all his seams, literally. Taken together, the monsters constitute an overwhelming gestalt, representing the intuitive left brain and the logical right, shadow and substance, superstition and science—the oddest of odd couples. There is almost no realm of modern culture in which they have not made their presence felt: in literature, in theatre, film, and television; in commerce and advertising; in social, scientific, and

---

Bela Lugosi and Dorothy Peterson in Horace Liveright's 1927 Broadway production of *Dracula*. (*The Harvard Theatre Collection*)

psychological metaphor. Put simply, they are everywhere. Few imaginary beings have a higher recognition factor; they rival Santa Claus and Mickey Mouse as shared mental constructs. Their uses are endless. In the cereal guise of Count Chocula and Frankenberry, we feed them to our children as a playful form of daily dread.

Both the Dracula and Frankenstein stories had their literary genesis at the same moment: the celebrated house party held in June 1816 at the Villa Diodati near Geneva. The participants included Percy Bysshe Shelley and his second wife, Mary; George Gordon, Lord Byron; and Byron's friend and physician Dr. John Polidori. It was suggested that they all try their hand at composing a ghost story. Byron eventually produced a fragment of a novel concerning a Romantic revenant that Polidori elaborated as a popular novella, *The Vampyre* (1819), which was widely held to be Byron's work. Mary Shelley, after listening to her husband and Byron discuss speculative theories about the electrical basis of life and the galvanic reanimation of corpses, had a powerful waking vision that "arose in my mind with a vividness far beyond the usual bounds of reverie. I saw—with shut eyes, but acute mental vision—I saw the pale student of unhallowed arts kneeling beside the thing he had put together. I saw the hideous phantasm of a man stretched out, and then, on the working of some powerful engine, show signs of life and stir with an uneasy, half-vital motion." Her imaginings culminated in *Frankenstein; or, the Modern Prometheus,* first published in three volumes in 1816.

Reanimated corpses were also the subject of Bram Stoker's *Dracula* (1897), the story of a dead-alive Transylvanian warlord who migrates from his castle in the Carpathians to modern-day London in search of fresh blood. Stoker, whose primary vocation was that of business manager to the celebrated actor-impresario Henry Irving, wrote reams of potboilers in his spare time. One of the central conundrums of *Dracula* is just how the book came to rise so far above the mediocrity of his other work. Some commentators have suggested a fevered, Freudian burst of inspiration bordering on possession; a more down-to-earth possibility is that the manuscript was reworked by someone other than Stoker. H. P. Lovecraft, America's poet laureate of dark fantasy, suggested just such a scenario in 1932: "I know an old lady," he wrote, "who almost had the job of revising 'Dracula' back in the early 1890s— she saw the original ms., & says it was a fearful mess. Finally someone else (Stoker thought her price for the work was too high) whipped it into such shape as it now possesses." *Dracula* historians Raymond McNally and Radu Florescu have suggested that the book doctor was the popular Victorian writer Hall Caine, Stoker's close friend, to whom *Dracula* is dedicated (under his childhood nickname, "Hommy-Beg"). Since Stoker left no written account of *Dracula's* genesis, the issue is not likely to be resolved.

Despite its perennial popularity, *Dracula* is strangely incomplete in its evocation of the Count, which may explain why its stage and film adaptors have relentlessly embellished the story—and then embellished the embellishments. Stoker broke radically with the seductive, Byronic image of vampirism that had already been popularized on the stage and in penny dreadfuls like James Malcolm Rymer's *Varney the Vampyre* (1847); Dracula spends little time on social niceties and is physically repellent, a cadaverous old man who grows younger as he drinks blood but who never becomes attractive. The twentieth-century image of Dracula is a distinct hybrid, combining Stoker's Count with character traits borrowed from the brooding antiheros of Gothic romances, from *Don Juan, Wuthering Heights,* and elsewhere.

Where *Frankenstein* is literary and philosophical, *Dracula* is a naive entertainment engaging the emotions rather than the intellect. The narratives, however, contain nearly as many similarities as polarities: both stories hinge on novel forms of self-replication (Frankenstein creates his own doppelganger by piecing together tissue from graveyards and slaughterhouses; Dracula reproduces his kind by a mystical blood transfusion). Each dramatizes a primal encounter with a supine human form that is, paradoxically, both living and dead: Victor Frankenstein staring with horror at the final result of his handiwork, which he somehow had expected to be beautiful; and the shock of the real-estate lawyer Jonathan Harker, discovering his host Count Dracula undead in an earth-box. Both books are cautionary daydreams about failed attempts to overcome death, the scientist by rational enterprise, the vampire by irrational curse. Each novel has become an almost bottomless text for critical and cultural inquiry, and neither has ever been out of print.

Both *The Vampyre, Dracula's* prototype, and *Frankenstein* inspired numerous stage adaptations in the 1820s, both in England and on the Continent. Occasionally, the image of artifical man and human vampire would blur: Shelley herself refers to her monster as a "vampire" at one point in the novel; an 1887 burlesque, *Franken-*

stein; or, the Vampire's Victim, mixed both varieties of monster in
the public mind. After the publication of Stoker's novel, the word
"Dracula" became a virtual synonym for "vampire," and the Shel-
ley-Stoker creations became associated as two sides of a coin,
complementary high points of scary entertainment, like bread and
butter, gin and tonic—or blood and thunder.

Monsters often require mortal helpers—dupes, assistants,
agents—to achieve their designs in the world. The vampire and
the patchwork man waited more than a hundred years beyond
their literary conception before encountering the strangely driven
personality who would secure their twin niche in the twentieth-
century imagination.

The year was 1930, and Horace Liveright was broke again.

The forty-four-year-old publisher-producer was truly a self-made,
and self-undone, man; from inauspicious beginnings as a bond
salesman and toilet-paper entrepreneur, Horace Brisbin Liveright
had risen spectacularly in the 1920s as one of the most influential
forces in American publishing history, with a showman's energy
that spilled over into the literal theatre as well. In addition to
founding the Modern Library, and later publishing the likes of
Theodore Dreiser, Sherwood Anderson, Ernest Hemingway, and
Eugene O'Neill, Liveright made a considerable splash as a Broadway producer of attention-getting, if not always money-spinning,
plays, including *An American Tragedy* (a hit), the first *Hamlet* in
modern dress (a palpable flop), and, most notably and successfully, the 1927 stage adaptation of Bram Stoker's *Dracula* that had
earned over $2 million in New York and on tour.

By 1930, the *Dracula* money was gone, sucked away in the wake
of the stock-market crash. This season, there were no best-sellers.
Most galling of all was the growing Hollywood interest in *Dracula,* for which he had stupidly relinquished all film rights. *Dracula*
had been one of Liveright's pet projects, and he had gone to great
lengths to secure the American rights from Florence Stoker, the
author's combative and money-obsessed widow. Although he
hadn't yet produced one, Liveright knew that thrillers and mystery plays could be surefire box office. Among the nail-biters that
had drawn large crowds in recent years were *The Bat* by Mary
Roberts Rinehart and Avery Hopwood, which opened in 1920 and
ran for 878 performances in New York alone; Crane Wilbur's *The
Monster* (1922), which included a creepy mansion, a mad scientist,

Horace Liveright as a young man. *(The Bettmann Archive)*

and an electric chair, and would become a film vehicle for Lon Chaney; and perhaps the most popular melodrama of the day, John Willard's *The Cat and the Canary* (1922), another creeper of the "old dark house" variety that would enjoy extraordinary longevity on tour, in stock, and through three eventual film adaptations.

These plays all had "horror" trappings but, in keeping with the theatrical conventions of the 1920s, always took care to dispel the shudders as the work of some human agency, usually criminal. *Dracula* kept the trappings, but refused to explain away its terrors. Horace Liveright immediately grasped the potential audience appeal of a headlong dive into the irrational and sensational.

Given the difficulty of dealing with Florence Stoker, it would have been easier to chuck the whole business early on, but Liveright was certain he could make a commercial success of the lurid vampire melodrama. Mrs. Stoker had already licensed the dramatic rights to Hamilton Deane, a touring actor-manager, who produced a badly written but nevertheless highly theatrical adaptation that was the surprise hit of the 1927 London season. Despite withering notices, the crowds couldn't stay away. Even George Bernard Shaw made the pigrimage to José Levy's Little Theatre★ in Adelphi to partake of the thrills (though afterwards, when asked for his opinion, he said only that "I'm awfully glad I didn't write it").

The widow Stoker was paranoid about the world's growing interest in *Dracula*—she seemed to regard Liveright, especially, as some unsavory American variation on Nosferatu, the unauthorized German Dracula she had litigated against for years. Her reaction was not unique; one of Liveright's former employees, Maurice Hanline, would later publish a sizzling roman à clef, *Years of Indiscretion,* in which a sensitive young writer comes under the thrall of Medici-like publisher Jason Pertinax: "I don't like this man, thought Mark, he's not human . . . He's a handsome Dracula, he'd laugh at my poetry, though he might publish it if he thought there was money in it, I think I'm going to like him, I hate the bastard . . . Can I get to the door without vomiting?" (To be fair, it must be noted that Hanline himself would be likened by at least one acquaintance to "a referee at a snake race.")

In order to bring *Dracula* under his control, Liveright had enlisted John L. Balderston, an American playwright and newspaperman

---

★The Little Theatre, London's premiere venue for thrillers in the twenties, might never have achieved its reputation had its building not first been wrecked by a fifty-kilo German bomb in September 1917. The former banking hall, which was being used as a club room for soldiers, was renovated and reopened by José Levy as an English Grand Guignol under the artistic direction of Sibyl Thorndike in 1920. Thorndike introduced the practice of stationing a nurse in the lobby, a stunt later borrowed by Hamilton Deane and Horace Liveright for their productions of *Dracula.*

John L. Balderston. *(The Library of Congress)*

living in London, to charm Mrs. Stoker. Balderston was about as British as an American could get, and, as a World War I correspondent, had lived on Cheyne Walk in Chelsea, not far from one of Stoker's former residences. In 1915, at the age of twenty-six, he had left his New York newspaper office for the European front.

He told *The Editor and Publisher* that he was headed for the war zone because he thought there were "too many war correspondents and journalists in the field and not enough reporters." Balderston promised to go after the war "in the same way that he would tackle a police story at home, and that he will not wear a wrist watch, cable descriptions of what he ate for breakfast, patronize the generals, and try to run the war." The correspondent-to-be pledged his determination to post those special stories "that will keep warm while coming across in the mails, like a thermos bottle, you know."

Resolution during wartime would prove to be good practice for dealing with Florence Stoker. It didn't hurt that Balderston was also handsome, cultured, and possessed far more tact and patience than Liveright ever would. The producer wanted Balderston to completely rewrite *Dracula*—Hamilton Deane's dialogue was hopeless—but it was important not to rub this in. Florence Stoker was testy enough without having her previous judgment and taste criticized. Once a legendary Victorian beauty, her admirers had included Wilde, Burne-Jones, Rossetti, and du Maurier. "You should see her," said actor Bernard Jukes, who originated the role of *Dracula*'s fly-eating maniac, Renfield. He recalled Florence Stoker's "little lace cap, tight waist, high stiff collar, puffy sleeves at

---

Newspaper cartoon of Raymond Huntley and Hamilton Deane in the original London production of *Dracula* in 1927.

the shoulder." Formidable in old age as Wilde's Lady Bracknell, she required a certain amount of handling.

Balderston's diplomacy carried the day, and *Dracula* went on to be a lucrative proposition for all concerned. But bringing the master vampire to life on stage was a tricky business. There was no male prototype for such a creature; only the Theda Bara conception of "the vamp" came close. They offered it to Raymond Huntley, a reedy twenty-two-year-old actor who played it in England with a middle-aged wig, but he declined Liveright's measly offer of $150 a week. Then another producer who had attempted unsuccessfully to bring *Dracula* to the stage recommended that Liveright consider the actor he had chosen for the unrealized production. "Hell," the producer reportedly said, "I heard that he even came from Transylvania."

The actor's name was Béla Ferenc Dezsö Blasko; born in 1882 in Lugos, Hungary, he arrived in America as a political refugee in 1921, performing under the name Bela Lugosi. He had been a versatile and well-known performer at the Hungarian State Theatre in Budapest, but in New York was cast primarily as exotics: Arabs, bandits, fakirs, apaches. Lugosi's English was terrible, essentially nonexistent; he learned American parts phonetically in a resonant, accented baritone that would become one of the most instantly recognizable, imitated, and parodied voices in theatrical history.

Lugosi's failure to realize the potential drawbacks of his self-perpetuated language barrier may have led to a messy legal entanglement in 1924. He had managed to obtain an assignment as the director of a play called *The Right to Dream,* a title that certainly described Lugosi's blind faith in his ability to stage a play in English. Dismissed in no time, Lugosi sued the producer, Hubert Henry Davis, for breach of contract, and demanded a trial by jury. Davis responded that Lugosi had proved "utterly unfit" as a director and had misrepresented both his abilities and professional connections. The court sided with Davis, and Lugosi, who couldn't or wouldn't pay a $69.56 judgment against him, had the contents of his West 55th Street apartment sold at auction to pay for court costs.

Lugosi's pigheaded streak would be noted by his coworkers throughout his career. The trait probably also contributed to his intensity as a performer: he acted in a language he didn't know through titanic willpower. Almost anyone else would have just taken English lessons.

The critics were not unanimous in their praise of Bela Lugosi as

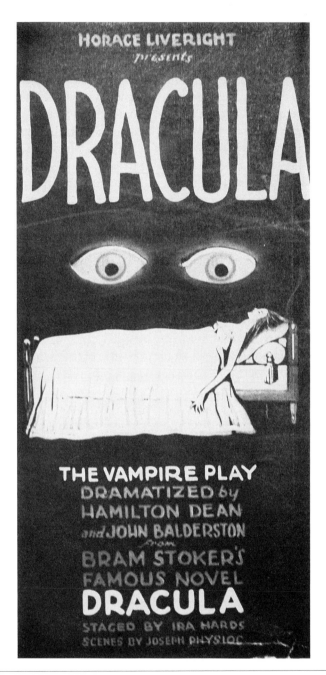

Original promotional art for Liveright's *Dracula*. *(The Free Library of Philadelphia Theatre Collection)*

Dracula when Liveright's production opened on Broadway in October 1927. This was, after all, a new and peculiar kind of character on the American stage, and there was no standard against which to evaluate it. Count Dracula had crossed the Atlantic with some changes in his appearance and wardrobe: beginning with Lugosi, Liveright's stage Draculas would have their faces painted green. The cape, lined in crimson for London audiences, featured purple satin in New York, as if to avoid holiday connotations. The *New York Post* noted that "Mr. Lugosi performs Dracula with funereal decorations suggesting . . . an operatically inclined but cheerless mortician." Alexander Woollcott, in *The World,* felt that Lugosi spoke in "that incongruous accent which American playgoers have come to associate with lovable and threadbare music masters." And the *Herald Tribune*'s Percy Hammond reported that "the torments of the first American performance might have been more alarming had the demon been illustrated less stiffly. . . . It was a rigid hobgoblin presented by Mr. Lugosi, resembling a wax man in a shop window more than a suave ogre bent on nocturnal mischief-making."

Such reservations did not deter audiences, and *Dracula* made a hit. It was one of those jazz-age thrill-machines that audiences couldn't resist, sort of a theatrical equivalent to the Coney Island Cyclone, another 1927 invention that was attracting record crowds. *Time* magazine noted a certain dissonance between the Victorian age that produced the story and the Roaring Twenties that now feasted on it. "The world, or at least that particle of it which is represented in the audiences at Manhattan theatres, has come a long way in 25 years. Now maidens can see grisly horror, and withdraw between the acts to smoke a cigaret and talk calmly of their minor vices."

The play ran thirty-three weeks at the Fulton Theatre (later the Helen Hayes), followed by two separate touring companies the following year. As part of Horace Liveright's traveling horror carnival, Bela Lugosi achieved a unique distinction as America's reigning death-symbol. "It was the embrace of Death their subconscious was yearning for," Lugosi said of his fans. "Death, the final triumphant lover." Smart conversation during the flapper era was increasingly peppered with half-baked Freudianisms. Since Horace Liveright, as a publisher, had popularized *A General Introduction to Psychoanalysis* in America, it was only appropriate that

Freud's pitchman would be the cause of a monumental encounter between America's queen and king of eros and thanatos. Without Horace Liveright, the self-appointed ringmaster of the American id, it never would have happened.

Comedian Jack Oakie recalled Clara Bow's excitement when she rushed out of her Los Angeles house on a summer day in 1928, and announced to the guests assembled around the pool that they were all going down to the Biltmore Theatre to see *Dracula*—now. She had evidently managed to get last-minute tickets to the sold-out show. "She was so excited, she didn't stop to dress," Oakie wrote in his 1980 memoirs. "She just threw a great long mink coat over her swimsuit and we all got into her chauffeur-driven black Packard limousine." Bow was well read on Lugosi, Oakie remembered. "I want to meet that man," she said. "Do you know he doesn't know how to speak English?" She was fascinated by the idea that the man could perform eight shows a week in a language he didn't understand.

All through the performance, the "Brooklyn Bonfire" squirmed seminude under her fur "and we watched Bela Lugosi in his monstrous makeup," wrote Oakie, "chewing on gals' necks all evening. Then we went backstage." The comedian recalled that Lugosi indeed spoke no English, "but no language barrier could hide his thrill at meeting Clara Bow." The Hungarian explained (somehow; Oakie didn't give communicative details) that he memorized his lines from cues, but if another actor would accidentally give him a wrong line, he would be lost for the rest of the performance. Like Bow, Bela clearly had his own way of doing things. She invited him home immediately.

Lugosi's affair with Bow continued for at least a year. He apparently commissioned a nude portrait of her (from an artist who had also painted him, clothed); the canvas would hang on Lugosi's living-room wall two marriages later. Little is known about the details of their relationship, but writer Adela Rogers St. John made some observations at the time that may have some bearing on the issue. "When men fall in love with Clara Bow, they seem to go a bit mad. They write things on pictures, for example, that surely no sane man would write."

Bow had a darker side than her "makin' whoopee" screen persona would suggest. To the public, she was the rebellious, fun-loving flapper (an icon first popularized by Horace Liveright's publication of *Flaming Youth* in 1922). But, like Marilyn Monroe, whose Hollywood tragedy would be prefigured by her own, Bow had a sad and difficult childhood that her biographer David Stenn described as "Brooklyn Gothic." Commenting on her ability to cry on cue for the camera, Bow once said, "All I hadda do was think of home." Bow's mother had been subject to "spells." "I think I'll kill ya," she would blurt to young Clara. "This is a terrible world. You'd be better off dead." One night the girl was wakened from a deep sleep by her mother, who was brandishing a butcher knife with which she intended to cut off her daughter's show-business aspirations for good. Fortunately, the woman passed out before she could complete the task.

The public's fascination with Clara Bow had an ambivalent dimension: a flapper was akin to a vamp, and a vamp was just a step away from a literal vampire. Bow received enormous publicity in 1926 when an obsessive suitor aptly named Robert Savage claimed she had kissed and bit his lips "until they bled." His advances

Eros and thanatos: brought together by Horace Liveright's *Dracula,* Clara Bow and Bela Lugosi soon found that opposites attract.

spurned, Savage draped himself on a divan, and lightly cut his wrists so that his blood could drizzle on Bow's photograph. Bow called a press conference, and pulled off a public-relations coup to rival Theda Bara. How dare Savage insult her with such an epicene display—a real man, she said, would have used a gun.

Lugosi's affair with Bow did not preclude him from simultaneously wedding a wealthy San Francisco widow, Beatrice Weeks, for a marriage that lasted all of three days. New York's *Daily Mirror* reported the details in a November 1929 story that unfolded in the tones of a seasoned carnival barker: "Clara Bow, flaming-haired siren of the screen, has at last met with true romance—a romance, which, ghost-like, sprang from the ashes of another woman's love.

"Folks, meet her fiancé, and husband-to-be; Count [sic] Bela Lugosi, Hungarian actor, the male vampire who took the leading role in the blood-curdling drama, *Dracula.*"

Readers who stepped right up to the newsstand learned that Mrs. Charles Peters Weeks, widow of a noted California architect, had filed for divorce in Reno, naming Clara Bow as the other woman in her husband's life. Lugosi, she told the press from her luxurious suite at the Riverside Hotel in Reno, became violent on the second day of their marriage: "He slapped me in the face because I ate a lamb chop which he had hidden in the refrigerator."

Sparks began flying immediately after the nuptials, she told the scribbling journalists, when the man who was Dracula demanded her checkbook as well as the key to her safe-deposit vaults. "He told me that he was King; that in Hungary a wife and all she possessed were placed at the husband's disposal; that, in effect, she was nothing but a servant." Being the strong-minded heiress of a $2,500,000 estate, she objected to such an arrangement. The bride fled their San Francisco apartment while Lugosi was out impersonating Dracula at a leading west coast theatre, she said. The breaking point came when Lugosi had decided to furnish his own bedroom—afterwards informing her that if she didn't equip quarters of her own, she could sleep on the floor.

But worst of all—given the bizarrely detailed emphasis she placed on the matter—Lugosi's "table manners were terrible. He would break an apple in half and crowd one of the portions in his mouth, unable to speak or to swallow, until he had chewed it up fine." And that wasn't all. "He constantly used his fingers in place of a fork and was addicted to similar habits that simply frayed my nerves." As for Clara Bow, she wished her "all the luck in the world." However, she added, "I cannot see any happiness for her if she marries my husband, unless he improves his manners."

Lugosi had a rather different perspective on the story. He didn't know that the woman he had married had a more primary attachment in her life—the gin bottle. The hopeless marriage transpired during the penultimate days of the roaring decade, and the image of the once stylish, now drunken socialite who hurled herself at the image of Dracula was a fitting climax and comment on the wild years that had just passed. Clara Bow would soon follow her mother into breakdown and Bedlam.

And then, in October 1929, came the crash.

Horace Liveright, whose personal and professional identity had revolved around the tremendous energies of the wild party that had been New York in the twenties, had always had a genius for following his instincts and landing on his feet. According to Louis Kronenberger, "If he had neither an artist's sensibilities nor a critic's cultivation and judgement, he had a feeling, and indeed a flair, for what bubbled and stirred in the world he aspired to." Another employee, Edith Stern, recalled that his flashes of intuition, when they flared, could "seem almost visible, like lightning."

What Horace Liveright sensed bubbling and flashing was *Frankenstein*.

And why not? The theme of Promethean overreaching had a certain timely relevance at the end of the Roaring Twenties, both for the culture and for Liveright himself, who took relish in cultivating a public image of devilish, if not divine, presumption. Perhaps what Broadway needed now was a good old-fashioned morality play . . . or the semblance of one. Let the audiences tsk-tsk the blasphemous doctor, all the while swooning over his brooding good looks. Liveright knew how to put on a show. He also loved casting himself as a romantic literary rebel, or patron of the same, as reflected in an authorized (and self-published) caricature-sketch:

HBL, Publisher—Put him down a product of that American ferment: of that already distant and romantic age in which our country, cut off momentarily from its European outlets, began to sizzle and stew in its own juice; in which theaters, books and magazines of verse rose like an enzymed scum to the surface of our life—and countless youths, perched on the garret-tops of Greenwich Village, found voice and shouted: "Hail, Nietzsche. Hail, Ibsen; Hail Dostoievski—we are come!"

If it wasn't exactly Shelley, the growing signs of hubris, at least, were unmistakable.

Liveright had a long-standing interest in fantastic and sensational themes that teetered on the edge of propriety and often drove the censors into fits of apoplexy. One of the firm's big best-sellers in 1923 was *Black Oxen* by Gertrude Atherton, which brought together Dorian Gray and Frankenstein themes in the story of Countess Zattiany, who cheats death and finds eternal youth through a "scientific" X-ray treatment of the ovaries.* The book's sales were rivaled that year only by Emily Post's *Complete Etiquette*. (A film version in 1923 marked Clara Bow's screen debut, as a flapper.)

Liveright evidently took a bemused, ironic attitude toward much of what he presented the public, in print and on stage. He once told Eugene O'Neill that *Dracula* was a "lousy little play," while proudly pointing out that it made more money touring in Newark than O'Neill's newest drama was earning on Broadway.

As a Manhattan sophisticate, Liveright's sensibility was, to a certain degree, that of a cynic, but it came nowhere near the outright misanthropy of another literary figure of the twenties, who also had a stake in horror. H. P. Lovecraft, then emerging as the prince of the dark pulps like *Weird Tales,* found it "hard to conceive of anything more utterly loathsome than certain streets of the *lower* East Side. . . . The organic things—Italo-Semitico-Mongoloid—inhabiting that awful cesspool could not by any stretch of the imagination be call'd human. They were monstrous and nebulous adumbrations of the pithecanthropoid and amoebal; vaguely moulded from some stinking viscous slime of the earth's corruption, and slithering and oozing in and on the filthy streets or in and out of windows and doorways in a fashion suggestive of noth-

---

*Atherton herself had undergone a dubious form of X-ray therapy, and, pleased with the results, seems to have become a militant partisan of weird science in the jazz age. "We live in an age of scientific marvels," she declared, "and those who do not take advantage of them are fools and deserve the worst that malignant Nature can inflict upon them." For more, see her *Adventures of a Novelist* (New York: Liveright, Inc., 1932, p. 562).

ing but infesting worms." For Lovecraft, the twenties didn't roar; they dripped and festered and screamed. One strains to imagine Liveright and Lovecraft having a drink at one of the former's favorite speakeasies, trying to find any common ground among their monsters. Nonetheless, both men contemporaneously did much to promote the cause of the dark gods in America.

From the other side of the Atlantic, Hamilton Deane had been pestering Liveright, as well as John L. Balderston, for almost two years about a stage adaptation of *Frankenstein* by a certain Miss Peggy Webling which he was touring in rotating repertory with his *Dracula*. In November 1928, Deane wrote Balderston: "One of the biggest professional disappointments I have had recently, was when I failed to interest you sufficiently to revise *Frankenstein*. I have now revised it myself and the business we are doing with the new version is every whit as big as we did with *Dracula* previous to the London production. Both the press and the public say that it 'out-Draculas *Dracula.*' " The box office, Deane wrote, was "talking" and "we are having as many faints as we did in the old days." Since Deane was known to have planted paid swooners in the stalls for *Dracula,* this last could not have impressed Balderston, who sent Deane's note to his agent Harold Freedman, commenting that "two London theatres have been offered for the play, but Deane is holding it up until he sees me. It is inconceivably crude, but I suppose *Dracula* was about the crudest thing that ever went on and made a hit."

Peggy Webling, author of Hamilton Deane's production *Frankenstein: An Adventure in the Macabre,* had indeed written a stilted, fussy, preachy piece of theatre. But beneath her script's problematic surface were some original and revealing insights, not derived from previous dramatizations. She was the first playwright, for instance, to see the dramatic possibilities of the doppelganger subtext of *Frankenstein* (although she may well have been influenced by Thomas Edison's 1910 film adaptation of the story, which used the gimmick and was exhibited in England). Webling intentionally named her *monster* Frankenstein (saving the name Henry for its creator, and completing a gestalt.) It was as if Webling intuited the "mistake" of future generations that would insist on using the names of monster and maker interchangeably. Though physically monstrous, Webling's creature wore a costume identical to that of Henry Frankenstein, and nearly all the characters in the play were doubled in one way or another. The splitting of Henry's character creates an emotional confusion for his fiancée, Emily, who tells her betrothed, "He is part of you and part of myself, and we are all one."

Although he considered the Webling version of the play "illiterate," Balderston entered into an agreement with the playwright in March 1929 to adapt *Frankenstein* in order to improve its commercial chances in London and New York. That Balderston paid Webling only £20 for the adaptation rights may be a gauge of his interest, or lack thereof; in any event, he agreed to complete a script by September of the same year. However, he seems to have put the project in a drawer and largely forgotten about it. Peggy didn't.

Who, exactly, was Peggy Webling? And what influences led her to set in motion a chain of *Frankenstein* adaptations that would culminate a few years later in one of the most indelible cultural icons that Hollywood would ever produce?

In her 1924 memoir, *Peggy: The Story of One Score Years and Ten,* Webling paints a word picture of a charmed Victorian childhood steeped in books and playacting. Born on a New Year's Day (she does not reveal the year, informing the reader that such facts are surely inconsequential), Peggy, along with sisters Rosalind and Lucy, proved so youthfully adept at amateur theatricals and poetry recitals that they were soon in demand throughout London, precocious thespian homunculae on display at all the best salons. The Webling sisters drew attention from lofty realms of Victorian arts and letters. Peggy was "captivated and haunted" by Ellen Terry, who doted on her, and whom Peggy loved to watch from a distance as she took her strolls in Kensington Gardens. John Ruskin was another admirer, and presented Rosalind a complete set of Byron bound in blue morocco. Peggy surreptitiously read *Don Juan* in stolen minutes.

Soon, the trio was receiving requests for audiences. "Somebody had told Lewis Carroll, at the time of our first success, about the little girls who were reciting his inimitable verses." An appointment was arranged, but the dour C. L. Dodgson, when he arrived, proved a bitter disappointment. The creator of some of English literature's most fantastic beings, Webling recalled, was in reality a gloomy mathematician who "made me positively miserable by writing some difficult puzzles on a piece of notepaper and telling me to find them out." Peggy had no interest in puzzles and fig-

Left: **Peggy Webling** *(right)* **and her sister Lucy donned Gothic garb for one of their celebrated theatricals.** *Above:* **Peggy Webling in her twenties.** *(Collections of the Research Libraries, The New York Public Library, Astor, Lenox, and Tilden Foundations)*

ures, which "literally made my head ache." But their guest would not relent, nor would he offer any help. He just kept posing new puzzles and staring at the girls until they, and their mother, were utterly exhausted. "I wonder," Peggy wrote, "whether children were *quite* so devoted to him as their parents said they were."

Later, she turned down the chance to meet Edward Lear, another admirer. "As the author of 'The Mad Hatter' had 'amused' me with terrible puzzles, perhaps the inventor of 'The Dong with the Luminous Nose' might suggest that we 'play' at spelling or sums."

Peggy and her sisters seem to have shared an ironic, slightly perverse sensibility from an early age. ("I'm glad to say we always scoffed at goody-goody books . . . Lucy, aged six, once shocked a tea party by announcing that she 'hated morals.' ") Nonetheless, morals, or their appearance, were the fashion of the time, and were often imparted to young people through morbid and frightening chapbooks and verse. One poem they especially disliked was accompanied by a drawing of "a horrid little boy" at the top of the page; at the bottom, a portly gentleman descended a steep hill with a feeble old lady: "Mother, guide my little steps/Gently while you can./Guide me up the hill of life/Till I grow a man./Mother, when I grow a man,/Good, and strong and brave,/I'll lead my mother down the hill/Kindly to the grave."

Peggy and her sisters soon wrote their own version: "Mother, guide my little steps/Harshly while you can,/Kick me up the hill of life/Till I wed a man./Mother, when I wed a man/Stout, and rich, and brave,/I'll trot my mother down the hill/Quickly to the grave."

The Weblings crossed the Atlantic with their theatricals, touring Canada in their teens with some success. But they found upon their return to London that they were no longer in fashion. Peggy turned her energies to writing, and soon was submitting stories, poems, and articles to dozens of periodicals—and frequently having them accepted. Her first book, *The Blue Jay,* was published in 1906, and was followed by over a dozen novels and collections. She wrote sporadically for the theatre in the 1920s, and, making the acquaintance of former Dubliner Hamilton Deane, who had been having a great touring success with *Dracula* in the provinces, obliged him when he asked her if she would like to adapt *Frankenstein* as a companion piece.

And so it happened, in December 1927, that the dark twins of the Villa Diodati—the Byronic vampire and the Frankenstein monster—were restored to earth in a dynamic fusion amid the threadbare trappings of Hamilton Deane's traveling repertory. It was a humble nativity, but a momentous one—for the first time, the interdependency of the Dracula and Frankenstein images was formalized and successfully exploited. It was the beginning of a formula that would continue to capture the public imagination for the rest of the twentieth century.

In an early, theatrical phase of his career, the well-known film historian Ivan Butler spent several years in various capacities with the Hamilton Deane Company, and in late 1990 recalled the inception of *Frankenstein*. "I remember well the first rehearsals, which took place on tour, in a small Welsh town called Porthcawl. It took place in the private room of a pub, very cold, and we were all wrapped up. Deane made his first 'entrance' in an overcoat and bowler hat—and from the very start held us spellbound." As the junior member of the company, Butler started "on the book"— that is, as the prompter. Later, when the play opened in London, he would take over the small role of Victor Moritz, originated by Desmond Greene.

Butler vividly remembered Deane's unusual makeup, "a strange mixture of blue, green and red—with thick red lips." The singular face was topped with a tangled fright wig, and Deane inserted lifts in his boots to exaggerate his six-foot-one-inch height. Deane's makeup may have been partially inspired by accounts of Thomas Potter Cooke's celebrated stage interpretation of the monster in *Presumption; or the Fate of Frankenstein* (1823). Contemporary accounts included descriptions of Cooke's "green and yellow visage, his watery and lack-luster eye, his long-matted, straggling black locks, the blue, livid hue of his arms and legs, his shriveled complexion, his straight black lips, his horrible ghastly grin."

Engravings of T. P. Cooke as the monster reveal his costume to be a neoclassical, toga-like garment; a century later, Peggy Webling's characters were costumed in high Regency style, the monster's appearance mirroring that of his master. Webling made numerous revisions to her script between its December 1927 premiere and its West End debut in February 1930. In particular, the monster's destruction was completely reconceived. In the first version, the creature destroys itself by leaping off a precipice upstage.

The "birth" of the monster (Hamilton Deane) is witnessed by Dr. Waldman (G. Malcolm Russell) and Victor Frankenstein (Henry Hallatt). *(Courtesy of Ivan Butler)*

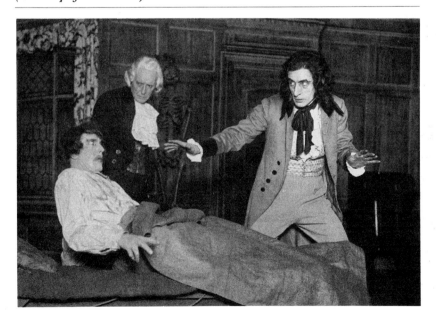

But the plunge fell flat. "It was very tame indeed," Ivan Butler recalled, "more so because of Deane's very tentative jump!" The revised script was much more in keeping with the blood-and-thunder tradition of José Levy's Little Theatre, which had, after all, presented both Sybil Thorndike's English Grand Guignol and Hamilton Deane's *Dracula*.

"The final version," recalled Butler, "was quite a bloodthirsty affair, with the monster apparently tearing his maker's throat out before being destroyed by lightning. Old Deanie revelled in it." The actor concealed in his strangling hand a sponge soaked in cochineal, a red food dye. "The staining was hideous," Butler remembered. "I have no idea why they used it." The cataclysmic "lightning bolt" was something of a challenge in the intimate theatre. Butler described the mechanism of disaster: "Downstage, up in the flies, a sort of long narrow stretcher or hammock of canvas reached across the width of the stage: the two long poles were fastened (a foot or so apart) to battens or rails. The body of the stretcher was filled with pebbles and small stones, dust and pieces of lightweight rubbish, and, I think, Fuller's Earth.

"On cue, one pole was released (it hung high above the proscenium arch and so was not visible), releasing the stuff on the stage—the cast meanwhile having moved slightly upstage to avoid being stunned." The spectacle proved a crowd pleaser, Butler remembered. "Accompanied by yells and cries, thundersheet, big drum and flashing lights, it was very effective."

Although Butler knew playwright Webling only on a "Good Morning and smile" basis when she came to visit Deane, he remembered her as "a gentle little gray-haired lady who seemed the last person to write such an adaptation." Years later, Butler was surprised to come across one of her children's books in a secondhand store—its subject was the lives of the saints.

Like *Dracula,* Deane's production of *Frankenstein* was not warmly welcomed by the London critics. *The Times* was typical in its appraisal: "Miss Webling, translating into terms of the theatre Mary Shelley's one lasting and original conception, has unquestioningly succeeded in bringing the monster to life; but the play in which she exhibits this wild beast is as flimsy as a bird cage." One of Deane's "improvements" to the original Webling script, the deus ex machina lightning bolt that destroys the monster, was especially criticized: "The death of Frankenstein seems to settle noth-

Deane in makeup as the
Frankenstein monster.
(Courtesy of Ivan Butler)

ing, and the stroke of lightning appears to cut a knot which it would have been interesting to see unravelled.

"Mr. Hamilton Deane's monster," the unsigned review concluded, "is nearly all of the play that is worth watching, but that is much. It is an extremely fine study in the macabre. The rest of the play that is worth watching consists of the pleasant, flamboyant flashes of Mr. Hallatt's Frankenstein. Nobody else has a chance, or can be expected to succeed in making one."

Ivan Butler recalled that Deane gave a sensitive and nuanced performance, "magnificent by any standards," reciting the speaking monster's lines in "a curious accent of his own invention. There was a scene in which the creature released a dove from a cage, telling it to 'fly away.' I still remember the unusual way Deane pronounced the word—'floy.' " According to Butler, "Deane played the monster very much for sympathy—indeed, he could bring tears to one's eyes—and except for the final moments of the play there was little horror as the word is usually understood."

By this time, of course, Balderston's option on the play had expired, and he saw his mistake. He had never dreamed that Deane would produce Webling's version in the West End. On February 11, 1930, he wrote Horace Liveright: "In a letter dictated this morning I enclosed the morning paper notices of *Frankenstein*. Here are the evening's, all raves. It does take the biscuit, for you never saw such a text or such actors." Balderston, however, was now prepared to set aside his distaste for the production and do what was necessary to sell the property to Liveright. Deane, Balderston told the producer, already had one American offer, and "the *Dracula* thing makes it fairly certain there will be others and perhaps from good people. Miss Webling is totally ignorant and inexperienced . . . That's why we have to shake some cash under her nose and sew her up quickly."

But first Balderston had some negotiating of his own to do. Peggy Webling had first been miffed at his failure to midwife a new *Frankenstein* script, but the seeming success of the Little Theatre production had increased her self-confidence. "She thinks she's written a hell of a play and [that] I would probably spoil it," Balderston wrote to his agent. But he was evidently able to charm the lady sufficiently to regain control of the American rights within a week. With some trepidation, Liveright cabled an offer for the play, sight unseen and without a producible script—a $1,000 advance against a sliding scale of royalties. Balderston did his best to assuage

Liveright's anxieties, sending him photos of Deane in the production and more press cuttings ("Note particularly the notice *Punch* gives Deane, and two lines in *The Nation & Athenaeum* . . . two highbrow sheets I should not have expected to notice the play at all.") Balderston urged Liveright to make a contract with Deane as well, because "this show is really a vehicle for Deane. It will be a much better show . . . than *Dracula* when I get through with it, better because it has a psychological development and an astonishing, in some ways even a great performance by Deane, while there isn't any punch or thrill in *Dracula* that this lacks. But this show, unlike *Dracula,* does need a star."

Balderston encouraged Liveright to also bring over Henry Hallatt to recreate his role as Henry Frankenstein: "He's a young, good, honest, handsome, old-fashioned ham with a rich and sepulchral voice, and you'd have trouble in picking up anybody like him in New York, especially because the play requires the monster to bear a physical resemblance to his creator . . . This actor does look like Deane, although he's a fairly big fellow he's only about three-quarter Deane's size, but then Deane's as big as Carnera." (Balderston was referring to Primo Carnera, the then-reigning champion of heavyweight boxers.)

Two faces of Hamilton Deane's monster. *(Left: Courtesy of Ronald V. Borst / Hollywood Movie Posters. Right: Courtesy of the Dracula Society)*

Aside from the lead roles, there were six more characters in Balderston's version: "Henry Frankenstein's father and boy friend, cheap and easy types, a little ingenue sister of Henry ditto, a maid-servant, a priest, who goes through the play disapproving of the proceedings, a good part, for somebody convincing like Van Sloan★ in *Dracula,* and finally Henry's fiancé, who gets raped and mur-dered. This lady should have a lot of force and guts and a good scream. You want for her a fairly good second-rate actress, and the rest of the casting is a cinch and cheap."

By the time Liveright scheduled a trip to London in late March to see his new pig in its poke, the closing of *Frankenstein* at the Little Theatre had already been announced. Despite all the good notices for Deane, the play failed to build up the momentum of *Dracula.* Nonetheless, Liveright saw the play on March 21, 1930, and was enthusiastic. "Horace likes Deane enormously and wants him in New York," Balderston noted. "Unfortunately you know Horace, and while Deane was eating out of my hand and thinks me a great playwright . . . Horace talked to him as though he were writing the play himself and was prolific in fool ideas." Deane was an English actor/manager used to controlling all aspects of a production, and Balderston knew there could be trouble. And as Deane was running a very profitable touring company, he had very little incentive to drop his activities in England merely to accommodate Horace Liveright's questionable brainstorms. "If Horace would only be tactful with him now the whole thing could be fixed up, but Horace talks like a Napoleon of the theatre and Deane saw through him at once." (One indication of Liveright's affinity for "fool ideas" was a rider he added to the February 26 *Frankenstein* contract with Balderston and Webling, granting him, along with stage and film rights, the additional option of present-ing *Frankenstein* as a musical comedy.)

Whatever rapport existed between Horace Liveright and Ham-ilton Deane deteriorated rapidly. On April 9th, Balderston wrote his agent in New York that "Horace thoroughly messed up the situation with Deane, who so cordially dislikes him that he would not sign up even though offered what amounts to a thousand dol-lars a week if the show does any business." Liveright responded by signing the noted Shakespearean actor Lyn Harding, who had

---

★Edward Van Sloan (1881–1964), the American actor who originated the role of the vampire hunter Abraham Van Helsing in Horace Liveright's production of *Dracula.*

Lyn Harding, Horace Liveright's choice for his Frankenstein monster on Broadway. *(The Free Library of Philadelphia Theatre Collection)*

been set to play the monster in a second London production that never materialized.

Balderston was also perturbed at having his close working relationship with Deane shattered. "Horace barged in and commenced giving instructions as to how the play was to be rewritten. He sat through it three or four times and each time it was Horace who was giving the orders. This was too much for Deane. I kept pretty quiet and kept my temper, as Horace is the sort of chap with whom a personal row probably means finish." Liveright, in Balderston's estimation, had "no feeling at all for theatrical values." The playwright was offered a momentary respite when Liveright left London for Berlin on business. "Unfortunately," Balderston wrote, "he is coming back."

Balderston was reasonably certain he could afford to keep his temper, since whatever Liveright's objections, his contract stipulated that Balderston was to adapt *Frankenstein* "in accordance with his own ideas" and the Dramatists Guild would back him up in any dispute with the tempestuous producer.

As with *Dracula,* Balderston undertook a wholesale rewrite of the London script, retaining Webling's skeleton while fleshing out his creation with crisp, argumentative dialogue and a distinctly theological preoccupation. Scarcely a page passes without some discussion of the proper relationship of man and God—there are over sixty direct uses of the word "God," and nearly as many other religious references. (It should be noted that this was an essential subversion of the Shelley original; Romantic Prometheanism was by its nature antithetical to Christianity.) Hollywood, predictably, would initially steer fairly clear of theology, but it would seize upon other Balderstonian touches: the crackling electrical apparatus, for example (the playwright realized that a life-inducing elixir somehow lacked stage presence). He also dramatized for the first time the partial creation of the monster's mate.

The Balderston script embellished and expanded upon many incidents that Webling had barely realized. One, the monster's accidental drowning of Henry Frankenstein's sister Katrina, is transformed by Balderston into a moment more than slightly reminiscent of the drowning in *An American Tragedy,* Liveright's biggest stage hit before *Dracula.*

Balderston sent Liveright a draft of the first two acts of the play by midsummer 1930, and received a terse cable in reply on July 17: DEEPLY DISAPPOINTED SCRIPT FRANKENSTEIN DO NOT BELIEVE CAN BE PRODUCED SUCCESSFULLY UNLESS YOU WILL COMPLETELY REWRITE ACCORDING TO OUR IDEAS OR ALLOW COLLABORATOR FAILING THIS DO YOU WISH TO TAKE OVER PLAY AND HARDING CONTRACT GOING TO HOLLYWOOD 23RD AND MUST MAKE PLANS QUICKLY

By this time Balderston was completely fed up with Horace Liveright, who was already falling behind on *Dracula* royalties and whose other business interests were rumored to be very shaky. The rumors were right: Liveright was essentially wiped out, was on the verge of selling out his interest in Boni & Liveright and being removed as its president. He was about to take a position as production associate in the Paramount Publix Corporation in Hollywood, "on such a loose and fantastic basis that it would be impossible for me to tell you just what my activities are going to be. All I can say is that they have wanted me very much and are paying me very high. . . . Of course people will say that Liveright has gone theatre, or Liveright has gone movie. To a certain extent this is true." His real interest in *Frankenstein* may have been the movie option, to which—quite unlike *Dracula*—he now held a firm 50 percent claim—as long as he could mount the stage version. He told Balderston he was already "dickering" with the film people. Regarding the play, Balderston told his agent, "I am so certain that he will make a hash of it that I don't care what terms you make." Balderston consented to a collaborator, who turned out to be Louis Cline, the general manager of Horace Liveright Theatrical Productions. Cline, a former press agent and theatrical jack-of-all-trades who had engineered most of *Dracula*'s ballyhoo (and later claimed to have contributed materially to the script), outlined some of the boffo play doctoring he had wrought upon *Frankenstein*:

> The Monster is to tear off Amelia's wedding gown, which gown is a breakaway affair, and leaves her as nude as the censors will allow. Then he is about to mount her in a rape. Before the scene gets too frankly sexy, the Monster is interrupted by a noise outside the window or door. He looks off stage, or goes to the door or window whichever it may be, and at this point Amelia escapes and runs out . . . Then we hear her clattering up stairs (off stage). The Monster runs after her, and we hear his boots (off stage) clumping up the stairs. Then we hear the door slammed by Amelia. The monster hammers on it. It gives with a splintering crash (all of this now is off stage), there is a wild shriek.

On the basis of such sensational material, Cline felt sure that sufficient investor money could be raised to produce *Frankenstein* on Broadway before the rights reverted to the playwrights on February 1, 1931.

Liveright was nominally employed by Paramount Publix, and one wonders what his higher-ups thought about the amount of time he must have been spending over at Universal, where *Dracula* was being produced as a film—he even ended up in a publicity still posed on the winding staircase of Carfax Abbey. Balderston's wife Marion cabled him in early December, shedding some surprising light on Liveright's machinations: HORACE ASKS EXTENSION OPTION BELIEVING UNIVERSAL WILL BACK PRODUCTION BUY FILM HIMSELF PERSONALLY DIRECTING. Liveright indeed intended to "go movie." What better vehicle could there be than *Frankenstein* to realize his mad ambition? Carl Laemmle, Jr., the new, twenty-one-year-old production head at Universal, had announced plans to begin developing plays on the New York stage for later production as films; the scheme would eliminate costly negotiation for screen rights to established stage properties. However, as Liveright had no experience whatsoever in film production, it is unlikely that Universal took him seriously, save for the option he momentarily held on

Frankenstein. The studio might well have considered him an irritation and a fool; incensed by Universal's $40,000 purchase of *Dracula* (a deal to which he might have been a part, had he not stupidly waived the film rights), Liveright threatened a nuisance suit, on the basis that the film would infringe on his stage rights. He settled for a $4,500 payoff, which he insisted be paid by Stoker's widow, Deane, and Balderston, but which Universal actually paid just to be rid of him. When he walked up the Dracula staircase he was, in a sense, as much a phantom as the plaster castle's fictional inhabitant.

It soon developed that Horace Liveright was no longer in a position to bring a Broadway, much less a Hollywood, *Frankenstein* to life; the spark, the flair, the bathtub-gin alchemy that all came so easily in the twenties were all pretty much extinguished. Shortly after the *Dracula* payoff, Mrs. Stoker and the playwrights moved against him for nonpayment of royalties, and reclaimed the property. Liveright, without whose efforts *Dracula* and *Frankenstein* would likely never have achieved their success in the twentieth century, was never able to reclaim his former fire. His stay in the film colony was disastrous, and he returned to New York about the time *Frankenstein* was released as a film, without a penny in his pocket. He made a monstrous match in a brief, tormented marriage to a disturbed actress, Elise Bartlett, in a union marked by violence from the outset. At their wedding reception, his nose was bloodied by an emissary of his wife's former husband, Joseph Schildkraut (who would later be her husband again): "There were rumors that their domestic life did not lack drama," remembered Louis Kronenberg, recalling a vicious gash that appeared on Liveright's hand a few weeks after the wedding. Another story hinted at a shooting. Liveright announced impossible plans for new theatrical projects with dark marital themes: *Hotel Alimony* was one, a musical comedy based on *Lucretzia Borgia* was another. All came to nothing. And the Promethean genius of publishing was stranded on the rock of Manhattan, his liver eaten daily not by a vulture, but by the ravages of bootleg gin. A *Variety* column once suggested that Liveright would make an ideal subject for an opera of the 1920s; if so, one can imagine a jazz-age variation on *Don Giovanni,* with Dracula and Frankenstein as the tempting demons who escort the charismatic libertine to hell.

He would live for only a few more years, forgotten by the public and abandoned by the twin demons to whose dark star he had, for a while, hitched his volatile fortunes. But monsters, Horace Liveright found, made fickle mistresses, ever likely to turn on their masters. Risen from slab and box, jolted alive by jazz-age energies, they were strong enough to make their own way, in a bleak and transformed America.

It was a moment the dark gods had waited for. In a new world of social upheaval and economic eclipse, their night could be endless.

Horace Brisbin Liveright, publisher, producer, monster-maker. *(The Billy Rose Theatre Collection, New York Public Library at Lincoln Center, Astor, Lenox, and Tilden Foundations)*

Chapter Five

1931: THE AMERICAN ABYSS

"And then in the morning,
I felt so weak. It seemed
as if all the life had been
drained out of me."

Helen Chandler in *Dracula*
(1931)

LIKE A HOLLYWOOD version of Dr. Abraham Van Helsing, Carl Laemmle, Sr., adamantly opposed Dracula. But unlike the fictional vampire-hunter, he was ultimately no match for the bloodthirsty Count, whose shadow had been hovering outside the gates of Universal City for quite some time, watching and waiting. Vampires, according to legend, require an invitation before they enter a house. Afterwards, they can come and go as they please.

Laemmle delayed his invitation as long as he could. He opposed morbid entertainment generally. He didn't understand why a play like *Dracula* was cleaning up on the road, or what strange gratification audiences derived from it. Even the pictures he had produced featuring Lon Chaney in his most terrifying disguises were, in the final analysis, *human* stories. This *Dracula* was about a bloodsucking demon from hell! Laemmle's son, Carl, Jr., to whom he had turned over the reins of the studio, insisted that the thing would be surefire at the box office. Had the public gone mad?

A hood ornament for a wrecked economy: Boris Karloff as the Franken-stein monster (1931). *(Photofest)*

If not exactly crazy, the public mood had changed—and changed radically. The crack in the fabric of reality known politely as the year A.D. 1931 appeared to many Americans to be the end of all earthly possibilities. The economic free-fall that had begun in October 1929 was about to hit bottom. Within a year the industrialized world's unemployed population would reach an estimated 30 million people. A popular song of the time, "Life Is Just a Bowl of Cherries," contained more than a hint of sour grapes. As Gilbert Seldes noted in *The Years of the Locust,* "The phrase . . . came into common use because it expressed a common state of mind. The bottom had fallen out of the tubs into which America had poured its hopes and faiths; the great horn of plenty had voided itself and all that was left of its unimaginable riches was a bowl of cherries."

Beyond bitterness was fear. The wreckage of the jazz age was a forbidding new landscape. Millions waited for a scapegoat or a deliverer. A new and controversial kind of entertainment—the gangster picture—served as a lightning rod for public anger and cynicism; audiences vicariously took part in adventures outside the law and standards of fair play that now seemed utterly irrelevant. The popular interest in gangsters wasn't an entirely vicarious identification: Prohibition, after all, had literally turned millions of otherwise law-abiding citizens into criminals.

But the most lasting and influential invention of 1931 would be the modern horror film. Monster movies opened up the possibility of psychic lawlessness; a monster, for Hollywood, was a gangster of the id and unconscious. Cataclysmic junctures in history usually stir up strong imagery in the collective mind, and the years following the 1929 economic crash were no exception. Salvador Dalí had risen to preeminence among the surrealist painters, and his 1931 canvas *The Persistence of Memory* defined the movement for much of the public. Dalí's flaccid timepieces depicted a dreamlike meltdown of history itself. Horror films served as a kind of populist surrealism, rearranging the human body and its processes, blurring the boundaries between Homo sapiens and other species, responding uneasily to new and almost incomprehensible developments in science and the anxious challenges they posed to the familiar structures of society, religion, psychology, and perception.

By January 1931, the vague fears that had haunted the economy for the previous year became real: President Hoover's Emergency Committee for Unemployment Relief confirmed the figures—the Depression was real, and worsening daily. A few months later the Austrian national bank failed, triggering the economic collapse of Europe. In Germany, the ensuing crisis would contribute significantly to the embryonic nightmare of National Socialism.

Movies offered an instinctive, therapeutic escape. As Gilbert Seldes noted, "The rich could still go to the South Seas Islands; the intellectuals went to Mexico; the poor went to the movies." The massive shared hardship of the Depression galvanized motion pictures as a dominant form of cultural expression.

During a twelve-month period that coincided with the darkest hours of the Great Depression, four Hollywood horror archetypes were released or readied for public consumption. America's worst year of the century would be its best year ever for monsters.

If Universal was not prepared to buy *Dracula,* Metro-Goldwyn-Mayer was, and the thought of a rival studio snatching the property away finally overshadowed Carl Laemmle's qualms about the subject matter. He finally gave the project a green light with a single proviso: that Dracula be played by Lon Chaney, a superstar whose box-office appeal would guarantee the film's success, morbid or not.

Chaney's dazzling ability to effect physical transformations did not, however, extend to his own health. He had for some time been bothered by a throat ailment that made him hesitant to do a talkie. Some years later, in a retrospective analysis of horror films, *The New York Times* reported that "Chaney wanted to act *Dracula*" from the early 1920s, "and often discussed the part with Tod Browning. . . . Chaney had a full scenario and a secret makeup worked out even at that early date, but Browning held out for a talkie." The actor and the director had competition, according to the *Times:* "certain Teutons saturated with post-war Weltschmertz." This may have been a reference to Universal's resident director of mysteries, Paul Leni, who had produced *Waxworks* (1924) in Germany and *The Cat and the Canary* (1927) stateside. Leni worked closely with Universal associate producer Paul Kohner, another European with an impeccable eye for production values. Kohner and Leni's *Dracula* would have had one powerful link to the *Caligari* tradition in the person of its star. "My husband wanted

Conrad Veidt for *Dracula*," recalled Lupita Tovar Kohner in 1991, "but something happened and Veidt went back to Germany." Two things happened: Paul Leni died unexpectedly, and Veidt, unsure of his English, did not want to take on the talkies.

Chaney finally did make a talking picture, a remake of *The Unholy Three* (1930), but his throat problems flared up again. During the spring of 1930, when executives and agents on both coasts were trying to convince Chaney to take up residence in Dracula's earth-box, he likely knew that the coffin was more than just a metaphor. His throat and lung cancer was diagnosed in June of 1930, and two months later he was on his deathbed. The MGM switchboard was flooded with offers from fans to donate their blood to the Dracula who never was. There were many transfusions, a final blurring of boundaries between the actor and his public. But the last hemhor-rhage came on August 26 and could not be stopped. And although Lon Chaney had never served in the military, his coffin would be draped with an American flag, as if he had fallen in war.

Just days after Chaney's death, *Variety* ran a devastating pan of *Outside the Law,* which Browning had directed for Universal with Edward G. Robinson taking the Chaney role. "No excuse for this," the review began bluntly, calling the film "one of the worst examples of claptrap since sound came in. Not a thread of conti-nuity. The thing rants on, an on-the-cuff script, players obviously as bewildered as the director." To add to the insult, Browning's name appeared nowhere in the body of the influential trade paper review.

Such notices did not bode well for *Dracula,* though the picture was on the schedule, and somehow was going to happen. Colonel Jason S. Joy (the wonderfully named administrator of the newly instituted—if barely enforced—Production Code) was personally sent copies of the Stoker novel and the Deane/Balderston play. Universal associate producer E. M. Asher wanted to get Joy's "censorship angles" on the story, which Universal would charac-terize as a "tale of horror and mystery, with love theme for relief." Aside from the enthusiasm of Carl Laemmle, Jr., the heir apparent of Universal who rammed through *Dracula* over his father's objec-tions, there wasn't a lot of support for the project. Most of the reader's reports on the play and novel had been highly negative, and almost all worried about censorship. The story contained "everything that would cause any average human being to revolt or seek a convenient railing," according to one story-department

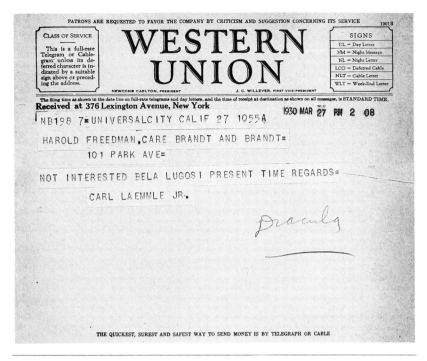

PATRONS ARE REQUESTED TO FAVOR THE COMPANY BY CRITICISM AND SUGGESTION CONCERNING ITS SERVICE   1201§

WESTERN UNION

CLASS OF SERVICE	
This is a full-rate Telegram or Cablegram unless its deferred character is indicated by a suitable sign above or preceding the address.	

SIGNS	
DL = Day Letter	
NM = Night Message	
NL = Night Letter	
LCO = Deferred Cable	
NLT = Cable Letter	
WLT = Week-End Letter	

NEWCOMB CARLTON, PRESIDENT   J. C. WILLEVER, FIRST VICE-PRESIDENT

The filing time as shown in the date line on full-rate telegrams and day letters, and the time of receipt at destination as shown on all messages, is STANDARD TIME.

Received at 376 Lexington Avenue, New York

NB198 7=UNIVERSALCITY CALIF 27 1055A   1930 MAR 27 PM 2 08

HAROLD FREEDMAN,CARE BRANDT AND BRANDT=

　　10 1 PARK AVE=

NOT INTERESTED BELA LUGOSI PRESENT TIME REGARDS=

　　CARL LAEMMLE JR.

Dracula

THE QUICKEST, SUREST AND SAFEST WAY TO SEND MONEY IS BY TELEGRAPH OR CABLE

Universal's original plans for *Dracula* did not include Bela Lugosi. But the studio's first choice, Lon Chaney, Sr., was struck down by cancer.

report. Colonel Joy, however, seemed to find nothing in *Dracula* except a novelty entertainment. Since supernatural movies did not yet exist in Hollywood, they had never created controversy. And there was nothing in the Production Code about vampires.

Bela Lugosi, despite his magnetism on stage, had no track record in Hollywood and was the last person Universal wanted in the title role. The list of actors tested or talked about for the part included Chaney, Ian Keith, Paul Muni, William Courtenay, Chester Morris, and Arthur Edmund Carewe. Browning, for his part, liked the idea of casting a completely unknown actor as Dracula—and keeping him unknown. "I favor getting a stranger from Europe, and not giving his name," the director said. The studio cast Lugosi at the last possible moment, after he had given up on winning the part. He had, almost simultaneously, been announced for a principal role in *Luxury,* a Fox production starring Clare Luce. The film was to have a gimmick plot touching on the human drama swirling around the creation of a wealthy woman's evening gown. Fortunately for Lugosi, the film fell through, and he was able to trade in the evening gown for the cape he had been born to wear, and would wear to his death.

Lugosi wasn't the only also-ran to be cast in *Dracula*. The role of Jonathan Harker (transformed over four screenplay drafts from the hero of the piece to an ineffectual bystander) went to the thirty-year-old David Manners, a borrowed contract player from First National. Lew Ayres, the star of Universal's *All Quiet on the Western Front* (1930), refused the role. He wanted to play the part of Renfield, Dracula's insect-eating slave, but it wasn't the image the front office had in mind for him.

Manners' manager drove him over to the Universal lot to meet Tod Browning, who wanted to consider him for the part of Harker. It seemed they were having a hell of a time with the casting; filming had already begun, and they were still filling major roles. "I didn't do a test, or even read for the part," Manners recalled. They paid Manners $2,000 a week for *Dracula,* four times what they were paying Bela Lugosi for the title role.

In a 1991 interview, on the eve of his own ninety-first birthday, David Manners recalled Lugosi as insufferably vain and pretentious, standing in front of a full-length mirror on the set, velvet cape wrapped over his shoulder, almost literally hypnotized by his own reflection. Unlike the fictional vampire, here was a Dracula who couldn't get enough of his image in the glass. "I *am* Dracula," he would intone, parading up and down the soundstage. Asked whether he ever felt that Lugosi's aloofness might have been due to his shaky handle on English, Manners replied, "I don't really know. He never got close enough for me to notice." (Manners would work with Lugosi on two other films, *The Death Kiss* and *The Black Cat,* and found Lugosi's demeanor equally odd, even without the cape.)

Nicholas Webster, later to be a feature, documentary, and television director, was the seventeen-year-old son of *Dracula*'s "script girl," Aileen Webster, familiarly known to her coworkers as "Webby." Nick had worked as an extra in Universal's most recent hit, a triumphant adaptation of Erich Maria Remarque's *All Quiet on the Western Front.* He still remembered vividly, in 1991, how Carl Laemmle, Sr., eager for realism, returned from a trip to Germany with 200 pairs of soldier's boots, only to find that 190 pairs

Darkness in the doorway: the image of Bela Lugosi's Dracula ushered in the Great Depression. *(Courtesy of Ronald V. Borst / Hollywood Movie Posters)*

were both left-foot. A student at Hollywood High, Nick visited his mother at the studio after school, and, with Tod Browning's permission, spread out his homework on one of the coffins in Dracula's crypt. He vividly recollected the massive, cobweb-bedecked sets. "They scared the hell out of me," he said.

Bela Lugosi, Webster recalled, approached his mother for off-set assistance in learning his lines. Webby, unsure of Lugosi's intentions, asked her son to accompany her. They arrived at the appointed place, Lugosi's house on North Hudson Street over-looking Hollywood. Webby knocked, and a portal slid open. "I remember how *those* eyes appeared," said Webster. "First they locked on my mother. Then they focused on me, and I had the distinct impression that he was very disappointed I had come along." As Nick's mother coached Dracula with his lines, the teenager couldn't help but think that "this man was somehow slightly mad, as if he actually thought he *was* Dracula."

Tod Browning, in Webster's recollection, was an "intense" presence, with a bristling mustache and ever-present, trailing scarf. Once Browning asked Nick what he wanted to be when he grew up. "A director, like you, Mr. Browning," the boy replied. "Well,"

said Browning sternly, "you have to start at the bottom." ("In retrospect, it was a terrible piece of advice," said Webster.)

The shooting of *Dracula,* in David Manners' memory, was "extremely disorganized." Auteurist partisans will shudder at the actor's contention that Tod Browning had nothing to do with the direction of his scenes, remaining a dim figure "back in the shadows." Karl Freund, nominally the cinematographer, actually directed much of the film, and everything that involved Manners. This included the concert hall sequence (with some of Lugosi's choicest dialogue), several drawing-room episodes (including the famous mirror-smashing scene), and the chase and destruction of Dracula in the cellars of Carfax Abbey. Since none of the other principal performers are now living, it cannot be ascertained how much else in the film Browning did or didn't direct. Manners' recollections corroborate the *Hollywood Filmograph*'s eventual observation that "we cannot believe that the same man was responsible for both the first and latter parts of the picture." The *Filmograph* had been a great booster of the film during preproduction, and evidently followed *Dracula*'s politics carefully.

To complicate matters even further, Manners remembered that

Dracula: **David Manners, Helen Chandler, and Edward Van Sloan** *(opposite)* **puzzle over the mysterious draining force that has entered their lives, while Bela Lugosi orchestrates the malaise.**

the German-speaking Freund directed his share of *Dracula* with the aid of an interpreter, who, Manners recalled, was a strikingly formal presence. "He wore white gloves on the set," Manners said. Given the difficulties of communication, it is little wonder that much of *Dracula* has the bizarre quality of a slow-motion dream.

The studio politics of *Dracula* were thickened by the simultaneous rendition of a Spanish-language version of the film, produced at night on the same sets. At the helm was none other than Paul Kohner, the young producer whose ambitious plans for the English-language version had been derailed by the death of Paul Leni and the ascendancy of Carl Laemmle, Jr. While Browning fumbled, Kohner effortlessly upstaged the American version with an entirely separate cast, crew, and mise-en-scène, completed at a fraction of the cost and in a fraction of the time. Kohner also used the film to woo and glamorize his wife-to-be, the beautiful Mexican ingenue Lupita Tovar, who took the female lead. Kohner had perfected his technique—both with Tovar and foreign-language production—in a similarly atmospheric Spanish version of *The Cat Creeps (El Voluntad del Muerto)* the year before. George Robinson's cinematography was highly ambitious for the time and amounted to a lush, nonstop parade of artfully arranged shadows. Kohner's director, George Melford, spoke no Spanish and employed an interpreter. If David Manners' recollections of Karl Freund are accurate, then both versions of Universal's *Dracula* were essentially created across language barriers.

In 1991, Lupita Kohner hinted at the intriguing possibility of the sideline involvement of F. W. Murnau, the director of *Nosferatu*, in the Spanish *Dracula*. The Spanish film contains numerous visual references to and borrowings from *Nosferatu*; Mrs. Kohner remembered that her husband-to-be was quite friendly with Murnau, who was then working in Hollywood, and often saw them talking together at Sunday get-togethers. Given Paul Kohner's passion for European cinema, it is almost inconceivable that he didn't take the opportunity to compare notes with Murnau on their respective versions of *Dracula*. Murnau died in an auto accident shortly after the film was released.

During filming of the English-language version, David Man-

Doppelganger cinema: Carlos Villarias was Bela Lugosi's stand-in for the Spanish-language version of *Dracula*.

ners became quite friendly with Tovar's American counterpart, Helen Chandler. The actress had recently married the screenwriter Cyril Hume, who eventually scripted *Forbidden Planet* (1956). "If he hadn't married her, I certainly would have," Manners recalled, sixty years later. Chandler shared his disdain for the production, and they giggled offscreen over the absurdities of the script. Behind the laughter, a genuinely dark scenario was taking form around the wistful ingenue. By day she fell victim to the mesmeric advances of the fictional Count Dracula; by night, her husband acted out another malignant role, Manners recalled. Cyril Hume, in his opinion, was a Prohibition-era Svengali of alcohol. The marriage did not last, but for Chandler, chemical dependency was a permanent part of the divorce settlement. Her life from the early 1930s onward was a downward spiral of drinking, pills, and sanitariums. Among many other things, *Dracula* is a story about a particularly destructive and compulsive form of drinking; in the ensuing decades vampire stories would be colored increasingly by the metaphors of addiction.

The effect, if any, of Tod Browning's drinking on *Dracula* is not known, but the film was certainly marred by inattentiveness and cut corners—not to mention budget pressures. One of the most dramatic sequences, the horrifying sea voyage from Transylvania to England, in which Dracula stalks and kills the ship's crew, was almost completely fudged with outtake footage of rain-soaked windjammers (most likely lifted from Universal's 1925 maritime melodrama *The Storm Breaker*). In the end, Universal was less than pleased with Browning's version of *Dracula,* and ordered the film tightened and reedited. William S. Hart, Jr., son of the famous Western star and Browning's friend for decades, recalled in a 1972 interview that the changes included the addition of numerous—and now famous—close-ups of Lugosi's penetrating gaze. According to Hart, it was Browning's intention to keep the vampire a shadowy, largely unseen presence. Over ten minutes may have been cut from the film, judging from contradictory records of *Dracula*'s running time. Some cuts are extremely clumsy, such as two that actually garble the story line—Renfield's attack on the maid and the fate of the vampire's first victim, Lucy, are simply left unresolved. A jarring jump cut occurs in the second reel as Dracula's wives glide across the flagstones toward their unconscious victim. The shot is already slow without the cut; Browning must have intended to have the women move with the pace of glaciers. When *Dracula* was finally shown on television in the late 1950s, Browning was still grumbling about the studio mutilations.

One piece of evidence suggesting that the studio was unhappy with Browning, even from the time of preproduction, was the caption that appeared on at least one batch of early publicity photos distributed by Universal before shooting began, identifying *Dracula* as "Edwin Carew's superproduction." Carew (no relation to Arthor Edmund Carewe, the actor mentioned for the title role) had just produced two blockbusters for Universal, *Ramona* and *Resurrection,* and would have been a natural choice to replace Browning if the studio felt the production was in trouble. But Carew was also one of the most expensive directors in the business, making at least $200,000 per production on a percentage basis. Did Universal really plan to dump Browning from *Dracula,* only to reconsider in light of finances? The truth may never be known.

The Motion Picture Producers and Distributors Association received numerous complaints on *Dracula.* "I cannot see one redeeming feature in this picture. It is the most horrible thing," read one unsigned appraisal. "The author must have had a distorted mind and I cannot understand why it was produced. I cannot speak too strongly against this picture for children." Another denounced the film as "unwholesome and ghastly, morbid, inhuman and pointless. In this day of high pressure living, strained nerves and constant excitement it seems too bad that such pictures with [a] strong influence on the emotions should be allowed a showing anywhere." Still another saw an immediate social danger in *Dracula*: "This picture should be protested by every previewing organization. Its insane horrible details shown to millions of impressionable children, to adults already bowed down by human misery, will do an infinite amount of harm." Marjorie Ross Davis, PTA report chairman, told the MPPDA that she knew the theme of the picture and "saw the first fifteen minutes of it and felt I could stand no more . . . It should be withdrawn from public showing, as children, [the] weak-minded and all classes attend motion pictures indiscriminately."

Dracula was rejected by censors in Singapore, British Malaya, and in British Columbia, where officials had requested extensive cuts, including elimination of the vampire women at Dracula's castle; Renfield's dialogue about flies, spiders, and rat's blood; the crying of a child in a cemetery; and even the reading aloud of a newspaper account of the child's offscreen victimization. Closer to home, Massachusetts censors insisted that two brief shots—one showing part of a skeleton in a casket as well as one of a beetle-like insect emerging from a miniature coffin—be excised for Sunday showings.

One of the long-standing criticisms of *Dracula* centers on its unbroken silences that seem to link the film with the pre-talkie Hollywood in which Browning had flourished with Chaney. Browning may have indeed been trying to stop the clock. In a 1931 interview at the end of his contract with Universal, he commented, perhaps a little defensively, "The addition of sound may increase suspense, but I think sound and dialogue should be used sparingly, perhaps 25 per cent sound and 75 per cent silence. This means that the bits and touches we used to put in our silent pictures and since have dropped—the speed, the pantomime, the subtlety of earlier days—need to be reinstated on the screen once more." (Actually, *Dracula* is not so silent as it has seemed—a 1991 restoration of its soundtrack revealed eerie, ambient wind effects during the Transylvania sequences, an atmospheric touch that had been buried in the accumulated audio noise of six decades.)

Many commentators consider *Dracula* as atypical of Browning's oeuvre. However, several elements place it firmly within the established themes of the Browning canon. Dracula, after all, is the ultimate charlatan and con man. He is a "castrated" seducer who cannot penetrate in the conventional way; all sex energy is displaced to his mouth. Instead of providing stimulation, repeated encounters only drain and depress his lovers, who can barely recall his visits. Unconsummated in normal terms, their passion soon becomes undead as well.

Carl Laemmle, Jr., was apparently uncomfortable with some of the homoerotic displacements of the script ("Dracula should only go for women and not men!" he wrote in his copy of the final screenplay) and sex in general was toned down. The play, for instance, contained directions for a long, passionate lip-lock between Dracula and his victim, leading up to the bite; in the film, Lugosi does no more than stiffly kiss Helen Chandler's hand.

Some of the press coverage of the film implied a link between *Dracula* and other Browning obsessions. A purported interview with Lugosi in *Motion Picture Classic* reads suspiciously as if the actual person interviewed was Browning. Entitled "The Feminine Love of Horror," the author, a woman, immediately comments on the actor's aura that suggests a "rank miasma" with "the atmosphere of charnel house and carnival surrounding him." The women of America, Lugosi (Browning?) said, "are unsatisfied, famished, craving sensation, even though it be the sensation of death." They "go to circuses and cast restless, unseeing eyes on clowns and trapeze artists," favoring instead "the place of the Strange People, the Freaks, and stand there, mouths agape, transfixed." There is, of course, "a profound biological reason. Before a woman bears a child she goes through successive phases of horror, lest the fruit of her body be a monstrous thing." (The zoophagous Mr. Renfield, in his resemblance to a sideshow geek, provides another correspondence between Browning's *Dracula* and the freak pit.) And even war mutilation figured into the *Motion Picture Classic* discussion of *Dracula*'s appeal: "During the war," Lugosi said, "women fought, maneuvered, bribed and schemed to get into the frontline trenches. In their hearts, in their conscious minds, they believed that they were striving for that place in order to provide deeds of duty and mercy. . . . But mixed in with this high motive was the ghoulish compulsion to see men torn and bloody and in agony . . . the need to look upon suffering, which is part of their destiny."

In the original studio press book for *Dracula,* Browning directly gave his opinion on popular taste. "Ninety percent of the people are morbid-minded . . . I am not sure that the average should not go higher. O. Henry once remarked that more people would gather to look at a dead horse in the street than would assemble to watch the finest coach pass by, and this homely observation comes very close to representing the actual fact." Browning then remarked on the particular fascination of car wrecks, probably the only time in his career he was quoted on the subject for publication, speculating that "more fainting spectators are carried away from automobile accidents than injured participants."

Despite Browning's apparent willingness to ballyhoo *Dracula* Universal gave it almost no publicity or advertising for its west coast premiere. The only public appearance Lugosi seems to have made was for the premiere of the Spanish-language version, when he walked onto the stage of the California Theatre to congratulate its stars. Not surprisingly, there is no mention in the press coverage of Browning having attended the event.

Dracula would eventually be recognized as a key American film, though not for the usual reasons. In the European tradition of filmmaking, the irrational and macabre had been part of the cinema since its inception. For all its artistic deficiencies, *Dracula* liberated the dormant impulse in America, reestablishing an essential connection between film and the unconscious, and quietly transformed our imaginative life forever.

One of the most powerful and disturbing images in *All Quiet on the Western Front,* Universal's biggest success of 1930, was a bodiless pair of hands, clinging to a barbed-wire fence, the rest of their owner having just been blown away before the viewer's eyes. Universal produced a similar pair of dismembered hands the following year, and it grafted them onto Boris Karloff for what would become the most famous horror movie of all time.

A one-reel *Frankenstein* had been produced by Thomas Edison in 1910; another, extremely free adaptation called *Life Without Soul* appeared in 1915, and the story was considered by First National in 1928 as a special-effects vehicle for Willis O'Brien, who had animated the dinosaurs for *The Lost World* and would achieve his greatest fame as the head technician on *King Kong.* The O'Brien conception of *Frankenstein* would have involved a stop-motion monster in miniature, thus allowing for superhuman feats impossible for an actor or stuntman to achieve. The film never got past the planning stages.

Three years later, Carl Laemmle, Jr., vindicated by the box-office success of *Dracula,* proceeded with his plans to film Mary Shelley's *Frankenstein.* Universal had purchased the rights to the John L. Balderston and Peggy Webling adaptation on April 8, 1931, a scant seven weeks after the release of *Dracula.* Balderston's agent, Harold Freedman, had been unable to extract anything near the $40,000 he had negotiated for *Dracula*; Universal was in terrible financial shape. Artfully, Freedman suggested a compromise: Balderston and Webling would accept a far smaller sum—$20,000, to be precise—in exchange for a one percent interest in *Franken-stein*'s gross earnings as a film. By preempting the stage rights, Universal would be able to produce *Frankenstein* without competition or delay. And having spent good money for the title to a solid and provocative dramatization of a literary classic, the studio then followed time-honored Hollywood procedure: they threw the thing away.

The French director Robert Florey was first announced as the man charged with creating *Frankenstein,* and he developed a script in which the monster emerged as a pure brute, devoid of even the half-articulate pathos that Balderston and Webling had given it.

Florey was intent on creating a stylized and expressionistic film in the *Caligari* manner, and filmed a couple of test reels on the standing sets of *Dracula* to show off the style. Bela Lugosi was the reluctant monster, heavily puttied and painted, and possibly with massive wig or headdress in the style of *The Golem*. Several accounts of this lost test makeup have been published, and almost all are contradictory. The wig, however, is a persuasive detail in that virtually every description, drawing, or photograph of stage and screen adaptations of *Frankenstein* from 1823 through 1930 present the monster with a flowing, flying, or tangled mane of hair. Lugosi bridled at being assigned a nonspeaking part, and Florey was being eased out of the project by James Whale, a stage director from Britain who had come to Hollywood prominence through three war pictures: for Howard Hughes' *Hell's Angels* (1930) Whale, uncredited, directed the dialogue sequences when Hughes, caught in the transition to sound, was forced to reshoot the picture with a sound track; *Journey's End* (1930), based on the hit London play by Robert C. Sherriff (which Whale had also directed on stage); and *Waterloo Bridge* (1931), his first picture for Universal, also based on a play (by Robert Emmet Sherwood) about the encounter of a wounded soldier and a prostitute in London at the end of the war. The film so impressed Carl Laemmle, Jr., that he offered Whale the pick of any project to which the studio owned the rights. Out of thirty-odd properties, Whale chose *Frankenstein,* but only because nothing else interested him. At least, he reasoned, it wasn't another war picture.

Frankenstein, though, would owe a debt to Whale's time in the cinematic trenches (as well as the real ones; his earliest attempts at theatrical production came about in a prison camp near Hanover during the last year of the war). After Universal had considered Leslie Howard for the title role, Whale chose Colin Clive, a haunted, highly strung actor who had played the tortured Captain Stanhope in the stage and film versions of *Journey's End*. He realized that Clive's nerve-racked intensity was also the perfect quality for Henry Frankenstein—a man on the edge if there ever was. And Mae Clarke, the prostitute from *Waterloo Bridge,* would be his fiancé, Elizabeth. Finding a monster took a bit longer, however. The new concept of the creature required an actor of some range and sensitivity. Whale's shooting script, by Garrett Fort and Francis Ford Faragoh, used the Florey script as a skeleton, but added a deep note of pathos throughout.

"It does not walk like a Robot," the script took pains to spell out. "Its first offscreen sound was to be "haunting, piteous . . . like that of a lost animal."

"I spent ten years in Hollywood without causing the slightest stir," Boris Karloff recalled in later years. "Then one day I was sitting in the commissary at Universal, having lunch, and looking rather well turned out, I thought, when a man sent a note over to my table, asking if I'd like to audition for the part of a monster."

Whale's companion David Lewis had suggested that he look at Karloff, who had recently made a striking gangster in *The Criminal Code*. Karloff, the former William Henry Pratt, sometimes drove a truck for a lumberyard between acting assignments. He had no illusions about the film industry owing him a livelihood, and no expectations whatsoever that his name would soon become a household word for horror. Whale thought Karloff's face had interesting possibilities; an amateur painter himself, the director sketched the actor, experimentally exaggerating the bony ridges of Karloff's head. He showed his ideas to Jack P. Pierce, head of Universal's makeup department since 1926. Pierce had been responsible for Conrad Veidt's hideous grin in Universal's *The Man Who Laughs* (1929), based on the Victor Hugo novel, and had created the Lugosi makeup for the Florey screen test of *Frankenstein*.

Pierce was considered a genius by those who worked with him, although perhaps an egotistical one; he never publicly acknowledged Whale's part in developing the *Frankenstein* makeup. Perhaps the closest he came to acknowledging the debt was his 1939 comment to *The New York Times*, "I didn't depend on my imagination." He said that he had spent three months of preliminary research in such areas as anatomy, surgery, criminology, and electrodynamics. The final Frankenstein design, he maintained, was a more or less logical result of these efforts.

In retrospect it seems clear that Pierce, and Whale, also drew less consciously on design considerations than from the stylized machine-age aesthetic which, by 1931, had become a dominant force in the applied arts. Eclectically inspired by cubism, expressionism, and architectural theories of the Bauhaus, the zig–zagging style soon elbowed and angled its way into the worlds of advertising, decoration, and industrial design. The movement had begun in 1925 in Paris, at the Exposition Internationale des Arts Décoratifs et Industriels Modernes, and the show's title gave birth to the

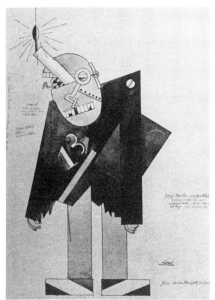

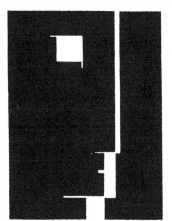

BAUHAUS-AUSSTELLUNG
WEIMAR, JULI - SEPT. 1923

Cultural precursors of Hollywood's Frankenstein monster: Bauhaus post-card (1923), George Grosz's design for a theatrical dummy in Iwan Goll's *Methusaleh* (1922), and Westinghouse Laboratories' mechanical man, "Televox" (1928). *(Grosz design © 1993 ARS, N.Y. / ADAGP, Paris)*

two names used most often to describe the movement: Art Deco and Art Moderne. American designers further refined the aesthetic, and *Fortune* later recalled that Fifth Avenue shops soon filled their display windows with the "grotesque mannequins, the cubist props, the gaga designs" that would define the style.

"Grotesque mannequin" well describes the Frankenstein monster, an amalgam of conventional bodies torn apart and reassembled according to new, logical-angular, electromechanical principles. The square head—a common motif in advertising graphics of the time—powerfully evokes the plight of an old consciousness forced to occupy a new paradigm, a round brain bolted uneasily into a machine-tooled skull. As the script described its structure: "The top of its head has a curious flat ridge like the lid of a box. The hair is fairly short and quite obviously combed over the ridge to hide the defect of the joining where the brain was put in." The monster is a modernist designer's nightmare: the seams show, the clamps and bolts stick out. Form follows function, but just barely.

Beyond Whale and Pierce, various other designers in Universal's production and even in its promotion department had contributed visual concepts for the monster-in-development. Two recurring elements were especially notable: the protruding brow, suggesting evolutionary regression, and the paradoxically futurist design of a completely mechanical man along the lines of "Tele-vox," an automaton developed by Westinghouse Laboratories in the late 1920s. The most "mechanical" concept, by Universal's poster illustrator Karoly Grosz, first introduced the notion of a steel bolt through the neck, a detail that in itself would come to symbolize the total Frankenstein mythos. As art historian Sidra Stich has noted, this kind of stylization, seen in the work of Max Ernst, "displaced, suppressed, and reshaped humans to conform with the machine world," a tendency that followed the world's first completely industrialized war. And finally, the Pierce-Karloff monster owes an obvious debt to Conrad Veidt's stark postwar silhouette in *The Cabinet of Dr. Caligari* (Whale had studied the film in preparation for *Frankenstein*) and, unwittingly, reaches back even further to the "Man or Machine" carnival prototype that first inspired Caligari's writers during the war years.

The Karloff monster, of course, undermines the principles of the machine aesthetic while drawing inspiration from them; although the creature is decidedly modern, he's certainly not deco—something more, indeed, like a battered hood ornament for a

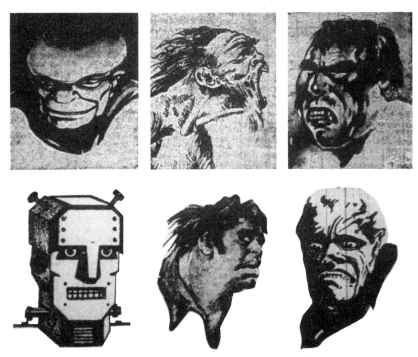

Preliminary concepts for the *Frankenstein* makeup by Universal artists in the summer of 1931. *(The Library of Congress)*

wrecked economy. Like a gargoyle on the Chrysler Building (completed in 1930) the Frankenstein monster is yet another inevitable culmination of the machine aesthetic: a looming and unforgettable piece of vernacular architecture.

"We were all fascinated by the development of Karloff's face and head," recalled actress Mae Clarke, who had a ringside seat at the construction site. "White putty on the face was toned down to a corpse-like gray. Then there was a sudden inspiration to give the face a green tint. It awed us and gave Boris and the rest of us a different feeling about the whole concept." (Karloff himself is said to have suggested the heavily puttied eyelids, which added a dimension of pathos and incomprehension.)

When the makeup was ready for a screen test—in black-and-white—Karloff had no idea how effective the finished product would be. Would it inspire horror . . . or laughter? "I was thinking this, practicing my walk, as I rounded a bend in the corridor and came *face-to-face* with this prop man.

"He was the first man to see the monster—I watched to study his reaction. It was quick to come. He turned white—gurgled— and lunged out of sight down the corridor. Never saw him again. Poor chap, I would have liked to thank him—he was the audience that first made me *feel* like the monster."

The story, as it was filmed, drew freely on a number of sources: the Shelley novel, the films *The Golem* and *Caligari,* and earlier dramatic adaptations of *Frankenstein.* Frankenstein's assistant Fritz (played by Dwight Frye, *Dracula*'s Renfield, memorably described by writer Stefan Kanfer as "a hyperthyroid actor with a stage whisper the size of Pasadena") was first depicted on the London stage in 1823. The character had been revived by Horace Liveright and Louis Cline in their unproduced rewrite of the Balderston script, which they sold to Universal. Liveright's contributions to the modern horror genre, therefore, included not only the resurrec-

The final makeup emerged as a subtle exaggeration of Boris Karloff's natural features. At left, Karloff's appearance in *The Criminal Code* (1931), the role that brought him to Universal's attention for *Frankenstein.*

tion/exploitation of its two major icons, but the popularization of the "laboratory hunchback" motif as well.

Frankenstein's opening credits appear over a half-distinct, demonic face approaching the viewer through a field of wheeling eyes, perhaps inspired by similar designs used on stroboscope discs, the whirling Victorian toys that anticipated the motion picture. The effect immerses the viewer at once in a primal kind of experience, simultaneously infantilized and terrified. The opening scene in a cemetery contained what was, for 1931 audiences, a visceral jolt: the sound of earth crashing on the lid of a coffin. The microphone itself was placed in the casket, the better to magnify the reverberations. David Lewis remembered: "The film has been imitated so much that today, these scenes don't bother people. But in 1931, it was awfully strong stuff." At a preview in Santa Monica, some audience members voted with their feet. "As it progressed," Lewis said, "people got up, walked out, came back in, walked out again. It was an alarming thing."

Pieced together from graveyard, gallows, and medical-school scraps, the monster is brought to life in a machine-age orgasm of crackling machinery. In 1818, Mary Shelley had made a passing reference to "a powerful engine"; in 1931, her dream-image took on the pop-sculptural reality of the present. *Frankenstein*'s gleaming lightning-arc generators, created by electrical engineer Kenneth Strickfaden, were a wholly fanciful, high-wattage commentary on the machine age. "The styling all depended on what kind of junk I had at hand," he said fifty years later, though his interest in electricity, its uses and metaphors, was far from flippant. "Electricity is life," he told interviewer George E. Turner. "We're just a bunch of sparks with various quantities of air." His sentiments reflected the distinctly reductionistic, mechanical-leaning tendencies of much cultural expression since the war. Untold millions had been left with the feeling that modern life—and death—was nothing but an anonymous, crushing assembly line.

Whale's film depicted a monster squarely in the grip of this confusion, a pathetic figure caught, as it were, on the barbed wire between humanism and mechanism. The exact time period is vague—it *seems* to be the present; the women, for instance, wear 1931 fashions, and although the film is "about" science, all of the trappings of technology and industrialization—cars, radio, telephones—are totally absent, as if their energy has been displaced totally into Frankenstein's laboratory equipment. The film is set

Wedding-night blues: machine-age science threatens the traditional reproductive paradigm. *(Courtesy of Ronald V. Borst / Hollywood Movie Posters)*

in a German village, which is also peopled (as if during the war) with characters speaking with British and American accents. Since the village sequences were shot on the same outdoor sets as *All Quiet on the Western Front,* no doubt many audience members experienced a certain level of déjà vu, whether or not they consciously equated *Frankenstein* with the celebrated war picture.

One of the most famous sequences of *Frankenstein* is one that was not seen in its entirety for almost fifty years. The monster encounters a little girl at the edge of a lake. Unfrightened, she leads him in a game of throwing flowers on the water to see them prettily afloat. The monster, carried away with delight, throws the girl in after the flowers, but unlike the daisies, she sinks and drowns. The scene ended up being radically cut. Karloff insisted in later years that the scene didn't work because James Whale had insisted that he throw the child with a brutal, overhead motion, rather than set her gently on the water. Karloff, who had some back problems, was incapable of hurling the girl very far, and the resulting, compromised action looked buffoonish. Fortunately, just the idea of the child's death was sufficiently upsetting ("No little girl is going to drown in one of my pictures!" Carl Laemmle, Sr., is reported to have fumed to his secretary) so that the scene was cut for many engagements, ending with the monster reaching out for the child (and, ironically, leaving some viewers with the impression that they had been spared the spectacle of some shocking molestation).

Many misconceptions have taken root about the extent of *Frankenstein* censorship in the United States. Most of the notable excisions—the drowning of the little girl, Colin Clive's line "I know what it feels like to be God," etc., were demanded cut by the MPPDA only upon the film's proposed rerelease in 1937. The six states with censor boards, of course, could, and would, snip as they pleased—Kansas was particularly bad. But in censor-lite California, the film seems to have been shown intact—Clive's "God" line, for instance, was quoted in a San Francisco review. And the drowning scene was apparently still in place when Universal submitted the film to the MPPDA for reissue clearance; the industry censors made their formal objection to it on June 9, 1937. (The scene, found largely intact at the British Film Institute, was finally restored to a videodisc version of *Frankenstein* released by MCA in the 1980s, but still lacks close-ups of the child sinking, etc.—details the English censors marked for excision.)

Frankenstein created a major flap with the Quebec censors, Catholics who raised religious objections to the film's theme of divine presumption. T. B. Fithian at Universal arranged to show the picture to two Catholic priests in Los Angeles, who were of the opinion that *Frankenstein* in no way offended Catholic doctrines. But they agreed with Fithian's suggestion that the best way to get the thing past Canadian censors might be "through the agency of a suitable foreword or some preface that would indicate the picture was a dream. Perhaps we could open it on the book with the off-scene voices of Shelley and Byron and Mrs. Shelley discussing a fantastic tale and dissolve into the picture. We would be willing to do anything like this." Essentially, Universal was proposing to do the same thing the Germans had done with *The Cabinet of Dr. Caligari* a decade earlier. But diplomacy prevailed and the Canadians finally approved *Frankenstein* in essentially its original form. A short prologue was, however, appended to all prints of the film, spoken by Edward Van Sloan, the actor who played Henry Frankenstein's mentor, Dr. Waldman. (Universal had used Van Sloan in a similar epilogue to *Dracula*.) Several of Universal's contract writers, including newcomer John Huston, contributed to the speech:

> Mr. Carl Laemmle feels it would be a little unkind to present this picture without just a word of friendly warning. We are about to unfold the story of Frankenstein, a man of science, who sought to create a man after his own image, without reckoning upon God. It is one of the strangest tales ever told. It deals with the two great mysteries of creation—Life and Death. I think it may thrill you. It may shock you. It may even horrify you. So if any of you feel that you do not care to subject your nerves to such a strain, now is your chance to . . . Well, we've warned you!

The curtain-raiser did little to mollify many censors, and the film was banned in Belfast, South Australia, Czechoslovakia, and, for a time, in Sweden. Domestically, one particularly pesky state was Massachusetts, which requested so many cuts that the film would have been utterly unintelligible. Among its most laughable requests: "Eliminate scene showing body on slab coming to life." In Texas, one exhibitor saw the publicity value of the controversy and drummed up Dallas audiences by publicly threatening to cancel his contract with Universal unless they allowed him to screen the film intact.

Frankenstein, of course, lent itself to novel and outrageous exploitation stunts. In addition to the techniques ushered in by *Dracula*—nurses on duty, free "nerve tonic," and the like—elaborate advance publicity included, in one venue, the firing of a gun backstage to startle the audience out of its collective seat just as the trailer began to play on the screen. Robert Sparks, who managed the Arcadia Theatre in Temple, Texas, advertised for a woman who would agree to sit alone in the darkened theatre for an advance preview of the film in exchange for a cash reward. "Eighty-five women made application for the privilege," reported *Motion Picture Herald,* and the prize finally went to the selfless soul who offered to give her prize to charity. In Omaha, an out-of-control crowd for a midnight screening shattered a theatre's plate-glass window, generating more publicity and interest.

"Morbidity is not without its claim to a high place among humanity's respectable emotional interests," wrote *Motion Picture Herald* in its discussion of *Frankenstein.* The film had arrived, "if the psychologists can be believed, at the familiar psychological moment. Say the savants, people like the tragic best at those time when their own spirits are depressed, and the economists tell us that even more than their spirits are at a low ebb."

Frankenstein, evidently, was just what the doctor ordered.

The close relationship between children's stories and the literature of horror is nowhere better demonstrated than in the career of Robert Louis Stevenson, whose two most famous works are a pirate adventure, *Treasure Island,* and a grim novella of scientific Gothicism, *The Strange Case of Dr. Jekyll and Mr. Hyde* (1886). *Jekyll and Hyde* was inspired by the true eighteenth-century story of Edinburgh's Deacon Brodie, a respected citizen by day and a ruthless criminal by night. Stevenson's freely updated version of the story would introduce the second great pair of nineteenth-century doppelgangers to emerge from the British Isles, following Frankenstein and his monster and anticipating Dorian Gray and his portrait. (Bram Stoker's *Dracula* would also embody aspects of the doppelganger, though its doublings and splittings would be more subtle and diffuse.)

The Stevenson story was almost immediately seized upon by the theatre. Thomas Russell Sullivan adapted *The Strange Case* for the actor Richard Mansfield, who essayed the dual role for the first time in Boston in May 1887. (It remained part of his repertory until his death in 1907.) The first film version of *Jekyll and Hyde* was produced by the Selig company in America in 1908, the second in 1909 (Denmark), a third version by Laemmle in 1912, a fourth and fifth in 1913 (U.S. and Britain), and a sixth version from Starlight appeared in 1914. Four separate versions were made in 1920—the first starred John Barrymore and was produced by Famous Players-Lasky; the second, by Pioneer, starred Sheldon Lewis; the third was a comedy produced by Arrow; and the fourth, filmed almost simultaneously in Germany by F. W. Murnau, starred Conrad Veidt, and featured, in the role of his butler, Bela Lugosi. To hide its source, the unauthorized adaptation of the Stevenson original split its identities even further, assuming the guise of *Dr. Warren and Mr. O'Connor* in Austria. In total, eleven silent film versions appeared.

It is interesting that both America and Germany, in the years immediately following the war, found *Jekyll and Hyde* to be a viable commercial subject. The story of a man's—and by way of audience identification, a country's—descent into bestial violence had a clear metaphorical link to the conflagration just past. The Murnau film does not exist in any known archival collection and is likely lost for good. The Barrymore film (directed by John S. Robertson from a screenplay by Clara S. Beranger) formalized the dramatic conventions that would influence adaptations for the rest of the twentieth century. Many of these conventions had nothing to do with Stevenson, owing instead a certain debt to Oscar Wilde. Four years after Stevenson published his novella, Wilde brought out his own great work of doppelganger terror, *The Picture of Dorian Gray*. Wilde's title character had a rather more roundabout way of splitting his personality; the physical ugliness was held out of sight in an attic-room portrait that grew progressively hideous. Dorian Gray's outward appearance—that of an unchangingly beautiful young man—allows him to go about his evil unobtrusively. Wilde never reveals the precise nature of Dorian's transgressions, but they are profoundly sociopathic. The young man seduces, then cruelly abandons, an actress named Sibyl Vane, and is clearly the cause of her ensuing suicide. For the Barrymore film, screenwriter Beranger consciously or unconsciously borrowed Wilde's subplot and, with a few modifications, grafted it seamlessly to Stevenson's original story. As Mr. Hyde, Henry Jekyll also found a woman of the theatre to exploit and destroy . . . and the presence of a dance-hall girl became a part of the Jekyll/Hyde equation that would never be erased.* As was the case with Bram Stoker's *Dracula*, stage and screen adaptors saw—craftily—that the element of overt,

---

*The give-and-take between adaptations of *Dr. Jekyll and Mr. Hyde* and *The Picture of Dorian Gray* was far from finished. When *Dorian Gray* was finally filmed by Hollywood in the forties, the character of Sibyl Vane was socioeconomically downgraded from a Shakespearean actress to a music-hall Cockney, as if to bring the story more in line with the conventions established by film adaptations of *Dr. Jekyll and Mr. Hyde*.

fatal seduction, missing in the original story, was necessary to realize its full imaginative and commercial potential. They were right, of course.

Barrymore filmed *Jekyll and Hyde* by day in New York while performing *Richard III* at night, a grueling physical combination. Tallulah Bankhead recalled that Barrymore had originally offered her the female lead. Bankhead was also achieving some prominence on the New York stage, and was flattered, but she was also leery of his motives. She went to his dressing room at the Plymouth Theatre, where, true to the Jekyll/Hyde atavism, Barrymore began to emit "little animal noises." Bankhead interpreted these as an indication of "his desire to shred the seventh commandment." The Great Profile took her hands "and started to lead me to a convenient couch. With such dignity as I could simulate under these fiery circumstances, I declined."

Much of the fun of the stage versions of *Jekyll and Hyde* involved seeing how far an actor could take a transformation without resorting to makeup (Richard Mansfield apparently used only facial contortions and lighting). Barrymore likely saw Mansfield in the part; the actor was a close friend of his father Maurice. For his own transformation, Barrymore did use a startling, snaggle-toothed, pointy-headed disguise, but contrived to apply the paint without stopping the camera, making efficient use of each doubling over and convulsion, of which there were many. The actor extended his fingertips with rubber appliances that may well have influenced the makeup of Max Schreck in *Nosferatu* the following year (Barrymore was an international star, and the film was widely shown in Europe). The creepy fingers, which looked at least five knuckles long, did have their practical drawbacks, however; during one particularly violent convulsion, a disembodied digit can be observed flying across the screen. Perhaps the most wonderful moment in the film is Hyde's removing his pointed hat, revealing that it conforms all too neatly to the shape of the head beneath.

Barrymore finished the film (which was not as much praised as was his performance) but the combined rigors of simultaneously playing the bunchbacked Richard III and the equally crabbed Mr. Edward Hyde ended in Barrymore's nervous collapse and an off-stage stint in a White Plains sanitarium.

A decade later, in the wake of *Dracula* and in a race with the almost simultaneously produced *Frankenstein,* Paramount entrusted an elaborate remake of the film to the theatrical director Rouben

Mamoulian. Paramount first wanted Mamoulian to use the character actor Irving Pichel as Jekyll, but the director refused. "I insisted that he be somebody young, [because] rebellion and transformation is more interesting when it is the result of the ferment of youthful aspirations," Mamoulian recalled in 1971. He chose Fredric March, who many in the industry considered a lightweight. He was about to show them otherwise.

March's casting is notable in that he is so obviously an American. A recurrent feature in thirties horror films is the injection of American characters and performers into nightmarish "European" situations. As Frank McConnell has noted, "The 'England' of *Dracula* is transparently New England, even to the accents of most of its major characters."

Dr. Jekyll and Mr. Hyde was filmed at Paramount while Universal was wrapping up *Frankenstein,* and would place a similar emphasis on a tour de force of monster makeup. One of Mr. Hyde's test faces was a close cousin to that of Lon Chaney's vampire in *London After Midnight,* including a shock of hair under a tall hat and horrible protruding teeth. Mamoulian claimed credit for the Neanderthal conception that was finally used. Like another classic horror makeup—that of Max Schreck in *Nosferatu*—Hyde's features become progressively hideous as the film unreels.

The transformation scenes were ingeniously filmed, and relied on the manipulation of color filters that would be undetectable in the black-and-white film. The first signs of Hyde's distorted features—wrinkle lines, enlarged nostrils, etc.—were painted directly on March's face in red makeup. Photographed through a compensating red filter, the makeup was invisible to the camera. As the filter changed gradually from red to blue, monstrous details seemed to erupt from the actor's face. The trick had originally been devised by cameraman Karl Struss for *Ben Hur,* where, used in reverse, it created the miraculous "healing" of lepers.

Today's lightweight foam latex makeup effects were unknown in 1931, and March's facial prosthetics had to be painstakingly built from sometimes unfriendly materials. Actress Rose Hobart, who played Jekyll's fiancé, recalled that the test makeups were "*too* mask-like," immobilizing the actor's face. "So they just put liquid rubber on his face—*that* was the makeup. And when they took it off, his face came with it! He was lucky he wasn't ruined for life."

In addition to literate dialogue and uncommonly lush production values, Mamoulian's *Jekyll and Hyde* added an unprecedent

Dr. Jekyll and Mr. Hyde: the two faces of Fredric March. *(The Stephen Jochsberger Collection)*

Mr. Hyde triumphant.
(Photofest)

edly explicit sexual element to the horror. The throwaway dance-hall girl of the Barrymore version was developed into a major character, a prostitute named Ivy (Miriam Hopkins) who tempts the good doctor, not knowing she is also inviting Mr. Hyde to come out and play. How these amazingly suggestive scenes made it past Colonel Joy and company is not at all clear; during pre-production, the MPPDA had objected only to some dialogue (a man calling Ivy a "mucky wench") and a scene calling for Hyde to drop a kitten into a river. Stills exist documenting that Mamoulian filmed the ugly sequence from the Stevenson original in which Hyde stomps on a little boy on the street. Paramount, possibly wishing to avoid a *Frankenstein*-style child-abuse debacle, removed the scene before the film ever reached the censors.

By the time the MPPDA had the chance to view the finished version of *Dr. Jekyll and Mr. Hyde,* Universal's *Frankenstein* had just opened to astonishing business, leading the industry to realize that *Dracula* was not a fluke, and "horror movies" (the term was not widely used previously, and was in many ways an invention of 1931) formed an important and profitable new category. Jason Joy let his thoughts be known to Paramount's B. P. Schulberg on December 1, 1931. "Because it is so well established a literary classic the public and the censors may overlook the horrors that result from the realism of the Hyde make-up," Joy opined, "though we are frank to say we cannot estimate what the reaction will be to this, or to the other horror pictures. Certainly we hope that the excellence of the production will offset any apprehension that the theme is too harrowing."

The film opened in New York on New Year's Eve, 1931. *Variety* found it admirable, but overlong, and complained that its "labored adornment of the original simplicity weakens the production for mob appeal." The film would be cut by seventeen minutes for later engagements—probably less for the benefit of audiences than that of theatre managers, who could thereby squeeze in an extra daily showing. Curiously, *Variety* ran a split-personality review; a sidebar feature called "The Woman's Angle" reinterpreted some of the perceived flaws as plusses for women. "Classic shocker loses much of its stark horror and consequent unpleasantness for women, by growing logical with psychoanalytical motivation and daringly presented sex appeal. Latest version made enticing instead of repellant to the girls."

March's performance elevated the horror film one notch further when he was named best actor of the year at the 1932 Academy Awards presentation. In other countries, the consensus was not so admiring; *Dr. Jekyll and Mr. Hyde* was rejected outright by censors in Finland, the Netherlands, Rhodesia, and Czechoslovakia.

With *Dracula, Frankenstein,* and *Dr. Jekyll and Mr. Hyde,* the psychic landscapes of castle, crypt, and laboratory were definitively mapped. Only one locale, that primal circus tent from which all the mad doctors and walking corpses had made their entrance into the cinema, remained to be explored. And there was only one man qualified to lift back the flap.

"My God, my God, this is a broken doll!"

John Eckhardt could not possibly have understood the first words spoken about him on this earth, but the Baltimore midwife who delivered him was trying to express with words what she had just witnessed on the night of August 27, 1911. The first of a set of identical twins, Robert Eckhardt, had come into the world normal. The second, John, emerged from his mother with the bottom part of his own body missing below the rib cage. And lived.

Johnny was complete enough internally to continue living and growing in a halfway normal fashion. Unable to explore the world in the ways of other children, he embarked on his own imaginative adventures. He loved the Sundays when his mother would carry him down to the railroad tracks. "I'd spend the whole afternoon lying there watching those trains, and more than anything in this world," Johnny remembered, "I wanted to be an engineer, up there in the locomotive, going someplace." At the age of eleven, he and his brother caught the carnival bug after a stage magician offered to break them into show business. Their brief working relationship turned out to be exploitative, and it ended, but the boys' desire to run away with the show did not. Most kids entertained such fantasies, but had no means to realize them. Bob and Johnny Eck had everything it took. Sometimes less was more.

Their work in midway shows and carnivals was interrupted by the onset of the Depression. Their original, shady manager ingratiated his way back into their lives and booked them into the 1931 Canadian Exposition. There Johnny was approached by men who introduced themselves as talent scouts for a Mr. Browning at Metro-Goldwyn-Mayer studios. Johnny didn't know anything about a

Mr. Browning, but filmed a screen test in which he showed off his powerful arms and balancing skills. The test also featured another sideshow attraction, a forty-five-pound Norwegian rat.

The boys traveled to Hollywood by train, first-class. Their manager didn't tell them that the film deal had come through—they thought they were going to work in a circus. Their manager also didn't tell them that they were only going to receive 10 percent of the $1,000 per week MGM was willing to pay for their presence. Finally they were introduced to the Oz-like man who had summoned them to the dream palace. A whole make-believe circus top had been erected on the movie lot, just waiting for them.

"Welcome to the family, welcome," said Tod Browning, intoning majestically. Eck recalled that "from that time on he never called me Johnny Eck, he called me 'Mr. Johnny.' " (If either man was aware of another, common slang meaning of "Mr. Johnny," they didn't comment on it.) In a 1980 interview, Eck remembered Browning telling him, " 'I want you to stay as close to me as possible, and *all* the time. . . . Whenever I have an empty seat or an empty chair, *you* are to sit alongside of me while we shoot.' "

And shoot they did. Tod Browning's *Freaks* was sped into production to capitalize on Universal's 1931 horror bonanza, but the story had been in development well before the rival studio had even committed itself to *Dracula*. In 1929, MGM had bought the rights to Tod Robbins' short story "Spurs," which had appeared in *Munsey's Magazine* in 1923. The studio paid the author $8,000

Johnny Eck, the "half-boy" of *Freaks* (1932).
(The Museum of Modern Art / Film Stills Collection)

for the strange little tale of a French circus midget, Jacques Courbe, who inherits a large estate and immediately proposes marriage to Jeanne Marie, a statuesque bareback rider he has admired from afar. Jacques' circus act is a clownish shadow of hers; he also rides, but his steed is a wolfish dog named St. Eustache. Jeanne Marie is really in love with her riding partner Simon Lafleur, but being dowerless knows he will never marry her. In the belief that midgets are apt to die young, she accepts Jacques' offer and they are married. Their wedding feast, held in a circus tent, degenerates with drink into a virtual riot among the sideshow freaks. Jeanne Marie forces her groom to perch on her shoulder like a monkey, boasting that she can carry him "from one end of France to the other." Jacques never forgives her. A year later she reappears at the circus and Simon does not recognize her; she is haggard and aged. Jacques has held her to her boast, it seems; he has measured the exact distance "from one end of France to another," and every day, rain or shine, forces her to carry him on her back along the country roads as a punishment—literally spurring her on. She begs Simon to help her escape this torment, but they are interrupted by Jacques and his wolfhound, who mount a cavalry charge on Jeanne's ex-lover. Jacques mortally wounds Simon with his tiny sword, and Jeanne is resigned to continue her punishment. "It is truly remarkable," Jacques reflects, "how speedily one can ride the devil out of a woman—with spurs!"

Matching Tod Browning with a Tod Robbins story made some sense; Robbins, after all, had authored the novel that had been the basis of one of the greatest Browning/Chaney money-makers, *The Unholy Three.* Brooklyn-born Clarence A. "Tod" Robbins was an enormously popular writer of mysteries and thrillers in the twenties. (Six times married, Robbins would be described by *The New York Times* as "a familiar figure in Greenwich Village and Montparnasse." A tennis-playing, globe-trotting Francophile who made a fortune imagining the worst in human nature, he settled on the French Riviera. His refusal to quit France during the Occupation landed him in a German concentration camp for a long period. He died in 1949.)

"Spurs" had its problems as a story; it was really little more than a nasty anecdote, and all the characters were detestable. But all the "Browning elements" were present, and there was a good part for the diminutive actor Harry Earles, who had memorably played a midget thug disguised as a baby in *The Unholy Three,* and was keen for Browning to film the story. Metro announced in November 1929 that the director's next film would be "a side-show picture," though the production obviously did not pan out immediately.

Only after Browning returned in commercial success from Universal and *Dracula* did Irving Thalberg give the go-ahead to *Freaks*. Browning promised the studio the ultimate horror picture, and to Thalberg that sounded like a pretty good idea. Universal already had *Frankenstein* in preparation; this monster thing, certainly, was the big coming trend. Scriptwriter Willis Goldbeck showed Thalberg a treatment. After reading it, Thalberg reportedly dropped his head in his hands. "I asked for something horrifying," he groaned, "and I got it."

A good businessman knows better than to produce his own tastes. If the public wanted to scream—and pay for the privilege—Metro-Goldwyn-Mayer was pleased to help them.

Four writers in addition to Browning—who almost always took an active, if unbilled, hand in his scenarios—worked on the script for *Freaks*; Goldbeck shared screenplay credit with Leon Gordon, and additional dialogue was contributed by Edgar Allan Woolf and Al Boasberg. Woolf would later work on the script for *The Wizard of Oz,* in which some of the *Freaks* cast would be recycled as Munchkins.

The story they presented for final approval bore only a passing resemblance to "Spurs"; while the revenge theme was retained, the trapeze artist (now called Cleopatra) was now a plotting murderess, intent on poisoning her tiny husband, Hans. The story is structured around three couples, each contrasting, shadowing, or paralleling the others. Cleopatra is in love with the circus strong man Hercules, equally evil. Hans is officially engaged to another midget, Freida, but unable to resist the fantasy of "the most beautiful big woman I have ever seen." Phroso the clown is stuck on Venus, the seal trainer. Other, less conventional couplings are evident as well: a pair of Siamese twins is a problematic dyad, bickering about their love lives; and in Josephine-Joseph, the half-man, half-woman, the twinning is accomplished within a single body. The plot turns, and the dancers change partners in bizarre and frustrating sexual pairings. The clown is a good guy, but lacks equipment ("You should have caught me before my operation," he tells his girl). We know the midget can't possibly satisfy Cleopatra—we've already seen what she likes, and his name is Hercules. The Siamese twins' marriage plans are a joke. In Tod Browning's microcosmic circus, there are physical barriers to normal sex at every turn. It culminates in a bizarre wedding feast for Cleo and Hans in which the drunken bride rejects the freaks who have "accepted" her, and sets everyone straight about who stands where. "You—dirty, slimy, *freaks!*" she shouts, dousing them with the wine. From this point on, there are no jokes. The freaks discover her plans and hatch a plot of their own. If the "big woman" will not have them, then the solution is simple—Cleopatra will no longer *be* big. When her wagon crashes in the mud of a torrential downpour, they chase her, screaming, through the primal ooze. She takes cover under a tree. In the scene as originally filmed, lightning strikes, and the falling tree crushes Cleopatra's legs. Lit by flashes of lightning, the freaks swarm over her, taking care of the rest. In an epilogue, set years later, we see that she is now part of the sideshow, legless, broken-nosed, partially blind, and

Unbearably Oedipal: Harry Earles and Olga Baclanova in *Freaks*. *(Photofest)*

speechless. She can only squawk like a duck, and is displayed in a bird-like costume. Hercules is nearby, also on display, singing soprano.

The shooting script (judging from a detailed synopsis of it made at the time of the film's production) contained countless fascinating and disturbing touches deleted during filming or afterwards. The effect of the wedding feast was to have been enhanced by some sharp, ugly dialogue: Why should Hans be jealous if his bride kisses another man at their nuptial banquet? There's so much more of her than *he'll* ever use! To increase the sense of nausea during the famous "gooble, gobble" sequence, it was scripted that some of the freaks should drool into the loving cup of wine as it was passed along the table.

The nightmare image of a wedding night that revolved around the grotesque display of physical deformity was the climax of Tod Browning's career.

One person who was genuinely horrified by the script was Myrna Loy. She had made her film debut in 1927, but already she was trying to escape a pigeonhole of femme-fatale roles, and so was delighted when Metro offered her a contract. "I wasn't aware at first that Irving Thalberg had brought me to MGM. But even he, it turned out, wanted me for a very strange role: the ruthless trapeze star in *Freaks,* who marries a midget for his money, then poisons him. God Almighty! Even Thalberg! That's how difficult it was to shake that image."

Loy wasn't the only star Thalberg and Browning wanted for *Freaks*; Jean Harlow was the first choice for the role of Venus, and the strong man Hercules was a part intended for Victor McLaglen. Somehow, they all wriggled out of the peculiar assignment. Browning turned to Olga Baclanova, a fading silent screen vamp and former member of the Moscow Art Theatre. She certainly matched Tod Robbins' original concept of the character: "A tall blonde woman of the Amazon type, she had round eyes of baby blue which held no spark of her avaricious peasant's soul, carmine lips and cheeks, large white teeth which flashed continually in a smile." Baclanova had originated the Garbo role in Vicki Baum's *Grand Hotel* on Broadway, but was best known for her screen portrayals of "vamps, cruel ones, man-eaters, the kind who rested their hands on their hips" in the memorable description of film historian John Kobal, who conducted possibly the only retrospective interview with Baclanova, in 1964. "There was nothing wrong

Tod's little chickadee: director Browning enjoys a smoke with the "mutilated" Olga Baclanova during a break in the filming of *Freaks*. *(Courtesy of Ronald V. Borst / Hollywood Movie Posters)*

with Olga's Russian; there was nothing wrong with her English," Kobal noted. "The two just met head on and their collision sounded like the clinking of jewelry—heavy jewelry."

Baclanova was not a typical Hollywood star, and revealed her bemused "take" on the film colony to a west coast reporter not long after the release of *Freaks*. "Hollywood is a city of suffering," she said. "Everyone suffers there. This one suffers because he has no work—that one because he has too much work! With the next it is a misery because a certain picture has not been used in the papers. Such suffering! Russia, even during the revolution, held nothing to compare with it."

Browning was no doubt aware of Baclanova's appearance with Conrad Veidt in Universal's mutilation melodrama *The Man Who Laughs,* and approached the actress personally. "I loved him," she said. "He say, 'I vant to make a picture with you, Olga Baclanova.' " Baclanova liked the script—and Browning took her to meet the rest of the cast, asking her not to faint. "Why should I faint?"

she inquired. First he introduced her to Harry Earles, the adorable midget who, like Baclanova, spoke German. They took to each other immediately. "Then he shows me a girl that's like an orangutan; then a man who has a head but no legs, no nothing, just a head and body like an egg . . . He shows me little by little and I could not look, I wanted to faint. I wanted to cry."

The casting department had been deluged with the resumés and photos of hundreds of sideshow performers. Some, self-created freaks on the order of tattooed men, were not used; others, like Johnny Eck, with spectacularly photogenic deformities, were summoned immediately. The cast finally included the famous Siamese twins Daisy and Violet Hilton, who had received tremendous publicity for their frustrated attempts to obtain marriage licenses (a sham) and their lawsuit (real) to free themselves from the clutches of a guardian and manager who treated them like slaves. Prince Randian was an armless, legless man, the kind of oddity called a "basket case" or "human worm." He could roll and light cigarettes with his lips. Five pinheads were employed—Zip and Pip, Jennie Lynn and Elvira Snow, and the celebrated Schlitze, a particularly genial sideshow favorite, somewhat more intelligent than most victims of microcephaly, and a transvestite to boot. Presented as a woman, Schlitze was really a man, who wore a sacklike dress to simplify hygiene. (According to writer Faith Service, Schlitze was especially fond of the child actor Jackie Cooper, "much to Jackie's terror.") Among the "little people" were Daisy Earles (Harry's sister) and Angelo Rossitto, later a resident dwarf in the low-budget Monogram thrillers of the forties.

Gradually Baclanova became desensitized. "It was very, very difficult first time. Because I couldn't look at them . . . it hurt me like a human being. How lucky I was. But after that I started to be used to them." All except one, "who was like a monkey, she go crazy sometimes . . . They put her in the closet and close the door." One account of the filming includes a reference to a pinhead being "chained to his keeper."

Freaks was shot in about nine weeks, from mid-October to late December 1931. Screenwriter and novelist Budd Schulberg had the chance to observe Browning, who he suspected was an out-and-out sadist, at work. "There was a certain glee in the way Tod Browning went about making this picture that made us think of him as Count Dracula on Stage Ten. . . . He enjoyed it too much." The making of *Freaks* became the stuff of legend. One real-life

legend who stumbled into its careening path was F. Scott Fitzgerald. On the day following a humiliating episode at a soiree hosted
by Norma Shearer and Irving Thalberg that became the basis for
his short story "Crazy Sunday," Fitzgerald had lunch at the MGM
commissary with screenwriter Dwight Taylor. Fitzgerald had been
working on a script for Thalberg; he badly needed money to cover
the expenses of keeping his wife Zelda in a sanitarium. At the
producer's party, he made a fool of himself by singing an endless,
drunken song while the guests cringed in silence. He realized he
would probably be fired—the studio knew about his alcoholism
and had hired him with trepidation. He would, in fact, be dismissed within a week.

Arriving at the commissary, Taylor and Fitzgerald found it to
be full of freaks, "which must have added considerably to Scott's
distraught frame of mind," Taylor recalled. "Scott and I had no
sooner seated ourselves than the Hilton sisters, a pair of Siamese
twins joined at the waist, entered and took a single seat at the same
table. One of them picked up the menu and, without even looking
at the other, asked, 'What are you going to have?' Scott turned
pea-green and, putting his hand to his mouth, rushed for the great
outdoors."

In order to avert further nausea, a group of MGM executives
tried to have the film shut down. President Louis B. Mayer was
believed to be furious that Thalberg had approved such a monstrosity. Producer Harry Rapf organized a delegation to march on
Thalberg's office in an attempt to smother *Freaks,* but director
Jack Conway vetoed a formal protest. "Irving's right so often he's
earned the right to be wrong," he said. The producer continued
to back Browning and the film. "If it's a mistake, I'll take the
blame," he said. As a compromise, most of the freaks (with the
exception of Daisy and Harry Earles, and the Hilton Sisters) were
banished from the commissary to separate-but-equal dining tables
set up adjacent to their set.

Film editor Basil Wrangell rued the day he was assigned to the
production. "It was bad enough to see them during the day when
you'd go down on the set or have to go by their eating quarters,
but when you had to look at it on the moviola for eighteen hours
a day, it was enough to make you crawl up the walls."

In later years *Freaks* would be acclaimed as "sensitive" and
"compassionate," but the kind of quotes attributed to Browning
in publicity handouts was pure exploitation, emphasizing the alien

qualities of the performers and none of their humanity. Freaks
lived apart from society, even from other circus performers,
Browning said, and "learning their customs, traditions and language is exceedingly difficult. When I was with the circus, years
ago, I worked for months trying to gain their confidence, and
even then learned very little." Over the centuries, the freaks developed "a gibberish language of their own," some of which was said
to be included in the film. Midgets were especially exotic, according to Browning, who began verging on a geographic and medical
twilight zone with his fantastic claim that most of them "come
from the Carpathian Mountains in Austria, where some climatic
or other condition seems to affect the ductless glands of the body
in a way that arrests growth. . . . There are whole villages of them
in Austria, carrying on all kinds of activities." There were other
lies as well—freaks were the "monied aristocracy of the circus
world"—and hints of a grotesque anti-Semitism: Betty Green, who
performed as the Stork Woman, was described as "a Jewish girl
from Springfield, Mass." who resembled "a cross between a crane

The original front-of-house display for the New York premiere of *Freaks*
at the Rialto Theatre. *(The Museum of Modern Art / Film Stills Collection)*

and a shaved dachshund." She was said to own five apartment houses in Boston, and to be a rabid movie fan and autograph hound who collected inscriptions from all the major stars, most of whom—of course—had seen her act. One Hollywood celebrity had not made the pilgrimage to Green's sideshow tent, and "it was chiefly to obtain Ronald Colman's signature that she signed a motion picture contract."

Time magazine perversely saw fit to spoil the film's ending by running a picture of Browning posing with Baclanova in her climactic, feathery getup. "Swift and certain is the revenge of the Freaks," wrote *Time* in its backward-reeling style, "their faces sullen masks as they move through the underbrush." But *Time* expressed disappointment that "you are not told how they make of Baclanova the legless, drivelling idiot that you see in the end." In a separate circus article in the same issue, *Time* casually referred to a whole assortment of sideshow performers, including midgets, fat ladies, giants, Ubangis, and Bushmen, as "subhuman animals."

Motion Picture Herald ran one of the earliest appraisals of *Freaks* on January 23, 1932. "That the production is bold and novel in conception and execution is unquestioned," the trade paper admitted, but expressed serious reservations about "the taste that prompted it." More important, in the paper's view, was "the moral effect it will have upon the industry . . . [*Freaks*] is evidently aimed at the great god Box Office and may very well reach its target." But the *Herald* hoped that *Freaks* would repulse a sufficient number of people to prompt Hollywood to "stem this rising tide of goose-flesh melodrama."

On the west coast, Louella Parsons jumped on Browning's bandwagon. "For pure sensationalism, *Freaks* tops any picture yet produced . . . I came into the Criterion Theater from the gayety of Mrs. Gardner Sullivan's luncheon party and I felt as if I had suddenly fallen asleep and were having a weird nightmare," Parsons wrote, adding that "*Freaks* is a picture so different the public will want to see it."

Freaks had to be submitted twice to the New York State censors and was finally given a license only after nearly thirty minutes had been cut from the film. *Variety* waited until the New York opening in July to print its assessment. "Planned by Metro to be one of the sensation pictures of the season, *Freaks* failed to qualify in the sure-fire category and has been shown in most parts of the country with astonishingly variable results. In spots it has been a clean-up. In others it was merely misery." The paper noted some anomalies, other than the freaks themselves. The circus in the film was a one-ring affair, "but it carries three times as many high-class freaks as the Ringling show ever trouped in one season." *Variety* also wondered why the dressing tent was bigger than the main top, "a fault which probably will be noticed only by show people." As for the performances, the reviewer described Daisy Earles as "a doll-like little woman who reads her lines with extreme care, but seldom succeeds in acting."

The New Yorker called *Freaks* "a little gem," although a perverse one. "There isn't anything wholesome about *Freaks* . . . Its morbidity lies beyond the boundaries of anything like dear, simple sex," the reviewer opined, but was unable to imagine any unsocial acts the film might provoke, and thus justify the wrath of the censors. "Few, if any, have to be warned against meddling with the private life of circus freaks. Having enough difficulty with persons of normal characteristics—and a few subnormals, as I often think of them myself—I didn't need *Freaks* to remind me of the hazards of such a dalliance."

The freaks themselves had mixed feelings about the film. Only two, Johnny Eck and Angelo Rossitto, maintained any affection for the director in later years. Bearded lady Olga Roderick (whose real name was Jane Barnell) told an interviewer for *The New Yorker* that she found the film to be "an insult to all freaks everywhere" and regretted appearing in it. After finishing *Freaks,* she vowed never to work in Hollywood again. No mention of the film occurs in any of the Hilton Sisters' 1932 publicity releases or interviews (they traveled extensively in vaudeville) or in their published memoirs. (Other performers didn't live long enough to hold extended grudges. Prince Randian, the armless-legless man, performed a final evening show at Sam Wagner's 14th Street Museum on December 19, 1934. He collapsed and died almost immediately afterwards. Randian's obituary revealed that he was sixty-three, had been born in British Guiana, and lived in Paterson, New Jersey, with his wife, four daughters, and a son.)

The disastrous reaction to *Freaks* marked the end of Tod Browning's ascendancy in Hollywood. He would work for eight more years, but would never again be given the respect and autonomy that had permitted him to make personal, bizarre, and obses-

Tod Browning's production

Do the Siamese Twins make love?
—
Can a full-grown woman truly love a midget?
—
Do the Pin-Heads think?
—
What sex is the Half-Man, Half-Woman?

THE BIG EXPLOITATION NOVELTY SENSATION of the Year!

YOUR CHANCE!

Trying to salvage a disaster: a trade advertisement for Browning's debacle. *(The Free Library of Philadelphia Theatre Collection)*

sive films within the studio system. Browning had been lucky; all his earlier pictures, even sloppy ones like *Dracula,* had made money. But *Freaks* had broken the one inviolable rule of Hollywood: it was a financial disaster that didn't recover its costs. In retrospect, one must wonder whether *Freaks* would have been more successful, commercially and artistically, as the silent film it was originally intended to be. The freaks' glaring deficiencies in reading dialogue would have been obviated, and the heightened stylization of the silents, with the formality of intertitles and continual musical accompaniment, could have done much to cushion viewer response. The wedding-feast, shot "silent"—i.e., with much of the soundtrack added later—emerged as the finest part of the film.

Some of the audience discomfort with *Freaks* may have come from the spectacle of human beings grappling not only with physical disabilities, but with a pathetic inability to "make it" in movies. Publicity for the film stated that many of the freaks themselves were movie fans. The moviegoing public of the thirties had as little use for such comparisons as they would have for Nathanael West's *The Day of the Locust.* The uneasy line readings of the freaks served only to break the narrative illusion, and by extension the whole unspoken contract between the audience and Hollywood. And beyond the surface melodrama, the Cleopatra-Hans-Hercules triangle may have been an almost unbearably Oedipal configuration for many viewers, with Hans playing the universal role of Freud's seething, frustrated man-child.

Jean Harlow, at one time the intended star of *Freaks,* was weirdly pulled back into its thematic vortex in 1932 when her husband, producer Paul Bern, was found shot to death in their home, an apparent suicide. According to Samuel Marx, a story editor at MGM at the time, Bern was actually shot by a schizophrenic woman with whom he had had a common-law liaison before marrying Harlow. Louis B. Mayer and his aides, according to Marx, concocted a cover story that, while sordid in its own right, reinforced Harlow's public image of formidable sexuality. It also distinctly echoed the central conflict of *Freaks,* and the films of Tod Browning in general. Paul Bern, according to the story, was a little man who couldn't satisfy the big woman, and killed himself in sexual humiliation. The story became a Hollywood legend. By the time Irving Shulman published his best-seller *Harlow: An Intimate Biography* in 1964, Bern's impotence had a physical cause: Bern, according to Harlow's agent Arthur Landau, had "the sack *[sic]* and penis of an infant boy." (As Cleopatra said to Hans, "What are you, a man—or a baby?") Novelist Harold Robbins used the story in an even more brutally sensationalized form in *The Carpetbaggers* (1961). Robbins' stand-in for Bern was Claude Estes, a latent homosexual who, having failed the sex test with actress Rina Marlowe, castrates himself in the bathroom. "If he was not to be a man," Robbins explained to his readers, evoking the spirit of Josephine/Joseph, "at least he could turn himself into a woman." Louis B. Mayer may not have thought much of *Freaks* as a film, but he seemed to know that themes of genital insufficiency had their uses.

Freaks would go into enforced hibernation for a long time, but eventually would have as large an imaginative impact as any of its fellow creations of 1931. Scavenging through this unprecedented, twelve-month carnival of fear and fragmentation, the dark gods assembled all the pieces they needed for their continuing experiments. The four archetypes would recombine easily; all had sprung into mass consciousness in response to the trauma of the Great Depression. They contained perceptible, if unintended, metaphors of economic and class warfare. Dracula, a sanguinary capitalist, relocates from Transylvania after draining the local peasants. The bourgeois Dr. Jekyll exploits and destroys a woman of the lower classes. The freaks live in a literally unbalanced social competition—"big people" against "little people." And the Frankenstein monster is a poignant symbol for an army of abject and abandoned laborers, down to his work clothes and asphalt-spreader's boots.

The mood of 1931 was Spartan, celibate. It was a time of dustbowl sterility and economic emasculation. Not surprisingly, the year's monsters all revolved around fantasies of "alternative" forms of reproduction. Dracula eschewed conventional sex in favor of necks. Frankenstein pieced together the dead, the better to avoid his wedding night. Dr. Jekyll found a way to simply split in two, like a psychosomatic amoeba. And the freaks reinforced the undercurrent of sexual avoidance by demonstrating the horrifying possible outcomes of "normal" coupling.

1931's mass confrontation with terrifying masks, and its melodramatic, imaginative encounter with reproductive paradigms, had many of the features of a classic initiation ritual. The Depression was, indeed, a rite of passage for millions into an unknown realm of terror.

With a yearlong flourish, the monsters were loose.

Chapter Six

ANGRY VILLAGERS

"A good many things go around
in the dark besides Santa Claus."

Herbert Hoover
(1935)

HORROR WAS SPREADING like an unspeakable social fungus across
the movie screens of America by the end of 1931, and the censors,
like censors in all places and at all times, were very concerned.
Censors, of course, were primarily interested in sex, and sex was
fairly easy to contain, at least on the screen. The rituals of erotic
exorcism were, by then, firmly established. There were certain
words, elements of costume, cleavage, the proximity of a bed—
the danger signs were fully recognizable. But the ramifications of
this thing called horror were not so clear. The obsessively detailed
Production Code itself had been drawn up in 1930, before *Dracula*
had flapped its way out of Universal City. The document had
nothing to say about supernatural monsters, doppelgangers, or
pieced-together people, even though horror did have a vague and
unsavory connection to the libido, even if you couldn't quite figure out what kind of hanky-panky was being hinted at. It was a
sneaky, slippery thing, this horror.

1931 had proved especially disturbing to Colonel Jason S. Joy,
Hollywood's resident enforcer of the code. Joy brought an aura of

**Boris Karloff's monster was misunderstood by busybodies on and off the
screen. From the censor-beleaguered *Bride of Frankenstein* (1935).
*(Photofest)***

military action to his office; just as his boss Will Hays was always called "General," so Joy was a "Colonel," and sometimes posed for pictures wearing what looked like cavalry boots. Since the late twenties, Joy had represented the sensitivities, peeves, and prejudices of hundreds of community groups and social organizations, and used all his skills of diplomacy to steer the industry clear of the state and local censor boards. He became involved in the planning stages of many movies, and had, in fact, passed *Dracula* without objections. A year later, he was getting nervous. He shared his unease with Will Hays on December 5, 1931: "Perhaps it would be wise to obtain an early estimate of the audience reaction and critical opinion concerning *Dracula* and *Frankenstein* by Universal; *Dr. Jekyll and Mr. Hyde* by Paramount . . . all of which are in distribution or about to be distributed. Paramount has another 'gruesome' picture about to be put into production, and Metro-Goldwyn-Mayer has *Freaks* which is about one-half shot.

"Is this the beginning of a cycle that ought to be retarded or killed? I am anxious to receive your advice."

The arrival of the new year did nothing to alleviate Joy's moody fixation on horror films. Sex and crime were already being dealt severe blows by censors in and outside the industry. The early years of the Depression were accompanied by a puritanical backlash of censorship of all kinds; the three-year-long American court battle over James Joyce's *Ulysses,* for example, occurred precisely at this time. Hollywood censor Jack Vizzard noted the resurgence of puritanism in his memoir *See No Evil*: "With the crash, the party was over. In the littered debris of confetti and tickertape, an enormous sense of guilt set in. . . . In a mood of sobriety, a chastened citizenry reacted against those symbols of its great debauch and began to punish them."

Two kinds of groups were especially noisy: womens' clubs and religious organizations, and the Hays Office actively courted their input, if only to let off their steam. The Production Code was a tool of industry self-regulation; in order to head off threats of federal legislative action, the angry villagers milling beyond the studio walls needed to be humored, if not always placated. Monsters, unfortunately, were giving them one more thing to complain about. The Production Code had managed to tame displays of movie sex, at least to some extent. "If something equally as effective could be done about the so-called horror pictures we'd be very much happier than we are," Joy wrote to Hays in early January 1932. "The fact that the supply of such stories is necessarily limited will lead eventually to straining for more and more horrors until the wave topples over and breaks," Joy maintained, noting Universal's swelling schedule of fright films. The other studios, Joy wrote, "are much intrigued by the fact that *Frankenstein* is staying for four weeks and taking in big money at theatres which were about on the rocks." This amazing new source of much-needed revenue effectively hardened the studios against complaints. The MPPDA did not have the authority to actually block the production or distribution of a film, since its judgments were subject to review by a jury of the film producers themselves, who were sure to vote their pocketbooks. "Talking out here won't have much effect," Joy admitted, expressing hope that a general public resentment was being built up. "How could it be otherwise if children go to these pictures and have the jitters, followed by nightmares? I for one, would hate to have my children see *Frankenstein, Jekyll,* or the others . . . The latest picture of the type is *Murders in the Rue Morgue.* It lacks the punch of *Frankenstein*, but the idea of the ape pursuing the girl is sufficiently disturbing."

When seventeen-year-old Arlene Kazanjian arrived in Hollywood, the last thing she expected was to be murdered in the Rue Morgue. She was on vacation with her mother, visiting her friend Constance Cummings, who was already beginning a career in films. In the best Hollywood fashion, she was spotted in a restaurant by a Universal executive looking for "another face on the barroom floor." But she was excited enough by being offered the part of a Parisian streetwalker and the chance to work opposite Bela Lugosi, the world-famous star of *Dracula,* that she didn't stop to think about her family's possible reaction to such a lurid screen debut. It was a chance to break into the movies—every girl's dream. As it turned out, the *Rue Morgue* would prove a dead-end street for young Arlene, at least for the moment. Years later, Arlene Francis would be the highest-paid woman in television, no thanks to Edgar Allan Poe.

"They told me it was a small part, and there was something else—I would have to swim. I couldn't even float, but I kept my mouth shut," Francis recalled in a 1991 interview. The script called for her to be locked in a carriage with a libidinous ape, bled, crucified, and dumped face-down in a Paris sewer. She was to do her own stunts.

Straightaway, she arranged to use a friend's pool and practiced floating "until I was blue and waterlogged." She spent two days on the set, the first screaming her lungs out while two drunken sailors killed each other in a dispute at the edge of the Seine. In the completed scene (originally intended to open the film), Bela Lugosi, sporting enormous bushy eyebrows, a cape, and slouch hat, emerges from the fog to offer his dubious assistance to the "lady in distress." "Who are you?" Arlene whimpers. "Your hand is cold—it chills me!" This is the extent of her dialogue, but audiences today have no difficulty recognizing the familiar voice from hundreds of "What's My Line?" broadcasts.

Arlene tried to be friendly with Lugosi, whom she had seen and thrilled to in *Dracula,* but found it impossible to make even small talk with the moody, reclusive star. Lugosi may not have been happy with his assignment to *Murders in the Rue Morgue*; Universal had first planned to cast him as Dr. Frankenstein, then demoted him to the part of the monster, and then, following Lugosi's protests ("I'm an actor, not a scarecrow!"), pulled him completely from *Frankenstein* along with director Robert Florey. *Murders in the Rue Morgue* was a distinct step down from *Frankenstein* in terms of its budget. But it remains a fascinating companion piece to the Whale film, since Florey managed to employ much of the visual style and integrate much of the expressionist decor and fluid visuals he had originally intended for *Frankenstein*. *Rue Morgue* would, in fact, emerge as the purest homage to the *Caligari* style Hollywood would ever produce.

The film retained almost nothing of Poe (the start of a long Hollywood tradition in Poe adaptations) and instead borrowed its basic plot from *The Cabinet of Dr. Caligari*. Lugosi was cast as Dr. Mirakle, a sideshow mountebank who comes to Paris, not with a somnambulist in a box, but with an intelligent ape named Erik on a chain. The sideshow masks his true activity—the attempt to mix the blood of a woman with the blood of an ape, and thus prove an evolutionary link. (The film is in many ways a crazy artifact of the Scopes trial era.) Erik enters the bedroom of Camille L'Espanaye★ like a simian version of Conrad Veidt's Cesare, and carries her across the expressionistically distorted rooftops of Paris before killing his master and meeting his doom. Florey's cameraman for

★Sidney Fox, cast instead of Hollywood newcomer Bette Davis, who Carl Laemmle, Jr., insisted had no screen presence.

On photo (handwritten inscription): *Tor David Don't ever do this to anybody you like* *arlene Francis*

"Don't ever do this to anybody you like." Arlene Francis' inscription to the author on a publicity photo from *Murders in the Rue Morgue* (1932).

the atmospheric little film was Karl Freund, who was finally able to display his flair for expressionist composition and mobile camera work that had been largely wasted in *Dracula*. John Huston was one of the writers called upon to doctor the script. As he recalled in his memoir *An Open Book,* "I tried to bring Poe's prose·style into the dialogue, but the director thought it sounded stilted, so he and his assistant rewrote scenes on the set. As a result, the picture was an odd mixture of nineteenth century grammarian's prose and modern colloquialisms."

After viewing Universal's latest nightmare, Jason Joy cautioned Carl Laemmle, Jr., that his enthusiasm for horror might be getting out of hand. "Our feeling that the screaming of the woman of the street [while] she was being subjected to a test by Dr. Mirakle is overstressed, not only from the standpoint of possible audience reaction but also censorship objections . . . You ought to consider making a new sound track for this scene, reducing the constant loud shrieking to lower moans and an occasional modified shriek."

The New York State Censor Board was surgically precise in its judgment on the film: "Reel 2—Eliminate all distinct views (5) of girl bound and tied to cross beams . . . all views of her writhing in agony—all views of Doctor standing over her, holding her arm while he tortures her.

"Eliminate all sounds of girl and loud cries and moans of agony and fear, and accompanying dialogue . . . *Be patient. Are you in pain, Mademoiselle? It will only last a little longer . . . We shall know if you are to be the bride of science . . . Your blood is rotten—black as your sins! You cheated me—Your beauty was a lie.*"

Although the New York censors managed to eliminate almost all of Arlene Francis' role from the film, they could not restrain the management of New York City's Mayfair Theatre from decorating their lobby with elaborate life-size cutouts from the film, including one from the censored scene.★ It depicted Arlene, crucified in a torn undergarment, Lugosi kneeling before her, basking in her pain as if in a religious ecstasy. The display was quite an

★When *Murders in the Rue Morgue* was rereleased by Universal four years later, the controversy over this scene had not abated. On October 2, 1936, Joseph Breen informed Universal that if they wanted to exhibit the film at all, the entire sequence with the prostitute would have to be eliminated, as well as "all views whatsoever of [carnival] girls dancing—of two men watching them dance . . . with accompanying dialogue as follows: *First Roué:* 'Do they bite?' *Second Roué:* 'Oh yes . . . but you have to pay extra for that.' "

eye-catcher, one duly noted by the trade papers, as well as the actress' father, the distinguished New York portrait photographer Aram Kazanjian. It was not a display that appealed to his own visual sensibility in any way. He sent her a telegram: I HAVE SEEN YOU HALF NAKED ON BROADWAY STOP OUR FRIENDS HAVE SEEN YOU TOO STOP COME HOME AT ONCE.

Arlene called her father and tried to reason with him, but to no avail. He additionally insisted that she call the Mayfair Theatre and instruct them to remove the salacious cutout from their lobby.

"But I can't make them do that!" she tried to explain.

"Oh yes you can," said Aram Kazanjian.

Deeply embarrassed, as only a child can be embarrassed by a parent, she called the Mayfair Theatre by long distance. They laughed her off the line.

Arlene Francis was ultimately not destined to join the ranks of Fay Wray and other Hollywood "scream queens" of the 1930s, although she would fondly remember her work in *Murders in the Rue Morgue,* and the film itself, as "a gasser." Her real shudders came after the film was completed when other producers, eager to discuss her future in films, began wielding scalpels sharper than those of Dr. Mirakle. They would offer her riches, it appeared, but only if she would consent to give up a portion of her nose. Rhinoplasty was all the rage in a Hollywood that now placed a premium on robotic, standardized glamour in the Busby Berkeley mold. Dorothy Tree, for example, was a highly regarded Broadway actress of the late 1920s, but her strong profile relegated her to bit parts in films, shuffling around in a shroud, for instance, as one of Bela Lugosi's vampire wives. Finally, after leaving her original nose behind her in the vaults of *Dracula,* she began to get speaking parts and billing. Producers and casting directors were eager to prescribe and preside over surgical rearrangement of the female body, an obsession beginning to be weirdly echoed, or perhaps weirdly magnified, in horror movies and popular literature. Indeed, the persistent, essential connection between plastic surgery, self-mutilation, and horror had only begun.

Arlene Francis, however, had the good sense to know that there was nothing the matter with her appearance, and the good fortune to have a father who pulled her out of Hollywood before her nose was caught in the Hollywood machine stamp. But the strange affinity between the casting couch and the vivisectionist's table, once established, would prove to be permanent. As mad scientists pursued their bizarre on-screen experiments on innocent girls, so too would producers and their surgical henchmen seek to fabricate their own "brides of science."

On the occasion of the simultaneous openings of *Murders in the Rue Morgue* and *Freaks* in the nation's capital in February 1932, *The Washington Post* worried openly about the country's thickening atmosphere of morbidity. "Those neurotic individuals who find agreeable occupation in following ambulances and pursuing fire engines, find themselves, at the present moment, the beneficiaries of an era in the motion picture theatres dedicated largely to them and their quaint amusement tastes," wrote film critic Nelson B. Bell. He speculated that the "disquieting and startling manifestation of public preference" was likely tied directly to the state of the economy. "Many are without employment, many are employed only by virtue of having accepted drastic curtailment of income, many lead their lives in a state of constant dread of the disaster that may overtake them at any minute. This is a state of mind that creates a vast receptivity for misfortunes more poignant than our own . . . The end of horror pictures," Bell concluded wisely, "is not yet."

Karl Freund was essentially given the chance to "remake" *Dracula* when he directed a film conceived for Boris Karloff as *Cagliostro*, reworked for the actor and retitled *Imhotep* and finally released as *The Mummy*. The picture is a good example of the kind of creative conservatism the studio system fostered; virtually every plot element as well as key performers (not to mention some props and set decorations) were recycled from *Dracula* in the story of an ancient Egyptian returned from the dead to claim the soul of a young English girl and transform her into a living mummy like himself. Her more contemporary boyfriend is David Manners, who joins forces with Van Helsing–like Egyptologist Edward Van Sloan, who, like Manners, was also a *Dracula* alumnus. Zita Johann, a Broadway stage actress who resisted working in films, was persuaded by her then-husband John Houseman to do *The Mummy* for the money when it was offered.

There was much somnambulism evident in *The Mummy* and other thirties horror films; what had originally been a German metaphor for involuntary military conscription in *The Cabinet of Dr. Caligari* now reflected a more diffuse anxiety in America. The shuffling spectacle of the walking dead in films like *White Zombie*

(1932) was in many ways a nightmare vision of a breadline. "Unusual Times Demand Unusual Pictures" claimed an advertisement for *White Zombie,* an atmospheric quickie which also employed some of the sets from *Dracula* and recycled Lugosi in the vampire-like role of a Haitian witch doctor named Murder Legendre. Boris Karloff may already have eclipsed Lugosi in salary and Hollywood stature, but Bela Lugosi would forever be Dracula, the first monster, the fear that preceded fear, that shadowy harbinger of the Depression that was now at every throat. Millions already knew that they were no longer completely in control of their lives; the economic strings were being pulled by faceless, frightening forces. If the force had a face, it was likely to be that of zombie-master Bela Lugosi, commanding you mesmerically. Zombies were especially handy in the present economy, for, as San Francisco reviewer Katherine Hill quipped, "They don't mind about overtime." And as if to reinforce the notion of zombies-in-the-here-and-now, she noted that the theatre management had positioned costumed members of the living dead throughout the lobby like so many potted palms. "To my genuine horror," Hill recalled, "I discovered a lady zombie in the retiring room. Did you ever try to telephone with a zombie right behind you? It's too terrible, really."

A similarly reductionistic, Darwinian view of the human condition was advanced in Paramount's *Island of Lost Souls* (1932), an ambitious adaptation of H. G. Wells' novel *The Island of Dr. Moreau.* Charles Laughton starred as the crazed vivisectionist who accelerates evolution in his jungle laboratory, creating a race of half-human monstrosities. There is an evocative social metaphor here as well: the animals have been given the promise of progress and social elevation. They have dutifully played by their master's incantatory "laws." And yet it has all been an ugly trick; their elevation is simultaneously a degradation, and a bloody revolt ensues. Paramount fostered a sense of popular identification with the monstrous through the rather extensive publicity given to their scouring of Main Street America in search of the ideal "panther woman," whom they finally found working as a secretary in Chicago.

Charles Laughton, cast as Dr. Moreau, was already acclaimed for his 1928 stage portrayal of another mad vivisectionist in the Grand Guignolesque *A Man with Red Hair* at London's Little Theatre. It was in that production that he learned to crack a bullwhip, a skill also required for *Island of Lost Souls.* Laughton hated the

Richard Arlen and Leila Hyams encounter the shadow of the beast in *Island of Lost Souls* (1932). *(Courtesy of Ronald V. Borst / Hollywood Movie Posters)*

part, though it remains one of his most memorable, an epicene gentleman-monster in a white tropical suit. Exteriors were shot on Catalina Island, reached by boat in particularly choppy seas. Laughton's wife Elsa Lanchester recalled that beside the actors and crew, the passengers "consisted of a puma, a cheetah, two lionesses, a tiger and forty dogs. The sea was rough and the animals nearly all sick." The normal stench of confined animals, coupled with that of their vomit, turned the human company green. On the set, there was scant relief. Laughton recalled that "each horror and monster had more hair than the one before. Hair was all over the place. I was dreaming of hair. I even thought I had hair in my food." Bela Lugosi, who played the lead mutant known as the Sayer of the Law, no doubt also had hair on his mind. Following a test makeup that merely added a wolfish accentuation to his features, a decision was made to totally obliterate Lugosi's face with fur. His ego apparently somewhat tamed by the *Frankenstein* debacle, the actor made no recorded protest.

For his part, Laughton "has never really enjoyed a visit to the Zoo since," Elsa Lanchester recalled several years later. *Island of Lost Souls* was banned for twenty-five years in England, on the basis that its theme was a challenge to natural law. "Of course it's against nature," quipped Lanchester. "So's Mickey Mouse."

The film was also banned in Latvia, the Netherlands, India, South Africa, Germany, Tasmania, Holland, New Zealand, and Singapore. It was rereleased in 1941, but only with extensive cuts ordered by the MPPDA; when the ban in England was lifted in 1958, the censor still insisted that three scenes be trimmed.

Due to the growing and concerted efforts of community and church groups, censors both in and outside of the industry were becoming more insistent in their demands. Jason S. Joy left the Hays Office in September of 1932; the MPPDA's role would shortly be reorganized under the stewardship of Joseph Breen, who took a more restrictive view of what was permitted under the code.

In 1932–33, the New York censors dictated cuts in *Freaks, Murders in the Rue Morgue, Mystery of the Wax Museum, The Monster Walks, King Kong, The Mask of Fu Manchu,* and *Murders in the Zoo.* A pamphlet published in 1933 by the National Council on Freedom from Censorship revealed to the public for the first time the kinds of ideas and images that unelected public officials were judging in star-chamber secrecy. Nearly 36 percent of all films exhibited in New York State went under the censor's knife, but horror

pictures as a category faced a higher rate of interference. Aside
from scenes invoking sex and horrific violence, typical cuts included
any depiction of the "technique of crime." Poison labels on bot-
tles, for instance, might suggest criminal use, and could not be
shown, and words like "Get rid of the evidence" were routinely
deleted. In *Freaks,* the New York authorities demanded that the
close-up of Olga Baclanova pouring poison into a bottle of cham-
pagne be eliminated lest it incite real-life crimes of a similar nature.
(No pogroms against midgets were known to have resulted.) A
strange kind of tunnel vision took hold: the lighting of dynamite
fuses was verboten, although a fuse could be freely shown burning
after it was lit. In *Mystery of the Wax Museum* the New York censors cut the shot of a character lighting a piece of paper with a
cigar in preparation to burn the museum for its insurance money,
as if the audience needed protection from the knowledge of the
various means by which a flame could be produced.

The National Council on Freedom from Censorship, which
included such luminaries on its board as H. L. Mencken, Lewis
Mumford, George Jean Nathan, Maxwell Perkins, Eugene O'Neill,
and Sherwood Anderson, railed against the self-righteous political
paternalism that the censors embodied. "The New York Board
seeks to justify its function as part of the educational system,"
wrote the council's chairman, Hatcher Hughes. "But its very position tends to fix its ethical and esthetic standards for the whole
public at the intellectual level of school children." The censors and
studios resisted demands for an examination of their practices and
methods. "The film companies, doubtless wearied by past con-
tacts with the many social reform groups having an ax to grind,
looked upon us with suspicion and answered noncommittally. We
gathered the impression that reprisals in the form of unusually
severe censoring might result from any disclosure of such information," wrote Hughes. The censors finally relented after concerted legislative pressure. "If the censors accurately reflect current
standards of morality and decency," said Hughes, "they have
nothing to lose by a public inspection of their work."

One of the most active, and, to Hollywood's mind, most
obnoxious, state censors was Ohio's. B. O. Skinner, director of
education for the Ohio Department of Film Censorship, complained directly to Warner Brothers over *Mystery of the Wax Museum.*
"We are, as you know, approving this film with eliminations. I
wish, however, to register a formal protest against the film. It

contains so many elements we find objectionable, as setting fire to the museum to obtain insurance, naming a poison and telling how it could be taken to produce death, using of dope and also the general theme of horror.

"I feel it would be much better for all of us," Skinner concluded, "if the production of this type of film would be discontinued."

The story of a disfigured sculptor who embalms his female victims in wax, *Wax Museum*'s shocks were rendered all the more vivid by the use of two-color Technicolor (the prototype of modern color processes that had also been used to intensify the masked-ball sequence in Lon Chaney's *The Phantom of the Opera*). The professional purifiers were seemingly so preoccupied with the obvious

British censors found Lionel Atwill's burn makeup in *Mystery of the Wax Museum* to be the "most nauseating" they'd ever seen. *At left:* Fay Wray. *(Photofest)*

elements of physical horror that they failed to notice the story's almost transparent theme of necrophilia. British censors objected to Lionel Atwill's burn makeup as "the most nauseating and by far the worst of its type" they had yet had presented to them. The opening establishing title—LONDON 1921—was removed at British request. Despite such censorship difficulties abroad, *Wax Museum* was one of Warner's biggest money-makers overseas in 1933— only Busby Berkeley's *Forty-second Street* did better.

By 1933, horror themes had become so commonplace that they were fit fodder for gentle spoofing in *The Saturday Evening Post*. Norman R. Jaffray's "The Spine Chillers" summed up the mania neatly:

> How spooky the movies are getting!
> Their patrons are gasping for breath.
> The morgue is the usual setting
> For thrillers that scare you to death.
> We shudder at Frankenstein's creature,
> And maidens transmuted to wax,
> There isn't one hideous feature
> The present-day cinema lacks.
>
> Dark houses, and monsters and mummies—
> Strange islands of terror and pain—
> Suave villains with prominent tummies
> Who doctor the anthropoid brain—
> Black bats that attack you when dreaming—
> New versions of Jekyll and Hyde—
> All talking, all yelling, all screaming
> Until you are fit to be tied.
>
> In staging this orgy of terror
> That leaves you in dread of the dark,
> The movies are making an error;
> They're all overshooting the mark.
> Inured to the fiend and the killer,
> Our blood is refusing to cool,
> And sooner or later the thriller
> Is bound to be knocked for a ghoul.

Another great monster icon, albeit one quite different in its antecedents and evocations than the creatures of the *Caligari* school, was *King Kong* (1933), a film ballyhooed as being so "big" it required a dual premiere at the world's two largest movie palaces, Radio City Music Hall and the Roxy. *King Kong* harkened back not to expressionism, but to the prewar experiments of the French film magician Georges Méliès, who introduced virtually all the basic elements of modern trick photography at the tail end of the Belle Époque. Willis O'Brien, its head technician, had been honing his stop-motion technique of animation ever since he first brought a brontosaurus to life in 1914 for *The Dinosaur and the Missing Link.* The two direct antecedents for *Kong* were O'Brien's *The Lost World* (1925), which involved the capture and transportation of a prehistoric beast to London, where it runs wild; and a fragment of an uncompleted film, *Creation,* which RKO had planned during 1930–31. *Creation*'s screenplay called for human characters shipwrecked on a mysterious island to encounter just the sort of battling tyrannosaurs and pterodactyls finally immortalized in *Kong. Creation* was shelved due to producer Merian C. Cooper's feeling that it was technically impressive but essentially plotless. It was Cooper who first struck on the idea of using a giant ape to save the basic concept; a few years before, he had a vision of a giant ape battling warplanes while perched atop the world's tallest building. (During World War I, Cooper himself had been shot down and severely burned in the Argonne. Later, in collaboration with another war veteran, Ernest B. Schoedsack, he would become a celebrated producer of jungle pictures.) Unlike lumbering elephants or dinosaurs, an ape could approximate human emotion, and therein Cooper intuited the mass appeal of *Kong.* "I'll have women crying over him before I'm through," Cooper is reported to have said.

The result was pop culture history. Coproduced and codirected by Cooper and Schoedsack, *King Kong* remains one of the most famous motion pictures of any genre. In recent decades many critics have focused on its perceived sexual politics; there are few images of male domination in all of Western art more outlandish and unforgettable than the giant ape holding Fay Wray like a prize atop the delirious deco-phallicism of the newly constructed Empire State Building. But there were other, less apparent reasons for public fascination with *Kong* as well. To the beleaguered, there was a certain cultural *Schadenfreude* that accompanied the spectacle of America's greatest city being trashed. And on a deeper, eerily prescient level, there was the anxiety played for laughs in a filler piece in *The New Yorker* shortly after the film's debut: "The other night,

Advertising art for *King Kong. (Photofest)*

an elderly Jewish gentleman was among the audience which saw the picture *King Kong* in which a giant ape runs amuck *[sic]* in New York, knocking over buildings and wrecking an elevated train. 'Tchk, tchk, tchk,' " he said, shuddering. 'Vorse den Hitler!' "

The shadow of the Great War haunted the horror movies of the twenties and thirties, and was depicted in unusually sharp focus in Edgar G. Ulmer's *The Black Cat* (1934), a moody melange of Art Deco demonism and twisted eroticism that marked the first pairing of Karloff (as Universal now referred to him, like "Garbo" or "Nazimova") and Bela Lugosi. Universal had attempted ineffectively to develop filmscripts based on Poe's short stories "The Black Cat" and "The Fall of the House of Usher," but, as was discovered with *Murders in the Rue Morgue*, Poe was heavy on mood but short on the kinds of plots Hollywood required. Nonetheless the Poe name was considered to be a commercial gold mine.

Director Ulmer was almost destined to direct a classic horror picture. He had worked as a director for Max Reinhardt, whose stage aesthetics had a profound influence on German expressionist cinema, and had served as an apprentice on *The Golem* in 1920. Coming to America, he worked on set construction for *The Phantom of the Opera* and other Universal productions at the time that Paul Leni and Paul Kohner were toying with the idea of *Dracula*. Finally, Ulmer began working on scenarios and was in a position to pitch a winning concept for a film of his own.

In his definitive documentation of the making of *The Black Cat*, film historian Paul Mandell quotes Shirley Ulmer, the director's widow, to the effect that *The Black Cat* represented to Ulmer not just a studio assignment, but the culmination of a personal obsession. "He had a dark side to his character that was unbelievable," she said. "It took me a year or two to dig under and find the 'why' of it. You couldn't use the word 'crazy' in his presence; it would petrify him. Like Kafka, he always worked in shadows."

The Black Cat had shadows aplenty. Ulmer's story cast Karloff as Hjalmar Poelzig, a master architect who inhabits a gleaming Bauhaus fortress built on the site of a titanic and bloody war battle. Lugosi took the part of Vitus Werdegast (literally, "Life Becomes Guest"), an ailurophobe psychiatrist, betrayed and left for dead by Poelzig during the war. "For fifteen years I've rotted in the darkness," he tells the honeymooners who have inadvertently stumbled into the two men's reunion. Fifteen years, for 1934 audiences, is nearly the time that elapsed since the war and precisely the time passed since *Caligari*. A central point of *The Black Cat* is that the first world war has somehow not yet been resolved. A vertiginous plot ensues. The monster builder, it is revealed, killed Werdegast's wife (displaying her, necro-techno, in an upright glass coffin), married his daughter (whom he also kills), and conducts Aleister Crowley–like rituals with caped cultists in a Caligari-esque tabernacle. Both men covet the soul of the newlywed girl, and play a game of chess for the right to possess it. Finally Werdegast skins Poelzig alive and dynamites the house.

Presented with this singular scenario, the MPPDA's Joseph Breen met with Ulmer, producer E. M. Asher, and screenwriter Peter Ruric to object to the gruesomeness of the flaying scene. "It is our understanding that you propose to suggest this merely by shadows or silhouette, but . . . this particular phase of your production will have to be handled with great care, lest it become too gruesome or revolting." Ruric's shooting script apparently also contained some intimations of homosexuality among minor characters, which were deleted, and Breen further suggested that it "might be wise to change [a] derogatory reference to Czech Slovakians as people who devour the young."

Ulmer shot *The Black Cat* in nineteen days for less than $96,000. Actor David Manners, recruited once more to do his leading-man chores, found *The Black Cat* to be less objectionable than the other Universal horrors he had endured. Ulmer, he remembered, quite unlike Tod Browning, spent considerable time with the cast, discussing his overall intentions and the effects he desired. Manners also recalled the numerous on-set rewrites, with the actors being handed bits of dialogue on half-sheets of paper. ("But that wasn't unusual," Manners added. "All the studios worked that way.")

Some of the rewriting was done to soften Lugosi's character, originally conceived as diabolical and lecherous as Karloff's. Werdegast's portentous ailurophobia ended up as little more than a gimmick to justify the Poe title. As for Lugosi's demeanor on the set, David Manners found him as unapproachable as ever. Shirley Ulmer recalled Lugosi's recounting of a grisly war-related anecdote: that he had been a hangman in the Hungarian army. "He even spoke nostalgically about the thrill he got out of being one, and how guilty he felt about it later on!" Ulmer couldn't decide whether he was joking. Lugosi had, in fact, been an infantry cap-

Shadows in the Bauhaus: Bela Lugosi and Boris Karloff in *The Black Cat* (1934). *(Courtesy of Ronald V. Borst / Hollywood Movie Posters)*

Publicity stills often employed double entendres impermissible on the screen. David Manners teases Jacqueline Wells with a suggestive prop that appears nowhere in *The Black Cat*. *(Courtesy of Ronald V. Borst / Hollywood Movie Posters)*

tain, and was wounded three times before feigning concussion-caused insanity and being discharged. According to actress Anna Bakacs, to whom the actor proposed marriage in the late 1920s, Lugosi claimed to have escaped death on the battlefield by hiding in a mass grave under a pile of corpses.

What Ulmer couldn't get past the censors, the publicity department could attempt to compensate for—images that would be struck instantly from the body of a film itself often made their way into still publicity shots without comment. One especially memorable press photo for *The Black Cat* featured David Manners tickling his costar Jacqueline Wells with a feline statuette that elongated into something resembling a devilish dildo.

The Black Cat has been called the first psychological horror movie in America. Relentless in its over-the-top morbidity (one priceless Karloff line: *"Even the phone is dead"*) and almost bottomless in its resonating references to war, religion, film, theatre, architecture, psychiatry, and classical music, *The Black Cat* was the first and last feature that Edgar Ulmer ever directed for a major studio (despite its being Universal's top money-maker of 1934). The demons that inspired Ulmer to direct *The Black Cat* may also have helped to undermine his career, which would sink, like that of Bela Lugosi, into the mire of independent quickies. But in *The Black Cat* Ulmer created a kind of meta–horror film, its effect summed up in its famous subjective camera sequence where the audience itself "becomes" Boris Karloff as he prowls the basement of his haunted house, once the war room of a great military encampment. "Are we any the less victims of the war than those whose bodies were torn asunder?" he asks Lugosi, also invisible. "Are we not both the living dead?"

Universal was not the only site of Hollywood horror in the thirties, though it certainly dominated the field. These "B" films proved to be the studio's most consistently profitable product; since Universal was running in the red (1931 was its only officially profitable year during the entire decade, largely due to *Dracula*), the formulas continued to be reworked and resurrected. At MGM, Karl Freund directed an homage to German expressionism in *Mad Love,* a remake of the Conrad Veidt vehicle *The Hands of Orlac,* from a screenplay by Guy Endore, P. J. Wolfson, and John L. Balderston. In this version, Colin Clive (Dr. Frankenstein himself) is a French concert pianist who suffers a war-like mutilation, the loss of both hands in a train wreck. His wife is the leading lady of a Grand Guignol–style troupe, Le Théâtre des Horreurs. The worlds of high art and theatrical horror are thus presented as parallel and mutually reciprocal realities. The self-loathing but brilliant Dr. Gogol—a bald, pop-eyed Peter Lorre in his first American film and possibly his creepiest characterization ever—transplants the hands of a murderer onto the pianist, further reinforcing an image of high artistic sumblimation wrestling with its malignant shadow. Gogol is morbidly obsessed with Orlac's wife—he has his own box at the horror theatre and seems on the verge of orgasm as the woman is subjected to simulated tortures. He tries to drive Orlac crazy by impersonating the guillotined (and "resurrected") killer whose hands the pianist now owns. Speaking in a whisper, his neck in a rigid brace, and sporting a gleaming pair of "artificial hands," Lorre/Gogol becomes yet another incarnation of the fragmented modernist personality, torn apart and crazily reconstituted by weird science and the overpowering dream-logic of the cinema.

By the time Universal decided to produce what it planned to call *The Return of Frankenstein,* censor interference was reaching a new peak, due to unprecedented grass-roots organizing, and the emergence of monolithic church-related groups like the Catholic Legion of Decency. Studio executives were eliminated as juries of last appeal, and the MPPDA empowered the Production Code Administration, which itself could stop a film from being exhibited. Finally, the code had teeth. As for the state censors, while only six were formally constituted, their effect was magnified by the larger, multistate "exchanges" through which the studios distributed their films. If one state in an exchange area demanded cuts, it was logistically expedient for the studio to expurgate all prints of the film shown throughout the entire region.

Given the headaches caused nationally and internationally by the original *Frankenstein,* the new censorship paradigm required a great deal of diplomacy on the part of the studios and individual directors, as well as a pronounced willingness to suffer fools. James Whale had, in the four years since *Frankenstein,* become a more confident and much more personal director. *Frankenstein* today seems austere and humorless compared to the sardonic wit Whale began to display in films like *The Old Dark House* (1932) and *The Invisible Man* (1933); for the *Frankenstein* sequel he planned to do a black comedy almost from its inception. The story (eventually retitled *Bride of Frankenstein*) was, at least for the record, a collaborative effort between the successful Broadway playwright William Hurlbut and John L. Balderston. Balderston's stage adaptation of *Frankenstein,* which Universal acquired the rights to in 1931, included the attempted creation of a female monster (drawn from the original novel), but the story element was not employed.

Though *Bride of Frankenstein* is today considered a genre masterpiece, it had an extremely bumpy development. One early treatment, by L. G. Blechman, fancifully exploited the horror genre's roots in carnival weirdness, and had Henry and Elizabeth Frankenstein change their name to Heinrich and run away with a traveling carnival, posing as puppeteers. The monster, not dead after all, catches up with them and demands a mate for himself. A carnival wagon hooked up to a high-tension wire becomes a makeshift laboratory. The resultant bride is short-lived, and the monster dies in a battle with an uncaged lion. Writer Philip MacDonald moved the action to the then-present, and had Henry Frankenstein trying to sell a death-ray device to the League of Nations. The war machine brings the dead monster back to life, and later destroys it.

John L. Balderston, who should have known better, contributed a grim and plodding script, utterly devoid of the pervasive and idiosyncratic humor for which the film would ultimately be famous. Balderston assembled his monster bride from hacked female parts dug out of a train wreck, ladies' limbs amputated in

Grand Guignol delirium: Peter Lorre and Frances Drake in *Mad Love.* *(Courtesy of Ronald V. Borst / Hollywood Movie Posters)*

a mortuary, and, most bizarre of all, the head and shoulders of a hydrocephalic circus giantess who has committed suicide in a fit of sexual despondency.

James Whale threw out Balderston's work entirely, save for a prologue featuring Mary Shelley, her husband, and Lord Byron, but even that was radically trimmed. William Hurlbut fashioned the story that was filmed almost completely from scratch, save for some scenes based on an earlier treatment by Tom Reed. The new script was tailor-made for Whale, who wanted to treat the film as a "hoot" and had a number of colorful character actors already in mind for key parts. He saw the film as a cartoony sex parable (the idea of a female monster, for instance, he found "highly amusing"), ripe with possibilities for outrageous satire.

The changing role of women in a world driven by male scientism is an arguable subtext of the Mary Shelley novel, as dozens of feminist analyses of *Frankenstein* in recent years amply attest. James Whale instinctively dipped into the feminist subtext of *Frankenstein* for his sequel, decades before any formal feminist inquiry.

Frankenstein is a visionary novel dramatizing, among many other things, a feminist writer's anxiety over scientific man's desire to abandon womankind and find a new method of procreation that does not involve the female principle. As Anne K. Mellor points out in *Mary Shelley: Her Life, Her Fiction, Her Monsters,* "At every level, Victor Frankenstein is engaged upon a rape of nature, a violent penetration and usurpation of the female's 'hiding places,' of the womb. Terrified of female sexuality and the power of human reproduction it enables, both he and the patriarchal society he represents use the technologies of science . . . to manipulate, control and repress women." The impulse is thus autoerotic ("With my own hands!" as Dr. Frankensteins are usually fond of saying, all the time wringing them in glee—or is it guilt?) and/or homoerotic—life created with the help of male assistants (often cowering dwarves who are seen sticking their heads through portals and trapdoors, who spill precious concoctions, "fuck things up," etc.). And the Karloff monster, with its stalking height and rigidity, is an obvious inversion-erection of the shrunken assistant.

James Whale, who was living openly as a gay man in Hollywood (not an easy thing in 1935, and not an easy thing now), presumably was well acquainted with the games heterosexuals play; his films are filled with the ironic sensibility known as "camp."

James Whale.

And it was this sensibility that allowed him, with the help of his screenwriters, to create a new and enduring mad-scientist icon that would playfully embody the sexual warfare that had been part of the Frankenstein brew from the very beginning. Conceived specifically for the celebrated British stage actor Ernest Thesiger, the role of Dr. Septimus Pretorious brilliantly elucidated not only the Faustian elements of the story but its sexual ambiguities as well: Pretorious, Frankenstein's mentor at school, would be a gay Mephistopheles. Waspish and epicene, with a long foxy nose that made him rather like a male stand-in for the actress Martita Hunt, Thesiger's portrayal is an over-the-top caricature of a bitchy and aging homosexual. In real life, Thesiger was married to the same woman for fifty years, and further belied stereotypes with his World War I combat record. One winter day, Thesiger recalled in his memoirs, his battalion was hiding in a half-ruined barn in France. While in the midst of sharing breakfast and the remains of his Christmas chocolate with his neighbor, a shell crashed through the roof of the structure. "There is a scene in *L'Aiglon*," Thesiger wrote, "where the ghosts of Wagram are heard calling out, 'My leg!' 'My arm!' 'My head!' and that is the scene to which I awoke. All around me my friends were groaning and telling the world of the wounds they had received." Thesiger realized that he was not dead, but was not sure that he could move.

Then my eyes fell upon my hands. They were covered with blood and swollen to the size of plum-puddings. My fingers were hanging in the oddest way, and I guessed most of them to be broken. I managed to stagger to my feet, wondering as I did so whether my breakfast companion had escaped before the explosion. I couldn't see him, but he had left his boots behind, and knowing that next to his rifle a soldier values his boots, I decided to take them to him. But how? I couldn't use my hands. Perhaps, I thought, I could lift them in my teeth. Still rather shaky on my legs, I stooped down carefully and then saw that in each boot a few inches of leg still remained. That was all there was of him with whom a few moments before I had been eating chocolate.

Images of this sort were part of the shared experience of untold numbers of young men in Europe and America. Most did not return to become involved with the horror industry. But many did. The *Frankenstein* pictures continued to be a cultural dumping ground for the processed images of men blown to pieces, and the shell-shocked fantasy obsession of fitting them back together again.

The expanded vigilance of the Production Code Administration now could involve elaborate wrangling with censors over the smallest nuances of a script, and the screenplay Whale presented for *Bride of Frankenstein* was a lulu. As if anticipating the familiar objections, the film would begin with a prologue featuring Mary Shelley (Elsa Lanchester; all the main parts were written for specific actors) reminding her husband and their guest Lord Byron that it had been her intention in *Frankenstein* to pen a "moral lesson." The prologue dissolves to the climax of the first film, where we learn that Frankenstein's monster (Karloff) did not die in the burning mill, but survived the conflagration in an underground cistern. Scorched and more horrible-looking than ever, he once more terrorizes the countryside, alternately brutalizing and being brutalized by the stupidly unpleasant townsfolk. After befriending a blind hermit and learning how to talk (an idyll ruined, of course, by the intrusion of ill-tempered locals) the monster meets up in a graveyard with the scheming Dr. Pretorious, who promises him a mate and uses him to blackmail Henry Frankenstein (Colin Clive) into collaborating on the unholy nuptials. Pretorious has also created life—miniature, toy-like beings in jars (a king, a devil, a mermaid) and wants to merge his techniques with those of his former

From *Bride of Frankenstein*: Dr. Septimus Pretorius tempts Henry Frankenstein from his marriage bed with the promise of an improved method of procreation. *(The Stephen Jochsberger Collection)*

student. Henry's wife Elizabeth (Valerie Hobson, later Mrs. John Profumo) is kidnapped by the creature, killed, and her heart transplanted into the she-monster. When the bride comes to life, she spurns her intended, who sets off a cataclysmic laboratory explosion that blows to atoms all concerned and assembled.

Whale was walking on thin ice with the Production Code Administration, but seems to have relished the challenge. "When Joe Breen wrote to a producer that a film . . . could not hope to receive a seal, a vaultlike door slammed shut," wrote Gerald Gardner in his book *The Censorship Papers*. Breen, a Catholic journalist prior to his appointment, immediately noted the story's irreverent tone. "Throughout the script," he wrote, "there are a number of references to Frankenstein which compare him to God and which compare his creation of the monster to God's creation of Man. All such references should be eliminated." Several months later, when a revised shooting script was submitted, Breen again requested numerous changes, most of which had to do with religious references and imagery. Whale proved to be a charming correspondent, even as the Breen Office tried to bowdlerize his film. Ever polite, and eager not to be perceived as "difficult," he even went so far as to remind Breen of his earlier objections that may have slipped his mind.

December 10, 1934

Dear Mr. Breen,
Herewith are the proposed changes, which deal with your letter of Dec 5, and also your letter of December 7th. As, however, the former letter is fuller, I think it best to send on the letter I had written immediately after the conference, as in your letter of December 5th there are several points about God, entrails, immortality and mermaids which you did not bring up again, and I am very anxious to have the script meet with your approval in every detail before shooting it.

All best wishes,
Yours sincerely,
JAMES WHALE

Woman as modernist construction: Hans Bellmer, *The Doll* (1934). (© *1993 ARS, N.Y. / ADAGP, Paris*)

Elsa Lanchester prepares for her role as the *Bride of Frankenstein* (1935). (*Photofest*)

Whale was intent on having the last laugh, and he would have it in spades. Under the apparent guise of "moralizing" the picture, the film's omnipresent cruciform imagery would finally make a statement more "blasphemous" than anything Breen ordered cut, i.e., the direct comparison of the Frankenstein monster to Christ. Whale made numerous adjustments and concessions (Elizabeth was allowed to live, and escapes with her husband at the end) but, due to his powers of diplomacy, was able to get the Production Code seal while keeping his most subversive material intact. Breen never picked up on the monster/Christ equation (not even in the finished film, where Karloff is trussed to a pole and raised aloft before a jeering mob), and the question of Dr. Pretorious' sexuality went similarly unchallenged (even when he swept into Henry Franken-stein's bedchamber, bitchily banishing the young man's bride and tempting him with the promise of an alternative way to create life.★ Like a character in Poe's "The Purloined Letter," Whale seemed to know that there were some things best hidden in plain sight. But his one misstep was an elaborate low-cut gown for Elsa Lanchester to wear while she rambled on about her "moral lesson." Any lesson implied was lost on Joseph Breen, who informed Universal that "the shots early in the picture, in which the breasts of the character of Mrs. Shelley are exposed and accentuated, constitute a code violation."

The studio agreed to eliminate the close-ups. Fortunately, Lanchester's second appearance, as the Bride, required no such trimming; she was covered from head to foot in bandages, and later in a kind of wedding-shroud. The publicity unit posed pictures of Lanchester and the other British cast members sipping tea in their costumes, but, as Lanchester later remembered, it was all for the camera. "I drank as little liquid as possible. It was too much of an ordeal to go to the bathroom—all those bandages—and having to be accompanied by my dresser."

Lanchester tartly recalled the persona of makeup artist Jack Pierce, who had with director Whale developed the techno-Nefertiti con-

---

★ In an elaborately embellished novelization of the screenplay by "Michael Egre-mont"—actually novelist Michael Harrison—published in England in 1936, Pretorious is more candid about his motivations in the laboratory. "Come," he says to Henry, " 'be fruitful and multiply.' Let us obey the Biblical injunction: you of course, have the choice of natural means; but as for me, I am afraid that there is no course open to me but the scientific way."

cept for the female monster. As the celebrated creator of the Karloff makeup, Pierce was "elevated even further in his own heaven
when a Bride was to be born. He had his own *sanctum sanctorum,*
and as you entered (you did not go in; you entered), *he* said good
morning first. If I spoke first, he glared and slightly showed his
upper teeth. He would be dressed in a full hospital doctor's operating outfit. At five in the morning, this made me dislike him
intensely." Pierce took his work as the culture's premiere mask-
maker with deadly seriousness, Lanchester wrote, "meting out
wrath and intolerance by the bucketful."

There was no shortage of intolerance among the various censors
when *Bride of Frankenstein* was released in May 1935. From the
tone of his comments, Breen had grudgingly granted the seal. He
had been "gravely concerned" over the first cut of the film, and
even after the further excisions he had demanded were complied
with, he predicted "considerable difficulty . . . wherever the picture is shown." He was correct; the self-appointed saints of the
provinces would indeed attempt to have their way with the body
of the *Bride.* Paul Krieger, branch manager of Universal's Cincinnati exchange, wrote to Sydney Singerman at Universal's home
office on May 7, 1935: "In accordance with my wire, I am attaching a list of eliminations ordered by the Ohio Censor Board . . . I
consider these very drastic and very harmful to the success of this
picture." Ohio's censorship czar, Dr. B. O. Skinner, had been
rushed into passing a judgment on the film, and had responded,
crankily, with an unusually lengthy list of demanded cuts. Universal appealed to Breen: would he have Will Hays intercede
directly? Breen obliged, but with some exasperation. He wrote to
Hays on May 8: "What responsibility, if any, have we to defend a
picture before political censor boards, where the studio deliberately refuses to accept our counsel in the matter and decides to risk
mutilation?" Hays evidently decided to take the industry's side,
and put Skinner straight; Ohio settled for the deletion of a single
scene and two bits of dialogue.

Bride of Frankenstein was rejected by Trinidad, Palestine, and
Hungary. "The deletions of the Swedish censors," wrote Gerald
Gardner, "were so numerous that the film seemed destined to be
released as a short subject." And Japan had one of the most memorable objections of all: the scene in which Dr. Pretorious employs
tweezers to capture his escaped, miniature Henry VIII and replace

him in his jar. The Japanese rationale: "Making a fool out of a king."

MGM avoided official censorship by unilaterally making cuts in *The Vampires of Prague,* released as *Mark of the Vampire* in 1935. The film was essentially a remake of *London After Midnight,* directed by the man at the helm for the original, Tod Browning. The "vampire" (revealed to be a fake, and part of a police investigation) apparently achieved undeath following an incestuous liaison with his daughter, which led to a murder-suicide. Browning and his screenwriter Guy Endore likely took some inspiration from Ernest Jones' pioneering psychoanalytic study *On the Nightmare* (1931), which explicitly linked vampire fantasies to incest guilt, and which also cited the legend of the Bohemian *Mora,* or vampire. (Such research gives further credence to the idea that Tod Browning's textbook-Freudian melodramas may have been deliberate and calculated, not unwitting revelations of his own conflicts.) Browning's new bloodsucker was Count Mora (Bela Lugosi), who sported a suicidal bullet hole in his right temple. The bloody wound made no sense in the film as it was released, since all references to incest were excised by the studio before the Breen Office even had a shot at it. Breen's sole suggestion to Louis B. Mayer: "There should be no suggestion that the Baron is guarding against leaving fingerprints." Otherwise, despite thick Gothic theatrics, *Mark of the Vampire* was squeaky-clean.

Mark of the Vampire was also in many ways a remake of Universal's *Dracula,* and Browning took some peculiar pains to recreate, or comment upon, moments in the rival studio's 1931 film, of which he had been the nominal director. There was the parallel casting of Bela Lugosi as Count Mora, of Helen Chandler look-alike Elizabeth Allan as the heroine, and even of character player Michael Visaroff as an innkeeper, a role almost identical to the one he had essayed in *Dracula.* Lionel Barrymore received top billing for his part as a Van Helsing clone named Dr. Zalen (Barrymore would have been a likely choice for Van Helsing in the production of *Dracula* Browning had planned for Metro, before Universal won the bidding war). Just about everything in *Mark of the Vampire* seems like a comment on *Dracula,* down to the absence of a music track and the bizarre, deliberate duplication of one of *Dracula's* weakest effects: a limp rubber spider being pulled up a wall on a string. Was Browning somehow thumbing his nose at Universal for a particularly unhappy experience? As the director never gave a career interview, we will never know. (An unverified story has circulated for decades to the effect that Universal threatened Metro with a copyright infringement suit.)

The real star of *Mark of the Vampire* is James Wong Howe, the cinematographer, whose moody compositions and lighting created several sequences that effectively define the "Hollywood Gothic" style of the thirties. Howe called Browning "quite a character . . . one of the old school who didn't know too much about the camera. He had the actors play 'at' the camera instead of moving around it, so the picture was very stagey and he used cutting to get him through." Howe shot test footage of Rita Hayworth as Count Mora's daughter, Luna, but the part went to Lugosi's young protégée, Carroll Borland. According to Borland, Howe's responsibilities were curtailed late in the production at the insistence of actress Elizabeth Allan, who was concerned that Howe's grand effects with the vampires were being achieved at the expense of her own glamour.

While the established censors found little to complain about in *Mark of the Vampire,* other camps would have their say. On July 28, 1935, the following letter from a Manhattan physician appeared in *The New York Times:*

To the Screen Editor:

There is a good deal of discussion of obscene and vulgar movies. Many of them are bad enough. But a dozen of the worst obscene pictures cannot equal the damage done by such films as "The Mark of the Vampire."

I do not refer to the utter senselessness of the picture. I do not refer to its effect in fostering the most obnoxious superstitions. I refer to the terrible effect that it has on the mental and nervous systems of not only unstable but even normal men, women and children.

I am not speaking in the abstract; I am basing myself upon facts. Several people have come to my notice who, after seeing that horrible picture, suffered nervous shock, were attacked with insomnia, and those who did fall asleep were tortured by the most horrible nightmares.

In my opinion, it is a crime to produce and present such films.

WILLIAM J. ROBINSON, M.D.

• • •

Incest after death: the studio sanitized the original relationship of Count Mora (Bela Lugosi) and his daughter Luna (Carroll Borland) in Tod Browning's *Mark of the Vampire* **(1935).** *(Courtesy of Ronald V. Borst / Hollywood Movie Posters)*

A few years earlier, *Island of Lost Souls* had offended fundamental-ist sensibilities with its merged images of men and animals, so it was not surprising that when Universal Pictures decided to film a werewolf story, ears pricked up. After reviewing Universal's script for *Werewolf of London,* Joseph Breen cautioned the studio explic-itly. "We understand that you will not show the actual transvec-tion from man to wolf, and that repulsive or horrifying physical details will not be used."

This, of course, was ridiculous: the major attraction of the world's first werewolf movie would be precisely to see a man turn into an animal, and the more horrifying the physical details, the better. Robert Harris of Universal subsequently defended script elements of *Werewolf* to the MPPDA, engaging in the particularly convo-luted double-talk that the politics of censorship dictated. In this kind of discourse, a writer or studio executive would contort lan-guage and logic in order to persuade the MPPDA to believe that what it thought it read in a script was not there at all. For instance, *Werewolf of London* contained no animal transformations—heaven forbid! As Harris put it, "Our transvections are merely from our normal players to people with hirsute tendencies," a process that naturally involved a "pointing of the ears and noses and a length-ening of the fingers, not dissimilar to what was done in the picture *Dr. Jekyll and Mr. Hyde.*" As for the refined beast's encounter with a short-skirted woman of the streets, "The girl, being of the lower class, is wearing a skirt which is not too lengthy, possibly having shrunk when she herself washed it, being quite without money to send it to be regularly cleaned."

The Netherlands finally rejected *Werewolf of London* because of its overall "degrading effect."

To the horror censors, monster makeup evidently took on the features of décolletage. A March 16, 1935, memo shows that the MPPDA took the unusual step of specifically passing approval on Boris Karloff's disfiguring cosmetics in *The Raven.* The film was the second pairing of Karloff and Lugosi under the wing of a Poe title; this time Lugosi was Dr. Vollin, a demented plastic surgeon obsessed with the works of Poe. He operates on an escaped con-vict, Bateman (Karloff), who demands to have his face changed, without bargaining for the mutilation that will result. Vollin rea-sons that the worse Bateman looks, the meaner he will be. The doctor has plenty of use for meanness, as we discover in an ensur-ing hour of gleeful sadism involving disfigurement, sexual obsession, and a basement chamber of horrors complete with a lethal descending knife borrowed from "The Pit and the Pendulum."

The London *Times* seemed to have films like *The Raven* and *Mad Love* distinctly in mind when it ran a lengthy editorial questioning the purpose of horror on the screen. The Elizabethans, *The Times* conceded, knew how to stuff their theatre full of horror, but even their most lunatic plots were redeemed by poetry. And where, *The Times* asked, was the poetry in Hollywood? And why were science and medicine being perverted?

> Very rarely is the purpose [of a movie doctor] to save a life or effect a cure . . . The favourite purpose of an operation on the screen is either disfigurement or the creation of a monster . . . Perhaps the most frightening aspect of this pseudo and sadistic science is its immaculateness . . . The blacker the heart of the surgeon the more fastidious he is likely to be in his professional methods . . . Ghosts and goblins that used to lurk in dark corners to pounce upon the unwary pale into ineffectual shadows before the grim figure of the demon surgeon brandishing his scalpel.

The Times did not notice (as did not most of the world) that medicine was becoming demonized along lines very much like those depicted in horror films, in the very country that had first introduced cinematic ghosts and goblins. Dr. Josef Mengele himself was in medical school at the time, poised with his fellow students to begin the medical purges that would lead inexorably to the Holocaust.

On August 23, 1935, the Associated Press finally ran a headline the studios had been dreading: HORROR FILMS TABOO IN BRITAIN— 'THE RAVEN' LAST. Edward Shortt, president of the British Board of Film Censors, had earlier warned the trade that such films were "unfortunate and undesirable" and needed to be curbed. *The Raven* created a firestorm of press controversy in England, with one prominent critic calling the film "quite the most unpleasant picture I have ever seen, exploiting cruelty for cruelty's sake."

Britain chose not to look at horror films from America, just as it chose not to look at another horror, much closer to home.

Despite the ban, Universal felt the domestic market was strong enough to support a sequel to its original horror talkie. In September 1933, two and a half years after Universal's release of *Dracula,*

Florence Stoker had sold a motion picture option on her late husband's short story "Dracula's Guest" to producer David O. Selznick. "Dracula's Guest" was in fact an episode from the novel *Dracula* deleted because of the book's length, an atmospheric fragment recounting Jonathan Harker's fleeting encounter with a female vampire on his way to Castle Dracula. It in no way represented this creature as Dracula's daughter or any other close relation, but Selznick apparently saw the commercial value of a female vampire with the Dracula name, if not to his own studio, Metro-Goldwyn-Mayer, then to Universal, which held the exclusive motion picture rights to the original novel.

Selznick's motives may have been more than a bit cynical; numerous legal opinions had been sought concerning the advisability of Metro's using the word "Dracula" in any way whatsoever, and none were positive. A flurry of ultra-confidential night letters and telegrams circulated in early 1933 between Selznick, Louis B. Mayer, and New York lawyers, and the legal consensus was uniform: Universal might well take action against Metro, enjoining the studio against any use of the D-word. The legal basis of such an action was somewhat vague; Universal had bought film rights to one, and only one, work by Bram Stoker, and "Dracula's Guest" was not part of it. But gray areas were exactly where the most protracted and unpleasant kinds of litigation might take place. The lawyers advised Metro to avoid the D-word even in correspondence, opting for the title *Tarantula* as a code word. And even *Tarantula*, it was feared, might sound too much like *Dracula* for full legal comfort. Nonetheless, Selznick drafted an agreement with Florence Stoker offering her a $500 advance against a purchase price of $5,000 for film rights to "Dracula's Guest." The contract contained a prominent clause specifically approving the alternate title *Dracula's Daughter,* and another concerning Selznick's discretion to resell the rights. In retrospect, one must wonder whether this was the point all along. Selznick had correctly anticipated the only logical basis for a screen sequel to Universal's *Dracula,* and now had placed himself as an expensive roadblock to Universal's producing it. This interpretation is given further credence by Selznick's hiring of John L. Balderston to write a screenplay treatment that could *only* be produced by Universal, since it used nothing at all of "Dracula's Guest" and took its plot inspiration, settings, and several characters directly from Universal's copyrighted film.

"In the three horror pictures with which I was associated as original playwright or scenarist, *Dracula, Frankenstein* and *The Mummy,* the last one-third of each dropped badly," Balderston wrote in early 1933. Balderston's idea for *Dracula's Daughter* was to reverse the process for once, increasing the thrills as the film progressed, like a roller coaster in which the dips grew higher and higher as if in defiance of gravity.

Since Bela Lugosi had been utterly destroyed by a wooden stake in the original *Dracula,* Balderston looked to the film's other, looser ends for inspiration. He seized upon the female vampires whom Lugosi left gliding around the flagstones of his Transylvanian lair, and postulated a new domestic arrangement for them. Where Lugosi kept them in line with stately, balletic hand motions, Dracula's daughter would employ another, more direct method. Cracking a bullwhip against the stone floors, she subdues her evil stepmothers like an animal trainer, and, in a scene borrowed directly from Stoker's novel, offers them a squalling infant in a sack to feed upon. But baby food is not enough. "We want love as well as drink . . . give us love, you keep that for yourself, men, young men." Dracula's daughter replies that *she* is their mistress while their master is away in England on business; they are only his paramours. They'll take what she brings and be grateful for it.

Scenes like this were pretty strong stuff in 1933, even for a speculative treatment, but Balderston was candid about his motives. "The use of a female Vampire instead of male gives us the chance to play up SEX and CRUELTY legitimately," he wrote. "In *Dracula* these had to be almost eliminated . . . We profit by making Dracula's Daughter amorous of her victims . . . The seduction of young men will be tolerated whereas we had to eliminate seduction of girls from the original as obviously censorable."

Balderston's justification of sensational plot elements gained momentum, sounding rather like a crusade. "Why should Cecil de Mille have a monopoly of the great box office value of tortures and cruelty in pictures of ancient Rome[?]" He added that he wanted to establish that Dracula's Daughter enjoyed torturing her victim-lovers, and that the men, while under her thrall, rather liked it. "The censors will stand this provided it is done by suggestion . . . It gives us a big box office value we lacked before." Dracula's Daughter, unlike her father, could find novel ways of obtaining blood, argued Balderston, who realized that the neck-bite was only a highly charged kind of euphemism. He proposed scenes in which the vampire's "loathsome deaf mute servants" stocked her boudoir with industrial-strength whips, straps, and chains. Nothing would be shown explicitly; it would be for the audience to guess what she did with them.

Balderston's treatment reclaimed the basic plot structure of the Stoker novel that Universal had made such a mess of in 1931. The proposed sequel would have Dr. Van Helsing return to Transylvania to destroy Dracula's vampire brides, overlooking the tomb of a fourth female vampire, Dracula's Daughter, who follows Van Helsing and his friends back to London where she assumes the identity of "Countess Szekeley" and victimizes a handsome young aristocrat, Lord Edward "Ned" Wadhurst. Ned's immaculate fiancée, Helen Swaythling, joins forces with Van Helsing for an exciting race back to Transylvania, where Dracula's Daughter is finally destroyed.

Everything about the treatment Selznick commissioned from Balderston violated a term of his agreement with Florence Stoker, namely, that *Dracula's Daughter* would employ no characters or incidents from any other work by Stoker besides "Dracula's Guest." And by early 1934, Selznick was baldly playing Metro against Universal, on one hand insisting that he wanted Metro to have first refusal on the property, while all the time knowing that they could do nothing but refuse. Selznick's contract reselling the rights to Universal was finalized in September 1934.

Universal "unofficially" sent a new treatment of *Dracula's Daughter* by Robert Sheriff to the Breen Office on September 5, 1935. Breen representatives met with Carl Laemmle, Jr., the following week. On September 13, Breen filed a memo: "This story, which was submitted to us 'off the record' by Junior Laemmle, contains countless offensive stuff which makes the picture utterly impossible for approval under the Production Code." Laemmle agreed to have Sheriff entirely rewrite the script, addressing the "dangerous" material. Especially dangerous, apparently, was the reinstatement of Dracula himself, seemingly in flashback sequences (as of this writing, an actual copy of this treatment has yet to surface).

On October 21st, Harry H. Zehner at Universal sent Breen Sheriff's second draft of *Dracula's Daughter*. Two days later he received in reply a six-page, single-spaced memo. The story, Breen regretted, still contained "dangerous material from the standpoint of political censorship." His main objection was that "there still remains in the script a flavor suggestive of a combination of sex and horror." There followed a detailed series of uniquely inept suggestions: ". . . in the early part of the script, where Dracula's soldiers sweep the countryside and bring to his castle a group of young women, with a sprinkling of men, that you affirmatively indicate that the purpose for which the young girls have been abducted is to provide dancing partners for the Count's assembled guests at the banquet." Or: "We ask that you eliminate the shot of Dracula in his chamber 'crushing the limp figure of a girl in his arms'—this to get away from the definite sexual connotation. Maybe the scene could show the girls dancing." In another scene, Universal was warned that Dracula's female victims would not be permitted to recline on couches, but would have to be bitten while sitting upright in sturdy chairs. Even minor atmospheric touches were to be sanitized: "Please eliminate the several rats referred to at the top of the page. The exhibition of rats on the screen at any time is generally considered to be bad theatre."

It became apparent that Dracula himself was the problem—what else was the vampire *besides* sex and horror? The studio began to reconsider whether they might be able to dispense with the character, while still retaining the publicity value of the name in the title. On January 14, 1936, Universal associate producer E. M. Asher informed Breen that the Sheriff script was being discarded entirely and that they would start over again from scratch. Breen replied that "we shall be happy to work along with you on the script when you have it ready; but we again warn you that the making of a horror picture at this time is a very hazardous undertaking from the standpoint of political censorship generally."

Dracula's Daughter was originally to be directed by James Whale, starring Bela Lugosi and Jane Wyatt. There were many delays and changes, and the picture was finally rushed into production with an unfinished script to beat a time limitation clause in David O. Selznick's option. Garrett Fort, who had worked on the original film, provided the final screenplay, which was quite a different affair from those conceived by R. C. Sheriff and John L. Balderston. Dracula as a character was dropped entirely, except for the cremation of a dummy early in the film. The film focused instead on Dracula's Daughter herself, Countess Maria Zaleska (Gloria Holden), who has followed her father to London. She seeks the professional advice of a psychiatrist (Otto Kruger). For the first time, vampirism was presented on the screen as a psychological compulsion as much as a supernatural affliction. There were also

Lesbian stereotype: Countess Zaleska (Gloria Holden) exerts a malign influence over a female victim (Nan Gray) in *Dracula's Daughter* (1936).

strong hints of lesbianism; one of Zaleska's victims (Nan Gray) is a street girl whom she invites to her Chelsea studio to model for a painting. Fort's script originally called for her to pose nude, with the resulting attack carrying an unmistakable flavor of lesbian rape. The Breen Office said no, and the actress kept her clothes on, but the scene is often cited as a classic "lesbian" sequence, although of a decidedly negative stripe. The homosexual aspects of vampire psychology (implicit since J. Sheridan Le Fanu's influential 1871 vampire novella *Carmilla*) would continue to gain prominence in the decades that followed. Interestingly, *Dracula's Daughter* was a direct inspiration for novelist Anne Rice, whose homoerotic vampire fantasies would find a huge mainstream audience in the 1980s and 90s.

Tod Browning, whose career had languished since the debacle of *Freaks,* found it ever more difficult to launch projects at MGM. *Mark of the Vampire,* a remake of two earlier, successful films, was just about all the risk Metro was willing to take. Browning spent a lot of time at the ballpark and racetrack in the early thirties, and veteran Hollywood writer Budd Schulberg (author of *The Disen-*

chanted and *What Makes Sammy Run?*) had a memory of another Browning pastime. "The marathon dance was in vogue then and we went a few times to the Santa Monica Pier to watch the young unemployed zombies drag themselves around the floor in a slow motion *danse macabre,*" Schulberg wrote in his 1981 memoir *Moving Pictures.* "Even more appalling than the victims on the dance floor were the regulars, affluent sadists in the same front-row seats every night, cheering on their favorites who kept fainting and occasionally throwing up from exhaustion. One of the most dedicated of the regulars was Tod Browning, who never missed a night and who got that same manic gleam in his eyes as when he was directing *Freaks.*" It has been said that Browning tried vainly to get the studio's backing for a film version of Horace McCoy's grimly existential novel *They Shoot Horses, Don't They?* (1935); the tawdry dance-marathon story could easily have been a signature Browning film, though it is difficult to imagine any studio producing the story as originally written. (Charles Chaplin was another director excited by the story's possibilities who never got the project off the ground.)

Browning planned a voodoo film called *The Witch of Timbuctoo,* but it was severely altered because of overseas censorship concerns. *The Hollywood Reporter* related on December 10, 1935, that "once again a foreign government has stepped in to censor a Hollywood script for political reasons." Great Britain had requested the removal of all black characters for fear that the witchcraft scenes would "stir up trouble" among blacks under British colonial rule. The film was finally revamped as *The Devil Doll,* a bizarre story of a Devil's Island escapee who employs miniaturized human beings to carry out a revenge plot. The film recycled several familiar Browning themes—the criminal who disguises himself as an old lady (from *The Unholy Three*), the obsessive, blinding thirst for revenge—but it was clear that Browning's days as an *auteur* who would determine his own projects were over. He remained an elusive enigma to most of the people who worked with him. Maureen O'Sullivan, who appeared in *The Devil Doll* and actually lived near Browning in the Malibu colony for a time, recalled that she never once saw him on the beach. Edgar Ulmer called him a "reticent and introverted. At night, after work, Browning got into his car and disappeared."

What didn't disappear throughout the entire decade of the thirties was the emphasis on motion pictures as a social scapegoat.

On November 16, 1938, Katherine K. Vandervoort, director of attendance for the White Plains, New York, public school system, left her City Hall office at approximately 5:15 P.M., only to be confronted on Main Street by a little boy "looking wildly into the faces of pedestrians." He begged the truant officer for directions home. "I could see that he was hysterical," Vandervoort wrote, and insisted on escorting him herself. "After we got in the car for the mile ride to his home, he kept chattering more or less incoherently. Until then I had thought he was a small boy who had wandered away from home and had become frightened to find himself out alone in the dark. At last, however, I began to listen to what he was saying and to one remark he kept repeating over and over again. 'I *know* he was going to kill her! I *know* he was!' "

"Kill whom?" Vandervoort asked, genuinely alarmed. She finally got it out of him that "Frank somebody" was going to kill a pretty little girl.

She realized, then, what had happened: the boy must have attended the matinee at Keith's. She had already noted "with amazement" the marquee, which she copied down verbatim:

WE DARE YOU TO SEE THEM TOGETHER
"DRACULA" WITH BELA LUGOSI
"FRANKENSTEIN" WITH BORIS KARLOFF

The nine-year-old had, according to Vandervoort, been "inveigled" into attending the screening by an older boy in the neighborhood. The next day, accompanied by "Mr. Duff, investigator attached to my office," Vandervoort made a visit to the theatre, where the unholy double bill was still running.

"As soon as school was out, the children arrived in droves. All ages were represented from toddlers who could scarcely mount the stairs to the balcony as we watched from the lobby below."

Sensing a snake that desperately needed scotching, Vandervoort "set aside other work and spent considerable time going from classroom to classroom in one of our elementary schools." To her dismay, if not her surprise, a large percentage of the children had been exposed to *Dracula* and *Frankenstein*. "Some were still wide-eyed with excitement and wanted to tell the whole story in detail. Others appeared more anxious not to talk about it and one little blonde girl who was seated in front of a larger boy said to me, 'He's got to stop talking about it—he's been talking about it all day.' "

The "dark twins" play Brooklyn Heights during one of *Dracula* and *Frankenstein*'s early double-bill revivals. *(Photofest)*

Perhaps most horrifying of all to Vandervoort's *in loco parentis* sensibility was the tale told by one boy who saw the show in the afternoon by himself, and went again in the evening with his parents because they had no one with whom to leave him.

White Plains was not alone in the fall of 1938; the dark twins of the Villa Diodati were everywhere, following the wildly successful pairing of *Dracula* and *Frankenstein,* initially just a desperate exhibitor in Los Angeles looking for a novelty attraction. The double bill broke all records and started theatre owners talking. "Grosses from the key cities indicate the horror revivals are mopping up everywhere," reported *Variety* on October 19. In Cincinnati, the demonic duo broke a six-year house record; in Indianapolis, the same combination was doubling the theatre's normal box office. In Manhattan, the Rialto ran *Dracula* and *Frankenstein* around the clock, filling the house to capacity ten times a day. "Other reissues, excepting old Valentinos," *Variety* noted, "have been duds in New York." The trade paper noted that the two films had done only moderate business when shown singly in Philadelphia a few months earlier, but did not speculate about the precise nature of the alchemy achieved when the beasts were brought together. Elsewhere, dual revivals of *King Kong* and *The Ghoul* with Boris Karloff were also working box-office magic.

A trade advertisement to exhibitors contemplating the resurrection of *Dracula* **and** *Frankenstein. (The Free Library of Philadelphia Theatre Collection)*

The success of the tandem reissue of *Dracula* and *Frankenstein* gave Universal the itch to revive the series. Foreign resistance was still strong, however. J. Brooke Wilkinson, secretary to the British Board of Film Censors, wrote Joseph Breen in November 1938 concerning Universal's desire to produce a second sequel to *Frankenstein*. "We have had so much trouble in [the] past with films . . . in the 'horrific' category that the trade have come to the conclusion that they are more trouble than they are worth . . . Representations have been made to us by the trade asking us to curtail this type of film as much as possible." In 1933, Wilkinson recounted, the British censors passed five horror films, in 1934, five films, in 1936, two films, and in 1937, only one.

Back in the States, some queasiness had already surfaced in *The New York Times* and elsewhere about the sheer amount of horror coming out of Hollywood before the British embargo. 1935 *had* been a particularly grisly year, what with *Bride of Frankenstein, Werewolf of London, The Raven, Mark of the Vampire, Dante's Inferno, Mad Love,* and other assorted unpleasantries. The *Times* critic André Sennwald noted the trend with mild alarm in a Sunday piece entitled "Gory, Gory Hallelujah." The increasing emphasis on pain and morbidity, Sennwald wrote, was "far from being an accidental and meaningless sort of thing" and might "be related very distinctly to the national state of mind. The screen is providing an acute emotional experience and, what is more important, vast multitudes are enjoying it even in the act of being shocked and revolted by it." Sennwald recalled the "mad, confused days which preceded our entrance into the World War [when] the cinema was satiating the blood-lust of noncombatant Americans with just such vicarious stimulants. Hollywood, always quick to reflect or stimulate a mass appetite, seems to be doing the same thing all over again."

Storm clouds were indeed gathering once more on the western front. In Europe, the great French filmmaker Abel Gance, best known for his monumental *Napoléon,* produced an antiwar film in 1937 that makes explicit, in retrospect, the link between the first great cycle of horror films and the first world war. Gance's film was called *J'Accuse* and it told the story of a war veteran turned inventor, who creates an impregnable kind of "steel glass" that he is sure will render war obsolete. When his employers decide to put the invention to direct military use, he summons the war dead back from their graves to march on the living. For his unnerving final sequence—completely irrational, but nonetheless a devastating moral statement—Gance recruited actual members of the Union des Gueules Cassées, and created a nightmarish montage of all the ruined faces that had been haunting the world's cinemas for the past fifteen years in the guise of "horror entertainment." The actual men are nameless, but they could easily be the living models for the masks worn by Lon Chaney, Boris Karloff, Lionel Atwill, and the others. As a conscious antiwar statement, *J'Accuse* is superior; as an unintentional revelation of horror's major subtext in the twenties and thirties, it is breathtaking.

Just as the horror cycle was coming full circle, rediscovering the genre that Tod Browning had helped bring to life in America, Browning himself could look forward to no such revival of his own career. Samuel Marx, the MGM story executive who had strongly opposed the making of *Freaks* on grounds of taste, had the chance to observe the entire arc of the director's career. "I knew Tod Browning well from my own early days at the Universal studio . . . right through his sad days when MGM finally let him go. I was very sorry for him at the end." Browning's final picture, *Miracles for Sale,* emerged as a gentle recapitulation of the career that had led up to it; it was a story of con artists and fake spiritualism devoid of the excoriating cynicism that had marked his earlier pictures. He even seemed to say farewell to the ugly motif of below-the-waist mutilation in an opening sequence played for laughs: a character in a stage show is "sawed in half" by a machine gun. Browning later did some scenario work at MGM. In 1942 he retired to Malibu forever.

The twenty-year horror cycle that began in Germany with *The Cabinet of Dr. Caligari* ended, appropriately, with an American film set in Germany that was influenced heavily by the mood and decor of the classic prototype. Universal's *Son of Frankenstein* (1939) is sometimes considered part of a new cycle, but its production style, mood, and theme look back and not forward. The film is visually stunning, and arguably one of the most visually ambitious American films before *Citizen Kane.* It would be the final time Boris Karloff would essay the part of the monster; he had no regrets about leaving the role behind him (although in a sense he would never leave it) and suspected, correctly, that the monster would be increasingly relegated to the role of a prop or buffoon. The creature that had originally been a stark black silhouette became, with Karloff's increasing age and size, bulky and monolithic, an

Three faces from *J'Accuse.*

Reopening a "war wound": Lionel Atwill loses an artificial arm to Boris Karloff in *Son of Frankenstein* (1939). *(Bottom: Photofest)*

approaching juggernaut. *Look* magazine noted the overtones of saber-rattling: "Movie producers attribute the public's current thirst for terror to the war scares of unsettled Europe. Quick to take their cue, they have started a race to produce blood chillers on a more lavish and fantastic scale than they have ever attempted before.

"Death rays, space ships, disintegration beams and other weirdly lethal instruments are being built in every property shop," *Look* noted. " 'Nightmares for everybody' is the Hollywood slogan for a more horrible 1939."

Basil Rathbone played the titular son, Wolf von Frankenstein, replacing the previously announced Peter Lorre. Bela Lugosi, originally signed to play a police inspector in the film, had the role of a lifetime literally improvised on the set—the broken-necked, snaggletoothed Ygor, the monster's demented shepherd. Gone completely was any hint of Dracula; here, for virtually the only time in Hollywood, was Lugosi as the versatile character actor he really was. Unfortunately, Hollywood paid little attention, and would never extend Lugosi such an opportunity again.

But perhaps the most fascinating feature of *Son of Frankenstein* was the character of the one-armed Inspector Krogh, (Lionel Atwill) maimed as a child by the rampaging monster ("One does not easily forget, Herr Baron, an arm torn out by the roots"). Amid the heavy expressionistic sets, an almost pure distillation of *Caligari*'s planes of light and shadow, he speaks of his frustration as a boy at having missed the war because of his mutilation. In the script's original, unfilmed climax, Krogh leads a heavy-artillery military action that saves the day.

The character, of course, never "missed" the war at all. He lived it again and again, as somnambulist-soldier, as field-hospital freak, as blood-seeker, werewolf, ghoul—one distorted creature after another, shadows chasing shadows through a terrifying primal battleground without beginning, end, or escape.

Except, of course, into a new kind of war—and monsters yet to be imagined.

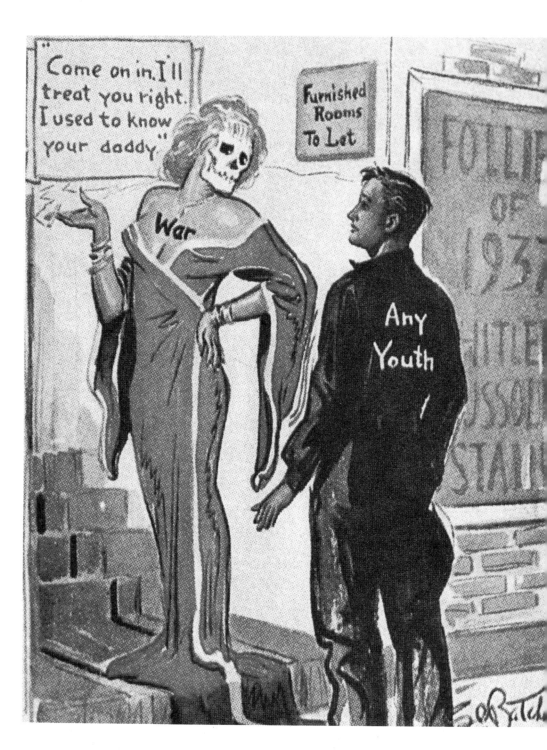

Chapter Seven

"I USED TO KNOW YOUR DADDY":
The Horrors of War, Part Two

"How dark it was inside the wolf!"

Little Red Riding Hood

IT WOULD PROBABLY have come as no surprise to the elderly Jewish man at Radio City Music Hall that one of Adolf Hitler's favorite movies was *King Kong*. The Führer couldn't get enough of it. He talked about the monster picture for days after it was first screened at the Chancellery (he liked to watch a film every night, if possible). Along with *Snow White and the Seven Dwarfs,* another favorite, *King Kong* occupied a place of honor in Hitler's private cinematic pantheon.

A figure like Adolf Hitler can probably never be completely understood, but politics and popular culture have always been close cousins, each with a finger on the pulse of the Zeitgeist. One of Hitler's enduring obsessions has an interesting resonance with a newly popular form of monster iconography introduced during the early years of World War II. According to psychobiographer Robert G. L. Waite,

Hitler was fascinated with wolves. As a boy he was well pleased with his first name, noting that it came from the old German

C. D. Batchelor's 1937 Pulitzer prize–winning cartoon mixed the threat of war with a scene straight from *Weird Tales*. (*The Library of Congress*)

"Athalwolf"—a compound of Athal ("noble") and Wolfa ("wolf"). And "noble wolf" he sought to remain. At the start of his political career he chose "Herr Wolf" as his pseudonym. His favorite dogs were Alsatians—in German *Wolfshunde*. One of [his dog] Blondi's pups, born toward the end of the war, he called "Wolf" and would allow no one else to touch or feed it. He named his headquarters in France *Wolfsschlucht* (Wolf's Gulch). In the Ukraine his headquarters were *Werwolf*.

Waite cites numerous other examples of Hitler's fetish for transforming people and things into wolves, including having his sister change her name to "Frau Wolf," naming the Volkswagen factory "Wolfsburg," identifying himself as "Conductor Wolf" for phone calls to Winifred Wagner, and his abiding affection for the Disney tune "Who's Afraid of the Big Bad Wolf?" which he liked to whistle.

The wolf is an ancient symbol, deeply linked to militarism and the battlefield, with special meanings in Norse and Teutonic mythology. The ancient warriors called berserkers were said to wear the skins of wolves and other animals to increase their ferocity. *Götterdämmerung,* the twilight of the gods, was envisioned as a wolf devouring the sun. A wolf guarded the gates of Valhalla. In Roman tradition, the wolf was an animal sacred to Mars, the god of war.

The wolf has also been a perennial symbol for other kinds of human aggression and predation besides war. According to Barry Holstun Lopez, in his remarkable study *Of Wolves and Men,* "The medieval mind, more than any other mind in history, was obsessed with images of wolves. . . . Peasants called famine 'the wolf.' Avaricious landlords were 'wolves.' Anything that threatened a peasant's precarious existence was 'the wolf.' "

The wolf as a species has received extremely bad press throughout history, and undeservedly. The classic "wolfish" traits of voraciousness and bloodlust are uniquely human characteristics, nonexistent in the animal kingdom. Healthy wolves in the wild do not attack people, nor do they kill for pleasure. According to Lopez, such negative wolf-lore is "almost completely a projection of human anxiety," the wolf being "not so much an animal we have always known as one that we have consistently *imagined.*"

Images/imaginings of anthropomorphized animals and animalized humans are ancient motifs; werewolf legends draw energy from both traditions. Historically, the werewolf is entwined with vampire beliefs; Bram Stoker's Dracula, for instance, was una-

A medieval werewolf.

bashedly a werewolf as well as a blood-drinker. The werewolf theme was largely eliminated from *Dracula* stage adaptations, due to the difficulties of convincingly presenting such a total physical transformation in the theatre. The vampire and werewolf became discrete in the public mind; Hollywood, beginning with *Werewolf of London* (1935), tended to link lycanthropy with the Jekyll and Hyde formula.

By 1940, wolf imagery was about to gnaw its way into popular consciousness. Universal Pictures, for example, wanted to do a picture called *The Wolf Man,* though it had no idea what the film would be about (the title had been kicking around since 1933, when Robert Florey suggested it as a vehicle for Boris Karloff). Screenwriter Curt Siodmak recalled, with no false modesty, how he was given—or gave himself—free reign in developing Hollywood's newest horror icon. "I targeted the screenplay to be delivered as late as possible," Siodmak wrote. "That gave the front office no time to engage another writer, who could mess up my screenplay. Also, Universal was stingy and didn't like to spend money for rewrites. That was the secret of getting a 'classic.' The writer's original screenplay reached the screen, unadulterated by 'improvements.' "

The Wolf Man, released in 1941, was yet another Hollywood nightmare of a geographically indeterminate "Europe" anxiously

blurring together elements of America, England, and the Continent, rather as the Great War had done literally, and the new war was in the process of doing all over again. The Europe of American horror movies was a nearly surreal pastiche of accents, architecture, and costumes, like the scrambled impressions of a soldier/tourist on a whirlwind tour of duty.

Lon Chaney, Jr., in the role of the werewolf Lawrence Talbot (who more closely resembled a wild boar than a wolf in Jack Pierce's elaborate makeup), was an oddly displaced American presence. Screenwriter Siodmak had originally intended the Wolf Man to be an American technician who travels to Wales to install an observatory telescope at Talbot Castle. At studio insistence, Siodmak changed the Chaney character to a Talbot himself, rationalizing his American accent as the result of a stateside education. More bizarre was setting the film in an up-to-date 1940s Britain where no one knew anything about the war, but soon would know absolutely everything about werewolves. Boundaries and credibility were also blurred by the Russian actress Maria Ouspenskaya as Maleva, an ancient gypsy traversing the Welsh landscape with her caravan. In *The Wolf Man* Ouspenskaya delivered some of the most famous lines from any American horror film, a memorable piece of pop poetry:

> Even a man who is pure in heart
> And says his prayers by night
> May become a wolf when the wolfbane blooms
> And the autumn moon is bright.

Autumn or not, Hitler's war was a springtime for wolfbane, at least in the realms of popular culture.

The bestial realities of war came as a shock to untold numbers of servicemen, but a widespread recognition of the inhuman conditions of the battlefield was systematically suppressed. In his book *Wartime,* Paul Fussell notes the methodical sanitizing of images that occurred throughout the conflict. In all the popular photographic compendiums published after the war, he writes, "no matter how severely wounded, Allied troops are never shown suffering what was termed, in the Vietnam War, traumatic amputation;

World War II's favorite monster: Lon Chaney, Jr., and Evelyn Ankers in *The Wolf Man* (1941).

everyone has all his limbs, his hands and feet and digits, not to mention expressions of courage and cheer." The reality of most battles involved human beings violently blown to bits. Following an exchange of shells, entire landscapes might be covered with rotting human flesh and body parts. There had never been such a widespread, macabre spectacle in the history of the world. Dealing with the dead, or the prospect of soon being dead oneself, could and did lead to madness. "Starvation and thirst among prisoners of the Japanese, as well as among downed fliers adrift on rafts, drove many insane," writes Fussell, "and in addition to drinking their urine they tried to relieve their thirst by biting their comrades' jugular veins and sucking the blood." (There is a grim irony in *Dracula* ranking as one of the most popular paperbacks distributed free to U.S. armed-services personnel in World War II, and, as Stoker biographer Harry Ludlam noted, the name "Operation Dracula" being given to an Allied excursion in Burma.)

The newsreels offered none of this; only in the melodramatic euphemism of Frankenstein movies was the public permitted to puzzle over fragmented bodies, the parts of which could always be snapped or stitched back together. With their replaceable limbs and brains, man-made monsters were the perfect toy soldiers to battle semiconscious fears. *Ghost of Frankenstein,* released in 1942, shattered box-office records for films of its type, despite poor reviews, to the surprise of both Universal Pictures and exhibitors. The brute image of the monster, able to dispose of any obstacle, may have provided a rallying point for morale-battered wartime audiences.

Images of devolved animal-men, often possessed of the wolfish traits so prized by the Nazis, were striking facets of horror pictures during the war years. (The "manimal" imagery wasn't restricted to horror movies; even Walt Disney's *Pinocchio* (1940) depicted unruly boys metamorphosing into donkeys in a sequence as hackle-raising as anything envisioned by Dr. Moreau.) The Wolf Man himself was resurrected for three more films throughout the war, beating out both Dracula and the Frankenstein monster for screen time.

The first sequel, *Frankenstein Meets the Wolf Man* (1943), elicited some immediate, if facetious, war parallels on the part of reviewers. *The Hollywood Reporter* observed that "Roosevelt meets Churchill at Casablanca, Yanks meet Japs at Guadalcanal—and yet these events will fade into insignificance to those seemingly inexhaustible legions of horror fans when they hear that *Frankenstein Meets the Wolf Man*. Yay, brother!" The film takes place in a monster-haunted Germanic never-never land called Visaria, which a resurrected Lawrence Talbot and his wizened gypsy sidekick (Maria Ouspenskaya) are somehow able to reach from Wales in a horse-drawn wagon. Exhibitors were encouraged by the film's press book to play up the "mechanical" and "animal" aspects in their lobby displays by lettering the monster names in metal and fur, respectively. "Metal and fur" was an apt, if unintentional, comment on the contradictions of modern warfare: the spirit of the ancient berserker pitted against high industrial sublimation. The Times Square premiere of the film was heralded by a huge lobby cutout of the dueling demons; on its base was a straightforward directive: BUY WAR BONDS AND STAMPS.

Talbot's four-film quest to put to rest his wolf-self is, in a strange way, an unconscious parable of the war effort. The Wolf Man's crusade for eternal peace and his frustrated attempts to control irrational, violent, European forces continued in Universal's *House of Frankenstein* (1944) and *House of Dracula* (1945). These two films, both of which featured Dracula (John Carradine, appearing on screen for the first time as Bram Stoker had physically described

Advertising art for *Frankenstein Meets the Wolf Man*.

the character), the Frankenstein monster (Glenn Strange), and the Wolf Man (Chaney), represented the last gasps of the studio's classic monsters, at least in a straight horror context (the icons would be reassembled one final time in the 1948 comedy *Abbott and Costello Meet Frankenstein*). The Wolf Man's saga was the most consistent and sustained monster myth of the war, beginning with the first year of America's direct involvement, and finishing up just in time for Hiroshima.

"Horror pictures have paid off handsomely for Universal," reported *Variety* in the summer of 1944. "By the end of this year the creepers and chillers will have poured not less than $10,000,000 [in] profits into the company's coffers for the 13 years which have elapsed since *Frankenstein* first reared his ghastly head." *Variety* noted that the market for monsters "has been largely confined to the American continent, England having barred all horror films for the duration on the declared ground that the dreadfuls were not good for general film audiences where there was so much wartime horror." But *Variety* opined that the lucrative market was "expected to be restored immediately after the cessation of war in Europe."

The Wolf Man spawned imitators, notably Twentieth Century Fox's *The Undying Monster* (1942) and Columbia's *Cry of the Werewolf* (1944). Other forms of devolution proved popular as well: Bela Lugosi appeared in Monogram's "poverty row" thrillers *The Ape Man* (1943) and *Return of the Ape Man* (1944).

One of the most memorable monster pictures of the 1940s, the reputation of which has grown with time, was *Cat People* (1942), a low-budget effort by RKO to imitate the enviably successful horror formulas at Universal. Like *The Wolf Man, Cat People* was originally a disembodied title, suggested by RKO's vice president in charge of production, Charles Koerner. Val Lewton, a thirty-seven-year-old former story editor for David O. Selznick with no particular fascination for the horror genre, was Koerner's choice for producer. Jacques Tourneur directed. Lewton—like Lugosi's Vitus Weredegast—was an ailurophobe, but nonetheless used the vehicle to inaugurate an artistically and financially successful cycle of atmospheric, psychological shockers, relying on shadows and understatement rather than obvious makeup effects.

Cat People had been originally conceived as a contemporary war story. In Lewton's first treatment, a Nazi Panzer division invades a Balkan village. The inhabitants put up no immediate resistence.

An advertisement for *Cat People. (Courtesy of Ronald V. Borst / Hollywood Movie Posters)*

They don't have to—at night they are able to turn into giant were-cats and kill their oppressors. Lewton imagined a village girl fleeing to New York, and taking the cat-people curse with her.

The Nazis were dropped, but the character of the cat girl remained the centerpiece of the final script, written by DeWitt Bodeen. Irena Dubrovna (the baby-faced French actress Simone Simon), a fashion designer in New York, marries a naval architect, Oliver Reed (Kent Smith) but cannot consummate their union because of her fear that sex will transform her into a predatory animal. She confesses her obsession to a psychiatrist, Dr. Louis Judd (Tom Conway), who finds her a personal as well as a professional challenge. As her frustrated husband begins confiding in another woman, Alice Moore (Jane Randolph), Irena's jealousy rises. The psychiatrist encourages her to surrender to the feelings that frighten her, preferably with him. Irena refuses. In the film's most famous sequence, Alice is trapped in a darkened hotel swimming pool while a snarling, unseen beast prowls its perimeter. When the lights come on, there is no panther to be seen—only Irena. When Judd enters Irena's apartment, hoping for sex, she responds by turning into a monster and tearing him to shreds. Wounded herself, she finds her way to the panther cage in the Central Park Zoo, an exhibit that has always fascinated her. She unlocks the cage, and the freed cat knocks her to her death.★

While *Cat People* was summarily dismissed by *The New York Times* as a tedious bore (a judgment that seems almost incomprehensible today, given its crafty, widely admired, and imitated mise-en-scène), the film was a popular hit, earning a $4 million return on its $118,948 investment—an amazing, nearly 3,500 percent profit.

Perhaps because of the film's overall understatement, the literal-minded censors gave *Cat People* scant trouble. The Breen Office objected only to details of one scene in a restaurant: "The drinking at this point should be minimized, and we suggest that Oliver be shown drinking *beer* instead of Scotch highballs. . . . It might be better to show them sitting at a table, rather than at the bar, and also be having some sandwiches." Panthers feasting on human tid-

---

★ The zoo sequences in *Cat People* are highly reminiscent of, and possibly inspired by, the scenes in Bram Stoker's *Dracula* in which the count displays a similar affinity for a caged wolf at the London Zoo. And the overriding theme of the film—the equation of a repressed woman's sexual awakening with predatory horror—also owes much to Stoker.

bits, apparently, caused no undue alarm—as long as they did their chewing in the shadows.

Lewton delved deeper into the psychological penumbra, producing several follow-up horror pictures at RKO, including *The Leopard Man* (1943), *I Walked with a Zombie* (1943), *The Curse of the Cat People* (1944), and *The Body Snatcher* (1945), featuring Boris Karloff in his finest screen role as a resurrection man in the best Burke and Hare tradition.

Lewton's technique of allowing an audience to create horrific details in its own mind was elaborately developed before and during the war years in another medium. A fifteen-minute radio feature, inaugurated on a Chicago station in 1934 by Wyllis Cooper, was taken over by writer-producer Arch Oboler who shaped the concept into the legendary radio drama series "Lights Out" on the NBC network. Oboler also wrote mainstream drama, but is best remembered for "Lights Out," the creepiest of the radio mystery programs, often crossing the border into pure horror with stories of giant chicken hearts that devoured the world, people turned inside out, or buried alive. Some of the appalling mental images were created by the simplest means. Sizzling bacon held up to the microphone became the sound of electrocution. Broken bones were simulated by cracking spareribs with a pipe wrench. Squishy cooked pasta could conjure cannibalism. Oboler's innovative use of sound effects to create terror and suspense was without equal—not surprising, since he pioneered many of the techniques himself—and they were showcased at their full emotional intensity when he dramatized Dalton Trumbo's 1939 antiwar novel *Johnny Got His Gun*. The story of a World War I soldier who returns without arms, legs, or face was a story that trumped Lon Chaney and Tod Browning in horrifying physical detail and was considered "unfilmable" for years. (A film version directed by author Trumbo was finally produced in 1971.) Radio, however, was able to circumvent censorship objections that would have been insurmountable in Hollywood circa 1940.

"Lights Out" played through the 1938–39 season on NBC, and was revived for 1942–43. By its return engagement the war was well underway, and Oboler's scripts (for "Lights Out" and other drama series as well) took on a propagandistic tone, delivered with the well-honed techniques of horror melodrama. Audiences were encouraged, with repetitious, almost hypnotic instructions, to visualize an America overtaken by the Germans, or Japanese soldiers lurking on the other side of the door. The shudders, needless to say, were surefire.

Until Pearl Harbor, America had been distinctly of two minds about entering the war. The antiwar, isolationist mood was summed up in C. D. Batchelor's Pulitzer prize–winning cartoon of 1937. A prostitute greets a callow young man on a staircase, telling him, "Come on in. I'll treat you right. I used to know your daddy." The boy doesn't seem to mind that a death's head tops her fleshy torso. The cartoon today looks remarkably like a vintage cover from *Weird Tales*. John L. Balderston, the writer of many a weird tale himself, who had been largely responsible for the stage and screen successes of *Dracula* and *Frankenstein,* was by this time essentially retired from monsters, and returned to his first professional interest, the politics of military engagement. Given his orthodox Quaker upbringing and schooling, Balderston's early career as a war correspondent is as intriguing as his fervent support for America's entry into World War II is surprising. He was nonetheless passionately convinced that America could not remain neutral in the European conflict, and lent his name to numerous organizations, petitions, and campaigns to break the isolationist gridlock.

There was a certain sense of fatality about America's eventual declaration of war, though Pearl Harbor came as the purest kind of cultural shock. Fritz Leiber, the noted horror and fantasy writer then just beginning his career, recalled how the permeating war anxiety affected the composition of his first novel, *Conjure Wife,* now considered a genre classic. According to Leiber, "There was this feeling of dread around me . . . doom and dread. The book picks it up."

By the last year of the war, both the vampire/battlefield metaphor that had inspired *Nosferatu* and the authoritarian-mesmerist motif of *Caligari* could be clearly discerned in a film titled—appropriately enough for the new conflict—*The Return of the Vampire.* Released by Columbia Pictures in 1944, it would mark Bela Lugosi's last appearance as a Hollywood vampire in a non-comedy film. *The Return of the Vampire* is one of those fascinating junk films that, relying on warmed-over clichés and aiming for broad popular appeal, becomes a vessel for unintentional historical subtexts. It tells the story of Armand Tesla (Lugosi), a vampire ravaging

London during World War I. Just in time for the Armistice, he has a spike driven through his heart and is buried in a secret grave.

Years later, during the blitz, the vampire's grave takes a direct hit from a German bomb. A cleanup crew assumes that the spike is a bomb splinter and pulls it out, releasing the vampire once more to drink during wartime. Tesla reclaims the soul of a previous victim, Andreas Obry (Matt Willis), who becomes a werewolf in service of the undead. Tesla assumes the identity of a scientist who has escaped a Nazi concentration camp, and sets about taking his revenge, nipping and sipping on the family that originally dispatched him. Another German bomb conveniently ends his plans for world domination. The reviewers took it all in stride. "In a place like England," wrote one New York critic, "where according to films the ancient burying grounds are practically sown with the corpses of vampires . . . it is a cinch that in the upheavals of the blitz period one of these stale characters should get tangled with the underground."

Lugosi toured *Dracula* on stage during the war, and, like many other Hollywood stars, made lunchtime morale-boosting appearances at defense plants along the west coast. His biographer Robert Cremer quotes Buddy Hyde, a special-services officer who organized the tours: "Eddie Cantor needed twenty minutes just to warm up. When Bela came on, the men cheered so long that he barely had time to make his pitch. He just made a quiet appeal; no Dracula takeoff or anything like that, but the audience loved him. I could have put some of Hollywood's glamorous stars out there, but none of them could have upstaged Bela. He got the warmest welcome of anyone connected with the morale program." Lugosi played more wartime villains than supernatural fiends in the early forties; one of his most flamboyant appearances was in *Black Dragons* as a plastic surgeon who alters the faces of Japanese agents sufficiently to allow them to impersonate a bevy of American industrialists.

Boris Karloff, while appearing on Broadway in *Arsenic and Old Lace,* also served as an air-raid warden in a basement room at the Beekman Hotel at 63rd Street and Park Avenue. His watch, recalled *New York Times* reader Nancy Farrell in a letter to the editor after the actor's death in 1969, began appropriately at midnight. "In the air-raid post, Karloff kept on his conservative coat of good British tweed. He wore rimless glasses. He looked thin and not especially tall. He urged us two wardens to hurry home and assured us he

Francis Bacon, *Three Studies for Figures at the Base of a Crucifixion* (1945). *(Tate Gallery, London / Art Resource, New York)*

was glad to go on duty early." Farrell was struck by his dissimilarity to the hulking Frankenstein monster that had frightened her as a teenager. "I thought only of the calmness and dependability of this courteous man who was responsible for the lives of thousands of his neighbors. I felt he would rather be an air-raid warden in London and that he was imposing on himself the same discipline that he would have observed in the blitz."

In the final days of the war, London was assaulted again, not by the Nazis, but by the horrific canvases of a self-taught painter, then almost unknown in art circles. Thirty-five-year-old Francis Bacon had himself not served in the British army (he had been rejected because of chronic asthma), but not since Picasso's *Guernica* had an artist managed to capture the primal nightmare of war in such a devastating fashion. Picasso had distorted the human form, but Bacon bypassed the human and went straight to the monstrous. Art critic John Russell described the impact of Bacon's *Three Studies for Figures at the Base of a Crucifixion* at the Lefevre Gallery in April 1945:

> To the right of the door were images so unrelievedly awful that the mind shut snap at the sight of them. Their anatomy was half-human, half-animal, and they were confined in a low-ceilinged, windowless and oddly proportioned space. They could bite, probe, and suck, and they had very long eel-like necks, but

their functioning in other respects was mysterious. . . . Common to all figures was a mindless voracity, an automatic unregulated gluttony, a ravening undifferentiated capacity for hatred. Each was as if cornered, and only waiting for the chance to drag the observer down to its own level.

Bacon's gallery monsters were twisted beyond anything ever presented to the public (save perhaps John Merrick, the horrendously disfigured Elephant Man who had captured the attention of Victorian society). For the time being, such extravagant nightmares were beyond the technical capability, and emotional tolerance, of the popular media. But their time would come. In the spring of 1945, the world had not yet heard of the atom bomb, and had barely begun to comprehend the reality of Auschwitz.

The Nazi doctors who administrated the death camps personified many of the psychological conflicts dramatized in prototype German horror films and the American genre they inspired. Psychiatrist Robert Jay Lifton, who has written extensively on the subject of adaptation to extreme stress, identifies the process of "doubling" by which a healer and a killer could inhabit the same person, the "good" doctor creating an autonomous "bad" doctor to carry out the dirty work of the death factory: "The second self functions fully as a whole self; for this reason it is so adaptable and so dangerous. It enables a relatively ordinary person to commit evil. It has a life/death dimension, in which the perpetrator overcomes his or her own death anxiety by involvement in the killing of others."

In *The Nazi Doctors,* Lifton explores this process of deadly mirror-imaging:

Doctors as a group may be more susceptible to doubling than others. . . . Doubling usually begins with the student's encounter with the corpse he or she must dissect, often enough on the first day of medical school. . . . Since studies have suggested that a psychological motivation for entering the medical profession can be the overcoming of an unusually great fear of death, it is possible that this fear in doctors propels them in the direction of doubling when encountering deadly environments. Doctors drawn to the Nazi movement in general, and to SS or concentration-camp medicine in particular, were likely to be those with the greatest previous medical doubling.

Lifton compares the Nazi doctor's situation to the Faustian bargain depicted in the German doppelganger film *The Student of Prague* (1913). In that story, a mirror image is given a life of its own, and becomes a killer. "Medical doubling" is also a good description of the underlying dynamic of *Dr. Jekyll and Mr. Hyde,* in which a healer begets a doppelganger/destroyer. Dr. Josef Mengele's ugly fascination with twins has a clear resonance with doubling and second selves; oddly, Lifton does not explore this metaphor in his detailed analysis of Mengele's personality.

By indulging sadism in the guise of dispassionate science, the pointless and atrocious medical "research" carried out by the Nazi doctors remarkably paralleled the typical activities of the mad movie doctors of the thirties and forties. In the movies, crazed scientists invented devices of mass destruction, or conducted cruel experiments, often to create races of new, altered, or superior beings (the *Frankenstein* films, *Murders in the Rue Morgue, Island of Lost Souls,* etc.). These madmen were usually obsessed with some dream of world domination (Lugosi's Roxor in *Chandu the Magician*), fixated on the purity of some theory *(Dr. Jekyll and Mr. Hyde)* or exaggerated aesthetic standards *(Mystery of the Wax Museum).* Pulps, films, and serials of the forties no doubt drew upon an actual, if partial, knowledge of the Third Reich's general aims vis-à-vis science, eugenics, and culture, but the presence of doppelganger-drenched science in the earlier films of the thirties suggests a larger modern ambivalence about the consequences of hyperrational scientism. In America the themes were trivialized as horror entertainment. In Europe they were invoked to summon real demons.

Eva Berkson, a British-born actress who had operated the Grand Guignol in Paris since 1937, fled to London in 1940 as the Nazis approached. Camille Choisy, the theatre's director in the late twenties, returned to the scene of his theatrical crimes, and found a profitable new audience in the occupying Nazi forces. According to Grand Guignol historian Mel Gordon, "Most of the repertory reverted to Choisy's old bills and the theatre became very popular with the enemy troops. Hermann Goering in particular enjoyed the productions; but, for the Gestapo and the SS elite, the Grand Guignol—with its gratuitous violence and lewd pornographic interludes—was a penultimate example of *Entartete Kunst* ('Degenerate Art')." Gordon reports that the Nazi censors vainly tried to close the establishment; one wonders what prevented them. Perhaps anything that pleased Göering's private tastes was unlikely to be challenged. While living at the Ritz, the corpulent Göering is supposed to have asked designer Coco Chanel to design him women's gowns, the better for the commander to relax in.

The image of Nazi storm troopers crowding into a Montmartre cul-de-sac to chuckle over horror plays that blindly paralleled the monstrous medical experiments then being pursued by German doctors is perversely surreal. Uglier still were the real-life Grand Guignol crimes of a collaborationist doctor, Marcel Petiot, who offered safe transport to Jews. After receiving payment, he incinerated them in his Paris basement.

Camille Choisy was said to have been a *collabo,* which also may have helped to keep the theatre open despite official disapproval. It was only his death, from natural causes, that prevented his being tried after the war. Eva Berkson returned after liberation, and reasserted her control over the Grand Guignol for another six years. But she found her audiences transformed. "Really," Berkson told *Time* magazine in 1947, "I've almost come to the conclusion that the only way to frighten a French audience since the war is to cut up a woman on stage—a live woman, of course—and throw them the pieces."

With the arrival of American troops, an eye-catching headline appeared in a Paris newspaper: "BLOOD AND GUTS" AT THE GRAND GUIGNOL. It wasn't a new play (as some patrons mistakenly thought); it was instead a report of a celebrity visit to the rue Chaptal. Old Blood and Guts himself, General George Patton, had replaced Hermann Göering as a guest of honor.

Europe had been liberated. And despite Eva Berkson's misgivings, the spirit of Grand Guignol was far from dead. Its life had in fact just begun, though it would never again seem quite so quaint.

Chapter Eight

DRIVE-INS ARE A GHOUL'S BEST FRIEND:
Horror in the Fifties

"HEH, HEH. I SEE YOU'RE HUNGRY FOR HORROR AGAIN. WELL, REST
ASSURED. YOUR APPETITE WILL BE SATISFIED. IN FACT, WHEN YOU'RE
THROUGH WITH THIS PUTRID PERIODICAL, YOU WILL HAVE LOST YOUR
APPETITE ENTIRELY. SO DON'T JUST STAND THERE DROOLING. COME IN."

Introduction by the Vault Keeper, a comic-book master of
ceremonies, to *The Vault of Horror*
(1952)

THE NEW AMERICAN prosperity of the early 1950s was won atop
the largest bone pile in human history. World War II had claimed
the lives of over 40 million soldiers and civilians, and had introduced two radical new forms of mechanized death—the atomic
bomb and the extermination camp—that seriously challenged the
mind's ability to absorb, much less cope with, the naked face of
horror at mid-century. And only five years after the fall of Germany and Japan, America was once again at war, this time a "police
action" in Korea haunted by the specter of the H-bomb, a looming
necro-technology now shared uneasily with the Soviets. If America in 1950 was filled with the smell of new cars, it was still permeated by the stench of mass death, and the threat of more to
come.

Juvenile delinquency goes Gothic: Michael Landon and his victim in
I Was a Teenage Werewolf **(1957). (Photofest)**

Most Americans found it easier not to face invasion/annihilation anxieties directly; they found indirect expression in McCarthyism, UFO hysteria, and, perhaps most pointedly, in the popular medium of lurid and sensational comic books that had been growing steadily in circulation since the end of World War II. They were a staple form of entertainment among enlisted men; in Korea, horror (and war comics) no doubt provided many soldiers with a *M★A★S★H★*-style escape valve of mordant humor and therapeutic social cynicism. The circulation figures for comic books during the early fifties are impressive even today: in 1950, 50 million comic books were being printed and distributed every month. They were being read mostly by adults (54 percent, according to one Dayton, Ohio, study), and by 40 percent of everybody in America above the age of eight. By 1953, horror and horrific crime accounted for approximately a quarter of the total comics-industry output. More Americans were reading horror comics than were reading *Reader's Digest* or *The Saturday Evening Post*.

Although they had their roots in established pulp-fiction traditions, and drew additional inspiration from radio melodrama and film noir conventions, horror comics were basically unlike anything that had ever been published in America. The most influential and imitated (but not the most numerous) were the titles published by the Entertaining Comics Group. The E.C. line of publications included *Tales from the Crypt* (1950–55), *The Vault of Horror* (1950–54), and *The Haunt of Fear* (1950–54).

The cataclysm of the plague in the Middle Ages had given momentum to the Dance of Death as a major cultural motif; the imagery of American horror comics in postwar America presented a strikingly similar popular aesthetic. Like the woodcuts of Hans Holbein the Younger, this new *danse macabre* took advantage of easily reproducible line art to disseminate images of rotting, revenant corpses who carry off the living. Although many other grisly stories were told, it was a rare horror comic that did not contain at least one story that followed the reassuring formula. Social satire was a strong component of the classical Dance of Death, and was prominent in the horror comics as well. Death, in the form of an animated corpse, was presented over and over as a judgmental and leveling force, one that made a mockery of human vanity and material greed. "It's strange how weird some of that stuff got," recalled Russ Heath, an artist for Marvel and DC Comics. "I didn't notice it at first, because it got progressively more bizarre until you had all this rotting flesh falling off ribs."

The stories inevitably introduced an element of personal revenge (a departure from the classical *Totentanz*), thus encouraging the reader to identify, rather gleefully, with Death as a sympathetic protagonist. While Holbein and others depicted the death-dance as a kind of funereal polonaise, the "dance" of the horror comics was their ritual narrative formula. If the rigid moralism of the core stories was not recognized by their (equally moralistic) critics, it was perhaps because the stories swung wildly between—and sometimes mixed together—moralism, sadism, and outright nihilism. In the horror comics view of America, morality was a state of grace attainable only by the living dead and the murderously insane. The world was made right only when a fetid corpse crawled out of its grave to revenge itself on the living, or when, in the comic-book clarity of psychosis, a hectored suburban spouse

Hans Holbein the Younger, "The Monk" from *The Dance of Death* (1534).

E.C. Comics (1951): an update on Holbein.

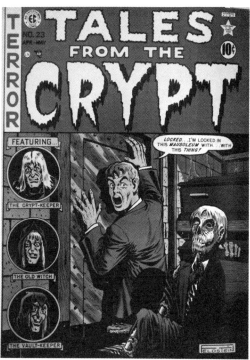

found postwar peace by barbecuing a husband or wife on a back-yard grill. For those unlucky enough to be living and sane, society was a noir film running in an endless loop. Marriage as an institution existed only as a setup for murder. No good deed would go unpunished.

The relentlessly grim worldview of Entertaining Comics was enhanced by the energetic rendering styles of artists like Jack Davis, Johnny Craig, and, perhaps most brilliantly, "Ghastly" Graham Ingels, whose fine-art training immeasurably enhanced the impact of stories in all three E.C. horror titles, especially *The Haunt of Fear*. Ingels, later described by a coworker as looking "like a dissipated John Kennedy," specialized in faces that were like Daumier caricatures from hell; even in relatively quiet, expository sequences, his sharp-featured characters seemed in the throes of epileptic seizures, nausea, and shock. A trademark of Ingels' seemed to be strings of spittle hanging like dripping cobwebs from his characters' open mouths; their bodies arched and contorted to fill each panel in the most uncomfortable poses imaginable. There was no respite from horror in an Ingels story; even his peripheral inking swirled in wavelike patterns reminiscent of Edvard Munch's "The Shriek."

One of Ingels' most memorable stories from *The Haunt of Fear* was "Wish You Were Here," a nasty update of "The Monkey's Paw" in which a wife's attempts to help her husband's failing business through a wish-granting jade statuette have hideous results. Her first wish, for money, results in the husband's death in an auto crash and a big insurance settlement. Remembering the mistake of the mother in "The Monkey's Paw" (who gets back her dead son, but as a mangled, walking corpse), she wishes for her husband to be returned to her as he was immediately *before* the accident. Again, she miscalculates: it turns out he died of a heart attack just before the accident, so she still has a corpse on her hands. Finally, she uses her last wish simply to will him alive. The husband wakes, screaming in pain—she has forgotten that he has already been embalmed, his veins burning with formaldehyde. She empties a shotgun into his twitching body. It does no good. She wished him alive, and alive he must stay. "Do something!" he cries. She goes to the kitchen and finds the largest knife . . .

AND EVEN WHEN JASON COULD NO LONGER MAKE A SOUND . . .
WHEN ENID'S FRANTIC HACKING HAD REDUCED HIM TO A MILLION

SEVERED SECTIONS, EACH SECTION STILL MOVED AND JERKED AND QUIVERED WITH LIFE. MR. SHINER FOUND HER THAT WAY WHEN HE RETURNED . . . CUTTING . . . CUTTING . . . CUTTING. . . . THE MEN IN THE WHITE COATS THAT CAME TO TAKE ENID AWAY . . . NEVER NOTICED THE TINY SEVERED SECTIONS PULSAT-ING . . .

The accompanying illustration (which the reader here will be spared) of the mad Enid kneeling over a casket brimming with fresh puree of husband represents either the zenith or nadir of E.C.'s visceral horror aesthetic, depending on one's point of view. The destruction of the man's body is so complete, so ferociously over-the-top that it is more like the damage inflicted by artillery or mortar fire than any kitchen utensil. These flashback-type images, like Enid's husband himself, apparently could not be stilled. Marriage and home could erupt into battlefield carnage at any moment. The story also sums up the *Totentanz* sensibility underlying most of the horror comics: material aspiration is an impossible, doomed folly—the postwar propaganda to the contrary.

Despite their gleeful show of blood and guts, the horror comics had a moralistic streak a mile wide, in the best tradition of Jonathan Edwards, or the medieval mural painters who inspired Holbein. But to a cadre of narrow-minded critics, such obvious nuances were lost entirely.

The leading foe of horror comics was Dr. Fredric Wertham, a Gramercy Park psychiatrist who, coincidentally, had been imported to America from Germany about the same time as *The Cabinet of Dr. Caligari* in the early twenties. At six-foot-three with piercing blue eyes, he was indeed a towering, intimidating, Nosferatu-like presence . . . at least from the standpoint of the comic-book industry. From the late forties onward, he had been publishing articles sharply critical of comics, which he saw as a direct cause of an upsurge in juvenile delinquency. His focus was monomaniacal, and appealing in its simplicity. Juvenile crime was not a product of the disrupted family patterns caused by the war, or of the uneven distribution of the postwar spoils, or of any other number of contributing factors: it was comic books that were doing the damage, directly inciting criminal violence, sexual perversion, illiteracy, and even eyestrain.

Wertham's evidence for his claims was purely anecdotal, rather like Senator Joseph McCarthy's knowledge of communists in government. Wertham eschewed the professional journals to make his case in the popular press—women's magazines often helped to spread his alarm—and his crusading culminated in a best-selling book, *Seduction of the Innocent,* published by Rinehart in 1954. He apparently tapped into a deep need of his audience to believe that society had turned into an unruly chamber of horrors, desperately in need of exorcism. "Children's play on the street is now of a wildness that it did not have formerly," Wertham wrote. "Children, often with comic books sticking out of their pockets, play massacre, hanging, lynching, torture." Wertham especially scorned horror, but was hardly less disapproving of other comic book genres ("What is the social meaning of these supermen, superwomen, super-lovers, superboys, supergirls, super-ducks, super-mice, super magicians, super-safecrackers? How did Nietzsche get into the nursery?"). He excoriated Batman and Wonder Woman for providing "homosexual" role models for children. The supposed children he quotes do not speak at all like children (in answer to a vocational question, one tyke chirped, "I want to be a sex maniac!"); but since they were clearly under the Svengali-like possession of the comic-book publishers, the weirdness of their purported conversations with the doctor could perhaps be overlooked.

Wertham included in his book some of the most sensational images he could find (and frankly he could have found worse). One illustration became a classic, and he displayed it with its caption before a Senate subcommittee hearing on the comics industry in April 1954:

so NOW you KNOW, fiends! now you know WHY there is a ball game being played in the moonlight at midnight in the deserted central city ball park. look CLOSELY. SEE this STRANGE BASEBALL GAME! see the long strings of pulpy intestines that mark the base lines. see the two lungs and the liver that indicate the bases . . . the heart that is home plate . . . see the batter come to the plate swinging the legs, the arms, then throwing all but one away and standing in the box waiting for the pitcher to hurl the head.

William Gaines, the publisher of the E.C. group (and later of *Mad* magazine), created quite a stir in the press when he gave rebuttal to Wertham's testimony on April 22. Senator Estes Kefauver,

Democrat from Tennessee, confronted Gaines with a cover of *Crime SuspenStories* ("Jolting Tales of Tension in the E.C. Tradition!") on which appeared a man with a bloody axe holding a woman's severed head.

"Do you think that is in good taste?" asked Herbert W. Beaser, the subcommittee's associate counsel.

"Yes," Gaines replied, "for the cover of a horror comic. A cover in bad taste, for example, might be defined as holding the head a little higher so that the neck could be seen dripping blood."

Gaines held his own, and made many well-reasoned points about the natural intelligence of children, and delinquency being the result of the real environment, not of fiction. "It would be just as difficult to explain the harmless thrill of a horror story to a Dr. Wertham as it would be to explain the sublimity of love to a frigid old maid," he said.

In an editorial called "Men of Taste," *The Hartford Courant* noted that "Mr. Gaines may have disappointed some of his public. He arrived without the company of a complement of vampires or werewolves, with the usual number of fingers, and with only one head. Even though he does gross close to a million dollars a year from this dirty business, Mr. Gaines is a man to be pitied as well as censured. For if he sees nothing wrong with the literary sewage that he helps create and distribute to small children, then he is indeed as strange as some of the creatures who stalk across the pages of his sardonically-named Entertaining Comics."

Frederic M. Thrasher, a New York University professor writing in *The Journal of Educational Sociology,* articulated the dissenting position. "Although Wertham has claimed in his various writings that he and his associates have studied thousands of children, normal and deviate, rich and poor, gifted and mediocre, he presents no statistical summary of his investigations. He makes no attempt to substantiate that his illustrative cases are in any way typical of all delinquents who read comics, or that delinquents who do not read comics do not commit similar types of offenses." The appeal of *Seduction of the Innocent,* of course, was not to clinicians, but to a general readership eager to hear "expert" voices in a confusing, rapidly changing decade.

The New Republic, another dissenting voice, criticized Wertham's argument as "a tissue of troublesome points." "His interview materials are presented with the scantest apparatus of criticism—in some instances they appear to record the uneasy spectacle of children telling their interviewer what they guessed he wanted to hear."

> Dr. Wertham's argument tacitly assumes, in a largely unjustifiable way, his comprehensive knowledge of social structure and culture. This may be why he displays so little interest in . . . broad cultural themes. . . . Could the connection between love and violence in popular literature and in comic books be indirect evidence of cultural change? Assume that our culture is shifting toward greater control by women over the conditions of their sexuality. Could the confusion between love and violence in fiction be a result, in part, of men's uncertainty about this change?

The New Republic concluded that *Seduction of the Innocent* "pivots mainly on the author's determination . . . to impress his readers not with professional argument, but with professional status."

The cartoony overtones of Wertham's worldview did not escape the notice of Robert Warshow, an associate editor of *Commentary* whose eleven-year-old son was an avid reader of E.C. comics. "Dr. Wertham's picture of society and human nature is one that a reader of comic books . . . might not find entirely unfamiliar," wrote Warshow, calling *Seduction of the Innocent* "a kind of crime comic book for parents." The similarities were many, including "the same simple conception of motives, the same sense of overhanging doom, the same melodramatic emphasis on pathology, the same direct an immediate relation between cause and effect." Warshow, who disapproved of his son's taste in reading matter, nevertheless concluded that horror comics were doing him no harm and it would be pointless to restrict him, or the books, since "surely something on an equally low level would appear to take their place. Children do need some 'sinful' world of their own to which they can retreat from the demands of the adult world. . . . Ultimately, one suspects, [Wertham] would like to see our culture entirely hygienic. I cannot agree with this tendency. I myself would not like to live surrounded by the kind of culture Dr. Wertham could thoroughly approve of," Warshow concluded.

In spite of a few well-reasoned objections to Wertham's diatribe, the popular press fawned over *Seduction of the Innocent,* and he became the darling of women's clubs, eager to surrender to his suggestions. In a sense, the 1950s housewife emerged as a somnambulistic "bride of science" summoned forth from her refrigerator-box by Dr. Wertham to do his bidding in a relentlessly hygienic world. (The Caligari-with-tail-fins milieu was depicted vividly in *The 5,000 Fingers of Dr. T,* Dr. Seuss' first and only foray into Hollywood in 1953. A colossal bomb at the time, but a cult favorite now, *The 5,000 Fingers* features a megalomaniac "piano teacher" played by ex–movie Nazi Hans Conried, who employs a hypnotized, Donna Reed–style mother to realize his fantasy of complete social control.) Fredric Wertham's dishonest, bullying "science" also had much in common with the increasingly sophisticated and cynical efforts of Madison Avenue to control the attitudes, anxieties, and consumption patterns of American women. And expanding postwar incomes was enabling psychiatry to make vast inroads into outpatient-land. The as yet unnamed category of drugs to be known as tranquilizers was already on the drawing boards, and would soon permit the psychiatric medicalization of a whole class of postwar discontents, many essentially social and economic in origin. As in some German expressionist film, a significant slice of society was ripe and willing to be treated as a madhouse, and the experts were only too eager to oblige the impulse.

By the fall of 1954, a cleanup of the comics industry was announced, with a restrictive code imposed by the newly formed Comics Magazine Association of America. No link whatsoever had been established between comics and delinquency, but the widespread bad publicity generated by Wertham's witch-hunt caused the industry to cave in. In addition to sex and violence, "scenes dealing with, or instruments associated with, walking dead, torture, vampires and vampirism, ghouls, cannibalism, and werewolfism are prohibited." Even the words "horror" and "terror" were taboo in titles.

But horror had its roots deep in the culture, and cracks in the pavement were plentiful.

While wisecracking "horror hosts" had become an endangered species in print, the new medium of television did not fall under the jurisdiction of the Comics Code Authority, and it was inevitable that the comic-book format would find a broadcast equivalent. In the spring of 1954 (the year that brought down both the horror comics and Joe McCarthy, and the year in which Bill Haley brought the words "rock" and "roll" into mass consciousness), Los Angeles rabbit ears began quivering in the direction of a strange new signal emanating from the transmitter of the local ABC affil-

Maila Nurmi as Vampira, television's original horror hostess. *(Courtesy of Ronald V. Borst / Hollywood Movie Posters)*

iate. The word spread quickly. *You've got to watch this.* And you did.

The show began at 11 P.M., like a late-night antidote to the prevailing blandness of prime-time fare—Milton Berle, "I Love Lucy," and "December Bride" had already colonized the living rooms of postwar America, and George Gobel was on the way. Much later, playwright Wendy Wasserstein would coin the perfect phrase to sum up the ethos of the era: it was a time, quite simply, when Dinah Shore ruled the earth.

But this was different. No sunny corporate theme song here. Instead, there was a rumbling peal of organ music—"Uranus" from Holst's *The Planets*—and then, in the pallid blue light of your bulky blonde-wood Magnavox console, a mist-filled corridor materialized. Advancing through the dry-ice miasma, there emerged a startling silhouette of a wasplike being. Could it be . . . a woman? From the impossible waistline swelled the cartoon bosom of a sex goddess, barely contained by the stiletto neckline plunge of a formfitting, tattered black rayon cocktail dress. The figure slinked past a floor-standing candelabra, fixed its gaze on the camera like a cobra seeking its prey. Three-inch-long black nails seemed to drip, rather than grow, from the ends of her fingers. Her eyebrows arched and loomed like boomerangs from beyond the grave. Nearing the camera, she raised talonlike fingers to serpentine hair.

And then she screamed—a piercing banshee's wail of anguish.

The reverberations subsiding, she composed herself, and spoke in sepulchral tones, a smoky amalgam of Marlene Dietrich and Tallulah Bankhead. "Good evening," she said. "I am . . . Vampira."

For Maila Nurmi, a thirty-one-year-old former coat-check girl, exotic dancer, necktie painter, and Broadway extra, the chance to introduce old horror movies on KABC-TV seemed like the break of a lifetime. The beautiful Finnish-born niece of the famed Olympic runner Paavo Nurmi was versatile in her aspirations, which had included both cheesecake and evangelism. Inspired by the *New Yorker* cartoons of Charles Addams, Nurmi had made quite a splash at a recent Los Angeles costume bash, the "Bal Caribe," winning first prize with a Victorian vampire getup assembled from a $3.67 remnant she cut with a pair of manicure scissors and sewed herself. Nurmi, and her screenwriter husband Dean Riesner, had hoped to attract the attention of Charles Addams himself, who might see the television possibilities of his mordant *New Yorker* drawings.

Instead, she made an indelible impression on Hunt Stromberg, Jr., son of the MGM executive, himself a television producer who had just been promoted to the position of KABC program director. He was looking for a way to build an audience for a somewhat listless lineup of late-night films. Movies on TV were a relatively new development, and the major studios, still competing with the fledgling medium, had not yet released their classic films for broadcast. Stromberg was working with independent poverty-row properties like *Devil Bat's Daughter.* There had to be some way to package the junk.

Then came the Bal Caribe, and the woman in the shroud who took the prize. Stromberg couldn't get her out of his mind. The problem was, he had no idea who she was. It took months before one of the costume-competition judges, designer Rudi Gernreich—later famous for the topless swimsuit—identified her: "Of course I know her! She's Maila Nurmi—the first woman in Southern California to wear backless shoes."

Nurmi went over to KABC. Stromberg told her what he had in mind, but was insistent on the need to not infringe on Charles Addams. Could Nurmi come up with a *different* kind of vampire? She mulled it over for a few days. The creature of the Bal Caribe had been deadpan drab, with all the sex appeal of an ironing board— in short, pretty much what Charles Addams had popularized in *The New Yorker.* Maybe she could turn it all inside out. As playwright Philip-Dimitri Galás would spin the phrase several decades later, it was all a matter of doom, gloom—and va-va-voom.

Nurmi didn't know much about movie vampires—her closest encounter with Dracula had been a near-collision with a roller-skating Bela Lugosi on Hollywood Boulevard (the actor had never learned how to drive, and had to improvise wheels in order to visit his favorite newsstand and cigar store). Nurmi drew instead on the Dragon Lady from "Terry and the Pirates," photographs of Theda Bara ("awe-inspiring"), and the evil queen in Disney's *Snow White,* which had come out when Nurmi was fourteen. For the makeup and costume, she turned for inspiration to a bondage and discipline magazine called *Bizarre,* full of cruel and corseted women. The Nosferatu-style fingernails were of her own devising. "There was a heavy plastic they made food containers out of, and I softened it with boiling water and shaped it to my fingers. I cooled them in an ice cube tray and later would affix them with airplane glue." To decrease her tiny waist even further, Nurmi mixed papaya powder (a main ingredient of meat tenderizer) with cold cream, and rubbed it on her midsection, which she further bound with a rubber inner tube. "My waist just melted," she recalled. "It was digesting my flesh."

The result was an inspired bit of cultural fusion. Death and sensuality had always had a deep affinity, but never before had they been so pointedly merged in a popular icon. Vampira's body was a landscape of cultural contradictions: simultaneously buxom and gaunt, well-fed yet skeletal, a paradoxical evocation of insatiable consumerism. She was especially well-suited to low-resolution television—no amount of fiddling with the contrast button could mitigate the stark planes and shadows that composed her. Her eyebrows were streamlined, jet-propelled parabolas—Gothic arches in orbit. Drawing energy from the quintessentially fifties nexus of automotive styling and the female form, Vampira was a souped-up hearse . . . with headlights. Breast-like projections on American cars had been introduced in 1953; their juxtaposition with the aggressively toothy grillwork already in fashion yielded a technological update on vampire-related images of ravenous womanhood. Vampira's daring décolletage effortlessly evoked vampirism as a kind of monstrous suckling . . . and the public, it appeared, was ready to feed.

National publicity quickly followed Vampira's debut in March 1954. By June, *Life* had run a four-page photo spread, and Nurmi's exaggerated physical dimensions (38-17-36) stirred debate in the letters column of *Newsweek*. "I defy any normal, full-grown, 31-year-old woman to say her waist measures 17 inches," wrote Marguerite Bonham of Norfolk, Virginia. "I say it is a physical impossibility." There was speculation that Nurmi had had ribs removed surgically, adding a Frankensteinian touch to the otherwise Draculean mystique. In reality, she was just very petite.

A typical Vampira program might feature the sexy ghostess taking a bubble bath in a boiling cauldron, or sharing her recipe for the Vampira Cocktail—one jigger formaldehyde and two jiggers vulture blood, served over dry ice and garnished with a glass eye. And while her corny brand of humor-in-a-jugular-vein may seem a bit tired today, it was, during its time, unlike anything audiences had ever seen. Ratings soared. "Many Angelenos, hardened as they may be to eccentricities, watch the horror films just to see 'Vampire [sic],'" wrote *Newsweek*. Nurmi's excellent comic timing and her punning wit were also pluses. Once, during a personal appearance at a beauty pageant, she pretended to mistake the sponsor, Rheingold's Beer, for the centerpiece of a Wagnerian funeral.

Vampira's fans could be found in all walks of Hollywood life and legend. Mae West liked to sit up and watch the show, and afterwards sent her chauffered offerings of Swedish meatballs. (West had apparently forgotten that she had once ordered Nurmi's dismissal as an extra from her Broadway show *Catherine Was Great*; Nurmi's wiggling, it seemed, upstaged her own.)

A pioneer postmodernist, Vampira blurred categorical distinctions by wearing her costume offscreen as well as on (at least for publicity purposes). Even Bela Lugosi himself, identified as he was with the Dracula role, didn't drive around Hollywood in a rented Packard convertible, shrieking at traffic lights from beneath a black parasol. Vampira did. In addition to tons of publicity, her kooky celebrity got her into expensive restaurants (where she couldn't eat a bite, lest she pop her waist cinch and vomit) and made her a fixture at L.A. jazz clubs and bongo joints. One favorite hangout was Googie's, at the corner of Sunset Boulevard and Crescent Heights, right next to Schwab's drugstore. Googie's represented the beginning of a new and uninhibited direction in commercial architecture: colorful, angular, gravity-defying—as crazily cantilevered as Vampira herself. If Vampira was Dracula in the vernacula, so, too, was Googie's a populist regurgitation of tired old formulas into something new and flashy.

One night, Nurmi was hanging out in Googie's with a camp follower named Jack Simmons, and an aspiring actor named Jonathan Haze, who would star in Roger Corman's low-budget classic, *The Little Shop of Horrors* (1960). Nurmi glanced out the window and saw somebody she wanted to meet. It was a young actor who had done a few films and, while not yet a star, was definitely on his way up. He was twenty-four years old and his name was James Dean.

"That's the only guy in Hollywood I want to meet!" Nurmi told Simmons. Her wish was his command. And so it came to be that James Dean, rumpled and scholarly-looking in the spectacles he didn't wear on-screen, was ushered into Googie's for an interview with the vampire.

He invited her back to his cluttered one-room apartment above a garage and read her a bizarre story about a mother-dominated boy who hangs himself. There was a noose hanging from the ceil-

James Dean in teenage monster makeup. *(Photofest)*

ing of the apartment. "He also told me about an opera he wanted to produce," recalled Nurmi, "a Kabuki kind of thing having to do with crystal chandeliers and hangings. And I said to him, 'What is this this preoccupation of yours with hangings?' He said, 'That's the way I'm going to die, with a broken neck.' "

No doubt, James Dean had a morbid streak. In the estimation of several biographers, his mother's suicide was a brooding influence. According to Warren Newton Beath, author of *The Death of James Dean,* the young man's leisure-time activities included the taping of "darkly imaginative ramblings about what it must be like to be casketed in a dank grave." While in high school, he had devised an elaborate Frankenstein's monster makeup for himself for a comedy revue called *Goon with the Wind.* The show was a huge success and helped pay for a class trip to Washington, D.C. The monster characterization stayed with him; years later he would still recall the strange sense of power he felt in the guise of the animated corpse. Like Frankenstein and Dracula in their movie incarnations, James Dean himself was a product of the year 1931. On the screen, he would portray just the kind of teenage trouble-makers that Fredric Wertham believed were products of the horror comics.

Nurmi firmly believes that James Dean was a supernatural being, an angel-teacher "brought here to serve as a kind of rosary bead for adolescents having trouble with authority figures." Indeed, James Dean would become the culture's surpassing icon of the postwar juvenile malaise that so disturbed Dr. Wertham and his zealous minions.

"I met him every night at midnight," Nurmi recalled. "On Saturdays I still had the Vampira makeup on, but I always took off the wig. We'd just go slumming around. Strange as it seems, we never talked about Vampira; in fact, we never talked about horror. Jimmy did come to the show one night—it was an especially good show. Like Carol Burnett, I did little vignettes and that night I was playing Vampira as a strict librarian who had to discipline someone with his back to the camera. And the crew saw Jimmy with his cowlick—they had no idea who he was—and said, 'Hey kid, put this on.' And he slipped on this tweed jacket and they shot over his shoulder while I rapped his knuckles."

Jack Simmons played chauffeur for what came to be known as "The Midnight Watch." Appropriately, he drove a converted Cadillac hearse, eagerly shuttling between Googie's, Tiny Naylor's, Barney's Beanery, and other favorite spots. Gossips quickly dubbed them "Vampira and her two Frankensteins." Although the relationship between Vampira and the Rebel Without a Cause was widely reported to be a romance, it wasn't. Speaking of the year of midnight rendevouz with Jimmy and Jack, Nurmi would later describe the friendship as "a ménage à trois without the sex." Jack was gay in any event; Jimmy was bisexual (at least according to more recent accounts), and Nurmi had a jealous husband.

At the beginning of the relationship, it was Vampira who was the star, receiving bushels of fan mail, but soon it was Jimmy who was getting the lion's share of attention. Vampira was a short-lived phenomenon, at least on KABC. In Nurmi's version of the story, her refusal to relinquish all rights to the character (she offered 49 percent, and no more) caused her to be blackballed. The Vampira show was off the air by November 1954, only eight months after its debut. Jimmy began to suspect that the waning TV star was attempting to cash in on her relationship with him. He gave a caustic interview to Hedda Hopper, who had fueled the romance rumors, telling her that "I don't date cartoons," and that Vampira was merely "a subject about which I wanted to learn." Nurmi was angry and hurt.

Following the failure of the Vampira show, Nurmi went back to New York, where she had found stage work in the forties. Maybe there was still some magic there. It certainly wasn't in Los Angeles, where, in desperation, she had sunk to cleaning friends' apartments for ninety-nine cents an hour.

New York, as it turned out, welcomed her with open arms. Arms right out of a horror movie.

On the night of June 20th, 1955, Nurmi answered a knock at the door of her apartment at 136 West 46th Street, only to have a man force his way in. "I'm going to kill you," announced the twenty-two-year-old intruder, Ellis Barber. Later, it would be revealed that one of his street names was "The Vamp." He grabbed her, began punching, choking, and stripping her. "How long do you think you're going to live?" he asked her. "Until I'm ninety-three," she retorted. But the Vamp assured Vampira that she wouldn't make it to dawn. The ordeal lasted over two hours. She broke away from him three times and got into the hallway, a flight up from the street. But Barber knocked her down three times, wrestled with her on the floor, once rolling all the way down the flight of stairs. Each time, he managed to scoop her up in his arms and pull her back into the apartment, repeating his promise that she'd be dead by dawn. She broke free on the fourth try. It was 1 A.M. She ran through the chill air, wearing only a pair of torn slacks. Her whole body was scratched and bruised, and her neck bore the red imprint of choking fingers. A man in a nearby store covered her up and they called the police. The attacker was stupid enough to come back, and they caught him.

The papers treated it as a novelty story. Had Nurmi "been wearing the ghastly attire she uses in her specialty act on stage and TV," one tabloid wrote, the intruder "might never have dared thrust his foot in her apartment door."

She went back to California. Liberace asked her to appear with him at the Riviera in his act in Las Vegas—his first choice, Bela Lugosi, proved too old and sick to be of use. "It was a cavalcade of music through the ages," Nurmi remembered. "Vampira would come on and introduce each era. I sang little couplets in a funereal, hollow way." Still trying to wring some publicity from the Vampira character, she posed for some "pinups" in and about an open grave at Forest Lawn. "They actually lowered me into a grave that was waiting for a funeral," Nurmi recalled. When the bereaved family showed up, the dead man's small children didn't want to

watch the burial—they had caught sight of the "vampire" nearby
and wanted her autograph. ("I was appalled," Nurmi said.) She
sent one of the pictures, which showed her seated primly at the lip
of the grave, to James Dean, who was working on location. She
inscribed the photo with a mordant gag: *Having a wonderful time—
wish you were here.*

Dean didn't get the photo—it had been confiscated by someone
in his entourage and described to him as a "threat." He called Nurmi
and confronted her. She told him that it was a joke that would be
spoiled if she described it before he saw it. She didn't know that
he had just posed for a photo of his own in an open coffin at a
funeral home, smiling, showing the "V" sign.

James Dean never saw Nurmi's photo. His neck was snapped in
a high-speed auto wreck on September 30, 1955, in Salinas, California. The scandal magazines jumped on the Vampira-Dean connection, and ran lurid stories with titles like JAMES DEAN'S BLACK
MADONNA. The grave photo was run prominently, with the
inscription altered to *Darling, come join me!* Nurmi was portrayed
as an actual witch, who had hexed the young actor and perhaps
even brought about his death. Dean's most famous picture, *Rebel
Without a Cause,* would be released posthumously, and much of
his celebrity took on the aspect of morbid cultism.

For years afterward, Nurmi told an interviewer in 1975, "I
couldn't attract anyone who wanted to live. Necrophiliacs would
send me erotic poems, leave decapitated animals on the front porch."
A particularly morbid admirer begged her to resurrect Vampira
one more time—and escort him to a Halloween party.

"Leave me alone!" she yelled at him. "My whole life has been a
Halloween party!"

She was lucky to have turned him down. At midnight on Halloween, he was said to have smashed his Porsche, an exact replica
of James Dean's death-car, into the wall of a tombstone factory.
Both the admirer and a companion were killed instantly. Or so
the story went.

Maila Nurmi thought she had created Vampira, but the character had taken on a life of its own, mocking its mistress. In cities
all across America in the late fifties, outlandish characters were
popping up on television to introduce old horror movies, and they
were making a lot of money—for somebody. Her now ex-hus-
band Dean Riesner admitted that he had "flushed a million dollars

down the toilet" by not properly managing and promoting the character. Vampira would be resurrected briefly a few years later for a mute role in the bizarre cult film *Plan Nine from Outer Space* (1959), directed by Edward D. Wood, Jr., widely considered one of the worst filmmakers of all time. Since no kinescopes of her original broadcasts survive, *Plan Nine* remains the sole archival film record of Vampira in full regalia. Nurmi, whose encounters with morbid fans made her reclusive, didn't see the film for decades. Once a friend tried to convince the manager of a Los Angeles theatre to allow her to stand in the aisle for a sold-out performance. "This is *Vampira,*" the friend said. "She hasn't ever seen the movie." The manager would have none of it. "Vampira's dead," he replied. Nurmi didn't argue the point, and went home.

The flurry of public interest over old-fashioned ghoulishness, as evidenced by Vampira's sudden rise to fame, excited the aging actor Bela Lugosi, who had not made a real studio film since *Abbott and Costello Meet Frankenstein* (1948). Hollywood was now making horror and science-fiction movies in color and even three-dimensions, largely to lure audiences away from their television sets with the promise of something that could never be experienced on the flat, black-and-white home screen. *Creature from the Black Lagoon* (1954) and *House of Wax* (1953) were two of the most successful of these eye-poppers; Lugosi had appeared in costume at the premiere of the latter, and was sufficiently impressed by the stereoscopic effect that he encouraged a letter-writing campaign to Universal-International, in which his fans pleaded with the studio to remake *Dracula* in color and 3-D. Lugosi thought the illusion of bats flying over the heads of the audience would be a grand effect. It probably would have been, but the studio didn't bite.

Audiences after the war were still interested in monsters, but the suave Mephisto in the black cape was no longer a compelling image for the modern moviegoer. Dracula's threat of a quaint, venous invasion was tired indeed when compared to the overwhelming border violations the world had so recently witnessed. An enveloping cloak was no longer an image of dread. But a mushroom cloud was. The threat of mass destruction was bigger than ever in America's mind, and so were its monsters.

Monsters came in two basic shapes in the fifties: gigantic, stomping mutations, explicitly the product of atomic testing; and alien invaders, sometimes overgrown themselves, but usually intent on some kind of brainwashing or ideological control. Fifties monsters personified the Bomb as well as the Cold War itself.

Godzilla (1954) is the key film of the mutation-metaphor variety. Produced, appropriately enough, in Japan (the only society to have actually endured nuclear attack), *Godzilla* grafted atomic trauma onto the *King Kong* formula and launched one of the biggest ritual displays of naive metaphor the world has ever seen. Oversized radioactive monsters were lightning rods for atomic-war anxiety, and one of the most successful and imitated Hollywood formulas since the Western. The basic premise was, of course, stupid: since irradiated marigold seeds, for instance, could yield humongous blossoms, then atomic testing could transform and gigantify anything, like a technological gypsy curse. Almost needless to say, the one thing the Bomb was capable of distorting and magnifying was cultural dread. Fear was only part of the picture, however—like all gods, atomic energy had the power to please as well as punish. Nuclear power plants, it was popularly believed, would eventually make electricity so cheap there would no longer be any reason to meter it. Propelled by the peaceful atom, a new age of unprecedented leisure and abundance was at hand. Highly stylized "atomic" imagery was everywhere: in fabric patterns, advertising graphics, even architecture. One of the most ubiquitous cultural mandalas of the fifties was the powerfully connotative graphic emblem of two or three interlocking orbital paths, electrons whizzing around like planets. Electrons, of course, do not really behave like planetary bodies, but it is significant that the atom was nonetheless regarded as a microcosm, the diagram of a new worldview. The symbol served a primal, nearly cruciform function, representing all the faith, hope, fear, and awe generated by the ambiguous postwar age. Or was it only a prewar age after all?

The public turned to magazines and consumer advertising for the sunny side of the atomic coin; for the bad news it turned to monsters. Even an incomplete list of giant-monster films of the fifties is impressive: *It Came from Beneath the Sea* (1955) introduced a jumbo octopus intent on devouring San Francisco. Oversized insects and arachnids were featured in *Them* (1954), *Tarantula* (1955), *The Deadly Mantis* (1957), *The Beginning of the End* (1957), and *Earth vs. the Spider* (1958). Huge flying horrors were on display in *Rodan* (1957) and *The Giant Claw* (1957). People were enlarged to

Putting a face on the Bomb: an original Japanese poster for *Godzilla* **(1954).**
(Courtesy of Ronald V. Borst / Hollywood Movie Posters)

the size of their anxieties in *The Amazing Colossal Man* (1957), its sequel *War of the Colossal Beast* (1958), and in the now deliriously campy *Attack of the Fifty-Foot Woman* (1958). Assorted big beasts could be seen in *The Attack of the Crab Monsters* (1957), *The Beast from 20,000 Fathoms* (1953), and in *The Incredible Shrinking Man* (1957), which reversed the formula with the same end result: because of radiation, normal animals became gigantic, mortal threats to the diminished Everyman protagonist.

Closely related to the Bomb scare was the Red Scare, and ideological otherness frequently went extraterrestrial. Mind-controlling monsters from space took the place of communists in numerous films. Of these, Don Siegel's *Invasion of the Body Snatchers* (1956) is the best, possibly because the social metaphor is ambiguous. The story of an invasion by vegetable pods who create drained human doppelgangers in a California town has a clear Cold War resonance, but Siegel knowingly indicts the tendency toward blind social conformity—what Erich Fromm called "the escape from freedom" that is a trait of industrialized societies generally. The enemy is them, *and* us.

The political metaphors of the film drew virtually no comment at the time of *Invasion of the Body Snatchers'* release. *The New York Times* declined to review it at all. But the vision of an all-encompassing conspiracy, understood only by disbelieved and persecuted protagonists, would eventually become a cultural fixture beyond the movie pages, as now evidenced by thirty years of assassination theorists. Oliver Stone's 1991 film *JFK* brought the theme full circle, back to the darkened theatres where grandiose conspiracies and takeovers first flourished as a stock element of fifties horror. Paranoid thinking may be flawed, but it does give a shape and meaning to the paranoid's embattled world. Science-fiction/horror movies of the fifties frequently pretended to scare audiences while delivering a perversely comforting message: the world *is* understandable, if only as a monstrous plot or cover-up. But rest assured you'll get the big picture, even if you become a pod in the process.

Moral guardians of the fifties—the hygienic minions of Dr. Wertham—were most troubled by the paranoid, subversive monsters. *Invaders from Mars* (1953), directed by William Cameron Menzies, is a film that can still disturb the sleep of some baby boomers. Despite some laughable special effects (e.g., a visible zipper up the back of a monster), *Invaders from Mars* succeeds in conveying the nightmare of a boy who suspects that the postwar world may be more fragile than it seems. A flying saucer lands in a sand pit near his house and carves out tunnels under the town; the alien invaders suck victims down into the sand and implant controlling gizmos in the necks of his parents and the police, who icily go about finding more slaves for the Martians.

PTA representatives were not pleased about *Invaders from Mars*. Wrote one: "Here, in science fiction form, is an orgy of hate and fear and futility, with no hope of escape, no constructive element whatsoever. The child with whom one is asked to identify is bereft of any security from father and mother, from constituted author-ity, and the adults burst into meaningless violence. . . . For a time we hope there will be an answer in this projection of the formless fears abroad in our world of technological annihilation and savage ideologies, but the terror and dread only pile higher." Another evaluator put things more succinctly: *Invaders from Mars* was "not exactly a family picture."

Mind-control themes in horror/fantasy films may have reflected the public's interest in and revulsion to the widely publicized brainwashing of American GIs that occurred in Korean POW camps in the early fifties. The idea that a patriotic American ("Even a man who is pure in heart . . .") could be transformed and con-trolled by foreign/alien puppet-masters was an update on *The Cabinet of Dr. Caligari*'s somnambulist-as-soldier metaphor. And whatever horrors are involved in personality surrender, the prom-ise of complete transformation/makeover is also a powerfully attractive fantasy, combining the "escape from freedom" motif with Cinderella and Horatio Alger.

Another extremely interesting facet of fifties monster films is the repeated images of bulging eyes and—especially—bulging brains. Together, they present an image of intense and unbearable visual-mental overload, a description that may have more rele-vance to the unprecedented level of media bombardment, (mainly by television) in the fifties, than to any possible physiology of extraterrestrial beings. Never before had the public been asked to witness so much, or absorb so many messages or quantities of information. The popular preoccupation with flying saucers may have been literally farfetched, but glowing visions were indeed traversing the sky and invading homes in the form of inescapable television signals. Enlarged, swollen brains were pictured in such films as *This Island Earth* (1955), *Donovan's Brain* (1953), and *The*

Eye-brain overload: an alien physiology as information-age anxiety. From
Invasion of the Saucer Men **(1957).** *(Courtesy of Ronald V. Borst / Hollywood*
Movie Posters)

Brain from the Planet Arous (1957). In *Fiend Without a Face* (1958),
the human brain is totally externalized as a snakelike thing that
crawls with a detached spinal cord which can also throttle its victims. *Invasion of the Saucer Men* (1957) boasted the most exaggerated eye-brain hypertrophy of all: aliens (played by dwarves) with

heads shaped like gargantuan light bulbs, their bugging eyes the size of baseballs. In the way that early movie monstrosities reflected a horror of physical fragmentation, these new creatures anticipated not the violent rending of the body but its withering and atrophy. The future was about watching images and processing information; the eyes and brain were the only useful parts of the human form left. Science-fiction magazines of the fifties loved to print lurid covers depicting never-ending onslaughts of bug-eyed monsters (affectionately known as B.E.M.s by their fans); ocular anxiety and depersonalization was similarly reflected in films like *The Beast with a Million Eyes* (1955), *The Crawling Eye* (1958), and *The Cyclops* (1957).

The new monsters on the block effectively displaced the old; a generation that had not experienced the 1930s was not likely to respond to horror icons generated in response to an earlier decade's economic and social traumas. Nowhere is the discrepancy in horror styles as evident as in the sad final years of Bela Lugosi, who had been typecast into a professional crypt. Unlike Boris Karloff, who had diversified profitably into stage work, television, and radio, Lugosi had not managed his career particularly well. One possibly apocryphal, but still revealing story tells of a desperate Lugosi receiving a lucrative offer for a show in Las Vegas—but only if Boris Karloff would appear on the same bill. Lugosi is said to have implored Karloff to join him, and Karloff is said to have refused. Dracula, by the mid-fifties, was distinctly the second banana in the Frankenstein-Dracula routine. Fifties horror was relentlessly right-brained and technology-obsessed; only rarely was an out-and-out supernatural theme exploited.

As an exemplar of the cobweb-retro style, Lugosi was long discarded by the major studios, working, when he could, in the lowest of low-budget films, often produced in a section of Hollywood known as Gower's Gulch. One of his last pictures—it was in fact his last speaking part in a film—was Edward D. Wood's *Bride of the Monster* (1955), in which a plot was concocted to blend the old Lugosi persona with an up-to-date atomic monster gimmick. The film failed to revive his career, for reasons unrelated to the film. During production, actor Paul Marco had to drive Lugosi home during a break. Lugosi was, in fact, the cause of the break—he needed to take his "medicine." In Lugosi's apartment, dominated by a huge oil painting of the actor at the height of his career in the thirties, he told Marco apologetically, "You're not going to like this, Paul. It's not very nice to watch, but I have to have my medicine."

> Directly in front of me there was a walk-in closet, and Bela pulled back the drapes and I saw that it was like a small room. . . . Bela took an apron, and he wrapped it around himself very daintily and slowly tied a bow. And then he rolled his sleeves and washed his hands, took a clean towel from a drawer and wiped them dry. Then he opened the sterilizer and took out his hypodermic and his "medicine." This was all so dramatic, it was like I was in a daze, in a fog. This whole heartbreaking ceremony. . . .

On stage and screen, Bela Lugosi had presided over countless rituals of blood-penetration; now he penetrated his own veins in a private drama of surrender to an outside force. Today, a struggle with chemical dependency is almost de rigueur for a star who wants to stay in the public view; a perverse reward of addiction, recovery, and relapse is mountains of sustained press attention. Lugosi may have been ahead of his time. He fought and won his own battle against drugs in 1955, but a demon after exorcism is not likely to command a lot of interest. A comeback never materialized. His fourth wife, Lillian, had left him in 1954; he married for a fifth time after his drug rehabilitation. The final bride of Dracula was studio editing clerk named Hope Lininger who had been writing fan mail to Lugosi since the early thirties. But Lugosi was only a shell of his former self, and the marriage was far from a dream come true for the younger bride. The yearlong liaison was reportedly marked by jealousy and bickering, which ended with Lugosi's death at the age of seventy-two on August 16, 1956. He went to his grave shrouded in the cape of Dracula, a stunning bit of performance art that has yet to be rivaled in its poignant audacity.

Hope Lugosi gave a peculiar, bitter interview to the *National Enquirer* the year following her husband's death, boasting that it was she who frightened Dracula, criticizing his legendary, self-dramatizing manner ("He was always acting"), and stating that she planned to use his life-size portrait in oils as a dart board. She was no less critical of his fans ("all boys—no girls. They wear makeup and hang around funeral parlors").

Lugosi's acolytes would have to wait a few years, until the classic horror films were released to television, for a revival of interest in traditional monsters. Meanwhile, horror would eschew the crypt, featuring more tail fins than bat wings.

Although young people had always composed a large part of the audience for monster movies, the fifties saw teenagers become a market segment unto themselves. By 1958, the twelve-to-twenty-five age bracket had jumped from 62 percent to 72 percent of the moviegoing public. Films like *I Was a Teenage Werewolf* (1957) and *I Was a Teenage Frankenstein* (1958) were exercises in pure demographic marketing; the producer, Herman Cohen, came up with the titles and ad campaigns before the pictures were even scripted. *Teenage Werewolf* took the *Rebel Without a Cause* formula and turned it supernatural; Tony, a troubled teenager (played by Michael Landon in his first film role), is treated by a psychiatrist, ostensibly to help him curb his aggression. In keeping with the best theories of Dr. Fredric Wertham, Tony's shrink knows that there is a fine line between adolescent and animal, and pushes Tony over the line with hypnotism and drugs. Producer Cohen perversely

Bela Lugosi: the final coffin (1956). *(Courtesy of Ronald V. Borst / Hollywood Movie Posters)*

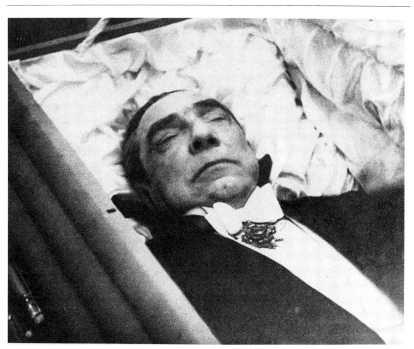

defended the story on grounds of psychiatric hygiene, quoting a California doctor's contention that horror movies were "self administered psychiatric therapy for America's adolescents." Cohen's teenage monsters were always made that way by evil adults, and the producer's mental-health defense contained a barely concealed rebuke to parents and authority figures: if they'd been doing their jobs, the movie companies wouldn't have to be providing therapy for their kids.

Cohen's films, which included *Blood of Dracula* (1958) and *Horrors of the Black Museum* (1959), were released by American International Pictures, a studio that specialized in low-budget, high-profit genre pictures. AIP also launched the Hollywood career of Roger Corman, the legendary "King of B-Pictures," who produced money-spinning films on almost insanely constricted schedules. *A Bucket of Blood* (1959) and *The Little Shop of Horrors* (1960), both horror spoofs, pushed his resources to the limit: each was produced for under $50,000 in five and two days, respectively.

The most extravagant shock-showman to emerge during this period was without doubt William Castle, who patterned his career aspirations after P. T. Barnum and Dr. Caligari, raising carny-creepy ballyhoo to the level of self-parody, and beyond. Born William Schloss in New York City, Castle as a boy wet his pants during the second act of Crane Wilbur's *The Monster* on Broadway. But a few years later he was ready for another try. "When I was thirteen years old, in 1927, I bought a balcony seat with $1.10 I had taken from my sister's purse, eager to see the play *Dracula* starring Bela Lugosi," Castle wrote in his memoirs. Mesmerized, he returned almost nightly for two weeks. "I sat in the balcony and listened to the frightened audiences scream. Soon I was no longer watching the play; I had more fun watching the audiences."

Castle's keen appreciation of the audience's sense of involvement served him well. While working in summer stock in Stony Creek, Connecticut, in 1938, he outrageously faked a "Nazi" vandalism of the theatre to publicize one of the company members, a German actress who had declined an invitation from Adolf Hitler to attend a Munich art festival. The stunt received national attention and won Castle a job offer from Columbia Pictures. He worked obscurely but steadily for a number of years, and showed a special flair for directing low-budget mysteries. *Macabre* (1958) was Castle's turning point. The picture itself was not a big deal; it was a morbid beat-the-clock thriller about a man trying to save his daughter, whom he believes has been buried alive. To make the picture more salable, Castle had convinced Lloyd's of London to insure every person on earth for $1,000 against death by shock while watching the film. Though Castle considered the gimmick nothing but publicity, staid Lloyd's was more cautious, insisting on the exclusion of some people with preexisting conditions, as well as mid-film audience suicides.

Variety reported that total distribution of the "insurance policies" passed the 10 million mark. *Macabre* was a hit, after which Castle pictures no longer had premieres—they had "screamieres." Next followed *House on Haunted Hill* (1958), accompanied by an audience-involvement gimmick called "Emergo," consisting of a glowing skeleton that sailed out over the audience during an on-screen blackout. The real, if unintentional, spook in *House on Haunted Hill* is postwar affluence. An American microcosm of haves and have-nots assemble in a modern-ancient house, with a wealthy eccentric (Vincent Price) exerting a malign influence over the lives of his guests. Each has been offered a prize of $10,000 if he or she can survive the night. Each is given a loaded gun as a party favor. In order to claim their cash, the guests are subjected to grotesque apparitions, a bloody head in an overnight case, a cellar vat full of acid, etc. No indignity is too great—in boom-time fifties America, anything is endurable in the pursuit of financial reward.

Vincent Price, a previously versatile actor with occasional forays into horror, made the genre firmly his own with *House on Haunted Hill*. Price could bring an arch elegance to the most insipid goings-on, a talent perfectly suited to Castle's next outing, *The Tingler* (1959). When his character's wife insists that a certain marriage will take place only over her dead body, Price, pouring a drink, takes it all in stride. "A bit unorthodox," he says, "but not impossible." *The Tingler* was built around another sensational Castle gimmick, this one called "Percepto." The Tingler itself is an imaginary centipede-like creature believed to coalesce around the human spine in moments of overwhelming fear; only screaming can dispel it. A highly contrived plot involving a deaf-mute woman (who cannot scream) allows a mature Tingler to be removed from her corpse and loosed on the audience. At the critical juncture, the movie itself seems to jump its sprockets and break, the shadow of the Tingler projected on the screen as if it is crawling all over the projector. Vincent Price's voice instructs the audience to scream

Vincent Price emerged in the fifties as America's new prince of horror.
From *House on Haunted Hill* (1958). *(Courtesy of Ronald V. Borst / Hollywood
Movie Posters)*

for its life, and in the blackout that follows, "Percepto" takes over.

"Percepto" consisted of electric vibrators attached to the under-side of theatre seats that would "tingle" unsuspecting viewers. According to screenwriter Robb White, "We didn't want to buy thousands of vibrators without knowing whether they would really work out, so we scouted around until we found a theater in the Valley that was running *The Nun's Story*." That film was sched-uled to close on Sunday, with *The Tingler* opening the following day. "We got in a huge crew of people to spend the day attaching the vibrators to the seats. But that night, just at the most tragic moments of *The Nun's Story,* somebody touched the master switch and the seats began vibrating in wave after wave. There was abso-lute pandemonium!"

Castle's gimmicks were part of the larger Hollywood move-ment in the fifties toward expansive presentational modes that could compete with television. CinemaScope, 3-D, Cinerama, stereo-phonic sound, and even the short-lived process called Smell-o-Vision were included in this trend. Flying skeletons, buzzing seats, and hokey insurance policies had the additional effect of turning impersonal moviegoing into a ritual of participatory live theatre, an understandable lure in a decade marked by suburban isolation and personal alienation. Castle's ultimate gimmick, he once said, would be a total sensory immersion: "The audience would taste the fog drifting through a cemetery. They'd smell the freshly dug grave. They'd feel the touch of ghastly fingers." Horror gimmicks provided audiences with a needed sense of contact, engagement, and recognition. Even if the dominant sensation was gooseflesh, at least it was a feeling.

A striking characteristic of fifties horror is its ambivalence about the good life, and the tenuous nature of material security and social identity. In film after film, people have their personalities stolen, are trapped inside or driven screaming from their flimsy homes, so easily demolished by monsters or other forces. Military readi-ness reassures, but it also threatens total destruction at any moment. Everything is shock, sudden change, disorientation, and bug-eyed information overload. The world of commercial horror painted a compelling shadow-portrait of America after the war, semicons-ciously exploring fears so basic and raw that it's amazing they were processed in any form at all.

The recognition, however, is in retrospect. At the time, it was

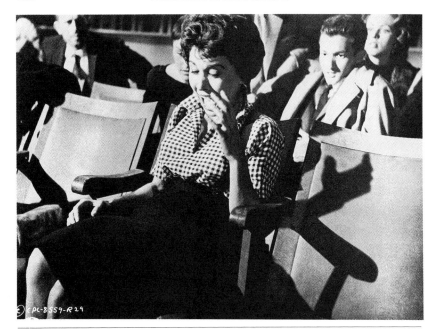

Audience participation: the shocks were palpable during *The Tingler* (1959).
(Courtesy of Ronald V. Borst / Hollywood Movie Posters)

the sunny side of the scream that received the most attention. In
1959, *Playboy* apprised its readers about the gathering momentum
of horror as a positive economic force: for nearly five years, monster movies had been the hottest thing in entertainment. Fifty-two
horror pictures—one a week—had been produced in 1957, seventy-five more in 1958, with a hundred planned for the 1959 season.

> If they are all actually produced, and there is no reason to imag-
> ine that they won't be, horror will account for over one third of
> all U.S. motion picture output. It will offer employment to three
> thousand men and women. It will use up 72,000 feet of film,
> reach one hundred million consumers (counting repeats), account
> for 150 hours of continuous entertainment, cost $10 million,
> and, unless the world ends, show a profit of $100 million. Which
> means, statistically at least, that horror is now one of the basic
> American commodities, like breakfast cereal or soap. In terms
> of finance, it is bigger business than the whole of hard-cover
> book publishing. In fact, if a single concern controlled all of the
> merchandise, that concern would be blue-chip.

"Thank God for the horror pictures," said the manager of a big drive-in theatre in San Fernando, California. "They've saved us. Before this kick we were thinking of shutting down two nights a week; now, with all the monster stuff, the place starts filling up at three o'clock. The kids go for it. The girls yell and hang on to the boys and sometimes you've really got to keep an eye on those cars . . ."

Chapter Nine

THE GRAVEYARD BASH

"DECORATE YOUR ROOM!
SURPRISE YOUR MOTHER!
CREATE YOUR VERY OWN CHAMBER OF HORRORS!"

*Advertisement by Aurora Plastics
for its line of movie-monster model kits (1962)*

HORROR AND HUMOR have been on intimate terms at least since the time of Elizabethan and Jacobean drama. Shakespeare's darkest tragedies were leavened with a gallows wit, and there are few examples of black comedy more mordant than Cyril Tourneur's *The Revenger's Tragedy* (1606). Produced shortly after London's plague-shuttered theatres had reopened, the play introduced a cynical protagonist, Vindice, who carries around the skull of his betrothed, dressing it up in women's finery as a horrid sex decoy that traps her killer. In its shifting moods, *The Revenger's Tragedy* demonstrates that the line between farce and tragedy is that flash point at which slapstick gets carried away into violence, or vice versa—the difference between *petit* Guignol and *grand*. Vindice's wisecracking asides and relentless morbidity defined sick humor almost three and a half centuries before the Crypt Keeper began his cackling commentaries over the revenge plots of E.C. Comics.

In 1958, horrid laughter and queasy comedy was showing up

TV's Cool Ghoul, Zacherley, enjoys an avalanche of "fang mail" at the height of his popularity. *(Photofest)*

everywhere. " 'Sick' was the magic word in American humor that season," recalled Albert Goldman in *Ladies and Gentlemen, Lenny Bruce!!* "Sick jokes and sick cartoons, sick singers . . . like knock-knock jokes and hula hoops that start with the kids, the subadolescents, and then spread like the measles." The sick sensibility is intimately related to the monster sensibility, and most of the "classic" sick jokes have a certain resonance with Hollywood horror motifs. One of the most famous sick jokes of all time—*"Can Johnny come out and play?" "But you know Johnny has no arms or legs." "That's okay—we want him to be home plate!"*—is almost pure Tod Browning, with a snickering glimmer of E.C. Comics thrown in to boot.

As Goldman elsewhere explained the phenomenon, "When sick humor erupted in the early Fifties, it came as a catharsis of the anger, fear and rebelliousness brought to a boil during the McCarthy era. No mere fad, the new humor revealed the great depth and breadth of the need to sound off and purge the soul of perilous emotion." In Goldman's analysis, the sick style was not so much intentional cruelty as a sounding off against the widening gap between painful social realities and the pious evasions of mass culture.

The comedian Lenny Bruce made an indelible mark on monster mania when he began injecting a Lugosi/Dracula shtick into his routines. In one famous bit, "Beautiful Transylvania," Bruce may have contributed nearly as much to the cultural evolution of the Dracula image as did Bela Lugosi himself:

> DRACULA *[to Bela Jr.]:* Alright, shut up and dr-r-rink your blood. And bite Momma goodnight. You hear me? Don bug us no more! Go to the next room and eat your blackboard and crayons. And pr-r-ractice on sister's neck.

> MRS. DRACULA *[nagging Jewish wife]:* Sure, that's a nice vay to talk to the child! Isn't it? Practice on sister's neck! That's all you think about, you degenerate you! Aghh! I can't stand to look at you any more! Phah! You know vat it means ven a woman can't stand to look at a man any more? Our knot is all gone, Bela. The stake is burned out. You Fancy Dan vit the vaseline in the hair, dirtying up the pillowcases . . .

> DRACULA: Go ahead. Go off by yourself, you freak! *Now,* you hear? Ve are going into the next room now, and I don't vant to be disturbed.

MRS. DRACULA: Sure, you're going to get high! You're gonna smoke some shit, some of those crazy zigarettes again, and eat up the whole icebox!

DRACULA *[a beaten old Jewish man]:* I'm not getting high—a coupla pills . . . Vy don't you leave me alone?

MRS. DRACULA: Sure, you stupid pimp, you—*phah! [to Bela Jr.]* You like vat your daddy does for a living? He sucks people on the neck. Hm hm! You like dat?

In a stroke, Lenny Bruce forever subverted the classic tuxedoed vampire. (A huge Dracula puppet was part of the stage backdrop for Julian Barry's play *Lenny,* produced on Broadway in 1971.) Other Jewish comedians would begin to do Lugosi impersonations and similar routines, with the end result being a standard Dracula impression that is vocally closer to Jackie Mason than to Bela Lugosi. It is nonetheless instantly "recognized" as Lugosi.

The iconoclastic worldview of the sick comics overlapped with that of the Beat writers. Jack Kerouac, for instance, was an inveterate Dracula fan, and had created an homage to the Lugosi-style of neck-biter in his 1959 novel *Dr. Sax.* Count Condu ("impeccably dressed, just-risen from the coff of eve, the Satin Doombox with its Spenglerian metamophosed scravenings on the lid") is one of many fantastic beings who inhabit the dream-life of Lowell, Massachusetts, Kerouac's real hometown as well as the locale of the novel. Dan Talbot, who ran the New Yorker Film Society, knew of the writer's interest in the undead, and invited Kerouac to prepare the program notes for the society's screening of *Nosferatu* in 1960. The problem was, "Jack was drinking so heavily by that time it was useless to try to screen the film for him in the evening." After a few frustrating tries, Talbot finally arranged a Sunday-morning showing. Just as it had foiled Nosferatu himself, sunlight dispelled Kerouac's own thirsty demon, but only temporarily.

One night in 1958, a woman described by *The Saturday Evening Post* as "one of Philadelphia's mainline dowagers" declined an invitation to bridge. The reason? It would interfere with her watching that week's installment of "Shock Theater," a package of fifty-two vintage Universal horror films just sold to television stations across the country. The hostess, however, had anticipated her invitee's response. "But my dear," she said, "of course you can come. Naturally we plan to stop playing when the program starts."

The program, when it started, was more than just an old film. The Philadelphia broadcast was hosted by a cadaverous-looking character in an undertaker's frock coat. He had hollow cheeks, a hollow laugh, darkly circled eyes, and lips that seemed to be sewn together like a shrunken head's. His name was "Roland"—accent on the second syllable, please.

Roland was, in real life, John Zacherle, a thirty-eight-year-old amateur theatre enthusiast who had never seen any of the classic horror pictures before he was called upon to host them. Given a choice, he would rather have spent his time tending his roses (he had won some prizes), but now, it seemed, Zacherle was going to spend his life pushing up daisies.

Four years earlier, of course, Vampira had pioneered the fine art of presenting horror films on television, but she was a localized phenomenon in Los Angeles and had no direct imitators. "Shock Theater" provided a whole new impetus for corn-on-the-macabre. Monsters of ceremonies began popping up independently on dozens of local stations throughout America.

"Roland" had his genesis on a daytime Western series called "Action in the Afternoon," produced in Philadelphia. Zacherle had been tapped to play a traveling undertaker who canvases the old West, profiting in the wake of all the bloody gunslinging. Ed White, a producer at WPLJ-TV, remembered the character and contacted Zacherle when the station acquired the "Shock" package. White scripted most of Roland's preternatural patter. The character emerged as a kind of necrophilic Soupy Sales, whose sidekicks included his vampire wife My Dear (represented by a wooden stake protruding from a dwarf-sized coffin) and Gasport, an unseen dead thing in a canvas sack. While Zacherle seemed to chew the scenery with ghoulish inspiration, he worked without specific role models— unlike Lenny Bruce, he had almost no previous familiarity with the classic horror icons.

"Shock Theater" was the inaugural event of Monster Culture, a phenomenon of horror-movie hoopla that began in the late fifties and continued into the mid-sixties. In Monster Culture, the participatory rituals surrounding the movies were every bit as important as the films themselves. The rites included the shared witnessing of the antics of horror hosts; an explosion of fan magazines that were read, reread, and traded among the cognoscenti; and even the creation of plastic model effigies. Most important, monsters materialized in the living room for the first time—not just reflected light in the movie theatres, but now a light *source,* a glowing electronic fireplace around which a generation could huddle and shudder and share.

In Philadelphia, Roland was successful beyond imagination. The station invited fans to attend an open house to meet "the Cool Ghoul"; a few hundred were expected, but a stampede of 13,000 showed up. John Zacherle moved up to New York's CBS affiliate, WOR-TV, dropping the name Roland in favor of a slight modification of his own name—Zacherley. One fan later reminisced about the Zacherley craze to *New York* magazine in 1978: "My God, I belonged to his fan club," recalled writer Peter Occhiogrosso. "I had an *operating table* in my basement. And test tubes, the whole thing. All the kids used to draw pictures of hypodermic needles and nooses in our school notebooks. The nuns actually confiscated my recipe for spider soup! It was against the Catholic doctrine. And every Sunday the monsignor got up on the pulpit and preached of the evils of 'Shock Theater.' We didn't care."

Zacherley also provided one of the earliest links between pop music and the macabre. Light years before Alice Cooper, Zacherley was a Halloween fixture of television's "American Bandstand." His novelty single "Dinner with Drac" was a top-ten hit in March 1958. (There was a certain fashion for bizarre and uncategorizable pop recordings around this time; other examples included "Flying Purple People Eater" and "Witch Doctor.") "Dinner with Drac" was basically a series of grisly limericks recited to a jazz guitar accompaniment. Dick Clark, the host of "American Bandstand," recalled the primitive studio techniques when he dropped in on the recording. "If they wanted echo they had to wait until everyone in the building went home, then they'd run a set of speakers down the hall and stick them in the john with a microphone."

Zacherley had the highest national visibility of any of the horror hosts, but he had plenty of company. WABC-TV in New York had a faceless host known only as "The Voice." Fort Worth was home to Gorgon, New Orleans to Morgus. San Franciscans left their hearts at Terrence's doorstep. In Chicago it was Marvin. In Baltimore, the airwaves lit up with Dr. Lucifer. Ghoulardi took Cleveland.

The horror hosts were shamans, storytellers, threshold figures, anarchists, deconstructionists before their time. In a 1991 interview, John Zacherle remembered the first time he actually became part of a movie, instead of being content to simply introduce it. "It was *The Black Cat*, with Boris Karloff and Bela Lugosi. There was a scene with a group of devil worshippers witnessing a rite. We decided to superimpose a shot of me in there with the group, making faces at the camera." The fans loved it. All across America, horror hosts started interrupting and intercutting the old features with irreverent commentary and outrageous film clips. The films winked at you, and you winked back. Kids were making monsters their own.

In the late 1940s, as an awareness of the nuclear age was dawning, Forrest J Ackerman, arguably the country's leading collector and fan of science-fiction, fantasy, and horror publications and memorabilia, got a call from the Los Angeles Public Library, which needed some cataloging assistance. Futuristic technology, wars in outer space, ghost stories, and Gothic romances had somehow all been occupying the same overcrowded niche, a section the library had for years called simply "Improbabilia." "Right next to a serious book about going to the moon would be *Dracula*," Ackerman remembered. "They thought rocket ships were just as improbable as vampires." Ackerman suggested that they consider everything looking toward the past—magic, wizards, sorcery, werewolves, etc., as the territory of fantasy, with a subcategory of horror, and everything forward-looking—space travel, extraterrestrials, and the like—as science fiction. While Ackerman could distinguish between genres, he collected omnivorously in them all. As a boy growing up in California, he corresponded with Carl Laemmle, Sr., who supplied him with all the posters, press books, and stills from Universal's classic horror and fantasy pictures.

Ackerman also worked as an agent, and in the late 1950s conducted some business with James Warren, a twenty-six-year-old east coast publisher. Warren (formerly Hymie Taubman of South Philadelphia), like so many young men of his generation, was starstruck by Hugh Hefner and his expanding Playboy empire. Warren founded his own men's entertainment magazine, *After Hours*,

Famous Monsters of Filmland **editor Forrest J Ackerman in his memora-bilia-filled "Ackermansion."** *(Courtesy of Ronald V. Borst / Hollywood Movie Posters)*

which published black-and-white cheesecake photos surrounded with articles by Ackerman's science-fiction writer clients, and pun-filled photo features by Ackerman himself that drew on his vast collection of fantasy film stills. Inspired by a special issue of a French film magazine that had been devoted to monsters, and encouraged by the volume of favorable mail *After Hours* had received on the Ackerman monster feature ("Scream-o-Scope is Here!"), they decided to create a one-shot publication first proposed as Wonder-ama. Warren had second thoughts about the title, and renamed it *Fantastic Monsters of Filmland.* The project's eventual distributor insisted on one final modification. Warren called Ackerman and told him, "You are about to become the editor of a magazine called *Famous Monsters of Filmland."* Ackerman recalled his reply: "Does that mean I'm going to have to put my name on it?"

Warren told Ackerman he'd be flying to Los Angeles to discuss the deal. "Actually," remembered Ackerman, "I found out later that he was so broke he took a Greyhound bus to Las Vegas, and then flew into L.A. on the New York plane." Gloria Steinem, who worked briefly for Warren as an office assistant in 1960, recalled him as "a great operator. We used to kid him about it—being a Sammy Glick–type character—you know, great big cuff links. I

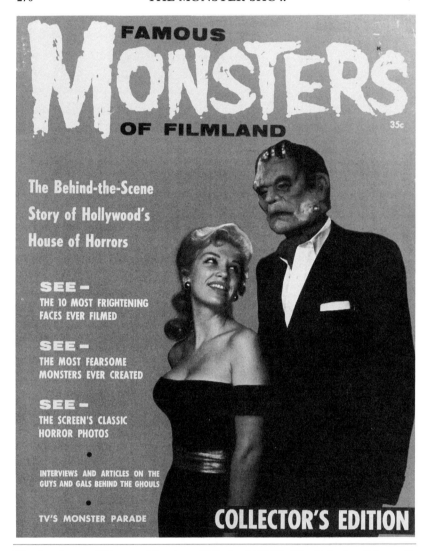

The first issue of *Famous Monsters of Filmland* (1958). The "playboy" beneath the mask is publisher James Warren. *(Courtesy of Ronald V. Borst / Holly-wood Movie Posters)*

don't know if it's true, but it's entered into the apocrypha of James Warren that he used to do things like ride around in the summer with the windows rolled up so people would think he had air conditioning."

Warren had such a salesman's flair that he found it unnecessary to solicit advertising. The sole advertiser was the publisher itself.

In the guise of the mail-order Captain Company, Warren Publications sold everything from rubber monster masks to eight-millimeter film clips to army-surplus high-altitude suits to real pet monkeys. A hundred and fifty thousand copies of the first issue of *Famous Monsters* were printed, featuring a Hefneresque cover photo: Warren himself in a green Frankenstein mask, the neck bolts wrapped in a dapper ascot. To his arm clung a bosomy blonde in a strapless dress.

Despite a raging east-coast blizzard on its February 27, 1958, publication date, the magazine was an immediate hit, selling out 90 percent of its print run and generating dozens of fan letters a day.

"I used to get five hundred letters a month during the heyday of *Famous Monsters*," said Ackerman. "My dear mother, who made it to the age of ninety-three, used to open and sort out the nonsense from the serious inquiries." One item that came in the mail was a single-page story called "The Killers" from a fourteen-year-old reader in Maine named Steve King. "At that point he was basically lifting story ideas from old copies of E.C. Comics and trying to convince himself that they were original."

Stephen King, born in 1947 in Portland, Maine, first encountered weird fiction as a kind of eerie gift from the father who had deserted him. Donald King—he had been born Spansky, but used the alias Pollack before legally coronating himself—was rather like the missing father in Tennessee Williams' *The Glass Menagerie* (a traveling Electrolux salesman "who fell in love with long distance"). One day in 1949, Donald told his family he was going out for a pack of cigarettes. He never returned. The younger King's first tangible connection with his father came when he discovered a stash of paperback books in the attic. His father, it appeared, was fond of pulp fiction, especially horror and science fiction. Along with the books were some unpublished manuscripts of his own, and rejection slips from men's magazines. At about the age of twelve, Stephen began submitting his own stories to the science-fiction pulps, as well as to *Famous Monsters*. He would have to wait until he was twenty for his first professional sale. Interestingly enough, the "lost-father" motif would recur frequently in his published work.

Another Steve, this one from Scottsdale, Arizona, found a major inspiration in *Famous Monsters*. Steven Spielberg's mother, Leah Adler, recalled the young *Famous Monsters* reader in a 1986 interview. "When he was growing up, I didn't know he was a genius. Frankly, I didn't know what the hell he was." Young Steven, according to his mother, was not cuddly. "What he was was scary. When Steven woke up from a nap, I shook." Not a good student ("Once, his teacher told me he was special—and I wondered how she meant it"), Spielberg drew a precocious energy from Monster Culture, and created numerous spectacular horror effects at home. His mother remembered him standing outside his sisters' windows in the dead of night, howling, "I am the moon. I am the moon." "They're still scared of the moon," she said. "And once he cut off the head of one of [his sister] Nancy's dolls and served it to her on a bed of lettuce."

Perhaps the most spectacular stunt the director's mother recalled might best be titled "The Cabinets of Mrs. Spielberg." In order to create the illusion of horrible ooze dripping from his mother's cupboards for a super-eight movie, he convinced his mom to pressure-cook thirty cans of cherries until they exploded all over the room.

In 1987, Spielberg himself recalled that *Famous Monsters* "sent me, as a youngster, scurrying for my father's eight millimeter home movie camera, my three younger sisters in tow, and seventeen rolls of dampened pastel blue toilet paper that I needed to wrap them up into mummies, filming until the toilet mâché dried and flaked all over my mom's shag rug. I credit Forry with much needed inspiration, and also blame him for all the punishment I received in ruining half the house I grew up in."

Joe Dante, a director who would make significant contributions to the genre with *The Howling* and the enormously popular Spielberg-produced *Gremlins,* was another product of *Famous Monsters.* "We all remember where we were when certain momentous things happened—where we were when Kennedy was shot, the moon landing, that kind of thing. Well, I remember the day, though not the date, when I found my first copy of *Famous Monsters.* It was in a Safeway supermarket in Parsippany, New Jersey. And here on the stand was this one-shot magazine printed on a sort of rotogravure paper. And it was all about monsters."

Dante, who was about eleven years old at the time, "lived in a kind of a vacuum. My friends and I went to see these movies and liked them, but we thought of ourselves as a little closed society. There wasn't anyone else out there interested in this sort of thing, or so we thought.

"But here, all of a sudden, was this magazine that was a validation that there were other people out there like us. It was written in a style geared to eleven- and twelve-year-old kids, but in a way it fostered a kind of serious film history study. It talked about films we hadn't seen, and it made them sound very exciting and mysterious. I remember going to the school library and getting all the film books out and trying to find any mention of *Frankenstein* or *Dracula,* and there weren't any—the films weren't considered worth studying. How times have changed."

Dante bought "probably eight or nine copies" of that same first issue of *Famous Monsters* over the next several months—they would regularly be confiscated by teachers or camp counselors. "I remember a counselor tearing one in half because it was 'trash.' I remember a school librarian confiscating one, again because it was 'trash.' " Dante's experience was hardly unique; given the frequency of anecdotes involving copies of *Famous Monsters* being shredded by authority figures—it amounts to nearly a primal scene for a generation—one can only conclude that parents and teachers artificially boosted newsstand sales, inadvertently guaranteeing the magazine's success.

Like almost every kid who read *Famous Monsters,* Joe Dante yearned for the recognition of having his name in print. The most obvious venue was the magazine's letter section, called "Fang Mail." "I fruitlessly wrote letters for a couple of years about *anything*— movies I'd seen, movies I hadn't seen, movies I'd made up, what monsters were really thinking, whatever. And none of them ever got published." He then tried to impress by sheer weight of verbiage. "I decided to write about the fifty best horror movies I ever saw, and that didn't get published. So I decided to write about the fifty *worst* horror movies I ever saw, and sent that in. And then one day I got this huge envelope in the mail and inside was *Famous Monsters,* only my letter is now a big *article,* completely rewritten and using words I didn't even understand. But now it isn't just the fifty worst horror movies I've ever seen, it's the fifty worst horror movies ever made. Now some of them, obviously, I hadn't seen, I just put them down because I couldn't come up with fifty.

"It was amazing. I couldn't believe it. It was the greatest thing that ever happened. I existed. I existed so much that Forrest J Ackerman pointed his finger at me from Hollywood and said, 'You are worth having your name and your writing in this magazine.' "

"I had the attention of malleable minds when, I guess, they needed a sort of father figure," recalled Ackerman. "Here I was, a grown man who didn't frown on their interests, and whom their parents could be sure was not going to encourage them to drink or to dope."

Ackerman was, and is, a master of the atrocious pun, and from its inception *Famous Monsters* was filled with wordplay and double meaning. A female freak was a "hunchback, notorious dame." A letters column was called "Reader's Die-Jest." There were even puns on top of puns. The "Ackermonster" (who lived in the "Ackermansion," in "Horrorwood, Karloffornia") had many playful names for himself, prominent among them "Dr. Ackula." This generated a second level of punning, a form of communication incomprehensible to the uninitiated—e.g., an editor's column called "Inside Darkest Ackula." The idiosyncratic and double-jointed diction convinced a large number of aspiring young writers that, hey, language was *fun*—a lesson transmitted all too rarely in the course of a conventional American education. The hidden and secondary meanings gave an encounter with *Famous Monsters* the sense of belonging to a secret society, with access to all manner of esoteric, elevating lore.

A quantum leap in monster consciousness occurred in the fall of 1962, when Aurora Plastics of Hempstead, Long Island, introduced a new line of plastic model kits aimed at young male hobbyists. They were a far cry from the replicas of fighter planes and ships that dominated the hobby-kit market; they were, instead, rigid plastic simulacra of the Wolf Man, Frankenstein's monster, and Dracula, their images officially licensed by Universal Pictures. They stood about nine inches high, while ads blatantly exaggerated their height to a foot. There were few complaints. If monsters weren't entitled to be bigger than life, then what was? Like glowering leprechauns, they soon stood guard at the bedrooms of thousands upon thousands of baby boomers. "Decorate your room! Surprise your mother!" trumpeted a full-color, full-page advertisement laid out like a circus poster in *Boy's Life,* the official publication of the Boy Scouts of America. In his 1975 novel *'Salem's Lot,* Stephen King's young protagonist Mark Petrie assembles these same model kits in his room while outside, real vampires decimate the town. The religio-mythic overtones are not concealed: "Mark glued the Frankenstein monster's left arm into the shoulder socket. It was a specially treated Aurora model that glowed in the dark, just like the plastic Jesus he had gotten for memorizing all of the 119th Psalm in Sunday school class."

Monsters have traditionally been part of adolescent initiation rituals, and the large-scale fascination with monsters in the early 1960s is recognizably a variation of age-old puberty rites involving horrifying masks and other monstrous trappings. In a 1975 essay, "Monster Movies and Rites of Initiation," commentator Walter Evans pinpointed some of the connections:

> Most of the definitive elements of premodern societies' initiation rites also function as definitive elements in the monster movie formula. Fascination with the distant past; the prominence of superstition or archaic religion; the focus on mythic beings who perform an initiatory function; the complementary focus on innocent and untested young people who are transformed by contact with these beings; the symbolic deaths and rebirths; the

---

In the shadow of Beatlemania, monsters provided another Cold War craze for baby boomers, as reflected in this 1964 cartoon. *(Copyright © by Gahan Wilson; reprinted by permission)*

GAHAN WILSON

"Charlie? <u>Forget</u> about the Beatles!"

A 1962 advertisement for the plastic model kits that gave the Cold War generation a "hands–on" experiment in horror. *(The Library of Congress)*

use of thunder, darkness and other motifs in elaborate scenarios designed to create terror; the emphasis on ritual passing on of archaic lore by learned elders; these are only some of the most important of numerous formulaic elements which point to the monster movies' crucial function in the vital process of initiation which modern American adolescents require and demand no less than their brothers and sisters of premodern societies.

Easily identifiable adolescent anxieties lurked barely concealed beneath the surface of the *Boy's Life* advertisement. As Evans noted in an earlier essay, "Monster Movies: A Sexual Theory," Hollywood's horror icons have distinct affinities "with two central features of adolescent sexuality, masturbation and menstruation. From time immemorial underground lore has asserted that masturbation leads to feeblemindedness or mental derangement: the monster's transformation is generally associated with madness; scientists are generally secretive recluses whose private experiments on the human body have driven them mad." The widespread, though nonsensical, belief that masturbation weakens the spine may account for "the army of feebleminded hunchbacks which pervades the formula."

Most of the pubescent boys for whom the monster models were intended were no doubt conducting private, one-fisted physical experiments, and, while the official Scouts' handbook frowned upon masturbation, the *Boy's Life* ad presented a subliminal tease: Dracula, in his typical mesmeric stance, strokes and pulls on the air; the Frankenstein monster is caught in a startled, "hands-off" pose, and the Wolf Man's hair-sprouting palms hardly require comment. Portentous revelations of "the secrets of life," disturbing physical transformations, nocturnal visitations/emissions, and moon-driven "curses" were all part of the appeal of Monster Culture to young Americans tottering on puberty's abyss. (Monster-boomer Stephen King would capture the public imagination in a big way with his novel *Carrie* (1974), a Gothic fairy tale about menstrual initiation gone haywire.)

There was, however, another abyss that threatened childhood in October of 1962, one that made movie monsters seem positively cuddly by comparison. Aurora Plastics' ad campaign, and the appearance of its products in stores all over America, coincided precisely with the apocalyptic shadow of the Cuban missile crisis.

The thirteen-day event was in itself a traumatic rite of passage for millions of children, adolescents, and young adults. In their book *No Reason to Talk About It,* David S. Greenwald and Steven J. Zeitlin note that parents of the period may have intensified their children's anxieties by not discussing the realities of the nuclear threat. Atomic annihilation joined sex as one of the adult world's dirty secrets. On the other hand, parents who shared their own terror didn't help things much. This author recalls the mother of a friend who, setting out the toast, told her children bluntly to "have a good day—it may be our last."

Educator Robert K. Musil, writing in *The Bulletin of the Atomic Scientists* in 1982, recalled the atmosphere of dread, the "duck-and-cover drills, and experienced an early disillusionment with, even disdain for, authority. In many ways, the styles and explosions of the 1960s were born in those dark, subterranean high-school corridors, where we decided that our elders were indeed unreliable, perhaps even insane."

If, as many commentators contend, meaningful initiation rites were already dysfunctional in postwar America, the Cuban missile crisis suggested that the adult world might be going one step further, into the ultimate anti-initiation of planetary extinction. The atmosphere was uncanny, even mythic: Saturn himself had never threatened to devour quite so many children.

Monsters—as this writer will personally attest—provided an element of reassurance. They were transcendent resurrection figures, beings who couldn't die. The traditional monsters were perversely Christlike (Dracula's most characteristic pose, with outstretched cape, is a blatant cruciform), offering an image of survival, however distorted or grotesque. And the more recent monsters did more than survive the Bomb; like Godzilla (and his many clones and cohorts), they were usually created by it.

Bobby Pickett grew up in Somerville, Massachusetts, where his father, Charles Pickett, operated a chain of movie theatres. As a child his father permitted him to press the button that alerted the projectionist to begin the show. In a 1991 interview, he remembered seeing *Dracula* and *Frankenstein* in one of his father's theatres when they were revived theatrically in the late 1940s. He was hooked.

"Other guys carried around pictures of their girlfriends in their wallets," Pickett recalled. "I had pictures of Boris Karloff and Bela Lugosi."

Following a stint in the signal corps in Korea, Pickett returned to the States and began to dabble in performance. For an amateur talent contest at an Irish-American club in Everett, Massachusetts, he prepared by downing a few vodkas in the bathroom, then walked away with a $25 first prize for his interpretation of the pop song "Little Darlin'," with its monologue section rendered in a fairly uncanny approximation of the voice of Boris Karloff.

Pickett migrated to California with some hometown musician friends, but tried himself to break into acting. When his agent died only two weeks after signing him, Pickett approached his songwriter friend Leonard Capizzi about producing a novelty song based on the Karloff voice. They wrote the song in a couple of hours and did a demo tape on an old Wollensak recorder. Bobby's first title was "Monster Twist." Lenny wanted to call it "Monster Mashed Potato," in homage to another recent dance craze. When they played the tape for the producer Gary Paxton, he suggested a further embellishment: "Mean Monster Mashed Potato." Fortunately, it was finally decided that less might be more.

"Monster Mash" by Bobby "Boris" Pickett and the Crypt-Kickers was produced by Paxton in a Hollywood recording studio that had been vacated moments earlier by "a guy named Herb Alpert." Bobby recalled that the song was done in one take with one pickup. "Cauldron" sounds were created by someone blowing into a glass of water through a straw. Hardware-store chains, dragged over a plywood board, effectively evoked a monster in shackles.

The record was flatly turned down by four major labels. Paxton had a thousand copies privately pressed and delivered them in person to radio stations up and down the California coast.

"Monster Mash" astonished everyone in the competitive, payola-ridden recording business by shooting out of nowhere by word of mouth to the top of the charts. London Records, which had initially turned it down, offered a contract, and an album was released by Garpax.★ It held *Billboard*'s number-one spot for two weeks in October 1962. Throughout the Cuban nuclear threat, America's favorite pop song celebrated a mad scientist who presided over a dance of death.

Pickett had the thrill of his life when Boris Karloff himself performed the song on the popular television music show "Shindig."

★In point of fact, there were two *Monster Mash* albums, one by Bobby Pickett on Garpax and one by John Zacherle on the Cameo label.

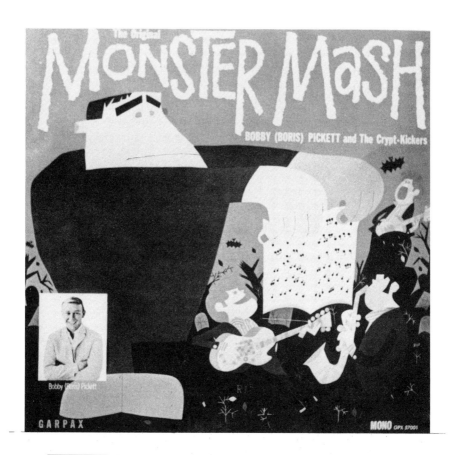

Right: Bobby "Boris" Pickett and a pair of alternate identities. *Above:* the original *Monster Mash* album. *(Courtesy of Stuart Hersh Entertainment and Bobby Pickett)*

Monster energy followed Pickett around; when he did a straight dramatic part on an episode of "Dr. Kildare," the show's star, Richard Chamberlain, walked around the set doing the Karloff voice for days. And one of the more interesting cultural validations of "Monster Mash" came from the White House. Having received a copy of the record, Jacqueline Kennedy's secretary wrote a thank-you note to Pickett—Caroline Kennedy, it seemed, was especially fond of monsters.

Thirteen months later, Jackie refused to change her blood-soaked dress in Dallas: "Let them see the horror," she said. Although she intended no larger significance than the immediate tragedy, America's preoccupation with the morbid and grotesque continued to escalate. We were a "sick" society, the pundits lectured endlessly. Following Cuba and the Kennedy assassination, the internalized image of a distinctly dysfunctional family/society—the nation of corpses we almost became—began slouching its way toward cultural expression.

Two of the major television networks decided, virtually simultaneously, that America was ready for a prime-time series in which the postnuclear family would finally face the death mask in the mirror—and laugh. On February 15, 1964, the television page of *The New York Times* announced to its readers the news: MONSTERS TO BE JUST PLAIN FOLKS. Joseph Connelly and Bob Mosher, the producers of "Leave It to Beaver," unveiled their plans for "The Munsters" on CBS. The series would present an all-American family whose members were unaware that they were monsters. "They know that they're being stared at," explained Connelly, "but they think it's because they're too fat." The ABC series was to be called "The Addams Family," a live-action version of Charles Addams' cartoons, a popular fixture in *The New Yorker* since their introduction in the war-clouded days of the late 1930s.

The shows didn't exactly mirror each other; they were more like negative and positive versions of the same delirium. The Munsters' household consisted of "real" monsters (with makeups based on the old Universal horror films), but they acted like a typical television sitcom family. Fred Gwynne played Herman Munster, a stand-in for Karloff's Frankenstein monster. His wife Lily was a shrouded vampire, played by the former screen siren Yvonne DeCarlo. Herman's father-in-law, Grandpa Munster (the family name, of course, makes no sense for an in-law, undead or not), was an over-the-hill Dracula portrayed by Al Lewis in a

borscht-belt style, completing the comic stroke begun by Lenny
Bruce. The Addams clan, by contrast, was comprised of real human
beings who were morbidly eccentric. (They did, however, keep a
supernaturally disembodied hand named Thing as a kind of pet or
servant.) John Astin and Carolyn Jones headed the cast as Gomez
and Morticia, names concocted by Charles Addams himself.

The general level of critical reception for the shows was not
high. *Variety* complained that the magic of Charles Addams' cartoons "lies in what is left unsaid (thus enabling the viewer to compound the macabre impact after digesting the Addams one-liners)."
By contrast, "the television version literally throws the book at
the audience. It's as though they're not quite sure whether the
viewer is going to get it, so it's laid on, and on and on." The New
York *Daily News* was similarly skeptical. "Is the television public
ready for The Addams Family? We don't think so. The ABC series
. . . offers viewers the most bizarre family this side of an halluci-
nation. The grouping makes The Beverly Hillbillies seem positively stuffy."

"The Munsters" was also widely panned, but both monster-
family shows achieved respectable ratings and were renewed for
second seasons. American families apparently enjoyed beholding
their image in the television glass, however darkly. Children
responded to the image of supremely dysfunctional families presided over by silly-threatening parents. Morticia Addams and Lily
Munster stirred together sexuality, housewifery, and death. The
overtones of sex and death, especially on "The Addams Family,"
were presented with a bluntness unimaginable outside of psychoanalysis. Despite the canned laughter, both families were generated out of death or death obsessions. The Munsters were literally
walking corpses; Herman was a stitched-together automaton who
had married into a family of vampires. Morticia Addams' pale
deathliness was presented over and over again as an aphrodisiac
for her ardent, necrophilic husband Gomez.

For some odd reason, network censors allowed the ghouls to
get away with sexual innuendo that would have been quickly scis-
sored elsewhere. "Gomez and Morticia were the first married couple on television who seemed actually to have a sex life," recalled
John Astin. "I had proposed that their romance be unceasing and
in the grand manner, that the slightest look or key word send
Gomez into raptures." Despite the heavy breathing, Addams Family
historian Stephen Cox has noted that it was the rival network's

Dead families: "The Munsters" *(left)* and "The Addams Family" *(below)* provided a bizarre cultural reflection from 1964 to 1966. *(Right: Photofest)*

horror couple, Herman and Lily, who were actually shown together in the same bed, previously an unchallengeable television taboo. Even little Eddie Munster's bed habits were tinged with horror. "Go to sleep—and don't forget to close the lid!" Herman Munster would remind him. (In retrospect, the missile-crisis admonition "Have a good day, children—it may be our last" would have been a perfect line for Morticia Addams.)

The series both ran two years, and were both announced and canceled within weeks of each other. The story lines were often remarkably similar—each series, for example, featured episodes in which the children were believed to have turned into chimpanzees, in which the families built robots, and parallel plots that turned on spacemen, beatniks, and amnesia.

One of the leading toy manufacturers, Remco Industries, marketed tie-in figurines of characters from both "The Addams Family" and "The Munsters," and found it was not necessary to do much paid advertising. The shows themselves proved promotion enough. *The New York Times* reported Remco's marketing research figures in late summer 1964, which anticipated that "The Munsters" would generate 982 million viewer impressions in its first year, with "The Addams Family" predicted to break the one billion point.

Remco claimed that its monster-related products had quadrupled in business during the previous year, while its line of educational science kits had languished. Other toy companies were not so sanguine. Mattel, Inc., one of the giants in the field, expressed skepticism and predicted that the fad would pass. "Children want toys which have play value and which last," said a Mattel spokesman. Little did he know.

Look magazine ran a cover story on the monster phenomenon, happily reporting that "Toyland '64 looks like a charnel house with all its ghoulish delights. There are monster models and monster games, monster dolls and all manner of monstrous cards, rings, by-the-number paint sets, costumes and masks. A battery-powered Frankenstein monster grunts, thrashes about, then drops his trousers and blushes in striped shorts. Little girls cut out ragged dresses for a hairy-limbed, cardboard Bride of Frankenstein doll, and legions of plastic uglies leer down novelty counters at cuddly trolls. There's a monster for every child, and toy dealers figure the ghoul game will pay a clammy $20 million this year."

In the shadow of monster mania lurked another dark figure, whose own fascination with distorted, freakish images had not yet achieved the notoriety for which it was ultimately destined. The publisher James Warren, however, was familiar with her photographic work and so hired her to document a group of his magazine's readers. The resulting photo, never published but described in a *Rolling Stone* feature in 1974, was titled *Bronx, New York, 1964: Meeting the Famous Monsters.* The photographer grouped the five young boys in front of a dilapidated house. Their faces were concealed by horrible masks. When one of the boys' hands nervously or inadvertently touched his crotch, the photographer released her shutter.

Diane Arbus, den mother of the damned, had found her image.

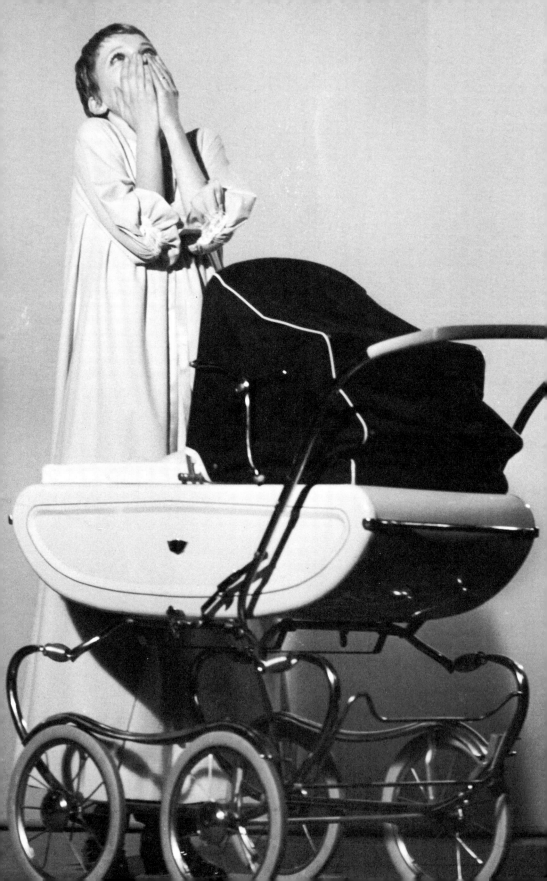

Chapter Ten

IT'S ALIVE, I'M AFRAID

"Hear, Nature, hear; dear goddess, hear;
Suspend thy purpose if thou didst intend
To make this creature fruitful.
Into her womb convey sterility,
Dry up in her the organs of increase,
And from her derogate body never spring
A babe to honor her. If she must teem,
Create her child of spleen, that it may live
And be a thwart disnatured torment . . ."

William Shakespeare
King Lear
(1605)

ALL MONSTERS ARE expressions or symbols of some kind of birth process, however distorted or bizarre. For decades before real scientists began tinkering with sexual reproduction on the molecular level, mad scientists in monster movies had been articulating similar designs. In the screenplay for *Bride of Frankenstein* (1935), Dr. Septimus Pretorious chides his former protégé for the inelegance of his cut-and-stitch methods: "Listen, Henry Frankenstein—while you were digging into your graves, piecing together your dead tissues, I, my dear pupil, went for my beginnings to the source of life . . . I grew my creatures . . . as nature does. I followed the

Rosemary's Baby: **Mia Farrow realizes, too late, that they don't make children the way they used to.** *(Photofest)*

process of Life, not the processes of death." Pretorious proposes that they join their techniques, having offered a toast to "a new world of gods and monsters."

And indeed, tinkering with human seeds would eventually inspire one of the monster show's most successful seasons ever. On May 11, 1960, the U.S. Food and Drug Administration approved a prescription birth-control pill, following four years of testing. Enovid, manufactured by G. D. Searle & Company of Chicago, would become one of the most widely prescribed medications in history.

Chemical birth control changed sexuality in dramatic and subtle ways, and was central to the "sexual revolution" of the sixties and seventies. On one level, women could now "control" their sex lives, or at least separate sex from reproduction. Less discussed was the element of subtle sexual coercion posed by the Pill; with the availability of cheap, easy, and (purportedly) safe chemical contraception, women also had less reason than ever before to refuse sex. The basic choice offered by the Pill was not whether or not to have babies, but instead, how much intercourse. Women's sexuality was thus radically reshaped along the lines of the Hefner-esque male's.

The primary scientists involved in the invention of oral contraceptives were all men, bent on "improving" female biology. In the view of some observers, the Pill was rushed onto the market without adequate safety-testing—a mad, mass experiment. By 1968, British scientists claimed to have found a link between the Pill and dangerous, even fatal blood clotting. By the early seventies, hormone levels were lowered in European versions of the Pill, but the original-strength prescription was not banned in America until 1988. In her women's-movement chronicle *Moving the Mountain,* historian Flora Davis notes that some American scientists who challenged the safety of the Pill actually lost their funding.

By the end of the sixties, the big American sex party was in full swing, thanks in no small part to chemical contraception. As in the twenties, sexual abstinence was distinctly unfashionable; the dangers of chastity were pointedly dramatized in Roman Polanski's horror-sex film *Repulsion* (1965), with an advertising campaign promising to reveal the "nightmare world of a virgin's dreams." A related cultural signpost was the science-fiction film *Village of the Damned* (1960), in which sex has nothing to do with reproduction anymore, rather as in real life. British women are impregnated by a force from outer space and subsequently give birth to blond, blue-eyed children with monstrous powers of psychic control. The film cost only $300,000 to make and earned $5 million in theatrical rentals, indicating a resonance between its outlandish story and a theme already in the public mind—namely, the creeping sense that women's reproductive functions could be hijacked by futuristic male science.

Within two years of the Pill's introduction, the official, benign image of chemically mediated reproduction received a deep jolt. Another "safe" medication, this one prescribed to pregnant women in forty-six countries, had horrific consequences. Thalidomide, a mild tranquilizer prescribed as a treatment for morning sickness, resulted in some of the most profound birth defects modern medicine had ever seen. Taken during the first trimester of pregnancy, thalidomide could disrupt the formation of fetal limb buds, leading to babies born without arms or legs, or with stunted, flipper-like projections at the shoulders and hips. Brain damage and gross facial deformities were common. In their book *Suffer the Children,* the reporting team of *The Sunday Times* of London described one of the worst thalidomide cases in England: "He had a deformed

Brave new children: *Village of the Damned* (1960). *(Photofest)*

and shortened arm and a hand without a thumb. The other hand had one extra finger. His palate had a gaping hole in it. His face was paralyzed on one side. One ear was completely missing, the other grossly deformed. For the first eighteen months of his life, he vomited his food across the room with projectile-like force. It soon became clear that his brain was damaged, that he was deaf and dumb."

The nightmare tragedy riveted the world. Never before had so many human beings been exposed to the images of such cruelly distorted human forms. In August 1962, the West German Health Ministry estimated 10,000 defective births, with half the babies surviving. Legal dramas gripped the public: in Belgium, a mother was acquitted—to thunderous spectator applause—after killing her armless baby with barbiturates mixed with milk and honey; in America, television and newspaper audiences vicariously participated in the quest of Mrs. Sherri Finkbine to obtain a legal abortion. The spectacle of monstrous birth in the 1960s effectively put the abortion issue on legislative front-burners.

Thalidomide jolted awake America's deep-seated fascination with freaks. The tabloids took the place of actual sideshows, with cover photos of NEW THALIDOMIDE MONSTERS given a pornographic air by the blotting out of genitalia with black squares, like strip-show pasties. Given the lurid carnival mood, it was inevitable that Tod Browning's long-suppressed *Freaks* would wriggle its way back into the spotlight.

The film's distribution had been given over by MGM in the 1940s to an exploitation specialist, Dwain Esper, who exhibited the film as a curiosity in itself, often under alias titles like *Nature's Mistakes* and *Forbidden Love*. Audience responses were unpredictable. Exploitation filmmaker David F. Friedman recalled a disastrous screening of the film under the *Forbidden Love* title at a North Carolina drive-in during the spring of 1947. The film unreeled during a torrential downpour, and by the end of the film, the audience, like the freaks themselves, was ready to revolt. Friedman remembered them "blowing their car horns, flashing their headlights at the screen, yelling and screaming out rolled-down windows, and yanking car speakers off the posts. Although they had seen a film now classified as one of the great screen shockers . . . they hadn't seen any skin." The audience whose voyeurism had not been satisfied by *Freaks* was quickly placated by the hastily arranged screening of a nudie flick.

Tod Browning never gave a retrospective interview on his career, even after films like *Dracula* found a new popularity on television in the late fifties. He couldn't talk if he wanted to. Throat cancer had necessitated a tongue operation as well as a laryngectomy; the angelic voice that had amazed turn-of-the-century Louisville churchgoers was stilled forever. At the 1959 Louisville funeral of his brother Avery, Browning, apparently unwilling to display the results of his surgery, withdrew to a private room at the funeral home and refused to let family members see him. The mourners were reportedly angered and alienated. Mute and mutilated, Tod Browning had returned, in a sense, to his silent film world of physical violation, brought down by the same disease that killed Lon Chaney thirty-two years earlier. He died alone in the bathroom of friends who had taken him in, on the morning of October 6, 1962.

It is not known whether Browning learned of, or was even in a state to appreciate, the revival and reception of *Freaks* at the 1962 Venice Film Festival, but the momentum toward canonization, once begun, would not stop. *Freaks* probably reached its greatest popularity at the height of the Vietnam War, as a midnight movie favorite of a counterculture that had claimed the title word itself as a badge of identity. *Variety* reported that in Pittsburgh, "street people who call themselves various kinds of 'freaks' are in theory giving the old Tod Browning Metro film, *Freaks,* a healthy run." In Los Angeles, a revival of *Freaks* at the Los Feliz Theatre set a new non-holiday house record.

Real freaks weren't so enthusiastic. Montague Addison, a tattooed dwarf, complained to *Films in Review* in 1971. "Freaks are people, individuals. The movie doesn't understand this and presents them as a homogenized collection of semi-imbeciles. Freaks value their individuality and dislike being placed in a niche by bleeding hearts." Addison had avoided the Browning film for years on the advice of his friends. "When I finally did see it my worst fears were realized. While pretending sympathy and understanding for a defenseless minority group, *Freaks* actually exploits and degrades us in a manner that is hokey as well as offensive." Addison compared Browning's exploitation of circus freaks to the stereotyping of blacks. "But there are not enough of us to make any difference should we organize a protest."

The rise of the auteur theory of film, with its often sweeping assumptions about the extent of directorial intention and control, helped to fuel positive revisionist assessments. The rediscovery and rehabilitation of *Freaks* became almost a cause célèbre in the film journals beginning in the early sixties. Once considered crass and tasteless, the film was now "compassionate" and "sensitive." In a way, the appreciation of *Freaks* became a politically correct way to indulge a morbid curiosity about thalidomide-style deformities, while still being able to feel self-righteous and progressive.

By the mid-sixties, disturbing images related to reproduction had been piled up high in America's reservoir of dreams. Beyond thalidomide and *Freaks,* the earlier horror icons (all aggressively resurrected and exploited in the early sixties) also dealt in one way or another with fantastic alternate forms of human replication. That a new monster myth would develop in response to this psychic stockpile was virtually inescapable.

Without realizing it, Americans were already supplicating the dark gods, offering their prayers for *Rosemary's Baby.*

Ira Levin's neo-Gothic thriller was published by Random House in the spring of 1967; it became one of the most widely read and talked-about books of the year. With its quickly readable, pared-down prose, *Rosemary's Baby* was a new kind of best-seller, one that was virtually a screenplay in book form and could be read in about the time it took to watch a movie. The eventual director of the film version, Roman Polanski, took his scenario and dialogue almost verbatim from the novel; it would emerge as one of the most literal, scene-by-scene film adaptations of a book in cinema history.

Rosemary's Baby tells the story of Guy and Rosemary Woodhouse, a young married couple in Manhattan who move into a Gothic apartment house (the Bramford, patterned after the real-life Dakota). Guy is an actor who gets a big break when his rival for a part is mysteriously struck blind. Rosemary, meanwhile, is concentrating on getting pregnant. The couple befriend an elderly next-door couple, Roman and Minnie Castavet. Rosemary has a strange dream in which she is demonically raped. She conceives, but her term is painful and difficult. She begins to suspect a plot involving the Castavets, her husband, and virtually everyone they know. Her suspicions prove correct: Guy has made an evil pact to advance his career, sacrificing her to devil worshippers who have forced her to literally bear a son to Satan. But instead of destroying the thing, Rosemary's maternal instincts prevail and she accepts the golden-eyed monster as her own—horn-buds, tail, and all.

Author Levin told *Publishers Weekly* that he couldn't remember exactly when the idea had come to him, but that the story had been germinating since the early sixties. "I don't think any pregnant woman should read it," Levin said. Elsewhere, Levin said that he had plotted the book backwards. "I started with a woman pregnant with something that wasn't quite right and eventually came around to the witchcraft. It was the only thing I could think of to account for the pregnancy except outer space."★ Random House had actually played with the idea of using a similar warning for publicity, but had abandoned the approach as a tad too gimmicky.

Whether Levin's strategy was conscious or not, the plot of *Rosemary's Baby* was a brilliant metaphorical distillation of the widespread ambivalence and anxiety over sex and reproduction, concerns overshadowed by the garish glare of the swinging sixties. On a simplistic level, both Rosemary and the reader share lingering doubts about the chemical-occult tinkering with their reproductive systems. Rosemary drinks the stinking tannis-root cocktail that her neighbor provides while the reader (likely) swallows the magic candy of birth-control pills. Neither has a deep understanding of the effects of either substance on their bodies and their lives; they rely trustingly on patriarchal authority. Rosemary Woodhouse is led repeatedly to believe she is making her own carefully considered reproductive choices, but the decisions are all being made for her. No matter what assurances are offered, no matter what charms and preparations she uses or ingests, she is not really safe. One of many indelible images in the film version of *Rosemary's Baby* is the pregnant but wasted-looking Mia Farrow dashing out against the light into midtown traffic, an apt metaphor for childbearing under socio-technological siege.

In June 1968, the National Catholic Office for Motion Pictures, formerly the Legion of Decency, slapped *Rosemary's Baby* with a "Condemned" rating. To attend the film was now an official act of venial sin for Catholics, a stain on the soul that could only be removed by a priest in the confessional. But times had changed so

★Rosemary's baby wasn't the only strange fetus hypnotizing film audiences in the summer of 1968. The enigmatic star-child of Stanley Kubrick's *2001: A Space Odyssey* also fueled the public's growing fascination with uncanny embryos.

much since the Breen Office days that the body's ruling probably did more to publicize the film than to hinder it. The film's nudity alone would have condemned the film. "Much more serious, however," said a representative of the office, "is the perverted use of fundamental Christian beliefs, especially surrounding the birth of Christ, and its mockery of religious persons and practices. The very technical excellence of the film serves to intensify its defamatory nature." Producer William Castle reported receiving vicious hate mail in the aftermath of the film's release, including the following: *"Rosemary's Baby* is filth and YOU will die as a result. Lover of Satan, Purveyor of Evil, you have sold your soul. *Die. Die. Die."* Castle had some health problems afterwards, and couldn't help wondering about curses.

After Rosemary had her baby, virtually all births in the popular media would be monstrous or demonic; normal childbearing was virtually banished. This was not a totally new development; the germ of the tendency can be observed as far back as Mary Shelley's reverie on asexual procreation, and even in Bram Stoker: the vampire women at Dracula's castle who devour a baby in a bag are, thematically at least, clearing the decks for a new form of baby-less blood-reproduction. In the post-Pill age, "normal" childbirth ceased to exist, at least in our collective dream-life. Reproduction crossed over into the realm of Gothic science fiction. Women would become pregnant by demons or computers, tinkered with by genetic engineers. Pregnancy was an act of war, a violent invasion by the enemy. These fearful images were rarely part of the debate over reproduction technology and abortion rights, but they provided a persistent subtext worth examination.

Suddenly, in the sixties, the womb was the new graveyard from which the horror mavens would take their raw materials for the new put-together monsters. As Dr. Pretorious exhorted his former pupil in *Bride of Frankenstein,* "Leave the charnel house and follow the lead of nature."

Many books and films that did not directly invoke reproduction imagery nonetheless managed to make the reader-viewer uneasy about the prospect of parenthood. William Peter Blatty's *The Exorcist,* published as a novel in 1971 and released as a film in 1973, is, stripped of its demonic-possession theme, a cautionary tale of a beleaguered single mother who believes she can endure no more, but who, with the aid of Catholic doctrine, to which she has previously been indifferent, manages to endure everything. Unlike *Rosemary's Baby, The Exorcist* escaped Catholic condemnation.

The film became a highly publicized cultural ritual exorcising not the devil, but rather the confused parental feelings of guilt and responsibility in the Vietnam era, when—at least from a certain conservative perspective—filthy-mouthed children were taking personality-transforming drugs, violently acting out, and generally making life unpleasant for their elders. Critic Pauline Kael, who hated *The Exorcist,* used her *New Yorker* review to raise another generation-gap question. After noting that director William Friedkin claimed to have looked at five hundred child actresses before choosing Linda Blair, Kael wondered about "those four hundred and ninety-nine mothers of the rejected little girls [who] must have read the novel; they must have known what they were having their daughters tested for. When they see *The Exorcist* and watch Linda Blair urinating on the fancy carpet and screaming and jabbing at herself with the crucifix, are they envious? Do they feel, 'That might have been my little Susie—famous forever'?" (Linda Blair, who was thirteen when she acted in the film, later told an interviewer that she suffered no harm over the role. "I didn't think of what the movie was about. . . . We would do the screen tests for testing the pea soup and I got to vomit on the first assistant director who wore rain gear and goggles. That was very funny from *my* point of view.")

The Exorcist proved to be one of the biggest boosts to the horror genre since the days of *Dracula* and *Frankenstein,* particularly in its whetting of the public appetite for elaborate makeup effects. Women's wombs were colonized by monstrous fetuses in films like *Humanoids from the Deep* (1979); sometimes the fetuses were just symbolic homunculae—devilish puppets or animated dolls. In the "Amelia" episode of the 1975 television film *Trilogy of Terror* we first meet Karen Black as the title character, and watch her enter her apartment carrying a chest that looks remarkably like a baby coffin. We overhear a tense phone conversation with her mother, from whose smothering energy she is unsuccessfully trying to distance herself. The object in the chest, we find, is not a dead baby, but rather a baby-sized Zuni fetish doll that comes to life and assaults her repeatedly. Following a horrific standoff, Amelia makes a fatal miscalculation and hurls the thing into her oven, where its evil energy explodes, devouring Amelia's soul. (Had she

It's Alive (1974): a mother's worst nightmare.

been appraised of the Freudian overtones of the kitchen appliance, the doll, perhaps, would not have possessed her.)

The sick-humor styles of the fifties shared a symbiotic energy with Monster Culture, and in the sixties and seventies another distinct sick-humor cycle provided an uneasy counterpoint to the growing tide of gynecological horror images in books and films. The dead-baby joke was a dubious, but prevalent, institution among American adolescents in the decades surrounding and following the sexual revolution, the Pill, thalidomide, and unstable family structures, as well as the emerging abortion-rights struggle.

It would be simplistic to assume that dead-baby jokes are "about" infanticide in a literal sense. The "dead baby" under discussion is often a stand-in for the joke teller; adolescents are, in a sense, "dead" to childhood. With adulthood, they will similarly be dead teenagers. One must wonder if the ritual being shared in the slasher subcategory of horror movies is, finally, not the puritanical punishment of sexually active adolescents—the standard interpretation—but rather a dysfunctional initiation rite: the collective witnessing and reenactment of childhood's murder by premature, media-driven sex.

Dead-baby jokes are frequently set in kitchens, and involve destructive appliance/orifices—ovens, food processors, garbage disposals. In a much-sanitized form, these images would eventually be recycled by baby-boom horror maven Joe Dante for the famous kitchen scene in *Gremlins* (1984), wherein pint-sized terrors are reduced to slime by a housewife's blender, microwave, etc. Folklorist Alan Dundes, who has authored a book-length study of the sick-joke phenomenon, notes that "no piece of folklore continues to be transmitted *unless* it means something," but adds that, in the case of jokes, "it is usually essential that the joke's meaning *not* be crystal clear. If people knew what they were communicating . . . the jokes would cease to be effective as socially sanctioned outlets for expressing taboo ideas and subjects." The taboo subjects include fear of parenthood, guilt over abortion, and resentment of children coupled with the desire to remain a child oneself.

By the late 1970s, these forbidden topics had become the visible substance of one horror picture after another. *It's Alive* (1974) featured a clawed mutant requiring no slapping at birth; it takes the aggressive initiative itself and slaughters the entire delivery-room team. By the sequel, *It Lives Again* (1978), childbirth has become an almost paramilitary operation, with SWAT teams and firearms attending each contraction. The parents are confused throughout the film: are they supposed to keep their baby, or are they supposed to kill it? Official advice seems untrustworthy. One character, the original father from *It's Alive,* wants the creature to survive; he insists he is only "protecting this woman's right to have a baby" when he interrupts a government-sanctioned abortion at gunpoint. "Lots of people call their baby 'it,' " says the new father at one point, trying to make sense of things. (A second sequel, *Island of the Alive,* was delivered in 1988.)

Another "it" was introduced in *Eraserhead,* with which filmmaker David Lynch launched his career in 1976. Genuinely nightmarish (and still difficult for many viewers to sit through), *Eraserhead* depicts human reproduction as a desolate freak show, an occupation fit only for the damned. The film's central image is a monster baby that appears to be an actual fetal calf or lamb, tightly swaddled and somehow manipulated from inside like a puppet (Lynch refuses to discuss any technical details). The geeky, incompetent parents go through the motions of caring for the thing, but cannot cope. The thing becomes sick (the fleshy prop may actually be rotting in these scenes), explosively vomits blood, and fulminates a mountain of cheesy crud. "They're still not sure it *is* a baby," says the mother, early on. Elsewhere *Eraserhead* features a surrealistic set piece of a grinning doll-woman on a music-hall stage. On the verge of breaking into song, she is repeatedly interrupted by ropy, spermlike organisms that drop from above onto the checkerboard stage floor. Still smiling, desperately eager for an unseen audience's approval, she squashes the things with mincing dance-steps, while white fluid spurts on the stage.

Eraserhead's sick dream, aimed at the midnight art-house circuit, nonetheless had much in common with the increasingly fetal and gynecological obsessions of commercial horror films. (Lynch's work on *Eraserhead* would lead to his directing the commercially successful but similarly obsessed *The Elephant Man* (1980), another story about a monstrous accident of birth.) The public was responding as never before to images of reproductive nightmares.

In 1979, David Cronenberg, a Canadian filmmaker who was emerging as a master of the literalized metaphor, released *The Brood,* an ambitious and unusually intelligent horror film that might be considered a Rosetta stone of modern reproductive anxieties. Although the director has since brilliantly elaborated on similar themes (most notably in 1988's *Dead Ringers*), *The Brood* remains one of his most personal and powerful efforts; Cronenberg has described the film in several interviews as having been partially inspired by his own divorce and child-custody battle, in progress at the time of production. *The Brood* introduces Dr. Hal Raglan (Oliver Reed), a charismatic psychotherapist notorious for his theory of "psychoplasmics," a process in which the patient's pent-up rage can be physically externalized. In some patients the result is stigmata-like lesions, in others, cancer. In one, Nola Carveth (Samantha Eggar), the shape of rage manifests as a murderous "brood" of child-like homunculae, who act out her unconscious impulses. Nola, like a pampered termite queen in Raglan's cult-like clinic, gestates the monsters outside of her body in huge, bubo-like sacs. Her own mother and father are the first to die—the brood are, in a sense, fetuses who abort parents. Their life span is limited; they draw their energy from nutrients contained in a camel-like hump. They have no navels, and no need for genitals. A patholo-

Samantha Eggar examines her fetal excrescence in *The Brood* (1979).

gist, examining one of the spent creatures, notes, "This thing has never really been born—at least not the way human beings are born." "Jesus!" exclaims Nola's husband, in an epiphany of sorts. Virgin birth, made literal, is not for the fainthearted.

Cronenberg's Hitchcock-like attention to detail enhances all his films, and *The Brood* is no exception. When the brood jealously kills a schoolteacher who has befriended Nola's husband, her bloody face is covered with one of her pupil's drawings that in itself is a child's innocent evocation of a fertility rite, its caption reading WE PLANT PUMPKIN SEEDS. (Halloween pumpkins, as it turned out.) Nola's external womb was an elaborate makeup effect designed by artist Dennis Pike, fashioned from part of a weather balloon filled with a rubber fetus, studio blood, and spaghetti. Shots of Eggar biting open the membrane were too much for the notoriously nosy Canadian censors, who demanded cuts. "I had a long and loving closeup of Eggar licking the fetus that was quite fantastic," recalled Cronenberg. But with the censor's abrupt hacking, "a lot of people thought she was eating the baby! That's much worse than I was suggesting. . . . [The image is] not sexual, not violent, just . . . gooey and disturbing. It's a bitch licking her pups. Why cut it out?"

It was clear that the director considered Nola to be a bitch on any number of levels. Canadian critic Robin Wood maintains that Cronenberg is a sexual reactionary, and interprets *The Brood* as a cautionary male fantasy about burgeoning radical feminism. Wood notes the implied message: that women's "activeness and rage *must* remain repressed—their release would be catastrophic." In London, the *Observer* wondered about the meaning of "a crazy housewife whose externalized aggressions become homicidal dwarves . . . *The Brood* has something pretty terrible to tell us about the state of family life today and about the fears [of] North American males."

But the crowning image of reproductive horror was yet to come. The poster art for *Alien* (1979) was deceptively simple and evocative: a cracked egg in a dark void, and the tag line IN SPACE, NO ONE CAN HEAR YOU SCREAM. Whether the space was internal or external was not made clear.

Directed by Ridley Scott, *Alien* is a brilliantly manipulative film (Scott had earlier been a highly regarded director of the most manipulative media form of all—the television commercial), creating an unprecedented horror frisson by superimposing technological and reproductive anxieties. A deep-space cargo ship, the *Nostromo,* is a bland womb for a crew of equally bland techno-babies. Their controlled-environment dream comes to an abrupt end when they investigate a derelict ship that is less a mechanism than a living-dead organism. Based on disturbing designs by the Swiss surrealist H. R. Giger, the alien ship consists of vagina-like portals and womb-like caverns. (Giger's unnerving artwork, in which everything looks like mechanized sex and death, developed a large cult following after *Alien,* for which he shared an Academy Award.) In the innermost regions, the *Nostromo* team discovers the ship's egg chamber, and one of its members, Kane (John Hurt), is attacked by a manta ray–like "face hugger" which inserts something down its victim's gullet. Back at the home ship, Kane seems to recover, only to have a rapidly growing alien burst from his chest, showering the crew with gore.

The *Nostromo*'s impersonal, artificial, and utterly controlled environment thus becomes a breeding ground for the Gothic-organic—the sterility of the environment is almost a red flag signaling the irrational, destructive forces lurking nearby. The alien has mechanical traits, startling in their juxtaposition with sexual-skeletal, insectoid features. The chest-bursting scene, the single most talked-about sequence in the film, became the seventies' surpassing evocation of reproduction as unnatural parasitism. Proving one's mettle by enduring this scene turned out to be an immensely popular rite of passage; not since the shower murder in *Psycho* (1960) had a shock scene generated so much word-of-mouth publicity. The film prompted a good deal of repeat business—individuals challenging themselves to "handle" the scene, or bringing friends to watch their reactions. The violent trauma of Kane's birthing / dying is never overcome; the alien matures, but it is always the fetus-as-bogeyman, an ever-growing, shape-shifting nightmare. The culture's growing but guilty hostility toward birth is transformed into a monstrous fetal parasite hostile to the culture itself. *Alien* was a validation of something already suspected: that reproduction was a kind of death, a devastating insult to the body and personal autonomy; that sex and technology had come together in a weird and ugly way. Relief came only when the beast was aborted from the mother-ship's body, sucked away by the vacuum of space. By the time of *Alien*'s second sequel in 1992, the themes were even more starkly presented. Ripley (Sigourney Weaver), embattled survivor of the first two films, is now

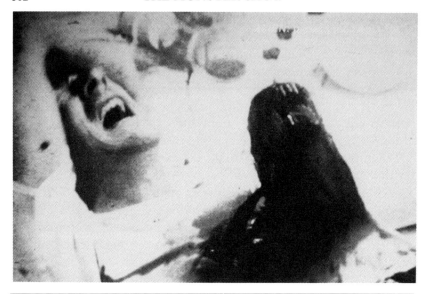

Fanged, phallic, fetal: the "chest-burster" from *Alien* (1979). *(Photofest)*

a desexualized feminist cartoon, holding her own against a microcosmic prison-world of male psychopaths and the alien monster
she is involuntarily carrying to term. Ripley's spectacular self-
immolation—one is tempted to call it *Sigourney's Choice*—had the
unintentional quality of a last-ditch political protest of the Supreme
Court rulings undermining abortion rights, handed down just before
the release of the film.

John Frankenheimer's 1979 film *Prophecy* featured Talia Shire as
a pregnant woman whose anxiety over giving birth (her environ-
mentalist husband thinks the world isn't a fit place to populate any
longer; she learns she has inadvertently ingested a gene-twisting
mercury compound) is wildly externalized as a mutated, man-eating bear in the Maine woods. Like *Alien, Prophecy* employed an
egg-like image in its advertising art, out of which a fanged fetal
thing stares at the potential ticket buyer. Unlike *Alien,* the Frankenheimer film failed to find a large audience, likely because it
spent more time preaching than punching buttons.

The demonization of fetal images does not lend itself to a simplistic ideological interpretation—monster children are not exactly
pro-life or pro-choice, but, like the sick joke, articulate unspoken
aspects on both sides. Abortion-rights advocates rarely discuss any
negative emotions surrounding pregnancy or pregnancy termina-

tion; the issue is presented as a consumer-style "choice," the selection of a life-style–enhancing brand name. The images of popular culture suggest that the issue is far more muddled; why else does the public flock again and again to anxiety-provoking stories of fetal beings who kill or must be killed? The right-to-lifers, in their eagerness to enforce pregnancy as a kind of ideological punishment (and in its glaring lack of interest in child welfare after birth), reveal their own hidden hostility to children, who seem to be nothing but throwaway political weapons. From the extreme puritanical perspective, children are the penalty to be paid for sex, a scourge not much different than the "punishment" of AIDS. From a liberal perspective, children are socioeconomic baggage that can drag you down. Both sides consider the unborn warily, and one good horror image may communicate more about modern reproductive ambivalence than a dozen formulaic abortion-rights debates.

Monstrous children, horrific pre-children, and abused (i.e., aborted) children became staple commodities in mass-market horror fiction in the seventies and eighties. V. C. Andrews' Gothic child-abuse novels, beginning with *Flowers in the Attic* (1979) and its coyly named "Dollanganger" family, became huge best-sellers. The presence of children on the cover of horror paperbacks is a genre cliché; now menaced, now menacing, it doesn't really matter—the unrelenting sense of dread that revolves around the image of a child is the point. By the late 1980s, the concept of a wounded "inner child" had become a fixture of pop psychology; simultaneously, wound-inflicting inner children were externalizing themselves everywhere, in films like *Children of the Corn* (1984) and, most extravagantly, *Child's Play* (1988) in which a murderous doll named Chucky knew how to get you before you could get him. *Child's Play* spawned two numbered sequels, the second of which caused a New York semi-scandal in 1991, when it was learned that a Brooklyn elementary school was using violent Chucky videos to keep classrooms quiet. A teacher justified the practice, explaining that cat-and-mouse cartoons no longer did the trick. "They're beyond the sweetness stage," she told the *New York Post*. Some of the same children may have spent time swapping a series of trading cards called the "Garbage Pail Kids," an intense but short-lived craze of the eighties featuring images of freakish small fry in repulsive situations. The idea that American children found a sense of identification with the debased and disposable Garbage Pail Kids— the name itself carries a strong connotation of abortion / infanticide—is worth considering, along with the earlier eighties craze for Cabbage Patch dolls, a phenomenon that based its appeal on a fantasy of asexual reproduction. Like Frankenstein, who also tried to subvert the traditional reproductive paradigm, American parents (more than their children) became obsessed with the Cabbage Patch doll and its unexamined, horror-related metaphors.

Shadowing the increasingly shrill abortion debate in the eighties

Chucky, the murderous doll of *Child's Play* (1988).

and nineties, commercial horror fiction began employing fetal imagery far beyond any visual shock tactics employed by the right-to-life faction. In F. Paul Wilson's 1991 short story, "Foet," the reader enters a near-future Manhattan peopled with shallow socialites for whom designer handbags made of foetal skin are the latest rage in status acquisitions.

> "Do you have any pieces without all the stitching? Something with a smoother look?"
>
> "I'm afraid not. I mean, you have to understand, we're forced by the very nature of the source of the material to work with little pieces." He gestured around. "Notice, too, that there are no gloves. None of the manufacturers wants to be accused of making kid gloves."
>
> Rolf smiled. Denise could only stare at him.
>
> He cleared his throat. "Trade humor."

The accumulated weight of birth-related horror imagery amounts to an undeclared war between the living and the unborn. There may be more to the matter than metaphor; the unconscious likely makes no distinction between geographical invasions and physical violations. *Your body is a battleground,* a feminist slogan widely popularized in a postmodernist art poster by Barbara Kruger, is, not uncoincidentally, the subtext of innumerable horror-movie posters and paperback book covers.

Embryonic imagery, by the 1980s and 90s, was as firmly established as the walking corpse as a method to elicit horror. Generation, it seemed, was as repulsive as decay. To the modern, technologically identified mind, it was no longer death that frightened, but the whole spectrum of biological phenomena. The unborn had merged with the undead, and the villagers gathered in a frightened dream to offer their babies in bags at the foot of Dracula's castle.

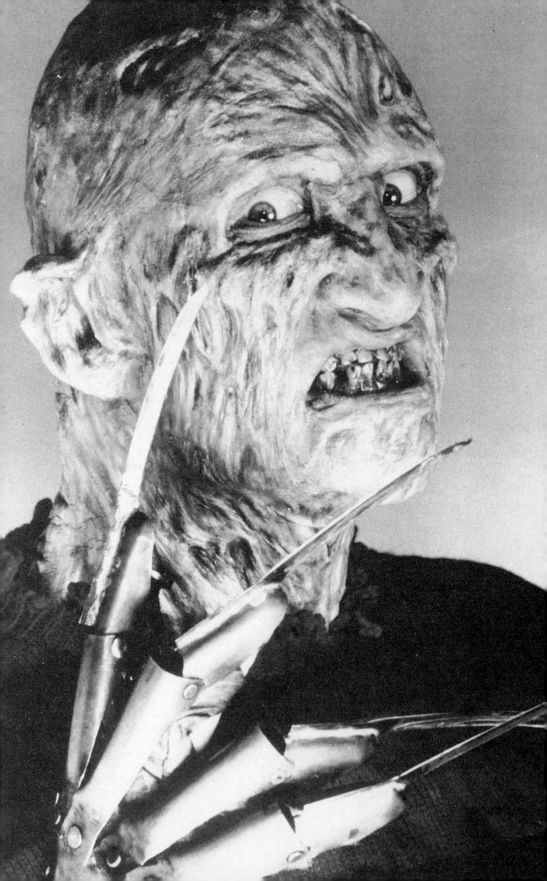

Chapter Eleven

SCAR WARS

"Building up your features with nose putty or mortician's wax is one of the most important and exciting make-up techniques because it really changes the shape of your face. Nose putty is a sticky, flesh-colored modelling material sold in the form of small sticks or in tins. Mortician's wax is a much softer, flesh-colored paste, sold in tins. Although it was designed for undertakers' use to restore injured faces, it is also used by make-up artists."

Dick Smith
Do-It-Yourself Monster Make-up Handbook
(1965)

TOM SAVINI DIDN'T want to go to Vietnam. He wanted to make movies, and a friend of his in Pittsburgh named George Romero was about to make a low-budget first feature to be called *Night of the Living Dead* (1968). Savini had grown enthralled by horror movies, and enjoyed creating makeup effects. Lon Chaney, Sr., was his idol.

"I had already enlisted in the army, in the 'Hold' program in order to stay out of Vietnam," Savini remembered. "It was a program in which you picked your own training, and I had chosen

---

Freddy Krueger (Robert Englund) got under America's skin with
A Nightmare on Elm Street **(1984). (Photofest)**

the photography school at Fort Monmouth. The army called me in before George started shooting *Night,* and after I finished photo school they sent me straight over to Vietnam as a combat photographer. So that was how I missed doing *Night of the Living Dead."*

There were no horror movies in Nam, but there was plenty of horror. "I saw a lot of bloodshed there," Savini recalled in a 1982 interview, "and my job was to photograph it. I did continue to practice makeup by working on the soldiers just for laughs." Savini had carried a makeup kit through basic training. "I turned my drill sergeant on to nonflexible collodion, a liquid plastic that will dry and shrink on the skin, forming scars. He wanted to use it on his face to scare the next batch of trainees coming in."

Collodion wasn't needed in the battle zone. Shock effects were plentiful. Savini recalled how he "walked around and nearly stepped on a human arm, one end of it jagged and torn, its fist clenched and grabbing the ground," and visited hospitals, seeing friends who'd had "certain private parts of their bodies blown off. . . . Perhaps my mind was seeing it as special effects to protect me.

"It was a funny thing," Savini said. "Your mind just takes care of itself under extreme conditions. It shuts off. But it caught up with me later on. Like everyone else who went to Vietnam, I was real screwed up when I got back. My marriage went instantly into the toilet."

Savini sought diversion in horror fantasy. "At one point, I remember I was playing the part of Renfield, the lunatic, in a production of *Dracula,* and I actually continued to play the character offstage. . . . The actor who played the attendant in the lunatic asylum saw me backstage and screamed 'What are you doing out of your cell?' I think he knew what I was up to. Vietnam changed my life; it made me want to escape from reality forever."

Savini's first movie assignment was a Canadian-made spin-off on "The Monkey's Paw" called *Deathdream* (1972), in which a Vietnam MIA named Andy (Richard Backus) shows up "alive" on his family's doorstep as a slowly disintegrating zombie-vampire. *Deathdream* (also known as *Dead of Night* and *The Veteran*) shows its low-budget seams, and it is difficult to determine if the parallel between the dying vampire and the dead-end, blood-draining Vietnam War itself was a conscious political statement. The film oddly echoes and inverts David Rabe's savage homecoming drama *Sticks and Bones* (1972), in which a blinded soldier

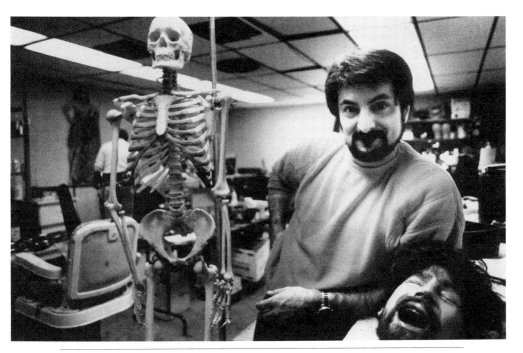

Tom Savini, master of grisly makeup effects, in his workshop for *Dawn of the Dead* (1979). *(Photofest)*

returns from Vietnam, and "sees" for the first time the essential monstrousness of his own family.

George Romero asked Savini to participate in his new production, *Martin* (1978), another contemporary vampire story which needed realistic stake-pounding and blood effects. A more important Romero assignment was *Dawn of the Dead* (1979), an elaborate sequel to *Night of the Living Dead*. The original film, a claustrophobic siege story filmed in vérité black-and-white, had relied on mood and shadow, with a few glimpses of butcher-shop entrails. The sequel would go whole hog. *Night of the Living Dead* was the last of the American gut-crunchers produced before the war-related political upheavals of 1968, and was, in a sense, the end of an era. Its post-Vietnam sequel was a remarkably different film in sensibility and execution, more complex, sardonic, and cynical. A razor-edged social satire, *Dawn of the Dead* peopled a shopping mall with flesh-eating zombies, an indelible image of consumerism gone mad. The special effects were grotesquely over-the-top: a head blown

The original storyboard for the shower murder in *Psycho*. (Photofest)

away by a shotgun blast, a zombie-husband taking a close-up bite out of his human wife's shoulder, another walking corpse given a gruesome crew cut, of sorts, by a whirling helicopter blade. The film was released without a rating. Savini told a magazine interviewer that "much of my work for *Dawn of the Dead* was like a series of portraits of what I had seen for real in Vietnam. Perhaps that was one way of working out that experience." Horror films of the seventies and eighties began exhibiting symptoms remarkably similar to some of those suffered by victims of posttraumatic stress syndrome: startle reactions, paranoia, endless scenes of guerrilla-like stalking, and, like traumatic flashbacks, endlessly repeated images of nightmare assaults on the human body, especially its sudden and explosive destruction.

In comparison to the visions of George Romero and Tom Savini, earlier excursions into violent movie horror had been positively genteel. Alfred Hitchcock's *Psycho* (1960) is usually considered the starting point for explicit media violence, even though its most famous sequence, the shower-murder of actress Janet Leigh, was achieved with virtuoso editing and a sprinkling of chocolate syrup. Hitchcock liked to tell interviewers that an elaborate rubber dummy of a naked woman, full of blood-tubing, had been prepared for the scene, but would not spurt properly when stabbed. No one else connected with the production, however, could remember any such prop.

Graphic designer Saul Bass, hired by Hitchcock as a visual consultant to storyboard and stage the sequence, originally conceived the scene as coldly stylized and completely bloodless. Hitchcock asked for some blood. Bass suggested ending the sequence with a single line of blood moving out from under the woman's face toward the camera as it pulled away from the victim's staring dead eye. The designer remembered that "we built a special tiled floor, sorta buckled it to create an imperceptible depression through which we could direct the route of the blood and stuff. It didn't work." Hitchcock settled for some chocolate sauce running down the drain instead.

Although *Psycho* was an extraordinarily influential film, explicit movie gore probably owes more to the blood-soaked, Eastman-color oeuvre of England's Hammer Films, which had begun cutting a distinctive red swath across audience retinae with *The Curse of Frankenstein* (1957) and *Horror of Dracula* (1958). Christopher Lee played the monster in both, launching his own horror career and forging yet another link of commonality between the twin icons. The first great Grand Guignol moment in an American film was provided by director Robert Aldrich in *Hush . . . Hush, Sweet*

Charlotte (1964), which opened with a close-up of actor Bruce Dern's hand being severed by a meat cleaver. His head followed, an action indicated rather poetically by a spurt of chocolate syrup (like *Psycho, Hush . . . Hush* was in black and white) on a carved cupid, an appropriate witness to a murder of passion. Advertisements for William Castle's *Strait-Jacket* (1963) promised audiences a film that VIVIDLY DEPICTS AXE MURDERS (even though the decapitations were fairly hokey—heads came off as if they were held on with masking tape). These films, and many resembling them, typically featured a "comeback" (i.e., resurrection) performance by veteran Hollywood actresses (e.g., Bette Davis or Joan Crawford). Like cinematic versions of Elizabeth Bathory (the sanguinary fifteenth-century Hungarian countess who believed that the blood of murder victims could restore her youth), Hollywood's new horror queens hoped to rejuvenate their careers by similarly bathing in blood.

In the wake of such flowing waves of establishment grue, and with the demise of many of the state censor boards which had traditionally given horror a hard time, the first true "splatter film" found its way into drive-ins and exploitation houses. *Blood Feast* (1963) was the brainchild of Producer David F. Friedman and director Herschell Gordon Lewis. Whether the film's endless simulated murders and mutilations (a mad caterer's twisted attempt to recreate a "genuine" Egyptian cannibal feast) are in any sense realistic may be a matter of debate, but no one will ever accuse the filmmakers of having been stingy with their brimming buckets of bright red goop.

Elaborate, unsettling cosmetic effects had been achieved in motion pictures since the days of Lon Chaney, but they took on a new level of realism with the perfection of a material that would become an almost alchemical substance of the late twentieth century. The use of that substance, latex foam, not only expanded the technical capabilities of the special-effects artist, but the resulting public spectacle of infinitely plastic human bodies paralleled and reflected the quantum growth of cosmetic surgery as a cultural activity and obsession during the same period.

Latex foam, in its finished state, is a solid, spongy material of variable density, and can be used to create models, masks, and prosthetics ranging from those tough enough to withstand violent stunt work, to tissue-thin facial appliances which register the most delicate expressions of the actor beneath. The processes involved seem improvisatory, almost homey (and were, in fact, perfected over the years by enthusiastic tinkerers working tirelessly in kitchens and garages, and happily sharing notes); household food mixers are used to whip the powdered latex, curing and foaming agents, and water into a batterlike froth. This fluid foam, with a gelling agent and color added, is poured into molds cast from real people or fantastic sculptures, and vulcanized in an ordinary kitchen oven. A misstep at any point can result in the heartbreaking equivalent of a fallen soufflé.

Foam latex and related technologies made possible fantastic distortions of the human body, almost as plastic as those previously achieved only by painters and sculptors. Many of the horror and science-fiction films of the seventies and eighties began showing signs of imaginative kinship to the earlier visions of Francis Bacon and Salvador Dalí. John Carpenter's remake of *The Thing* (1982), with special effects by Robb Bottin, subjected the body to the most surrealistic stress and strain ever seen outside a gallery canvas. At least one of Bottin's grotesqueries, in fact, closely resembles a panel from Bacon's seminal triptych *Three Studies for Figures at the Base of a Crucifixion*. In a sense, the entire twentieth-century history of increasingly abstracted human forms in fine art was recapitulated in the pop medium of horror, science-fiction, and fantasy films. Following their inspired foray into H. P. Lovecraft's *Re-Animator* (1985), filmmakers Brian Yuzna and Stuart Gordon pushed the approach even further in the Lovecraft-inspired *From Beyond* (1986), with climactic images of people reduced to writhing, snapping masses of protoplasm that recalled any number of Bacon's nightmarish paintings. The exploration of the connection between screen horror and surrealism is conscious and calculated; with his talented special-effects consultant Screaming Mad George, Yuzna borrowed directly from the imagery of Salvador Dalí for his horror satire *Society* (1990), in which the rich literally engulf the working classes like fleshy amebas.

By the 1980s, special effects in the popular media were the closest encounter with the miraculous that a secular culture could muster; the vast appetite for transformation illusions bespoke a deep, unmet hunger for images of transcendence and transfiguration. (As always, monsters proved themselves serviceable Christ-substitutes.) Not all the effects were preoccupied with formless flesh; some of the most ambitious work involved detailed, bravura cross-species transformations. When Lon Chaney, Jr., underwent

One of Robb Bottin's startling effects for John Carpenter's *The Thing* (1982).

his wartime werewolf metamorphoses, the camera technology involved was fairly straightforward: stop-motion lap-dissolves as layers of yak hair were painstakingly applied. Forty years later, two films produced nearly simultaneously, *The Howling* (1980) and *An American Werewolf in London* (1981), demonstrated the new shape of lyncanthropy, now more mechanical than optical. *The Howling,* directed by monster-boomer Joe Dante, introduced a state-of-the-art wolf man, whose flesh (latex skin, lined with inflatable air bladders, the work of Robb Bottin) could swell and stretch on cue, whose snout roared forward like a freight train, and whose talons emerged from his fingers like motorized switchblades. *The Howling*'s big transformation scene (added to the film as an expensive afterthought) turned out to be a powerful, word-of-mouth lure. Director Dante was pleased with the scene, but much later realized that it made no sense—the spectacular metamorphosis took so much screen time that the victim would have had ample opportunity to run away. Diverted by the display of effects, however, audiences made no complaint. The film was stuffed with affectionate references to genre movies, including a cameo appearance by Forrest J Ackerman, the venerable editor of *Famous Monsters of Filmland*. John Sayles contributed a particularly witty script.

John Landis' *An American Werewolf in London,* with makeup effects by Rick Baker, upped the ante with its first-time-ever depiction of a werewolf transformation in the nude. Individual wolf-hairs sprouted from human skin in microscopic close-up, while the actor David Naughton's complete skeletal structure was stretched and animalized beneath his exposed and vulnerable flesh.

An American Werewolf in London was seen and enjoyed by Michael Jackson, the singer whose first solo hit had been the title theme from the horror movie *Ben,* a winsome tale of psychically controlled killer rats. Jackson decided to ask John Landis and Rick Baker to create the title-song music video for his hit album *Thriller* (1982). In point of fact, the album was more than a hit—it was a runaway mega-phenomenon destined to be the best-selling album of all time, moving a half million copies a week at the peak of its popularity. CBS Records eventually sold 38.5 million copies of the album throughout the world; the recording was number one on the *Billboard* charts for thirty-seven weeks. Seven of its cuts were top-ten singles. The song "Thriller" included a rap sequence by Vincent Price that harkened back to the proto-rap novelty songs of John Zacherle and Bobby "Boris" Pickett; the spirit of "The Monster Mash" and "Dinner with Drac" had achieved an astonishing commercial apotheosis.

The fourteen-minute "Thriller" video, produced at a cost reported variously from $800,000 to $1 million, opens with a scene of Jackson as a fifties teenager on a date, shyly confessing to the girl that he's "different" and "not like other guys." The line elicits a homophobic titter from the audience followed by a scream from his date when he demonstrates exactly what he means, changing into a snarling yellow-eyed cat-creature. Before he can kill her, the scene is revealed as a film-within-a-film, Jackson and his date safely watching themselves on-screen in a movie theatre. On their way home, they pass a graveyard that belches up every rotting revenant from *J'Accuse* through George Romero, and Jackson metamorphoses again, this time into a dancing Frankenzombie. With its flashy display of boogying bogeys, "Thriller" was an almost literal *danse macabre* for the go-go eighties, a leveraged buyout of Hans Holbein the Younger by modern entertainment conglomerates. (The video was heavily financed by MTV and the Showtime cable network.)

Rick Baker recalled that Jackson was surprisingly unfamiliar with

The plastic body: David Naughton in John Landis' *An American Werewolf in London* (1981). Transformation effects by Rick Baker. *(Courtesy of Ronald V. Borst / Hollywood Movie Posters)*

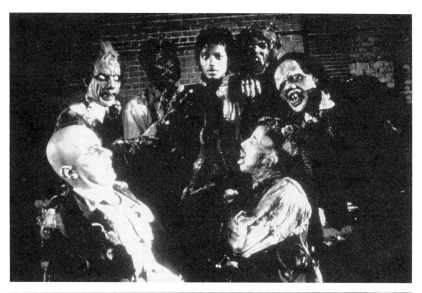

Nothing is real: the faces of Michael Jackson's video "Thriller" (1984).
(Photofest)

the horror genre; the sheer extravagance of the project suggested a heartfelt *hommage* by a true devotee. But when Baker and Landis learned that the entertainer had never even seen *Bride of Frankenstein,* "we started reeling off all these names of films, and it turned out he'd seen very few," Baker said. His complete exposure to the genre was *American Werewolf, The Hunchback of Notre Dame* (1939) with Charles Laughton (a special favorite), and *The Elephant Man* (1980).

The world came close to never seeing "Thriller," even after it had been produced. According to Jackson biographer J. Randy Taraborelli, the singer, a practicing Jehovah's Witness, became distraught when church elders objected to the demonic "Thriller" video. In a panic, he demanded that the unreleased video be destroyed. His manager, John Branca, reportedly told Jackson a story about Bela Lugosi—Jackson had never heard of the actor—in which he painted the performer as a deeply religious man who nonetheless could play Dracula with no resulting damage to his soul. Although there is no biographical documentation that Lugosi was particularly religious (but much evidence of personal and professional woe arising from the vampire image), Branca's ploy worked. Jackson allowed the video to be released with this disclaimer: "Due to my strong personal convictions, I wish to stress that this film in no way endorses a belief in the occult." (Taraborelli also reports director John Landis' alleged reaction to the flap: " 'Jesus Christ,' Landis is supposed to have said. 'This kid's in bad shape, isn't he?' ")

Evidently there was something about his own shape that Michael Jackson found troubling; he had already begun an obsessive odyssey with plastic surgery, and the public's first awareness of his real-life facial reconfiguration was juxtaposed with the fantasy monster transformations of "Thriller."

The rather obvious correspondence was not much commented on—perhaps it was too obvious, hidden in plain sight—though much was made of Jackson's surgery itself. Both plastic surgery and the monster iconography that propelled Michael Jackson to his greatest fame had their origins in World War I—the surgery as a medical response to the horrors of the battlefield, the monsters as the cinematic war metaphors of *Caligari* and *Nosferatu*.

People magazine was the first to report in late 1983 that Jackson had undergone a nose job; the story and before-and-after pictures made the wire services and built anticipation for the "Thriller" video, which debuted on MTV in January 1984. The fascination with the monster makeup was simultaneously a fascination with the surgical alteration—for both Jackson and his audience, it appeared. By his next album, *Bad* (1987), surgery alone would suffice. Jackson now had a skeletal, fashion-model look (many onlookers believed he was trying to physically transform himself into Diana Ross, one of his mentors and idols), and had carved away even more of his nose. "He has added an odd little cleft to his chin and made his lips thinner," *The New York Times* reported for the record, "desensualizing his features and blurring his racial heritage." His skin had a pallor that could only be the result of heavy makeup or, as many speculated, skin-peeling treatments designed to minimize natural pigmentation. Many found it creepy, though just about everybody found it interesting.

Perhaps it wasn't surprising that the star of "Thriller" should be intent on transforming his face into a kind of living skull. From some angles, the bone-white skin, cutaway nose, and tendril-like hair resembled nothing so much as Lon Chaney's Phantom of the Opera. The comparison is apt, because it underscores Jackson's and Chaney's parallel cultural function: the embodiment of a powerful transformation metaphors for a public basically unsure and

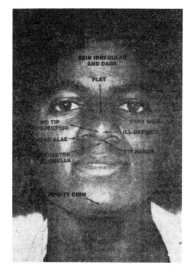
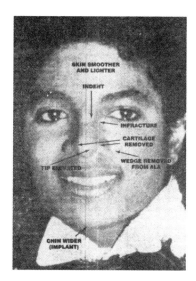
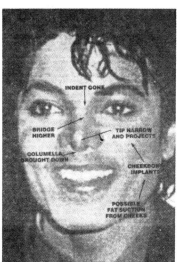
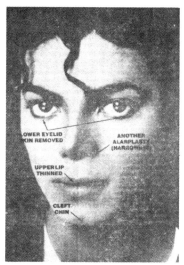

The new Lon Chaney? The changing face of Michael Jackson. *(Photofest)*

fearful about the actual prospects of change in a supposedly class-less and mobile society. A vast socioeconomic gulf separates superstar and audience, in Chaney's time as well as Jackson's, and belies the fantasy. It is not surprising that the gaps between expectation and reality consistently get gummed up with horror; Jackson has, indeed, used his enormous wealth for ghoulish media attention. In a 1987 publicity stunt, the singer offered the London Hospital Medical College $1 million for the skeletal remains of

John Merrick, the grotesquely deformed Victorian whose life was the basis for *The Elephant Man*. The December 1987 issue of *Playboy* responded with a joke report that John Merrick's descendants had made a much smaller offer—for the remains of Michael Jackson's nose.

Michael Jackson is often compared to Peter Pan, but Peter Pan is rarely acknowledged as the variation on Dracula that he is—a late-Victorian fantasy being who flew into young people's bedrooms with a problematic offer of life everlasting. (This concept was elaborated upon by director Joel Schumacher in his horror comedy *The Lost Boys* (1987), in which an alienated youth gang avoids growing up by becoming vampires.) The fantasy still flies. Rejuvenation and eternal youth are the driving illusions of the cosmetic surgery business, to which Michael Jackson's image is forever wed. *Standard and Poor's Industry Surveys* reported in 1988 that the industry of elective surgical alteration was a $300 million business, growing at a rate of 10 percent each year. The explosive growth of cosmetic surgery paralleled the unprecedented plasticity of the human body as depicted in motion picture special effects of the 1970s and 80s. The conventions of contemporary science fiction has similarly had an overwhelming impact on the way people view the workings of their minds. Once computers were tools of the brain, efficiently aping certain of its functions; today, huge numbers of otherwise intelligent people believe that the brain is "nothing but" a computer, and consciousness "nothing" but a by-product of a sufficient level of mechanical complexity. A metaphor, in short, is accepted as literal fact. If we take our cues on self-image from the fantasy images of popular culture, it is not surprising that somatic images are just as potent as their mechanistic counterparts.

Visions of men playing God with the bodies of women got rolling in American popular culture in 1930s horror films like Robert Florey's *Murders in the Rue Morgue* (1932) and, at its most spectacular, in James Whale's *Bride of Frankenstein* (1935). Creating or remaking women, and circumventing or modifying ordinary methods of reproduction, is a fantasy impulse dating back at least to the myth of Pygmalion; feminist critic Constance Penley links this tendency to Marcel Duchamp's concept of "the bachelor machine," which she describes as "a closed, self-sufficient system . . . Its common themes include frictionless, sometimes perpetual motion . . . electrification, voyeurism and masturbatory eroti-

cism, the dream of the mechanical reproduction of art, and artifical birth or reanimation." The dream-language of cinema allowed,
for the first time in human history, the elaborate mass workshop-
ping of such reveries, where they became the almost exclusive
property of mad scientists. A dominant iconography emerged: the
crazed doctor, obsessed with impossible, overreaching theories and /
or aesthetic standards, bends over the woman he has strapped to
an operating table. "And now, my dear . . ." his litany usually
begins. Anyone over the age of twelve can complete a serviceable
scenario: he's going to mate her with an ape, replace her blood,
transplant her head, shrink her into a doll, turn her into a wax
statue, etc. It is virtually impossible to catalog the frequency with
which our culture has gazed upon this image, attracted and repelled,
with attraction winning out, given the motif's perennial appeal. It
is a vision that has moved beyond mere fantasy construction, and
is now accessible in the course of everyday life.

According to Naomi Wolf, author of *The Beauty Myth,* we tol-
erate behavior on the part of cosmetic surgeons that would not be
permitted to Josef Mengele. Cosmetic surgical techniques, she
writes, "appear to be developed in irresponsible medical experiments, using desperate women as laboratory animals: in the first
stabs at liposuction, powerful hoses tore out of women, along with
massive globules of living tissue, entire nerve networks, dendrites
and ganglia. Undaunted, the experimenters kept at it. Nine French
women died." Wolf criticizes the lack of informed consent, the
element of psychological coercion, and, most important, the false
definition of healthy bodies as defective in the pursuit of medical
profits: "Looking at their actions strictly literally, not rhetorically,
it's clear that modern cosmetic surgeons are daily violating the
medical code of Nuremberg."

Both psychotherapy and cosmetic surgery increasingly push back
the boundaries of what kind of minds and bodies deserve "treatment" and "correction." Too often, the real point is to breed patient
dependence. Almost always, the goal is to make the patient accept
or conform to the conventions and fantasies of the larger society.
The fantasy of surgical release from social anxiety is a powerful
one. The relationship between the (usually) female patient and
(usually) male cosmetisurgeon is often morbidly eroticized along
horror-movie lines. The overtones were evident on a recent cable-
television program viewed by this author, a weekly "infomercial"

produced as self-promotion by a cosmetic surgeon. Two nervous, very young women discuss the unhappy state of their bodies with the doctor, who nods sympathetically, reinforcing their fears. The viewer sees nothing unattractive or misproportioned about the faces, but the women evidently feel freakish and disadvantaged. The doctor explains how he can inject a substance into their lips to make them appear more sensual. Their fear of "being cut" is discussed, and the doctor explains that they probably don't really need any "cutting" at this point, just a little touching up with collagen, which temporarily allays their fears while making them even more tense about the future. The ritual is seductive and manipulative; the viewer suspects that collagen is just heavy petting, that cutting is all the way.

For more adventurous consumers, a videotape of a breast augmentation procedure is shown, to desensitize the queasy. There is surprisingly little blood. The nipple itself is cut around the circumference and lifted like a bottle cap to allow insertion of the sac of silicone gel. No one comments on exactly what happens to the erotic response of a nipple whose nerve endings have been cleanly severed before the camera's eyes. (Although this is not the favored technique—the cutting is usually done in the fold under the breast—it is interesting that the imagery of nipple-mutilation is chosen for promotional purposes.) As in prostitution, the woman's sexual pleasure is not the point. The brides of science are there to please the scientist and lie on his table. Their bodies, in all likelihood, will never please him; he will cut them again and again, as in a slow-motion, socially sanctioned slasher movie in miniature. The effect is toned down several notches from that of a splatter film, but the essential ritual images are the same: a flash of a breast, followed by the flash of a knife. In the typical language of the cosmetisurgeon, women's bodies are deemed in need of "correction" (a transparent code word for punishment). "Being cut," of course, is the whole goal and point of the show, be it a cable television advertisement for plastic surgery, or a Tod Browning freakfest.

Perhaps the most extreme version of socially sanctioned vivisection occurs in the realm of transsexual surgery. Transsexuals are held to be persons literally trapped by an accident of birth in the body of the opposite sex. Only rarely is there true hermaphroditism or genetic evidence for such a diagnosis; but the deep anxiety over gender is real, and is addressed with the knife. As in horror movies, a metaphor is literalized. In the case of men, testicles are cut away and discarded, penises are hollowed out and inverted to become "vaginas" that have a kind of interior sensitivity that real vaginas lack. Psychiatrists told women for generations that they were supposed to have "vaginal orgasms"; finally, through transsexual intervention, doctors were able to create their fantasy in the flesh.

In *The Transsexual Empire,* Janice G. Raymond makes an excoriating argument against the practice from a feminist standpoint. "In its attempt to wrest from women the power inherent in female biology, transsexualism is not an isolated or aberrant medical procedure," Raymond writes. "It can be placed along a continuum of other male interventionist technologies such as cloning, test-tube fertilization and sex selection." To Raymond, transsexualism gives birth to not only a "she-male," but, more important, a "he-mother," Frankenstein restored to earth. The immensely popular cult film *The Rocky Horror Picture Show* (1975), a campy recap of horror characters and clichés, made a similar point in histrionic drag: *Rocky's* mad scientist, Frank N. Furter (Tim Curry), is a "transsexual transvestite from Transylvania," the very soul of gender-bending, in stitches.

Horror films in the sixties, seventies, and eighties did much to popularize the notion of sexual doppelgangers: *Psycho* still remains one of the most-seen black-and-white movies of all time. It would be revealing to learn the extent to which horrifyingly persuasive images of men and women sharing a single body influenced and legitimized the trannsexual procedure itself.

Cosmetic surgery is not the only contemporary locus of horror-related body anxiety. As evidenced by the large number of magazines, books, and information networks on the subject, the public interest in tattooing, scarification, piercing, and related body-altering activities is at an all-time high. V. Vale and Andrea Juno, editors of the recent compilation *Modern Primitives,* write that against a backdrop of an "almost universal feeling of powerlessness to 'change the world,' individuals are changing what they *do* have power over: *their own bodies.* That shadowy zone between the physical and the psychic is being probed for whatever insight and freedoms may be reclaimed." A less decorative form of body adornment (if that is the word) has been widely, but not exclusively, observed in the self-mutilating behavior among the jailed and institutionalized. According to two experts on the subject, Robert Robertson Ross and Hugh Bryan McKay,

> It would be reassuring to most of us if self-mutilation represented only the bizarre reaction of a small number of deranged individuals carefully sequestered out of the public eye . . . [but] such is not the case. Self-mutilation is not exclusively found in institutional settings, nor is it restricted to severely disturbed individuals. Just as there is no part of the human body which has not been mutilated, there is no setting where self-mutilation has not occurred.

The behaviors they describe range from crude self-tattooing to scratching, carving, biting, burning, outright amputation, and related acts against the self such as starvation and poisoning. Sometimes the point, as in the case of some schizophrenics, is simply to induce sensation in a body that feels itself "cut off." In other, more typical cases, such as those seen in homes for delinquent girls, there is a distinct social dynamic at work, including manipulation-provocation of authority and peer bonding. A permanent mark on the flesh, however disfiguring, is nonetheless a label, an identity, and an inarguable point of social reference.

Another, medical specialist, Armando R. Favazza, has extensively examined the historical, literary, and anthropological basis for self-mutilation. In *Bodies Under Siege* he notes the prevalence of mutilation imagery in cosmogenic myths, which "demonstrate the origins of social order from the body parts of dismembered primal beings." The mythic antecedents, of course, are easily observed in horror films of the fantastic-demonic variety. Mutilation has its initiatory functions as well, and it is of some interest to this discussion that one of the first uses of big-screen mutilation in an American film was the image of actor Richard Harris being hung by his pierced pectorals in *A Man Called Horse* (1970). That unforgettably gut-wrenching recreation of a Sioux initiation ceremony significantly raised the tolerance level for full-color physical horror in Hollywood, paving the way for later benchmarks like *The Exorcist*.

Whatever collective pathologies may be involved in today's pervasive imagery of mutilation and mutation, the individuals who make their livelihoods creating such spectacles are, in this writer's repeated observations, a friendly, cheerful, and levelheaded lot. Greg Nicotero, a young protégé of Tom Savini who had assisted on *Day of the Dead* (and whose own features were used on one of the film's grimacing, bodiless heads), dropped out of his premed studies to work on the Romero zombie film, and never went back. After working together on films like *The Evil Dead II* (1987), Nicotero went into business with Howard Berger and Robert Kurtzman, young men of a similar bent and background, and in 1988 founded K.N.B. EFX Group. Based in Chatsworth, California, an hour north of Los Angeles, the studio is one of several dozen in the L.A. area that cater to the entertainment industry's bottomless appetite for realistic corpses, wounds, detachable body parts—and monsters, of course.

In the reception area of their studio, a child's car seat is casually propped up against a wall hung with the realistic dissection cadavers that the team created for the film *Gross Anatomy* (1989). The main working space has multiple projects in progress, most of them having to do with rotting bodies and traumatic head wounds. At one work station, an illustrated pathology textbook is braced in a cookbook stand for ready reference. At first glance, it resembles a kind of surreal M.A.S.H. unit, where the point is to make the damage as bad as possible, not to stitch things up. Propped up on a shelf is the eponymous, barely-pieced-together torso from *Bride of Re-Animator* (1991), Brian Yuzna's ultimate, sardonic comment on the male urge to rebuild women. An odd dissonance of smells pervades the room—industrial chemicals sweetened with talcum powder (used to dust the finished appliances). There is an overall air of camaraderie, of shared mission—no one, certainly, would argue that these guys lack the fright stuff.

Nicotero, like virtually all the makeup-effects mavens, was enthralled with monsters as a child, and remembered how he challenged himself to return again and again to scary movies, even though they gave him nightmares. "I actually cut school to see *The Howling,"* he recalled. The shoulder-munching scene in *Dawn of the Dead* was another epiphany: "I never saw popcorn fly so high."

Once the province of individual free-lancers like Dick Smith, makeup effects are now created by forty increasingly competitive companies in the Los Angeles area. According to Nicotero, the effects budget for a horror fantasy film can range from $60–100,000 for an independent feature to over $10 million (nearly half the total production budget) for a big studio effort like *Gremlins 2: The New Batch* (1990), which consisted of almost nonstop Rick Baker puppet effects. Due to a glut of late-eighties splatter films which did not do well at the box office, producers retreated from the genre for a bit, and companies like K.N.B. started putting their technical know-how to use in much less gaudy films. Nicotero's shop created a group of amazingly realistic buffaloes for *Dances with Wolves* (1990), and an undetectable stunt dummy for actress Kathy Bates and broken legs for James Caan in *Misery* (1990). "The producers of both films told us they never wanted to see our work on the screen. It was important that nothing look like an 'effect.' " Horror-honed technology, in other words, has begun to invisibly set up camp in the mainstream.

Forrest J Ackerman, that ever-avuncular avatar of monster worship, scrupulously avoided unsavory manifestations in *Famous Monsters of Filmland,* and it was inevitable that his magazine would not easily survive the sex-and-violence splatter of the eighties. *Famous Monsters* gasped its last in the spring of 1983, following a downhill period of inattention by its publisher, James Warren, who withdrew into an unexplained reclusion.

Forry's fans had teethed well on the gentle humor of *Famous Monsters,* but now they wanted meat. Many of them—like Greg Nicotero and his partners—were especially interested in the technical aspects of special effects, an interest Ackerman had directly fostered with his regular and reverent homages to Lon Chaney, Sr., and, perhaps most influentially, with the publication of a *Famous Monsters* one-shot spin-off in 1965. Sold for sixty cents at newsstands across the country, the *Do-It-Yourself Monster Make-Up Handbook* was written by the then-leading professional practitioner, Dick Smith, who would later put to use absolutely everything he knew in *The Exorcist* (actress Linda Blair's head-whirling stand-in dummy is presently a prized possession of the Smithsonian Institution, a demonic cultural counterpoint to the *Spirit of St. Louis*).

Do-It-Yourself is almost uniformly cited by the leading special-effects makeup artists as having launched or influenced their careers, and is still fun reading, if only to see how far the industry has come in the intervening years. Unlike the modern techniques, which rely heavily on head and body casting, *Do-It-Yourself* preaches the old-fashioned gospel as practiced by Hollywood veterans like Jack Pierce. Chapters titled "Creating Weird Skin Textures" and "Nose

Putty and Mortician's Wax" showed young enthusiasts how to painstakingly build up fantastic disguises layer by layer on the skin itself. Some of them were pretty gruesome, but all within the established limits of the wholesome *Famous Monsters* formula.

The magazine that launched a thousand careers: Dick Smith's *Do-It-Yourself Monster Make-up Handbook* (1965).

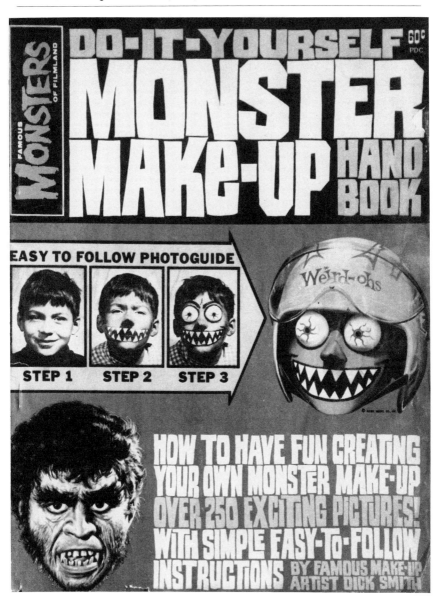

Not surprisingly, a new kind of horror magazine emerged in the late 1970s to respond to the new atmosphere of industrial-strength mayhem, and to readers eager to learn how it was all done. *Fangoria,* launched in 1979, caused controversy from its inception; not since *Mad* magazine had a publication aimed at young people raised so many eyebrows among their elders. Unlike *Famous Monsters, Fangoria* was printed in full color, the better to reproduce its center spreads and foldouts of lovingly photographed carnage, like a necrophilic parody of *Playboy.* ("It isn't exactly the kind of magazine you see people reading on the subway," said director Joe Dante.) Like *Playboy, Fangoria* balanced its eye-popping visuals with detailed, often highly technical articles and interviews with actors, directors, and, most important, makeup artists.

Those uninitiated in the textures and nuances of Monster Culture could not get past the pictures. After complaints, the magazine got pulled from the shelves of one Canadian convenience-store chain. In England, *Fangoria* caused a Nightmare in Downing Street for Prime Minister Margaret Thatcher, who called it "absolutely appalling" and urged a member of Parliament to determine whether the magazine fell under the Obscene Publications Act of 1959. It didn't. The episode recalled a similar moment from the fifties, when Winston Churchill officially summoned a batch of horror comics to the prime minister's residence in order to brief himself on the then-raging censorship battles. (He later claimed not to have had the time to read them.)

Fangoria's current editor, Anthony Timpone, is keenly aware of censorship issues, and frequently editorializes against the hostile encroachments of the Motion Picture Association of America, capricious guardian of the problematic alphabet soup that currently passes as a "rating system" to alert parents to the sex and violence in movies and videos. The MPAA is the latest incarnation of the MPPDA that gave such grief to the creators of *Bride of Frankenstein* and *Dracula's Daughter* in the 1930s, and, at its hypocritical heart, has changed not at all. Politically unable to win many skirmishes against the big studios, who provide its funding, but still needing to appear responsible to the public, the MPAA primarily inflicts its arbitrary and indecipherable standards on independent and low-budget features, where most of the horror is to be found.

Writer / producer Ken Sanders wrote for *Fangoria* a devastating article on the MPAA's cat-and-mouse games over withholding the all-important "Restricted" rating of his picture *Blood Salvage*

The visual shocks of *Fangoria* magazine are direct descendants of Dalí and Buñuel's *Un Chien andalu* (1928).

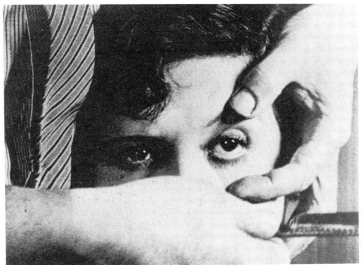

(1990). (An unrated, or "X"-rated film can run into crippling distribution and advertising problems.) In Sanders' telling, an inattentive ratings board relied on their *projectionist* to gauge middle America's potential reaction to the film. They then used the man's verbatim responses to demand cuts of some bloodless violence, which Sanders was able to successfully fight. Meanwhile, in an expensive studio effort like Twentieth Century Fox's *The Fly II* (1989), a gratuitous close-up of a man's head being crushed by an elevator in no way jeopardized its "R" imprimatur. Sanders similarly pointed out to the MPAA that an action film like *Lethal Weapon 2* (1989) contained ten times the on-screen violence of *Blood Salvage*. The morality guardians would not budge. "Your film is different," they said. Sanders agreed. "My film was a modestly budgeted, independently produced *horror* film. It wasn't a big studio production with big stars and loads of advance publicity. That's what made it a candidate for swift execution."

In addition to keeping readers abreast on the politics, personalities, and technical advances in horror, *Fangoria* sponsors an ongoing series of tribal celebrations. In January 1991, the Penta Hotel in midtown Manhattan was host to *Fangoria*'s "Weekend of Horrors," the latest installment of a continuing horror convention held in New York, Los Angeles, and around the country. A "splatterpunk" mood predominates. The attendees are what Manhattanites call a bridge-and-tunnel crowd (the monster-troll connotations duly noted): working-class, young, white. In addition to enjoying appearances by horror superstars like Robert Englund (the actor who plays Freddy Krueger in the *Nightmare on Elm Street* movies) and author-filmmaker Clive Barker (a charming ex-Liverpudlian whose tales of controlled, icy cruelty set new standards in the genre for themes of pain and domination), fans can tour a large exhibition hall full of monster memorabilia. Families look on approvingly while their wives, husbands, and children submit to what can only be described as a Georgette Klinger Salon of the Damned— temporary cosmetic uglification as status badge. The most remarkable tables are those that brim with latex rubber body parts— arms, legs, heads, whole hacked-apart torsos, laid out for sale like so much human sashimi. There are paperweights of realistic, yanked-out eyeballs sliced with razor blades and run through with straight pins. There is more, but these will suffice here.

Bizarre as it may seem, these homely handiworks are objects of true veneration, and not for incipient serial killers. They stand for something else entirely: a promise of personal transformation, recognition, and material reward. According to *Fangoria* editor Timpone, a large portion of his present readership is attracted to the magazine for a specific reason: they want to get out of whatever it is they're currently doing with their lives, and they want to get into the world of special effects. The Art Institute of Pittsburgh, where Tom Savini is a faculty member, offers an associate degree in media-effects technology, and has a tidy literature table set up amidst its far messier neighbors for those on a serious career track. In earlier cultures, mutilation rites symbolized a rite of passage. They still do. If one does it right, there is advancement, money, and prestige. The power to shock *is* power, after all. The mastery of a technically complicated plastic art *is* mastery, even if the results of that art strike some as the equivalent of blood-painting on velvet. A scream is recognition in its purest, primal form; in the world of splatter effects, it is the sincerest sound of flattery.

Entertainment is one of America's last viable and most visible exports, a fact not lost upon the young people who have no prospects in the industrial economy that produced them. The odds may not be in their favor. The point is made bluntly in *A Nightmare on Elm Street 3: Dream Warriors* (1987). A girl with show-business aspirations is confronted by Freddy Krueger, who erupts from the video monitor and pulls her toward the screen. "Here's your big break in TV. Welcome to prime time, bitch!" he cackles, and smashes her head through the picture tube. Or to put it another way: *I'm Freddy Krueger. And you're not.*

Horror, however, keeps hope alive. The Savinis manqués want to make a splash, and they aim do it in the most literal manner possible. Whatever working-class rage is lurking here, it is content, for the moment, to feed on illusory gore. The "Weekend of Horrors" is like a surreal populist casino where the slot machines turn up eyeballs and body parts, and the jackpot, when it comes, spills entrails on your shoes.

It is a perfect moment. The go-go eighties have gone gore-gore. There is talk of another war, this one in the Middle East. The economy has stalled, tottering. And as far as the eye can see, the only thing "trickling down" is make-believe blood.

Chapter Twelve

ROTTEN BLOOD

"Your blood is rotten! Black as your sins!"

Bela Lugosi in
Murders in the Rue Morgue
(1932)

"THE 'RED DEATH' had long devastated the country. No pestilence had ever been so fatal, or so hideous. Blood was its Avatar and its seal. . . ." Edgar Allan Poe's macabre short story "The Masque of the Red Death," first published (in its final, revised form) by *The Broadway Journal* in July 1845, required a cultural gestation of a century and a half before its full significance would be revealed to America, not in high-school textbooks, where it had long been relegated as a harmless, spooky fairy tale, but as an urgent plague parable for the age of AIDS. By the mid-1980s, all of America was living in Poe's dream in one way or another. "The Masque" is basically a story of denial in the face of catastrophe, the account of a gaudy, quarantined revel staged, *Decameron*-style, by an emblematic Prince Prospero, whose kingdom has been half-depopulated by a bloody plague. He seals himself off with a thousand

Nervous laughter in the age of AIDS: Dracula (James Woods) takes a cautionary blood sample from a prospective victim (Nora Dunn) during a skit on NBC-TV's "Saturday Night Live." (Courtesy of the National Broadcasting Company)

revelers. "They resolved to leave means neither of ingress or egress to the sudden impulses of despair or of frenzy within. The abbey was amply provisioned. With such precautions the courtiers might bid defiance to contagion. The external world could take care of itself. In the meantime it was folly to grieve, or to think."

The social and political response to the blood-borne epidemic of Acquired Immune Deficiency Syndrome had much in common with Prospero's self-defeating strategy of denial. Prospero denied the Red Death, and Red Death mockingly materialized in a hideous theatrical disguise. Prosperous America of the 1980s denied the reality of AIDS, locking its doors against victims of the plague, while monstrous images popped up everywhere in its collective dreams. The landscape of popular culture was awash with sanguinary themes as never before; splatter movies and blood-spilling serial killers became fixtures of the media, and images and metaphors of bloodstream poisoning—in product-tampering scares, in the obsession with cholesterol levels, in the backlash against chemical food additives, and even in the blood-purification fantasies of the skinheads and neo-Nazis.

Not surprisingly, vampires were a constant presence at the feast, if not the honored guests.

"When I was a little girl," the vampire intoned, "television was a very new thing. I think we were the first people on the block to get a television."

It is only appropriate that the vampire now lives on the outskirts of the television and film industry, on a quiet residential street in North Hollywood. An ample, apple-cheeked woman resplendent in a floor-length red velvet dress, Megan★ the vampire is a part-time actress who occasionally plays walk-ons on network sitcoms, usually cast as a housewife or aged into a cherubic grandmother. Millions have had a fleeting vampiric visitation in their own living rooms, without ever suspecting. The vampire likes it that way.

Megan introduces the visitor to her longtime companion, Douglas, as well as to Christopher, her donor. Douglas, it turns out, is not interested in donating to the vampire cause, although Megan has "been after him for years."

The vampire was born during World War II in southern Cali-

★Names and some identifying details have been changed. However, all persons described are real and not in any way composites or fictionalizations.

fornia. Her father had been born in London in 1897, the year Bram Stoker published *Dracula,* a fact Megan believes explains much. A naturalized American, "my father tried to shake his Britishness, but he could never really scrape it off his shoes," she said. "But his ideas on how to bring up a young girl came straight out of Edwardian England. The golden rule in our household was 'No.' "

When Megan was still quite young, her mother thrilled her with eastern European folk legends and ghost stories. "My grandmother was of Polish ancestry, and my mother picked up a lot of strange tales from her that she passed on to me in turn. And the happiest experiences I had with my mother were listening to her 'witch' tales. They didn't scare me. They delighted me."

But one kind of narrative was absolutely taboo. "Vampire stories gave my mother the willies," Megan remembered. And the forbidden nature of the subject, of course, made it all the more fascinating to Megan. She doesn't remember when she first saw Bela Lugosi in *Dracula,* but knows she was fully familiar with the movie before the age of ten. Universal had given the film a major rerelease in 1947, when Megan was five.

Unlike Dracula, who never drank wine, both Megan's parents imbibed heavily. Megan's father physically abused both mother and daughter, "but we fought back," she recalls. "I could never have any friends over, of course. So I created my own world to live in. I read a great deal. My mother had taught me to read and write before kindergarten."

Left alone one day while her parents drank in the kitchen, Megan started rummaging through her father's trunk. She didn't know exactly what she expected to find there, but was flabbergasted at what she did find: a pair of comic books, both of "a decidedly macabre nature." They were exactly the kind of publication that Frederic Wertham had campaigned against.

Read today, Wertham's interviews with "comic-book addicts" are less than convincing. It was too bad that he never interviewed Megan, who was "absolutely thrilled" by her father's secret stash of horror. As her parents were consumed by their stupor, she stole away to her bedroom and read the books from cover to cover. "One of them contained a story about a female vampire named Lila. It left a lasting impression. I felt very sympathetic toward the character. She was so beautiful."

Megan's delight with *The Vault of Horror* was short-lived. Her mother caught her poring over Lila's undead exploits and punished her severely. "She told me this was completely unsuitable reading material for a young girl. I was never to look at it again." Funny animal comics were okay, but even Batman was too close to another kind of bat-man for her mother's comfort. "She was determined to turn me into a happy, wholesome little girl." But, as in many dysfunctional families, Megan received contradictory signals. Despite the household prohibition on horror comics, her mother continued to tell her spine-tingling ghost stories until her young adulthood.

Megan maintained her "vampire" life on a fantasy plane that she could enter at will, with or without her parents' approval. "I began to play my vampire games," Megan recalled. "These were very

A comic-book vampire from the early fifties.

secret games I told very few people about. Only certain, selected kids who were creative enough, imaginative enough, or just 'odd' enough in some way to be receptive." Megan's vampires were never creatures of destruction. "They were always after the bad guys—beautiful women who took care of the villains of the world. I would act out the stories with the neighborhood kids—we would wander around in flowing nightgowns, things like that." Once, Megan's mother snapped her picture in a billowing garment, unaware that her preadolescent daughter was modeling not sleep-wear, but, to her own mind, a shroud.

Soon she started writing her stories down, in the form of serials she would read to trusted friends as delicious, shared secrets. She filled notebooks with the kind of vampire stories she could never find in published sources, stories in which the vampires triumphed and were clearly superior beings. On Saturday nights, she watched the horror movies hosted by Maila "Vampira" Nurmi. "I absolutely idealized her," Megan said. "I can still remember the introduction—'Fletcher Jones Chevrolet presents—Vampira!' She was like a goddess to me."

Megan's obsession with Vampira got her into trouble, at school and at home. "My parents had stuck me in a Catholic girls' school, unaware how stimulating I found the religion's blood imagery." From an early age, Megan had been receiving conflicting messages about religion and blood, love and pain. "It was good, it was bad, do it, don't do it. . . . My mother was raised a Catholic in the Polish tradition, and had the fear of God beaten into her by her own mother." In church, the children were taught that the wine the priest drank was blood, not just symbolic blood, but the genuine article. The nuns, however, failed to see the relevance of vampirism to a Catholic education.

"I used to come to school wearing dark fingernail polish. The other kids thought I was crazy and persecuted me for it." Even the girls in Megan's inner circle didn't share her fixation on the glamorous Vampira. "It was a full-blown secret identity—until I got busted." One of her girlfriends ratted to the nuns, revealing all the details of Megan's fantasy life. "The nuns interrogated me, and called my parents, who in turn decided to investigate Vampira themselves. They sat up one night, and watched the show in silence. Afterwards, I was told I was never to watch the program again. They brought out my precious stories and made me tear them up, one by one. If I ever so much as mentioned the subject again, they told me, they would take me to a doctor who would shrink my head down to size."

In practice, the embargo on the undead was short-lived, due to her parents' alcoholism. "I'd just wait until they got smashed on Saturday night, which they always did. They'd be so blotto they couldn't tell what was on television anyway." Then, like an unseen wraith in her own house, Megan would rise from her bed and drift past the semiconscious figures of her parents to commune with Vampira. The character's perverse contradictions—beautiful-ugly, sexy-deathly—echoed the unresolvable conflicts of Megan's family life. "In a way," she recalled, "Vampira was a kind of beatnik," a comforting, antiauthoritarian image.

Vampira turned out to be a brief phenomenon, a dark comet visible on the airwaves for less than a year. Her broadcast demise was one of two traumatic events for Megan in 1954. One day, Megan's mother left the house and was hit by a car, which crippled her for life. The accident ruined the family financially. Forced into a caretaker role at an early age, Megan began sublimating her dark fantasies. She was still an oddball and outcast at school, but now she read the Brontës instead of *Tales from the Crypt,* substituting a genteel Gothicism for the cartoony flamboyance of the Crypt Keeper and Vampira. Megan lived at home until she was twenty-five, taking care of her mother, whose injuries proved mental as well as physical. The older woman sank into depression, continued to drink heavily, and ignored her doctor's prescriptions for physical therapy. "She was committing slow suicide," Megan remembered.

With considerable emotional effort, Megan gave up the dark side, found a job that paid $50 a week, and moved into an apartment of her own. "I started to have fun," she recalled. "I became a hippie for a while, I smoked pot, I took acid, I had a ball. I learned a lot about life, and a lot about different levels of consciousness. Acid was a spiritual thing, it was ritualistic, religious." For a time Megan became one of L.A.'s many psychedelic gurus, a hippie earth mother nurturing others the way she had never been nurtured herself.

In 1971, Megan's mother suddenly died of a heart attack. And shortly afterward, her psychedelic experiences began to take on frightening, vampire-related imagery. "I thought I had given it all up. But it woke up again, stronger than it had ever been before. It was something so contrary to the earth-mother role I was playing at the time that it really freaked me out." The visions were "intensely religious, ecstatic, and frightening. I saw myself as a vampire, with an overpowering compulsion to drink blood from a lover. Male or female, it didn't matter."

Megan drifted through the seventies in a kind of trance. She knew that her vampire obsession was no whimsical childhood fantasy that had resurfaced, but something that was part of her fundamental nature, needing to be confronted and assimilated. But the only release she found was in domestic horror movies like *Count Yorga, Vampire* (1970) and *Love at First Bite* (1979) and the elegant imported nightmares of Hammer Films. At the same time she nursed her father through his final illness, numbing herself in the cold eroticism of Christopher Lee.

Rock music, which had interested Megan since her early psychedelic days, began appropriating the trappings of horror movies in the early seventies, beginning with Alice Cooper, Kiss, and other groups. Fused with the burgeoning punk sensibility, a disturbing hybrid emerged by the end of the decade, a new kind of shock-rock known generically as Gothic. Clubs began springing up in Hollywood with names like Theatre of Blood, the Veil, and Helter Skelter. One day Megan was walking down Hollywood Boulevard when she saw a handbill plastered on a wall: ONE NIGHT ONLY—CASTRATION SQUAD.

Megan had always been passionately fascinated by the legendary castrati of the opera world, an interest that had almost eclipsed her obsession with vampires, and the name of the group transfixed her. And although she didn't understand it completely at the time, the castrato and the vampire shared an underlying psychology— an oral displacement of genital sex, steeped and transformed in nineteenth-century Romanticism. Megan began hanging out with groups like Castration Squad, the Sleepless, 45 Grave, and Christian Death.

It was about this time that Megan received a call from Anne Rice.

Megan didn't know her, but they had a mutual friend who recommended the author contact her as part of her research for her new novel, *Cry to Heaven,* which concerned the castrati. According to Megan, they talked for hours, the way only two people who share a passionate, specialized interest in an arcane subject can. Megan made the novelist tapes from her collection of rare, turn-of-the-century discs of the last castrati voices ever recorded, and received an acknowledgment in print. Rice suggested that Megan might enjoy her first novel, which dealt with a related theme. The book was called *Interview with the Vampire.*

"I went out and found a paperback," Megan recalled. "And I couldn't put the damned thing down." A ripe, decadent story of vampires in nineteenth-century New Orleans that had already claimed a cult following, the book included an especially unforgettable character with a special resonance for Megan, a little girl transformed into a vampire and trapped in a child's undead body for eternity. Megan came out of her room only to eat. "I couldn't get enough of it—it was a revelation. At last, here was one modern writer who wrote a beautiful story and didn't destroy her vampires at the end. It was as if vampire literature had finally come out of prehistoric caves and into civilization."

Interview with the Vampire pushed Megan's life into a kind of critical mass. Suddenly, vampires were everywhere. And one day a "ghoulish little guy in whiteface and a full mortician's outfit" came into the L.A. newspaper office where Megan worked as a production artist. He was a musician with British pretensions, and called himself Jonathan Cape. His band was named Schreck's Bad Boys, after the actor in the German film *Nosferatu.* "I fell head over heels in love with him," Megan said. "He told me all about his dark self, secret things he did and got high on." Blood, he hinted, was one of them.

Megan also fell in love with one of Jonathan's singers, who used the name Desiree LeFanu. "She was so exotic, tall and thin. *Real* thin. She came up to me like I was her long-lost sister and stared at me with her strange eyes. She invited me to one of her poetry readings. And after I heard her perform she called me one night, à la Anne Rice, and we just talked for five and a half hours. It was a marathon phone call that totally changed my life. She talked about her poetry, her friends in the underground, her drug use, her dream life. And finally she said, 'Do you mind if I ask you a very personal question?' 'No,' I said. 'Are you *quite* sure . . . ?' she asked. I told her I was.

" 'Tell me, Megan,' she said, 'has anyone ever asked you . . . for your blood?' "

It was as if a dam had burst. Desiree revealed her personal history of vampirism, how she had been practicing blood-drinking from the age of twelve or thirteen. Megan felt the most powerful

An original handbill for one of Hollywood's first Gothic music hangouts in the early eighties. *(Courtesy of Paul Penser)*

surge of yearning she had ever experienced. To think that this beautiful creature, not a fantasy, not a movie, wanted to partake of her very essence!

Actual consummation proved more difficult. Despite her declarations of thirst, Desiree tormented Megan by putting off the crucial event. And then, in a kind of painful primal scene, Megan learned that her beloved Jonathan and Desiree had begun drinking each other's blood, that they were driven around the Hollywood hills in the back of a car, tearing the skin of each other's throats and lapping the flow. (Later Megan would learn of blood fetishists who played for higher stakes, who could only be sated by *spurting* blood, auto-vampires who knew how to safely puncture their own jugular veins, catching the leaping stream in their mouths.)

Jonathan's and Desiree's flirtations turned out to be a cruel tease. They were to remain the unapproachable, undead adults, and she the perpetual child. Jonathan further alienated Megan, and nearly everyone else, by his involvement with skinheads, Satanists, and neo-Nazis. "Nobody wanted to play with him anymore," Megan remembered. Thoroughly disillusioned, she withdrew from the orbit of Schreck's Bad Boys.

Eventually, Megan found a sympathetic donor in Christopher, an intense, dark-haired young man with a hawklike profile and a prodigious knowledge of punk, heavy-metal, and Gothic music. Christopher is what is known in vampire circles as a "passive" donor; he and Megan are soul mates, not physical lovers. His own erotic fantasies center on the classic Vampira-dominatrix image: Diamanda Galás, the intense and uncompromising performance artist who has made a stark theatrical connection between Gothicism, politics, and AIDS with her *Plague Mass,* is his most idealized female icon. Christopher, who is HIV-negative, gives Megan approximately 100 monogamous cubic centimeters a week, withdrawn by syringe for her private, autoerotic delectation. AIDS awareness is high in the vampire community, whose central rite is the exchange of bodily fluids, even though the disease itself is not readily spread by the oral ingestion of blood.

Many people have trouble seeing this kind of activity as anything but bestial. According to Christopher, "Although the Gothic movement may seem to be surrounded by a kind of violence, it is actually gentle, sharing, and nurturing. Gothic people are intensely alive—and honest enough to deal with images of death openly."

There are many "types" in the Gothic scene, said Christopher, "but the vampire occupies center stage. The vampire is the ultimate imaginative outcast, a lonely rebel against the establishment." Both Megan and Christopher decry the popular connection between vampires and satanism as misleading and stereotypical. "Vampirism is a pre-Christian idea," said Megan, and has nothing to do with modern religions or their satanic inversions. Like practitioners of wicca, or Druidic witchcraft, they feel that the vampire / Gothic movement has been unjustly maligned.

And exactly how many people are involved in this sort of thing? Megan and Christopher personally know a half dozen out-of-the-closet blood drinkers in Hollywood; estimates of the size of an "active" vampire community in America usually run into the hundreds. The closeted population seems to be much larger—large enough, in fact, that a 1-900-VAMPIRE phone service was inaugurated in 1990 for anonymous devotees.

Just who becomes a vampire? Is Megan's case typical? According to Norine Dresser, the California folklorist who broke the taboo on the subject with her book *American Vampires* in 1989, strong correlations have been made between early childhood abuse and a later acting-out of vampire fantasies. Blood-drinking becomes an overpowering metaphor for warm human contact. Dresser cites the unique research of Jeanne Youngson, Ph.D., who has collected correspondence with blood fetishists for the past thirteen years (Youngson's interest in vampires is decidedly catholic—as president of the Count Dracula Fan Club, she ministers to enthusiasts of all stripes, from movie buffs to the hard-core thirsty). Their histories are a litany of "abuse, neglect, abandonment, loneliness or molestation."

There is another way to look at it. Like mythical vampires, Megan is nothing if not a survivor, who has assembled from the wreckage of a tumultuous childhood a powerful sense of identity, albeit an identity many would find perverse. But their reaction might also contain a sense of recognition, for we all share Megan's larger world. There are those who have said for years that ours is a generation already raised living-dead in front of the television, drawing vicarious life and sustenance from images of violence and blood, real and imagined. We hardly need to share Megan's specific traumas to become "undead" ourselves. With or without the family, modern life itself can be supremely dysfunctional and abusive, cranking out a largely unchronicled generation of lost boys, and girls. And to them, finally, attention must be paid.

Two recent paperback horror novels throw a dark illumination on Megan's world, as well as ours. Issued by separate publishers, they feature strikingly similar covers. At a distance they might be mistaken for classic images of Madonna and child, but upon close inspection it becomes clear that the infants are not so interested in their mother's breast as in her throat. Their eyes seem to flicker demonically, and at the corners of their baby-lips there is something else—sharp, glistening, and white. Love and hate, blood and nourishment, obscenely juxtaposed. These are truly monstrous images, all the more so for their ambivalent depiction of the roots of the vampire in life's basic bonds and interdependencies. On this level, where we all have been, no one is safe.

Children of the night?

What music we make.

By the mid-1980s, more people were reading about vampires than at any time in history, and for the first time, they were identifying with them positively. At Dark Carnival, one of the country's largest fantasy bookstore-emporiums in Berkeley, California, vampire literature became sufficiently voluminous to merit an alcove all its own, with over a hundred titles in print. (Adjacent to the vampires are the serial killers, and another intriguing category called "Forensic Fun," consisting of illustrated pathology textbooks and the like. Proprietor Jack Rems said that young couples often peruse these shelves, "because it gives them a reason to start talking about bodily functions.")

Author Anne Rice was the undisputed queen of literary vampires in the eighties: two sequels to 1976's *Interview with the Vampire*—*The Vampire Lestat* (1985) and *The Queen of the Damned* (1988)—were instant best-sellers. Other popular titles included Chelsea Quinn Yarbro's *Hotel Transylvania* (1978) and its sequel, *A Flame in Byzantium* (1988), dealing with the vampire Ragoczy, Count Saint-Germain; S. P. Somtow's *Vampire Junction* (1984), set in the world of Gothic-rock music; and Ray Garton's audacious *Live Girls* (1987), in which 42nd Street vampire-hookers draw blood as well as semen from their male victims during peep-show sessions of oral sex.

The vampire fantasies were hardly limited to fiction. In a decade morbidly preoccupied with body fluids and sexually transmitted diseases, blood-draining metaphors appeared regularly in the rhetoric of Ronald Reagan and his economic advisors. The talk of cutting, slashing, and budgetary hemorrhaging was nonstop from the time of Reagan's televised debate with Jimmy Carter until the new administration had instituted its economic programs. Liberal policies, from the Reagan point of view, were sapping the body politic when not poisoning it. In a new age of puritanical austerity, social expenditures were suddenly seen to be toxic. In his book *Reagan's America,* the psychohistorian Lloyd deMause enumerates the various kinds of pollution, poison, and contagion that captured the public imagination, culminating in the media circus surrounding AIDS: herpes hysteria, Tylenol poisoning, dioxin, toxic waste dumps, etc., would soon be followed by seeping radon gas, carcinogenic food additives, and the radiation disasters at Three Mile Island and Chernobyl. Reagan's call for a mass purification struck a deep response in a public that suddenly believed much of the nation's blood was indeed rotten, and as black as its sins. Following the example of Bela Lugosi in *Murders in the Rue Morgue,* a blood-testing frenzy set in—testing for AIDS, testing for drugs, testing for killer cholesterol. As deMause writes, "Whenever nations have gone a long time since their last sacrificial cleansing, they choose a leader who easily entertains paranoid poison fantasies." DeMause also draws a provocative socio-psychological parallel between the sacrificial scapegoating of the Reagan years and the cannibal rites of the Aztecs: just as the Aztecs would gather to witness the spectacle of a heart being ripped from a living victim, Americans in 1982 fixated on the miraculous allegory of a heartless man, Barney Clark, kept alive by a "magical" mechanical pump.

Like Tod Browning, the director of *Dracula* and *Freaks,* Ronald Reagan also seems to have had a deep affinity, personal and professional, for castration imagery. Reagan's most famous film, *King's Row* (1942), would, in the hands of a perceptive film programmer, make an ideal triple feature, sandwiched between Browning's *Freaks* and *The Unknown.* In *King's Row,* Reagan is the victim of a sadistic doctor who, following an accident, unnecessarily amputates the young man's legs as punishment for desiring his daughter. Reagan's anguished cry at discovering his mutilation—"Where's the rest of me?"—became a trademark line, and he even used it as the title of his autobiography. His need to repeatedly screen the film led his first wife, Jane Wyman, to confide to Gregory Peck that the real reason for her divorcing the president-to-be was that "I just couldn't stand to watch that damn *King's Row* one more time." America had elected as its leader a man who was the Gipper on the outside, and Johnny Eck on the inside.

The specter of AIDS, meanwhile, loomed over the wreckage of the sexual revolution like the pestilential image of Nosferatu had once presided over a decimated Germany. AIDS, according to thanatologist Robert Kastenbaum, "has a way of speaking directly to powerful fantasies that usually remain under firm control and constraint." He notes that the AIDS epidemic has the power to stir up unconscious, vampire-related fears. "The vampire image," writes Kastenbaum, "may now have taken the all too palpable form of an unholy, sex-related, blood-stealing catastrophe."

The initial connection, in industrialized countries, between AIDS and gay men was paralleled on the plane of popular fantasy with a blurring of the image of the homosexual with that of the vampire. Homophobes had long held that gay people were evil predators with the Draculean power to corrupt and transform the sexually straight and virtuous. "They have to recruit, because they can't reproduce their own kind" was a common refrain on the right. The faded pop singer Anita Bryant, who sought to revive her career with an antihomosexual campaign in Florida, went beyond metaphor in her assertion that "the male homosexual eats another man's sperm. Sperm is the most concentrated form of blood. The homosexual is eating life."

The ugly stereotype had a fascinating flip side, however. One gay bookstore, Unicorn Books in West Hollywood, told this author that all its best-selling titles for a period during 1991 were vampire titles, with Anne Rice topping the list. In the three novels of her *Vampire Chronicles* series to date, Rice spins a seductive, evocative myth of gender transcendence among the living dead, consciously seeking a gay resonance. "Like the saints she had so strongly admired in her youth," writes Katherine Ramsland in her authorized Rice biography, *Prism of the Night,* "gay men exhibited an excessiveness that excited her and courage in the face of prejudice." Rice and her husband eventually moved to the Castro district of San Francisco, one of the most celebrated gay enclaves in the world. The first book, *Interview with the Vampire,* had been composed before the onset of the AIDS crisis, but it nonetheless had roots in an actual, blood-borne disease: the Rices' daughter, Michele, died in 1972 at the age of six from leukemia. The character of Claudia in *Interview with the Vampire,* a never-aging child-vampire who is one of Rice's most memorable creations, emerged (in the estimation of both Rice and her biographer) from a largely unconscious effort on Rice's part to process her grief.

While it would be simplistic to think that gay readers turn to Anne Rice novels as a conscious form of bereavement therapy, her sympathetic portrayal of an alternate, supernaturalized sexuality that survives a world of death conveys a complicated healing message to a community which has suffered, and continues to suffer, a concentrated level of human loss unprecedented outside of wartime—or medieval plague.

The vampire serves a coping function, symbolically representing a dreaded plague-death while at the same time triumphantly transcending it. In the early sixties, children turned instinctively to the resurrection figures of Dracula and Frankenstein as protective amulets during the death-looming days of the Cold War. In the age of AIDS, the vampire myth offers a similar strategy to adults (gay and straight) for processing the widespread, inescapable reality of death at an early age—a necessary form of psychological "bargaining." The vampire provides secular society with a quasi-religious engagement / exorcism of the demon Death, a function which could be discerned even in the pop humor of a late-eighties television commercial featuring a toy Dracula rising from his crypt with the aid of dry-cell batteries; vampirism, in other words, was equated literally with power, resurrection, and beneficial energy, an admixture of Halloween and Easter. Joyce Carol Oates, commenting on *Dracula* through the perspective of her own Catholic childhood, elaborated on the ceremonial religious function of the vampire. "The figure of Count Dracula as played so coolly by Bela Lugosi *is* priestly; his formal evening wear, high starched collar, ankle-length black cape suggest the vestments of a Catholic priest, as do his carefully choreographed movements, the precision with which he pronounces words, enunciates syllables, as if English was a foreign language."

The Catholic Church no longer persecutes witches and vampires, but in the age of AIDS adamantly opposes the advancement of civil rights for homosexuals. By the beginning of the nineties,

"Even I'm afraid of AIDS": Japan's first public-service campaign for AIDS awareness enlisted Dracula as its unlikely spokesman. *(Photo by Jack Chenet; reprinted by permission of* Newsweek)

confrontations between church officials and militant gays over AIDS issues became increasingly noisy and shrill. A strictly political reading of the conflict misses the complicated mythic underpinnings of these ritual clashes. The symbolic flesh-eating and blood-drinking of the Catholic mass has the same ancient roots as vampire legends; when gay demonstrators ("life-eating" monsters to the far religious right) disrupted the communion service at Saint Patrick's Cathedral in 1991, primitive and unarticulated blood-themes shadowed the publicly stated issues. The abortive attempt, in 1990, by a convention of religious fundamentalists in San Francisco to march against the "demonic" Halloween celebration in the Castro district was another illustration of the power of religio-mythic horror to irrationally influence human activity.

A surprisingly high number of vampire aficionados (gay and straight) do turn out to be Catholics or ex-Catholics—at least in this writer's extensive, if unscientific, observation. In *The Queen of the Damned,* Anne Rice calculatedly imbued her ambisexual vampire with the traits of a pagan / Christian savior: "The blood ran in tiny rivulets down his white face, as if from Christ's Crown of Thorns," she writes of an ecstatic rock concert given by the Vampire Lestat. There is no "as if" a few pages later: "Lestat was Christ on the cathedral cross. . . . The Vampire Lestat was God."

Just as the younger generation of gay activists reclaimed the epithet "queer" as a badge of honor during the AIDS wars, so was the negative vampire identification similarly embraced, rehabilitated, and defanged. Charles Busch's comedy *Vampire Lesbians of Sodom* was one of Off-Broadway's most remarkable hits in the eighties, running in Greenwich Village for years. Explicitly gay and lesbian vampires appeared in the small-press fiction of authors Jewelle Gomez, whose *The Gilda Stories* (1991) chronicles its title character's undead progress from 1850s Louisiana into the twenty-first century, and Jeffrey N. McMahan, whose far more escapist *Vampires Anonymous* (1991) depicts gay vampires in a modern world where AIDS is never mentioned (a narrative strategy which echoes the absence of World War II from the wartime Wolf Man movies). The link between vampirism and AIDS could be found without much difficulty by the end of the eighties, in venues ranging from avant-garde theatre to commercial television. The New York stage artist Ping Chong staged a disturbing "yuppie" version of *Nosferatu* in 1985, in which the vapid inhabitants of a high-tech Manhattan loft are set upon by a low-tech version of Max Schreck. Chong's

Nosferatu "comes from the Reagan years," he told *The New York Times* when the piece was revived in 1991, adding that "the vampire we confront has been born from our own neglect and denial" in response to AIDS and other social issues. NBC-TV's "Saturday Night Live" produced a sketch in which actor James Woods played an AIDS-obsessed Dracula who spends so much of the night testing the blood of his prospective victims that the sun rises and destroys him before he can suck.

In mainstream journalism, the AIDS story was shaped as a stereotypical horror movie scenario. A wasting malady involving blood is discovered, each victim capable of creating more of his kind. Conventional medicine is baffled. Highly authoritarian figures declare that the epidemic can only be controlled if traditional sex roles are observed; the monster is linked to sexual license and unconventional sexual arrangements. More monster-vampire coloration is added to the stew with the indictment of drug addiction as a contributing factor. Drugs are held to be yet another "plague" of the late twentieth century, centering on uncontrollable cravings and personality transformations. The addicts are popularly imagined to be vein-puncturing night-creatures, pariahs, outcasts, nocturnal urban predators. The irrational, vampire-related undercurrents of plague panic and blood taboos prompt a reactionary "scientific" response stirring up omnipotent male fantasies of the Frankenstein school—the solution is said to require nothing less than the control of basic life processes. The leading researchers show an excess of hubris. A virus is held to be the cause of the crisis (viruses are fashionable in medical research these days, and if one believes their publicity, account for almost every medical phenomenon, just as "galvanic energy" was the key to life itself during Mary Shelley's day). AIDS researchers carry out their work in paranoid secrecy, conducting experiments in genetic engineering with viral clones. (Clones—asexually created, genetically duplicated organisms—are, on one level, the latest, high-tech incarnation of the doppelganger, that ever-present force in stories of vampires and artificial beings.)

Clearly, "scientific" activity surrounding AIDS, as well as its media reportage, shows signs of having drawn unconsciously upon monster melodrama fantasies to solve a crisis that exists in fact. Susan Sontag, in *AIDS and Its Metaphors,* makes a related critique of the widespread use of the military metaphor in relation to AIDS, which "not only provides a persuasive justification for authoritarian rule but implicitly suggests the necessity of state-sponsored repression and violence . . . the effect of the military imagery on thinking about sickness and health is far from inconsequential. It overmobilizes, overdescribes, and powerfully contributes to the excommunicating and stigmatizing of the ill." The implicit horror metaphors do much the same thing.

Ten years into the AIDS crisis, the precise mechanism by which the putative AIDS virus was supposed to decimate the human immune system remained mysterious, and some perceptive cynics wondered if the huge and immediate profits from patented diagnostic tests and antiviral drugs were skewing basic research. The familiar schematic depiction of viral armies gobbling up helper T cells, as if in a video-arcade war game, eventually proved false. The sickest patients did not show particularly high levels of the virus, and though barely reported by the mainstream press, eloquent dissenting opinions on the role of HIV in the disease were published in leading medical journals. By mid 1991, even Luc Montagnier, the French "co-discoverer" of HIV, expressed doubt publicly that the retrovirus was sufficient to cause the syndrome. Official muttering about "necessary cofactors" started circulating. Non-HIV cases of immune deficiency began to be reported. But the HIV virus, demonized by science and freighted with monstrous metaphor, continued to mesmerize researchers while AIDS research, to some observers, began to resemble the never-ending, self-serving, and self-perpetuating war of Orwell's *1984*. Data that would seem to contradict or modify the HIV hypothesis was instead taken as evidence of the virus' complexity and craftiness. Dr. Kary Mullis, a biochemist and member of the newly formed Group for the Scientific Reappraisal of the HIV-AIDS Hypothesis, told *Spin* magazine that the "mystery of that damn virus has been generated by the $2 billion a year they spend on it. You take any other virus, and you spend $2 billion, and you can make up some great mysteries about it, too." Hollywood isn't the only place where weird science can be exceedingly profitable. As essayist Barbara Ehrenreich commented: ". . . from the point of view of the pharmaceutical industry, the AIDS problem has already been solved. After all, we already have a drug [AZT] which can be sold at the incredible price of $8,000 an annual dose, and which has the added virtue of not diminishing the market by actually curing anyone." Medicine, in other words, can be as predatory as disease.

Another notable socio-medical malady of the late twentieth century is anorexia nervosa, which has its own metaphorical parallels to vampirism. In the wasting syndrome of anorexia, as in vampire stories, the victim (almost always female) often feigns compliance with her rescuers, and accepts the psychotherapeutic equivalents of garlic and wolfbane—all the while secretly collaborating with the disease itself. Like a vampire, the dying anorectic finally achieves a controlling, draining power over those close to her. The syndrome resonates strongly with the Victorian penchant for eroticizing consumptive, wasted women, a common motif of classic vampire tales. Anorexia also illuminates the modern dance of death underlying the parade of skeletal female images in contemporary fashion media, which juxtapose vanity and mortality as disturbingly as any medieval mural painter. In the heavily symbolic world of female body starvation / transformation, the piercing, devouring liposuction nozzle is a high-tech vampire phallus that drains and reshapes women in the Dracula and Frankenstein traditions simultaneously.

The dark twins, in their long and codependent dance through Western culture, have rarely enjoyed the power they have today. Dracula and Frankenstein are significant modern myths, gods that have descended periodically into ineffectual kitsch, but only to rise again, stronger than before. Each icon defines the other; they rarely travel alone. They embody nothing less than the centuries-long war between science and superstition—Apollo and Dionysus at the Saturday matinee. In the age of AIDS they have spent an inordinate amount of time admiring each other, perhaps, in part, because they both "reproduce" as AIDS does—one through transfusion and one through transplantation. The dark twins are palpably present when the most advanced communication technology in history brings home, almost nightly, the most psychically primitive juxtapositions of blood, sex, and pestilence, a new kind of living-room war, a psychosexual Vietnam.

It is a bloody landscape, one of the most saturated the mind has ever beheld. As at Prospero's feast, there is nowhere to hide. The vampires that scratch at the windows of popular culture represent our own recent and restless dead. And unless we learn how to listen to them, they will only keep on scratching.

Chapter Thirteen

THE DANCE OF DEARTH

"What I want to see, above all, is
that this remains a country where
someone can always get rich."

Ronald Reagan
(U.S. President, 1980–1988)

"The Americans never use the word *peasant*."

Alexis de Tocqueville
Democracy in America
(1835)

THE FREEDOMS OF a democratic society have a threatening shadow-side rarely addressed in an open manner. Expectations of boundless opportunity and upward mobility, of acceptance and inclusion in a supposedly classless society, the potential for sudden economic transformation and the nirvana of endless consumption—all are familiar components of the American dream. Although there is little evidence that Americans are more likely than other peoples to transcend the castes into which they are born, the dream, like a long-running television game show, dies hard.

Carrie White (Sissy Spacek) has her social expectations shattered by an ugly prank in Brian De Palma's film adaptation of *Carrie* (1976). (*Photofest*)

One place the dream is permitted to perish, with noisy, convulsive death rattles, is in horror entertainment. The American nightmare, as refracted in film and fiction, is about disenfranchisement, exclusion, downward mobility, a struggle-to-the-death world of winners and losers. Familiar, civic-minded signposts are all reversed: the family is a sick joke, its house more likely to offer siege instead of shelter.

Since the end of the 1960s, the aims and programs of the Great Society have also been under siege, as political and demographic shifts strained and distorted baseline economic assumptions. For a generation raised in the unprecedented abundance of the postwar years, there was the expectation of a similar expansive future for their own families. But the dream began to fray, slowly at first, in ways that could be rationalized. Two-income families became more and more common, and finally the norm. The women's movement allowed wives and mothers to feel "empowered" by working outside the home—as if they had a real choice in the matter. For a big part of the postwar generation, the prospect that the future was not going to resemble the past was frightening. The idea was so disturbing that it was better not to think about it directly. As always, scary entertainment would be happy to do the worrying, Dorian Gray–style, on everyone's behalf.

Although Ronald Reagan was widely touted as the Great Communicator of the century's penultimate decade, the title more fairly belongs to the novelist Stephen King, who, in numbers and dollars, emerged as the most successful storyteller in human history. By day, Reagan told people stories about their social prospects they wanted to hear. By night, King told very different stories people didn't want to hear directly, but would devour if presented in the veiled images of vampires, werewolves, rabid dogs, demonic automobiles, geeky outsiders with vengeful psychic abilities, and the omnipresent favorite, the walking, rotting dead.

Horror writer and filmmaker Clive Barker, citing the estimated 90 million copies of King's books in print, commented, "There are apparently two books in every American household—one of them is the Bible and the other one is probably by Stephen King." King's emergence as a household brand-name coincided with large-scale economic shifts in the seventies and eighties. Not surprisingly, the accompanying human dislocations provided a fertile medium for images of dread. According to Landon Y. Jones in *Great Expectations: America and the Baby Boom Generation,* "The biggest and best-educated group of men and women in American history was beginning to feel as if it had entered some kind of negative growth cycle; the older it got, the worse things looked. Instead of rappelling itself up into adult society, it remained entangled in its own mass."

Stephen King exploded into public consciousness with his first novel, *Carrie* (1974). The title character, Carrie White, is in many ways the ultimate outcast baby boomer, an awkward New England high-school student who grovels under the domination of her religious-fanatic mother, while suffering additional abuse from her cruel, scapegoating classmates. Carrie also has a latent talent for telekinesis—the psychic ability to move objects at a distance—though the strange gift is not under her conscious control. When Carrie experiences her first menstrual period in the school locker room, she becomes hysterical—her puritanical upbringing has given her no preparation for the event, and she thinks she is bleeding to death. The other girls unmercifully pelt her with tampons. Mrs. White, in her fundamentalist fervor, offers no comfort to her daughter; menarche, to Margaret White, is nothing less than the beginning of an apocalyptic war between the spirit and the flesh. With mild demonstrations of telekinesis, Carrie begins to rebel against her mother, defiantly accepting an invitation to her school's spring ball. She doesn't know that the dance is a setup by her classmates for an appalling prank: moments after she is elected queen of the prom, Carrie is drenched in a stinking shower of pig's blood. The trauma detonates the full force of her psychic powers; like a vengeful primitive demon, she traps the assembled in the school gym and incinerates them in a gaudy *Götterdämmerung* that destroys half the town. Her mother, convinced that Carrie is a witch, stabs her when she returns home. Before dying herself, Carrie telekinetically stops her mother's heart. One of Carrie's surviving friends manages to flee the holocaust, but in the last narrative passage of the book she is left screaming in the middle of an open field, horrified at the sudden onset of her own menstrual flow.

In a 1981 interview, King discussed the real-life inspiration for Carrie as

> . . . a very peculiar girl who came from a very peculiar family. Her mother wasn't a religious nut like the mother in *Carrie*; she was a game nut, a sweepstakes nut who subscribed to magazines

for people who entered contests. And she won things—weird things. She won a year's supply of Bebop pencils. But the big thing she won was Jack Benny's old Maxwell. They had it out in the front of the yard for years, with weeds growing up around it. They didn't know what to do with it.

The girl eventually married. "She had three kids and then hung herself one summer," King remembered. The religious fanaticism of Carrie's mother, in other words, had its origins in a more secular American obsession: the strike-it-rich fantasy of rescue and transformation, of magical entitlement.

Carrie's fascination as a novel sprang from its fantastically exaggerated evocation of adolescent initiation rituals in a decade when America's social and economic rites of passage began to falter. The importance of initiation imagery, to the horror genre in general and to Stephen King's work in particular, cannot be overstated; all the hair-sprouting werewolves, rotting faces, and uncontrollable impulses of the horror tradition have obvious parallels in the biology and psychology of puberty.

In its ritual offerings of quasi-initiatory encounters, horror fantasy clearly fills an anthropological vacuum, especially among young males. The field had its most explosive growth in the 1980s, the same decade that saw a widespread interest in the idea of dysfunctional initiation; the poet Robert Bly generated a cottage industry of participatory seminars centered on male initiation as argued in his 1990 book *Iron John*. Bly's audience tended to be middle-class and affluent, but the entrenched problems of inner-city youth were also widely ascribed by social commentators to the lack of meaningful role models and coming-of-age rituals. With the exception of occasional exploitation films like *Blacula* (1972), horror did not particularly seek a minority audience; rather, its greatest following was found among the white blue-collar and so-called new-collar readers and viewers. The initiatory vacuum in this group may extend beyond specifically adolescent issues to a larger sense of exclusion from the socioeconomic initiations of college, graduate degrees, and entrance into the high-salary professions.

The Cinderella legend itself is a transformative initiation rite. In *Carrie,* Stephen King recycled most of the fairy tale's key elements: the dark mother figure, the tormenting stepsisters (here, Carrie's classmates), the transfiguring ball-promenade, and a supernatural intervention (telekinesis as fairy godmother). It is often forgotten that "Cinderella," at least as told by the Brothers Grimm, was a brutal story; in order to fit the glass slipper, the big-footed stepsisters amputated their heels and toes—a gambit worthy of Tod Browning—hoping the Prince wouldn't notice all the blood welling up in the shoe. Cinderella enjoys a delicious, displaced revenge: at the story's finish the bad sisters are set upon not by the heroine, but by angry birds who pluck out their eyes.

Carrie was especially raw in its depiction of the cruel and exclusionary rites of high school. The school can be viewed as a microcosm of American society, which at the time of *Carrie*'s publication had gone just through a severe economic recession that rattled the dream of "classless" inclusion. By the mid-seventies the lower-middle-class began to lose ground perceptibly. George Romero's *Night of the Living Dead* was well-established by this time as a fixture of the midnight movie circuit, a primal allegory of haves and have-nots (the "living" and "dead") struggling over the control and occupancy of an emblematic house. Stephen King himself identified the real anxiety reflected in the film version of *The Amityville Horror* (1979), in which a family's first, hard-won home is beset by one "supernatural" disaster after another. "Windows crash in, black goop comes dribbling out of the walls, the cellar stairs cave in," wrote King, "and I found myself wondering not if the [family] would get out alive but if they had adequate homeowner's insurance." King recalled a woman sitting behind him in the theatre, moaning, "Think of the bills . . ." The safety net of earlier decades was fraying rapidly for a large segment of the populace. A single income no longer sufficed for the average family, and, as mirrored in horror entertainment, American life looked more and more like a literal rat race—with Nosferatu presiding.

Carrie is a ferocious howl of the outsider, a cry of class resentment and social disenfranchisement that found its public at the precise moment a certain segment of the population began to suspect perhaps subconsciously, that its safety net was about to snap. Paradoxically, it was the nightmare of social free-fall and ostracism that allowed Stephen King to crash publishing's prom. As after any successful initiation rite, King's life, like that of the bookselling world, would never be the same.

King's childhood, at least as he has described it in interviews, lacked surface melodrama but was emotionally conflicted, with a classic "outsider" mood. "I often felt unhappy and different, estranged from kids my age," he told *Playboy* in 1983. Overweight and uncoordinated, King was raised on the edge of poverty by his hardworking mother after his father deserted the family when King was two. The Kings settled in Maine in 1958, coincidentally the year that *Playboy* told its readers that horror had become, for the first time, the equivalent of a blue-chip commodity. Like many baby boomers, King was fascinated with dreadful images in popular culture: E.C. Comics, *Famous Monsters of Filmland,* and the late-fifties spate of Hollywood horrors were special influences. After college, he worked as a high-school English teacher for $6,400 a year, selling short fiction on the side to men's magazines like *Dude* and *Cavalier.*

The composition of *Carrie* in the early seventies was King's turning point. In her retrospective introduction to a special edition of *Carrie* in 1991, King's wife Tabitha, herself a novelist, rekindles the Cinderella theme of her marriage: "In the winter of 1972 / 73, we lived in a trailer in Hermon, Maine. Steve wrote in the closet-sized room that was supposed to be the laundry room. We didn't own a washer or a dryer at the time. The little room was just big enough for a desk, a chair, a trashcan and a writer."

Harlan Ellison, the acclaimed scenarist, short-story writer, and essayist whose ferocious, just-get-it-off-the-page narrative style had an huge impact on science-fiction, fantasy, and horror writers from the sixties onward (and is still palpably evident in King's work), witnessed firsthand the publishing buzz that rose up around *Carrie* after the hardcover rights were purchased by Doubleday for $2,500 in 1973. "Xeroxes of the manuscript were run off; they were disseminated widely in-house; women editors passed them on to female secretaries, who took them home and gave them to their friends," wrote Ellison, a decade later. "That first scene bit hard." New American Library bit, too, and offered $400,000 for the paperback rights.

King's rise to pop-culture preeminence coincided with, and was undoubtedly helped by, the increased centralization of book marketing and distribution from the seventies onward. As large chain stores drove out independents, it became possible to issue first printings of hardback novels that would have been logistic impossibilities in earlier decades. ("Democracy," wrote Alexis de Tocqueville, "not only infuses a taste for letters among the trading classes, but introduces a trading spirit into literature.") *Carrie* had a first printing of 30,000 in 1974; *'Salem's Lot,* the following year,

Stephen King. *(Photo by George Bennett, courtesy of Viking Penguin and the George Bennett Studio)*

had an initial run of 20,000. By the late seventies, however, spurred by the exponentially expanding delivery system of the chain stores, King's public exploded. Following *The Shining* (1977), King's next three books, *The Stand* (1978), *The Dead Zone* (1979), and *Firestarter* (1980), had first printings of 70,000, 80,000, and 100,000 copies, respectively. His first book for Viking, *Christine* (1983), hit the quarter-million point, and, beginning with *It* in 1986, virtually all of King's novels have had first hardcover printings of one million copies or above.

As with many superstars, King maintains a great deal of control over the packaging and marketing of his name. When the sheer numbers loom as large as they do in the case of Stephen King, some of this control can have amusing consequences. According to sources close to the subject, King vetoed the $22.95 price tag proposed by Viking for his novel *The Dark Half* (1989), concerned that his fans deserved a break. He asked that the price be reduced to $21.95. The publisher gulped. The initial print run was one million copies. At Stephen King's whim, a million dollars in publisher and bookseller revenues had just been wiped out.

There was, in all likelihood, more than high-handedness to King's decision. He recalled in a 1985 *Publishers Weekly* essay that, following the paperback sale of *Carrie,* "All of a sudden I could afford to buy hardcovers," something that had previously been a luxury. Not having to wait for the paperback, King implied, was an important point of cultural validation. "I used to look into the windows of bookstores with the idle curiosity of, let us say, a construction worker looking at the necklaces in the display windows of Tiffany's."

Beyond pricing, King also avoids alienating his readers by eschewing any hint of "literary" style. His prose often has the rhythms and cadences of transcribed speech, a near-total informality of diction. (In an interview with *Fangoria* magazine, King commented that "a lot" of his fan mail—though not the majority of it—consisted of "these sort of labored, almost scrawled things in pencil, from people who obviously don't read much or write much. . . . This sounds like I've got a swelled head, but that's really the way they are: [wondrous voice] 'I can *read* this book. I *know* the words in this book!' ") A supreme populist, King almost always appears in his publicity photos casually dressed in jeans and sneakers, eager to chew the fat, ready to knock back a beer. We know he's incredibly rich, yet we know he's somehow one of us.

Like Michael Jackson, Lon Chaney, "The Beverly Hillbillies," and lotto, Stephen King is a classic American transformation myth, keeping alive cultural fantasies of personal metamorphosis—along with their corollary dark side of the outsider's resentment. King ultimately resembles his creation Carrie, the outsider who brings down the high-school temple through an angry display of mental energy. It is, perhaps, no coincidence that King employed his own odd talents to bend the publishing establishment to his own standards. King's career finds a humorous parallel in the Jerome Bixby story "It's a *Good* Life" (1953), about a little boy with omnipotent mental powers who remakes the world as a horrifying cartoon. The story was the basis of a celebrated "Twilight Zone" episode in the early sixties, and was lovingly recreated by director Joe Dante as a segment in *Twilight Zone: The Movie* (1983).

Writing in *The Atlantic* a dozen years after *Carrie*'s publication, Lloyd Rose identified another important element of King's appeal:

> His characters live in the worst possible moral universe: you're punished if you do wrong and you suffer if you're innocent. It's like the world of a child with crazy parents—whatever you do, they'll beat you, and you'll never know why. The confusion and rage at the center of this view of the world have a primal power that has nothing to do with King's hokey plots and monsters and that, boiling under them, gives them disturbing heat.

Horror entertainment's fixation on child abuse, child murder, and related themes in the eighties paralleled a swelling hysteria in the courts and the media over sexual molestation and incest. No sane person can deny the deplorable and tragic reality of child abuse, but the reality left a huge wake of weird fantasy that often blurred legitimate issues. The longest and most expensive court proceeding in U.S. history—the McMartin preschool case in Los Angeles—turned on accusations heavy with the trappings of cheesy horror movies. The case ended in acquittal. There was a striking similarity in a number of other abuse cases prosecuted across the country in the late eighties and early nineties, almost all involving owners or employees of day-care centers—that is, stand-in or surrogate parents. This aspect of "doubling" may have been crucial to the hysterical air of projection, scapegoating, and witch-hunting that permeated these cases. Day-care workers, in a sense, became doppelgangers. The trials generally involved anxious baby-boomer parents who, with the coaxing aid of therapists, drew out from their own children lurid stories of fantastic sex crimes committed by robed Satan-worshippers who killed babies and mutilated animals, molested their victims in secret tunnels and hot-air balloons, staged undetected nude orgies within earshot of authorities, etc. In one case documented on public television, children claimed to have been baked alive in microwave ovens, à la *Gremlins* or the dead-baby jokes.

One must wonder of how much of these pervasive fantasies of intergenerational abuse had more to do with the baby boomers' shifted resentment of their own children—not to mention their own parents. The pressures and difficulties of child-raising in the eighties were endlessly discussed in the media throughout the decade—guilt over reliance on day care, the inevitable lack of "quality" time in a two-career family, and the tendency to view children as a kind of middle-class entitlement rather than a financial responsibility. (This last issue was usually framed in terms of welfare mothers, to keep the matter at a safe distance, though the middle class could barely afford the children it was producing, either. How many parents in any income bracket would qualify for a mortgage to raise children if a means test was required?) On the other end of the spectrum, the boomers' parents' one-income, comfortably middle-class existence now seemed to mock the aspirations of their economically embattled children.

The painful sense of lockout, both Oedipal and economic, could not be addressed directly, so it was necessary to find the betrayed, battered, even "murdered" child somewhere else. In addition to the child-abuse witch-hunts, there were V. C. Andrews' novels and, especially, the Freddy Krueger icon of the *Nightmare on Elm Street* films. A child-killer in life, Freddy was lynched by a posse of parents, but lived on as a bogeyman in the community's dream-fantasies, a collective obsession.

Stephen King's books brim with images of sacrificial children. *Pet Sematary* (1983) found a wide audience with its story of a desperately guilty father who resurrects his dead son in a variation of "The Monkey's Paw." *Pet Sematary* (the title reflects a child's attempt at spelling the name of the locus of dread) was yet another example of a "Gothic" breakdown of the bond between between parents and children. But King saved his most ambitious and disturbing imagery of childhood under siege for his sprawling horror epic *It* (1986).

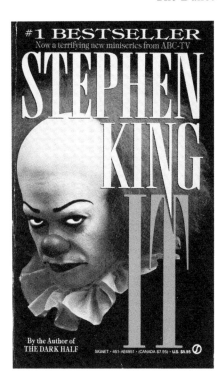

The dark carnival never dies. Cover of the paperback edition of Stephen King's *It*. *(Courtesy of New American Library)*

It plays its demographics flawlessly, flashing between the fifties and the eighties to tell the story of grown-up baby boomers who return to their monster-soaked childhood town to complete a rite of passage. In the town of Derry, Maine, they re-encounter and destroy a primal, shape-shifting, kid-killing evil that, more often than not, takes the shape of a Bozo-style clown called Penny-wise—a name which rather directly raises the idea of a materialistic, economy-driven horror. King makes some direct comparisons between Pennywise and corporate icons Ronald McDonald, Mickey Mouse, and Donald Duck. Pennywise also summons up the image of John Wayne Gacy, the notorious child-murderer who sometimes worked as a clown. The reader knows when the clown is about to kill, because he starts talking about floating. "You'll float down here," he says over and over, as if in a commercial jingle, as if they are all going to be rendered into Ivory soap. The idea of floating also connotes elevation or levitation, freedom, lack of restraints, a gravity-defying transcendence—the baby boomer's anxious, possibly unattainable fantasy.

The book's first shock comes in a storm drain, where Pennywise lures a six-year-old boy with promises of cotton candy, hot roasted peanuts, a whole subterranean circus. The scene is set up like prelude to supernatural sex abuse: "I'm not supposed to take stuff from strangers," the boy tells the clown, wisely, when he offers him a balloon. But, as in a lot of King's fiction, the threat of sex gives way to Grand Guignol violence: when the child is close enough to touch, Pennywise seizes the moment and rips off his arm. As in the life of Tod Browning, to surrender to the circus is to encounter a sideshow of horrifying mutilation. It is perhaps significant that King has elsewhere used the circus metaphor to describe the baby-boomer experience: "We were fertile ground for the seeds of terror, we war babies," he noted in his book-length essay on horror, *Danse Macabre* (1982); "we had been raised in a strange circus atmosphere of paranoia, patriotism, and national hubris." In *It,* King resurrects and celebrates the dark carnival motif that was first depicted in *The Cabinet of Dr. Caligari* and kept alive by Tod Browning and Lon Chaney. Chaney's oft-quoted observation, "There's nothing funny about a clown in the moonlight," informed the fiction of Ray Bradbury and the criticism of Leslie Fiedler. Horror, in the eighties, became the gold standard in publishing and Fiedler's hunch that America's soul could be found in a literature of horror for boys was finally realized.

The Christian Science Monitor's critic wrote that *"It* is to gruesomeness what the Sears Roebuck catalog is to things to buy." *Newsweek* identified the novel's buried engine: "Stephen King's apparent desire to be a literary heavy hitter wears down his already elephantine new novel. . . . The exciting and absorbing parts of *It* are not the mechanical showdowns and shockeroos . . . but the simple scenes in which King evokes childhood in the fifties."

King's major cultural function may be his validation of the lives and experience—especially childhood lives and experience—of a large segment of the population whose most vivid formative memories centered on homogenized mass-media rituals like E.C. Comics, "Twilight Zone," "Shock Theater," and *Creature from the Black Lagoon.* Stephen King's books reflect back the lives of his readers, especially the "intimate" media moments, and the result is a surge of pleasure and self-recognition. Whatever their literary merit, King's books may more passionately and viscerally *involve* their readers than much literary fiction. King readers groan, gasp, experience knots in their stomachs and tingles on the back of their necks. Historically, there has always been a degree of envy on the part of the educated classes toward their underlings, centered on the nagging suspicion that the lower classes are people of direct and vivid experience unattainable through the intellectual veil. Fiction like King's is sensual, pulse-pounding, immediate. It has almost nothing to do with the aims and goals of mainstream literary publishing, and constitutes a category of its own.

Not surprisingly, the critics have run very hot and very cold when it comes to the writing of Stephen King. In the summer of 1982, *Time* ran a full-page profile on the writer, with the acid headline MASTER OF POSTLITERATE PROSE. King said the article "depressed me for weeks afterward. But, you know, what really depressed me was the tone. The tone wasn't particularly angry, it was sort of sad. It was this guy saying . . . the Visigoths are in the crumbled remains of Rome, and they're pissing on the curiae and the steps of the Senate. And what he was talking about were these people who aren't very bright, who are reading these books, and I thought, My God . . . I wonder if he knows how elitist all this sounds."

He noted that alternative and counterculture papers had, early in his career, given him positive reviews, but by the early eighties a backlash had set in. Walter Kendrick, reviewing King's *Danse Macabre* in *The Village Voice,* wrote, "If you value wit, intelligence or insight, even if you're willing to settle for the slightest hint of good writing, all King's books are dismissable. . . . It's hard to tell which is worse—the utter vacuity of the ideas or the foolish flatulence of their expression." The scathing *Voice* notice was accompanied by an equally scathing illustration by the caricaturist Philip Burke; it depicted the author as a hairy, bespectacled pig, eating money out of a trough-shaped typewriter. Kendrick, however, was more than willing to admit that King was a genius at what he chose to do, and that his books could be addictive. After spending four hours "enthralled" with *'Salem's Lot,* Kendrick confessed that

> I hated myself in the morning. I felt glutted and dirty, as if I'd just swallowed a gallon of Cool-Whip. King's prose has a lot in common with this synthetic goo that can never go stale because it was never fresh; it's a featureless flood of clichés, uniformly tasteless and absolutely unthreatening, never asking you to feel

or think anything that isn't totally familiar. And though his books are always monstrously too long, somehow this is soothing, too, because you can slither through whole pages in a second, confident that the general drift suffices; the words don't matter.

Since King's work is so image-based, it was inevitable it would be adapted for film. Surprisingly, only Brian De Palma's stylish adaptation of *Carrie* (1976) starring Sissy Spacek has been a critical and commercial success. De Palma took a number of liberties with the story, and enhanced the package with several Hitchcock-style set pieces: the shower scene, the blood-baptism at the prom (filmed in agonizing slow motion), and a completely new death for Carrie's mother, now telekinetically crucified with kitchen utensils.

Other King adaptations repeatedly fell short of *Carrie*'s inspired élan; by 1991 eight Stephen King novels had been produced as theatrical films or television movies; *'Salem's Lot* (1979), *The Shining* (1980), *Christine* (1983), *Cujo* (1983), *The Dead Zone* (1983), *Firestarter* (1984), *Pet Sematary* (1989), and *It* (1991). Several of King's short stories also formed the basis for features or anthology films, notably *Creepshow* (1982), *Cat's Eye* (1984), and the non-genre *Stand by Me* (1986). *The Shining,* directed by Stanley Kubrick, was a major disappointment to King's fans as well as Kubrick's. Strangely, none of the King-based properties even approached a commercial success equivalent to that of his books. The jinx-like aura attached to King adaptations might have served as a warning, when, in the 1980s, the idea of producing *Carrie* as a Broadway musical was sent up like one of Pennywise's blood-filled balloons.

Given the enervated commercial theatre's marked tendency to adapt and recycle properties, the idea of a musical *Carrie* must have seemed like a winner. Stephen King, after all, was the most "bankable" storyteller of all time. The production would involve the prestigious Royal Shakespeare Company, which had coproduced the long-running hit *Les Misérables.* The West German producer of *Cats,* Friedrich Kurz, was raising money. A legendary Broadway vocal artist, Barbara Cook, would make her comeback as Carrie's mother. Lawrence Cohen, who wrote the screenplay for Brian De Palma, was signed to do the book. The music and lyrics were provided by Michael Gore and Dean Pitchford, who had collaborated on *Fame* 1980); Pitchford had also been the lyricist for the hit musical film *Footloose* (1984). The score, performed at backers' auditions without formal staging, was hauntingly effective, combining melodic ballads, pop songs, and high-energy dance music (Debbie Allen, *Fame*'s choreographer, would drive the dancing). Horror could be Broadway's hottest ticket, as Andrew Lloyd Webber's version of *The Phantom of the Opera* (1987) had amply proved. Part Cinderella story and part blood spectacle, *Carrie* the musical would also be a pop distillation of the decade's overriding obsessions: socioeconomic transformation and body-fluid fright.

The difficulties with *Carrie* may have begun with the Royal Shakespeare Company's involvement. In a sense, the real "bad mother" of *Carrie* was British Prime Minister Margaret Thatcher, whose Draconian cuts of government arts subsidies forced the RSC to look for sideline commercial projects. The British press was leery from the start. The *New Statesman* called the RSC's rationalizing its undertaking of *Carrie* "cynically pious: look what you made me do. '*Carrie* is the result of the government's new self-help policy,' a blunt spokesperson has said."

Terry Hands, the RSC's artistic director, knew from the start that the production deal guaranteed his company a profit, risk-free; should *Carrie* crash and burn on Broadway, the RSC would owe nothing. The production had found limited partners in Germany, Sri Lanka, Liechtenstein, and Australia. CBS was also a backer. The budget was nearly $8 million. Like the sweepstakes-obsessed mother of the girl who inspired King to write the original book, the backers must have been dazzled indeed by the prospects of hitting it big in the big casino of Broadway musicals.

Carrie had three weeks of performances at the RSC's Stratford-upon-Avon theatre, an experience which prompted Barbara Cook to withdraw from the production (her decision may have been helped along by a piece of opening-night scenery that came close to beheading her). As Cook recalled, "I thought, 'There isn't a chance in hell that they'll be able to pull this off.' " Cook initially had faith in Terry Hands as a director, believing that " 'This man is head of the Royal Shakespeare Company; if a scene isn't working, he's going to see it's not working.' Well, he didn't."

Nicholas de Jongh in *The Guardian* perhaps best picked up the hidden meanings of *Carrie*:

> *Carrie* is a cautionary fairy tale centered upon a middle-aged stage director called Terry Hands who seemed to have everything—looks, abounding talent, and the Royal Shakespeare Company.

> But one fatal day from a faraway place called America came alien folk offering his troupe money and a Broadway show. . . . Millions were spent, but vultures were sighted circling the theatre days before the opening, brought there by a rumor of that succulent dramatic feast, a still-born musical.

The advance word was not good—to say the least—but the anticipation in New York was keen nonetheless. A striking, minimalist show logo was created by the DeWynter Group in London, designers of graphics for all the major British musicals. A few simple lines suggested a girl's face, with a single red "teardrop" falling into a void. The image appeared on red-and-black posters all over New York with a simple message: CARRIE. THERE'S NEVER BEEN A MUSICAL LIKE HER.

No one would deny the claim. But few were prepared for the astounding mess that began previews at the Virginia Theatre in May 1988. Barbara Cook had been replaced by Betty Buckley, who had played the role of Carrie's gym teacher in the film version, and who had sung the most celebrated song ("Memory") in the smash musical *Cats*. Unlike Cook's earth mother, Buckley played the part of Margaret White like an austere dominatrix. Linzi Hateley, an appealing British newcomer with a big, Judy Garland–like vibrato, reprised the title part. The musical's book had been almost totally pared away, rendering the explanation of Carrie's telekinetic abilities incomprehensible to audiences who had not read the novel or seen the movie. The performers cast as high-school students appeared, on the average, at least ten years too old for the roles; the girls were costumed like vicious hookers, and the boys at one point like sadistic leather fetishists. The locker-room scene featured complicated hydraulic shower stalls with peekaboo frosting on the glass; the girls, nevertheless, "showered" in their bras and panties. The Dionysian hog-slaughtering number that opened the second act ("Out for Blood") was without question one of Broadway's greatest moments of high camp. Numerous special effects that couldn't be managed were simply abandoned, including demonstrations of Carrie's powers, which only confused things further. When it proved impossible to dump blood on Linzi Hateley without clogging her body mike, the whole climactic bloodbath of the prom was sacrificed on the altar of expedience; at the performance attended by this writer, an actor daintily

A baby boomer hits bottom: Carrie (Linzi Hateley) and her mother (Betty Buckley) meet their ends on a staircase to nowhere in the Broadway musical version of *Carrie* (1988). *(Photo by Peter Cunningham)*

daubed Carrie's cheeks with a few handfuls of red glop, unceremoniously plunking the empty bucket over her head. Eight million dollars had been spent, and no one had been able to work the bugs out of *Carrie*'s most crucial moment. In the final image of the Broadway production, Carrie meets her mother on a white-on-white staircase to heaven, and is stabbed to death—the sort of moment Florenz Ziegfeld might have come up with had a lunatic asked him to stage a Grand Guignol version of his *Follies*.

Newsday critic Linda Winer said the show was "stupendously, fabulously terrible—ineptly conceived, sleazy, irrational from moment to moment, the rare kind of production that stretches way beyond bad to mythic lousiness." Given the auto-destructive bent of the production, the acerbic John Simon could afford to be less caustic than usual in his *New York* magazine notice headlined BLOOD AND NO GUTS. "A musical based on a sleazy movie made from a cheap thriller need not be awful," Simon wrote. "One would have hoped for something spectacularly weird, dementedly arousing. Instead we get an unstable mixture that crumbles on exposure to the stage." Jack Kroll of *Newsweek* called the first-act duet in which Mrs. White "curses and slaps her poor daughter around, finally stuffing her into a trapdoor, one of the most repugnant scenes in the whole history of Broadway musicals." The *New Yorker* critic Mimi Kramer complained that Debbie Allen's choreography "isn't about joy or striving or aspiration, it's about T. and A.—a sort of sexualized aerobics: balletoporn."

In his book *Not Since Carrie: 40 Years of Broadway Musical Flops,* Ken Mandelbaum noted the perverse excitement generated by the show on opening night: "As the audience files out, some appear thrilled, others appalled; the word most frequently bandied about is 'unbelievable.' For show freaks, this has been a night unlike any other, the kind of show for which they have waited a lifetime. They cannot wait to get home to call their friends, and phone lines, particularly those on the West Side, will continue to steam for hours to come." For many, *Carrie* was a living, breathing equivalent of *Springtime for Hitler,* the imaginary "worst musical of all time" created by Mel Brooks for his comedy *The Producers* (1967). To the producers of *Carrie,* Stephen King was supposed to be a bank that couldn't fail; to the observers of New York's late-eighties speculative delirium, *Carrie* was something else: *The Hellfire of the Vanities*.

· · ·

Stephen King himself has not failed, though the reviewers seldom invite him to the critics' ball. The *New York Times Book Review* called King's most recent novel, *Needful Things* (1991), "the type of book that can be enjoyed only by longtime aficionados of the genre, people who probably have a lot of black T-shirts in their chest of drawers and either have worn or dreamed of wearing a baseball cap backward." The reviewer compared the novel to Bret Easton Ellis' ultraviolent, but upscale *American Psycho* (1991). The controversial book had been canceled in late 1990 by Simon and Schuster when a stink (or, perhaps more appropriately, a stench) arose over its impending publication. Assailed as nauseating and misogynistic by insiders who had read the manuscript, the book became a corporate hot potato for Simon and Schuster and its parent company, Paramount Communications, after the most violent murder scenes were leaked to the press. Paramount, which announced no plans to curtail the production and marketing of its *Friday the Thirteenth* series of slasher films, insisted that no corporate censorship had been brought to bear on its publishing subsidiary. *American Psycho* was almost immediately snapped up by Alfred A. Knopf for its Vintage Contemporary line of paperbacks. The press attention paid to the controversy was enough to enable Vintage to publish the book without having to advertise it.

The Ellis book, the *Times* concluded, "contains the same amount of senseless sadomasochistic violence" as Stephen King, but the lunatics in King's world "smear their bloodstained hands on duds from Sears, not Saks."

The class and money tensions that permeate modern horror are well illustrated by the publishing history of *American Psycho*. Ellis' novel, in which a twenty-six-year-old status-conscious investment banker, Patrick Bateman, is also a casual serial killer, reads like a parody of Stephen King in its endless litany of fashion labels and affluent consumer props. In what is perhaps its most infamous scene, Bateman prepares to introduce a live rat into his latest victim's vagina while playing her a videotape of an earlier murder. In the tape, Bateman tells us, "I'm wearing a Joseph Abboud suit, a tie by Paul Stuart, shoes by J. Crew, a vest by someone Italian and I'm kneeling on the floor beside a corpse, eating the girl's brain, gobbling it down, spreading Grey Poupon over hunks of the pink, fleshy meat." Elsewhere in the book, Bateman bites off women's nipples and gnaws fingers down to the bone.

Cannibalism as an upscale cultural motif was not exactly new;

it had been ushered in by the Stephen Sondheim musical *Sweeney Todd: The Demon Barber of Fleet Street* in 1979. The show provided a cultural overture to the Darwinian, dog-eat-dog age of Ronald Reagan, and was a steady draw throughout the eighties, adapted for television and entering the repertories of numerous light opera companies. It received an acclaimed Broadway revival in 1990, effectively bracketing the decade with dentation. An even more popular cannibal than Sweeney Todd was the flesh-famished psychiatrist Dr. Hannibal Lecter, introduced by novelist Thomas Harris in *Red Dragon* (1981) and reprised in *The Silence of the Lambs* (1989). Peter Greenaway's film *The Cook, The Thief, His Wife and Her Lover* (1989) outraged audiences and many critics with its graphic metaphors of man-eating, while Paul Bartel's *Eating Raoul* (1982) played the theme for laughs. By the time of *American Psycho,* cannibals were licking their chops in every corner of the newspapers; up front, the tabloids trumpeted the crimes of Daniel Rakowitz, who in 1989 killed and cooked his East Village roommate, and fed parts of her body in a soup to the homeless inhabitants of Tompkins Square Park. In Bill Watterson's widely syndicated cartoon strip "Calvin and Hobbes," a young boy, apropos of absolutely nothing, confronts his mother in the kitchen. "Hey Mom," he asks, "if we were cannibals, what parts of people would we eat?" The mother is aghast, but the kid keeps at it: "You know, where would the steaks be? Would legs be like drumsticks? Would kids be like veal?"

Leaving aside the occasional real-life people-eater, the mass obsession with cannibalism had little to do with a surging desire among the populace to dine on human hams. It is ancient wisdom among fortune-tellers that the Death card is never to be interpreted literally; it is similarly wise not to take the outlandish symbols of popular culture at their face value. As in the case of slasher movies, which can be profitably read as allegories of the media-murder of childhood, the cannibal image suggests other interpretations as well. Cannibalism, after all, represents the most primal kind of assimilation and inclusion imaginable; in an age when we are told at every turn that the basic social contracts are in jeopardy, is it any wonder that the cannibal and the vampire violently assert themselves as dysfunctional images of human connectedness?

Few people were willing to look for deeper meanings in *American Psycho,* which was a shame. It was fairly obvious that, for better or worse, *American Psycho* was intended as a scathing commentary on the dehumanizing social excesses of the decade just finished. Norman Mailer, no stranger to themes of violent aggression, offered the following assessment in the pages of *Vanity Fair*:

> *American Psycho* is saying that the eighties were spiritually disgusting and the author's presentation is the crystallization of such horror. When an entire new class thrives on the ability to make money out of the manipulation of money, and becomes altogether obsessed with the surface of things—that is, with luxury commodities, food, and appearance—then, in effect, says Ellis, we have entered a period of the absolute manipulation of humans by humans: the objective correlative of total manipulation is coldcock murder. Murder is now a lumbermill where human beings can be treated with the same lack of respect as trees.

Most critics, however, opted to ignore the endangered forest, Alfred Kazin confessed that *American Psycho* "confirms something I have long been afraid to disclose. It is perfectly possible to have a certain amount of literary talent yet to be dumb as hell." Concerning the conspicuous consumption, Kazin maintained that "Bret Easton Ellis doesn't know the difference between a novel and the Hammacher Schlemmer catalogue," and "is so heavy-handed that street ads for *Les Misérables* appear for 'ironic' contrast. Some limit in trendiness is reached when Patrick sneers at his pals for having the *American,* not the *original English recording* of the show."

The Los Angeles chapter of the National Organization for Women decided, with grim literalness, that *American Psycho* was not social commentary, but rather a "how-to" manual for the torture and dismemberment of women. The argument recalled Fredric Wertham, in a kind of feminist drag. A boycott of Knopf titles by NOW members was threatened, but never materialized. Ellis' satiric intentions in *American Psycho* are obvious, and perhaps too obvious. ("The Chinese dry cleaners I usually send my bloody clothes to delivered back to me yesterday a Soprani jacket, two white Brooks Brothers shirts and a tie from Agnes B. still covered with flecks of someone's blood. I have a lunch appointment at noon—in forty minutes—and beforehand I decide to stop by the cleaners and complain.") Simon and Schuster's catalog described the book as a "black comedy." But *American Psycho* is so bloated and overdone that potential appreciation of the author's intentions or control was blinded by the blood-spray. As pure concept, *American Psycho* must have seemed brilliant (one wonders what a master surreal stylist

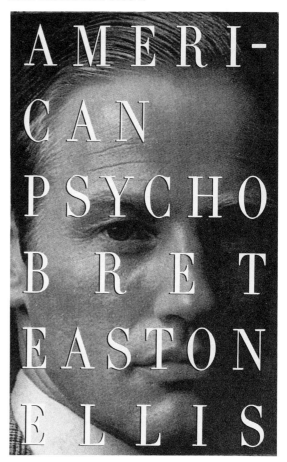

No advertising
needed: *American
Psycho* by Bret
Easton Ellis.

like J. G. Ballard would have done with it), but so did the idea of a musical based on *Carrie*.

Bret Easton Ellis has distinct narrative gifts, and an especially good ear for dialogue. A non-gruesome sequence in which Bateman and a manic-depressive woman have a totally miserable time performing "safe sex" in the age of AIDS is both hilarious and horrible, and probably the best-written scene in the book. Here Ellis brilliantly conjures a world of body-fluid terror without spilling a drop himself. The rest of the book, unfortunately, confounds readers who are otherwise disposed to defend it. The manuscript of Ellis' first book, *Less Than Zero* (1984), was reportedly cut in half with the help of Ellis' creative-writing teacher, Joe McGinnis. *American Psycho* seemingly received no such attention. The manuscript went on . . . and on . . . and on. Ellis' agent,

Amanda Urban, was said to have landed a $300,000 advance on the basis of a half-page outline. The deal was made, fortuitously, just before Ellis' second novel, *The Rules of Attraction,* was published and bombed in 1987.

Could a contract for a book like *American Psycho* even be thinkable in a world without Stephen King, Clive Barker, and the splatterpunks? It is doubtful. King's record-breaking deals for horror novels—his current contract is widely believed to be worth nearly $40 million—may well have convinced at least some publishing executives that grisly horror fiction had the same kind of speculation value as New York real estate. It was perhaps fitting that $300,000 was just about the price for a nice Manhattan co-op at the end of the eighties.

Both Stephen King and Bret Easton Ellis describe worlds of consumer horror. King does so literally and fictionally. His use of commercial brand names and other media references is one of his most recognizable narrative tics; he is also a brand name himself. While his push-button invocation of trademarks may well be lazy writing, it does illustrate the extent to which advertising and television have become a primary form of social glue in the late twentieth century, the last vestige of shared experience for millions as the shopping mall and television cable have replaced more traditional forms of human congregation and contact. King dangles his readers over the darkest abysses, letting them grab at media anchors for safety and comfort: Coca-Cola, the "Today" show, Dristan, Rolaids, Kaopectate, Preparation H, Midol, *Time* magazine, H & R Block, Sony, Kodak, "Family Feud," Datsun, Ford, Camel cigarettes, British Airways, and "Sesame Street" are just a random sampling of King's style of name-dropping as reflected in *It. It* also contains nearly three pages of permissions and acknowledgments for popular song lyrics quoted throughout the book. It is when the shopping cart is almost full, the anxiety nearly assuaged by familiarity and consumption, that Stephen King inevitably brings on the newest shock or monster.

American Psycho, on the other hand, uses consumer tags and designer labels to numb and overwhelm. Ellis, or his publisher, added a disclaimer in the front of the book: "This is a work of fiction. All of the characters, incidents, and dialogue, except for incidental references to public figures, products, or services, are imaginary and are not intended to refer to any living persons or to disparage any company's products or services." The products are all high-ticket: Giorgio Armani, Christian Dior, Bergdorf's—although on the book's opening page Ellis describes a McDonald's restaurant with a red-painted FEAR graffito. Although he often flubs his effects, Ellis occasionally makes the transition from banal consumption to equally banal violence startling and effective.

There is actually nothing in *American Psycho* in terms of explicit, degrading violence that had not already appeared in any number of books in the 1980s. Splatterpunk was well established as a subset of horror publishing, loosely embracing a range of writers from the best-selling Clive Barker to paperback newcomers eager to ride a trend. Over-the-top depictions of sadistic serial killings cropped up in the mystery field as well, notably in the psychosexual crime novels of James Ellroy—*The Black Dahlia* (1987), *The Big Nowhere* (1988)—which frequently approached the mega-Guignol in their descriptions of graphic evisceration.

None of this figured into the media circus surrounding *American Psycho*—for one reason. Simon and Schuster and Knopf were not genre publishers. To the offended sensibilities, it was permissible for the working classes to pork down on books like Rex Miller's *Slob* (1987), because the classes who read the books didn't matter. *American Psycho* was an upscale, gold-plated *Texas Chainsaw Massacre,* the purest kind of cultural collision. Although the whole incident was endlessly discussed in terms of taste, misogyny, and political correctness, a subtext of class snobbery predominated. The hideous progeny of Stephen King could be tolerated, or ignored, as long as they kept their place in the peasants' quarters in Brooklyn or New Jersey, but let them start tracking blood up the staircase of the Manhattan castle, and there'd be hell to pay.

Both Bret Easton Ellis and Stephen King depict, from radically polar perspectives, the monstrous spectacle of the consumer consumed. Ellis' world of blood-soaked designer labels recognizably upgrades the voracious mall zombies in *Dawn of the Dead*: they shop till they drop, eat your brains, then shop some more. Both writers are obsessively concerned with rituals of initiation and class identification. King's books, readily available at the supermarket display rack, forge a link between shopping, belonging, and the ultimate horror of not being able to do either.

In Stephen King's America, there is nothing that can't be profitably assimilated and aggressively exploited, where even a charnel

The consumer zombies from George Romero's *Dawn of the Dead*.

house can be refitted as a piece of Disneyland-style real estate. The seemingly opposing sensibilities of King and Ellis have a meeting of minds at the Universal Studios tour in Orlando, Florida, where a *"Psycho* soundstage" was recently installed as a family-style attraction, allowing vacationing Americans the chance to participate vicariously in the famous shower murder. That scene, it should be remembered, involved a monstrous, masked doppelganger and a violently interrupted ceremony of rebirth. Marion Crane (Janet Leigh), who has impulsively stolen $40,000 and run away, decides to return the money and return to society. The shower is the transitional symbol of her purification, of her reinitiation into the social group. Her murder, like Carrie's betrayal at the prom, became a powerful image of the collapse of basic social contracts and human relatedness: like us, Marion Crane wants advancement, security. She makes a mistake, but plays by the rules and seeks forgiveness-acceptance, only to have her cleansing transformation turned into a bloody sacrifice. There is no God, it seems—at least not a just one. The disturbing scene became one of the most influential images in film history with good reason: it undermined all expectations and formulas—just as the sixties themselves were doing on almost every social, political, and artistic level. *Psycho* is a keystone of modern horror, articulating the dread of ordinary people feeling trapped and immobilized in a world otherwise full of rapid change. The pace of economic and technological transformation only accelerated in the intervening years; *Psycho* has stubbornly refused to go away. The film has been processed and reprocessed through the mills of popular culture, imitated, sequelled, parodied, analyzed, deconstructed . . . and finally retired to Florida as a harmless tourist attraction. If your family is having difficulty being assimilated by the downsized nineties, take the kids to Orlando, where they can literally take a stab at the most destabilizing dream-moment of modern times.

By a similar process, Stephen King defangs his monsters and domesticates his horrors. It could be said that King doesn't just mine popular culture; in many ways he *is* popular culture. As the anxiety levels of the Cuban missile crisis are eclipsed by everyday angst, King's monstrous images have become reassuring reference points for millions, as surely as the "Monster Mash" provided a necessary buffer zone between the fallout shelter and the grave. With the end of the Cold War, the bombs that threaten are more economic than atomic, but the knot in the stomach remains; the dance of death is now a dance of dearth, the horror less a matter of rigor mortis than other forms of paralysis. King's novel *Gerald's Game* (1992) depicts the struggle with personal immobility in the most literal way imaginable: a woman playing bondage games with her husband in a remote cabin is left handcuffed to the bed when he accidentally dies. Horror, in late-twentieth-century, deficit-ridden America, is the realization that we may not be able to change our circumstances, and may well be stuck with what we've got.

Chapter Fourteen

THE MONSTER MILLENNIUM

"To a new world of gods and monsters!"

Ernest Thesiger in
Bride of Frankenstein
(1935)

AMERICA WAS DEAD again. The persistent flat line of economic indicators had, by the end of 1991, convinced a majority of Americans that something was seriously awry with the nation's fiscal health. Some economists believed that the current "recession" (an official euphemism coined in the thirties to control the rampant use of the word "depression") was a long-term malaise strikingly similar to the catastrophic, decade-long stagnation that had followed the stock-market crash of 1929. Indeed, 1991 and 1931 shared some striking similarities, especially in the realm of popular culture. To coin a *Famous Monsters*–style pun, if 1931 had been an American abyss, then its sequel, 1991, might best be regarded as Son of Abyss.

In 1991, the entertainment and communications worlds were filled with images of morbidity and dread. *Dead Again* was the title of a film. So was *Dying Young*. And, while people weren't flinging themselves from windows on Wall Street, an instruction book for painless suicide made it to the best-seller lists.

The new Frankenstein: Arnold Schwarzenegger in *Terminator 2: Judgment Day* **(1991).** *(Photofest)*

Universal's *Dracula* and *Frankenstein* were restored for sixtieth-anniversary theatrical screenings around the country, part of a $5.5 million advertising promotion by Miller beer and other sponsors. The monsters who had put a face on the Depression for millions of Americans in 1931 could be seen and heard in their nearly original condition, during a time of similar national turmoil. If the old monsters no longer provided catharsis, they were at least a reminder of how enduring the by-products of social crisis can be.

1991 found its own fictional monster who served an analogous function to the creatures of *Dracula, Frankenstein, Dr. Jekyll and Mr. Hyde,* and *Freaks.* The cannibal serial killer Dr. Hannibal Lecter, as portrayed by actor Anthony Hopkins in the film version of Thomas Harris' novel *The Silence of the Lambs,* was a striking amalgam of the classic monsters, and captured the public imagination in an electrifying way. Hannibal Lecter was, arguably, the most publicized and recognizable personality (real or not) in America during February 1991. (The media shifted with great enthusiasm from its promotion of *Silence of the Lambs* to its coverage of the Milwaukee cannibal / killer Jeffrey Dahmer a few months later; the public's evident appetite for human flesh blurred the distinctions between news and entertainment. One of ABC's radio reporters on the Dahmer trial was actually named Tony Perkins, as if in homage to *Psycho.*)

Like Dracula, Hannibal Lecter has a pronounced taste for human blood; like Frankenstein, he is a brilliant, but mad scientist; he has two personalities, like Dr. Jekyll and Mr. Hyde, both civilized and savage; and, like some sideshow super-geek, he is held and exhibited in a succession of zoo-like enclosures. *The Silence of the Lambs* itself provided a sideshow-like diversion in which all the traditional headliners in the monster show reassembled themselves like the pieces of a broken mirror. And the monster, this time, looked very much like us.

In March 1992, *The Silence of the Lambs* won a clean sweep of all the major Academy Award categories—best picture, best director, best actress, best actor, and best adapted screenplay. Actor Anthony Hopkins received a thundering standing ovation when he accepted his award for the cannibal role, and had been treated during the ceremony almost as a guest of honor, with an endless stream of flesh-eating jokes thrown in his direction throughout the evening. The nonstop, bloodthirsty humor was bizarrely juxtaposed with the red lapel ribbons worn by most of the presenters—symbols of compassion for people with AIDS.

A year earlier, when the film was first released, an advertisement featuring the cover of the March 25, 1991, issue of *Newsweek* filled with Hannibal Lecter's staring eyes was printed directly next to a *New York Times* article about the growing pessimism of American consumers. Citing a just-released study by Grey Advertising, the *Times* reported that consumers were feeling vulnerable "because of problems over which they had little control," including the Persian Gulf War, AIDS, pollution, and the growing ranks of the homeless. "Seventy-five percent of those polled questioned whether their hopes and dreams for the future would ever come true."

The Gulf War had its echoes in the world of media horror. Just as E.C. Comics had been read by servicemen in Korea, *Fangoria* accompanied many American boys to the front, if letters received

Dr. Hannibal Lecter (Anthony Hopkins) enjoys his hideous repast in *The Silence of the Lambs* (1991). *(Photofest)*

by the magazine (including one on Operation Desert Storm letter-head) are any indication. "Being deployed out here really puts a kink in my ability to check out the latest in horror / splatter films," wrote one private first class. *Fangoria,* he maintained, "is the best kind of support you guys can give the troops over here." After the pullout, a suppressed wire service photo of an incinerated Iraqi soldier in the hatch of a tank was reproduced on a poster protesting U.S. involvement. Its grisly effect was perhaps dulled by a too-close resemblance to any number of film posters featuring the makeup creations of Tom Savini. Such imagery was now commonplace, even banal. *The New York Times* was made a bit queasy by the Home Box Office cable television series "Tales from the Crypt" for war-related reasons. The reviewer, John J. O'Connor, expressed some discomfort that the show's skeletal puppet-host, the Crypt Keeper, looked a bit too much like a photo of starving Iraqi child. "Horror is not limited to comic books," O'Connor wrote. "Primal nightmares are rooted in reality, and the overlapping of images can be disorienting."

The public's perennial fascination with freaks was bubbling up everywhere. Daytime television talk shows had replaced the traditional sideshow tent; human oddities, be they physical or psychosexual, became prize attractions for programs like "Oprah," "Geraldo," and "Donahue." (Oprah Winfrey herself, in highly-publicized bouts of weight fluctuation, managed to embody the spirits of both the fat lady and the human skeleton.) At least one traditional traveling sideshow emerged, eliciting nationwide amazement and disgust with a performer who pounded railroad spikes into his nose, another who pumped his own stomach and re-imbibed his bile, and yet another who suspended heavy objects from his pierced nipples, tongue, and penis. Given horror's sideshow roots, it is not at all surprising that one of the most popular monster icons of the 1980s and 1990s is Clive Barker's "Pinhead" from the *Hellraiser* films. (The character's name evokes two sideshow images simultaneously—the classic microcephalon, as well as the self-made, self-mutilating freak who hammers nails into his head to attract a crowd.)

Two familiar horror images overlapped loudly in the summer of 1991 with the release of *Terminator 2: Judgment Day,* which, at a widely reported cost of $100 million, was the most expensive collective dream-ritual of all time. Arnold Schwarzenegger reprised his killer-android role from *The Terminator* (1984), which had made him the central cultural repository of Frankenstein energy. Schwarzenegger's Terminator was a mechanical steamroller of the traditional artificial-man school; the sequel pitted him against a new kind of monster—a plastic, shape-shifting being (Robert Patrick) who evoked the protean powers of Dracula. The left-brain / right-brain waltz of the Dark Twins had found an unprecedentedly vivid level of expression, and, as always, kept the world mesmerized.

Lifelessness and cannibalism, two hit motifs of the year, were both on prominent display again shortly before Thanksgiving, when a screen version of *The Addams Family* became the public's entertainment of choice. It grossed $25 million during its first three days of release, a record for a non-holiday weekend. Here was a household where everything was dead or dysfunctional. The children are given live animals in brown bags for their school lunches; the grandmother keeps a copy of *Gray's Anatomy* next to her cookbook. The parents are necrophiles. The macabre dislocations clearly struck a resonant chord with the public during America's worst year since the Great Depression. Brandon Tartikoff, chairman of Paramount Pictures, gave his initial reaction. "It's campy nostalgia for the adult part of the audience. For the kids, who don't really know the *New Yorker* cartoons or the TV series, what they see is a very weird, spooky family that's the original dysfunctional family. These are weird times, and these are weird people."

It's not just people who are weird. Our de facto gods, the beings with which we commune with before our home-video altars, to which we make offerings at the Cineplex, are weird, too—graven images if there ever were. "Horror films are rituals of pagan worship," writes Camille Paglia. "There western man obsessively confronts what Christianity has never been able to bury or explain away. . . . The horror film uses rot as a primary material, part of the Christian west's secret craving for Dionysian truths." Slippery things that they are, monsters also manage to reinvigorate Christian values. Leonard Wolf, who has written frequently and cogently on the subject of horror, noted during one of the monster cycles of the 1970s that

> the cinema of horror provides its highly secularized audience with their last—perhaps their only—opportunity to experience mystery and miracle. . . . The great frenzies of chaos, creation, disobedience, disaster, solitude and evil which have been ren-

dered vague or bland in the well-bred church and synagogue
services of the 70's are restored to their terrifying proportions in
the half-light of the movie theaters. Priests of the horror cinema
still recite incantations that count.

A good deal of this book has dealt with the long shadow of war
reflected and transformed in the shared anxiety rituals we call
monster movies. Wars tend not to resolve themselves, culturally,
until years after actual combat stops. The same is true of economic
depressions, fatal epidemics, political witch-hunts—the traumas
can linger for decades. World War I found a persistent symbolic
expression in horror entertainment, a tendency that never really
ended, and was only replaced by the symbol-distillations of World
War II. The American nineties are still haunted by the Vietnamese
seventies; the belief in the survival of Vietnam-era MIAs remains
a powerful fixation in many quarters, a tenet of faith that psycho-
logically concretizes at least one truth: that the Vietnam War was
never really resolved, not in the world and not in our minds.

Ghost-monsters of the Vietnam conflict provided nervous
laughter in the horror-comedy *House* (1986), in which a Stephen
King–like writer is stalked by a rotting, helmeted Vietnam casu-
alty; but it was not until director Adrian Lyne's remarkable *Jacob's
Ladder* (1990) that horror and Vietnam came together in an intelligent and visionary way. Jacob (Tim Robbins) returns from Vietnam, not knowing that he is already dead. The New York City
he inhabits becomes increasingly demonized, full of almost subliminal monstrosities, until Jacob comes to a final acceptance of
his fate. In his afterword to the published script, screenwriter Bruce
Joel Rubin enumerates the initial sources of inspiration for the
film's disturbing metaphysical visions, including thalidomide
deformities and the paintings of Francis Bacon. By consciously
humanizing monster-movie clichés, *Jacob's Ladder* avoids the usual
displacements and repressions of the genre, affording audiences a
genuine catharsis and closure—a marked contrast to the *catharsis
interruptus* of most commercial horror efforts. Francis Ford Coppola, who began his directing career with the horror film *Dementia
13* (1963), returned to his roots in a big way with *Bram Stoker's
Dracula* (1992) which depicted for the first time the vampire's origins
as a berserker-style warlord—an acknowledgment of horror's
genesis in primal human conflict. As horror attracts more mainstream talents—the trend seems inevitable—we may expect to

see more and more of the traditional cobwebs swept away from the mirror's spooky surface, revealing with an unprecedented clarity exactly where we stand in relation to our deepest fears.

The circumstances surrounding the creation of Hollywood's most enduring monster icons in 1931 are now at the very edge of living human memory, and this book may be one of the last to give a personal, anecdotal voice to their genesis. Interviews proved difficult; performers, producers, and directors who had not already died were often unwilling to speak. Johnny Eck, the "half-boy" from *Freaks,* became a recluse in his inner-city Baltimore home after being badly beaten by intruders in the early 1980s; one of the thieves was reported to have immobilized Eck by sitting on him like a pillow while his partner ransacked the house. "If I want to see freaks, all I have to do is look out the window," Eck told Forrest J Ackerman, the former editor of *Famous Monsters.* Johnny Eck died in early 1991.

Angelo Rossitto, the exuberant dwarf who offered the loving cup to Olga Baclanova during the wedding feast in *Freaks,* met this author at the Hollywood retirement home where he spent his last days. At first glance he was a highly theatrical figure in his brightly painted room—a classic Diane Arbus image, leaning on a walking stick and sporting oversized sunglasses. At second glance the Hollywood mood evaporated; Angelo Rossitto was disabled and blind. Clearly depressed, he decided not to talk about his career, and certainly not about Tod Browning and *Freaks.* "I don't want any publicity," he said. "When you look like me, walking down the street's enough publicity." A few months later, the trade papers contained the news of Angelo Rossitto's death.

Further up the coast, the author found a more gracious reception, and some final insights. "It's all rather like a haunting," said David Manners, on the eve of his ninety-first birthday. The former actor appeared at least twenty years younger, somehow turning around time, or at the very least, holding it still. In his homey room at a coastal California retirement community, he offered his guest a jar full of Hershey's Kisses. Sunlight streamed through the window, with no demons to destroy. There could not be a setting further removed from the claustrophobic expressionism of *The Black Cat,* one of the films in which he acted almost sixty years before. The discussion turned to war, economic collapses, the breakdown of the social fabric, AIDS, and finally back to horror films. "I still get letters from people all over the world," he said. "They write to me as if I were actually a character in *Dracula* or *The Mummy* rather than an actor named David Manners." Asked about his memories of World War I in relation to the theme of this book, he confessed that he tried to enlist but was rejected. "I always looked young for my age," he remembered. "I got in line with all the naked men, and an officer walked over to me and said, 'Go home, sonny—we don't take babies.' I went home to bed and cried my heart out." As a Hollywood actor making $100,000 a year in the early thirties, he barely felt the Depression. In World War II, he was again rejected by the army, this time because of flat feet.

Spared the horrors of war, and the dread of economic cataclysm, it is perhaps understandable that David Manners never developed a taste for or comprehension of the classic horror films in which he starred. He laughed at the suggestion that monster movies "meant" anything at all, and leaned forward to impart an additional bit of information with the quiet authority of a "century baby" who had seen it all. Well, not quite all.

"You know," he said, out of the blue, "I've never even seen *Dracula.*"

The visitor was stunned. Not *ever?*

"Never! I knew it was a stinker all the while we were making it, so I just never bothered to go."

The visitor started to respond, but Manners raised an authoritative hand. "I know what's coming next, and the answer is no! Before you even ask—please!—do *not* offer to send me a videotape."

He laughed again, proffering another piece of candy. And this time, the visitor laughed, too.

Acknowledgments

It is only appropriate that the task of researching and writing a book called *The Monster Show* was in itself a monstrous undertaking, one that could not have been accomplished without the help and encouragement of numerous institutions and individuals. I wish to thank especially my editor at Norton, Hilary Hinzmann, whose perceptive comments and suggestions helped me shape a book far wider in scope that I had originally imagined. My agent, Malaga Baldi, backed the project tirelessly from its inception, and the film historian and preservationist Scott MacQueen was a near-bottomless resource for my endless and often extremely obscure research questions.

Research collections consulted included the many divisions of the New York Public Library, especially the Billy Rose Theatre Collection at Lincoln Center; the Margaret Herrick Library of the Academy of Motion Picture Arts and Sciences; the Library of Congress; the Harvard Theatre Collection; the Free Library of Philadelphia Theatre Collection; the Theatre Museum; the Circus World Museum; the Oakland Public Library; the San Francisco Public Library; the British Library Division of Manuscripts; and the British Film Institute.

The reconstruction of Horace Liveright's attempts to produce *Frankenstein* as a play and film could not have been accomplished without the cooperation of the estates of John L. Balderston and Hamilton Deane in opening the negotiation files for my research. A special thanks to John Balderston and Ann and John Burton, as well as their agents, Robert Freedman in New York and Laurence Fitch in London. Ivan Butler, the last surviving member of Hamilton Deane's company, provided invaluable recollections by letter, phone, and finally in a delightful personal interview at his home outside of London. Bernard Davies and Robert James Leake of the Dracula Society graciously gave me access to their collection of Deane photographs and papers. Bret Wood and Elias Savada were most generous in sharing with me their unpublished biographical research on Tod Browning. As he did for my earlier book, *Hollywood Gothic,* Ronald V. Borst opened his incomparable collection of visual and printed materials. Film historian Philip J. Riley was equally obliging in helping me locate important data in his extensive collection of vintage scripts and memorabilia. With his encyclopedic knowledge of fantastic films, writer Tom Weaver quickly located answers to many cryptic inquiries.

Thanks are owed the following individuals for their diverse contributions, courtesies, correspondence, suggestions, and interviews: Forrest J Ackerman, Buddy Barnett, Anne-Marie Bates, Pat Wilks Battle, Barbara Belford, Richard Bojarski, Patricia Bosworth, Edward Bryant, Jonathan Sinclair Carey, Roz Celeiro, Samuel R. Crowl, Bob Damrocher, Joe Dante, Mark Dery, Norine Dresser, Arlene Francis, John Gallagher, Ian Grey, Roger Hurlburt, Maria Jochsberger, Lupita Tovar Kohner, David Manners, Samuel Marx, Raymond McNally, Maila Nurmi, Paul Parla, Paul Penser, Richard Peterson, David Pickman, David Pierce, Heriberto Quinones, Jack Rems, Garydon Rhodes, Laura Ross, Angelo Rossitto, Jay Sheckley, Sam Sherman, Stephen Speliotis, Daniel Talbot, Peter Thorpe, Anthony Timpone, George Turner, Ross Wetzsteon, Scott Wolfman, Jeanne Youngson, and John Zacherle.

Photographic resources appear adjacent to illustrations; unsourced photos are from the author's collection. Ron and Howard Mandelbaum at Photofest provided extensive help in locating hard-to-find images, and photographer Donal F. Holway contributed tireless darkroom assistance and advice. Commercial lab work was handled with careful attention by Galowitz Photographics, Inc. Arthur J. Walsh resurrected several brittle and damaged images that a lesser retoucher would have given up as irretrievable.

A penultimate thank-you is due Lisa Pliscou for her sure and perceptive copyediting of the manuscript, with a final, grateful acknowledgment to the legendary Edward Gorey for putting such a splendidly effective public face on my work.

NOTES

Introduction
A Sideshow in Camelot

16 SHE LEARNED ABOUT THE FILM: Patricia Bosworth, *Diane Arbus* (New York: Alfred A. Knopf, 1984), p. 162.

16 A MIDDLE-AGED VAMPIRE: Renee Tajima, "Emile de Antonio, 1919–89," *The Village Voice,* January 2, 1990.

16 DRINK IS MY MEAT: Mitch Tuchman, "Emile de Antonio: 'All Filmmakers Are Confidence Men,' " *The Village Voice,* May 17, 1976.

17 A DARK, UNNATURAL, HIDDEN SELF: Bosworth, *op. cit.*

17 AN ANXIOUS VISCERAL EXCITEMENT: *Ibid.,* p. 167.

18 WHAT IS EVIL: Hilton Kramer, "From Fashion to Freaks," *The New York Times Magazine,* November 5, 1972, p. 65.

18 WHO CALLED HIMSELF JACK DRACULA: Diane Arbus, accompanying text for photo of Jack Dracula, *Harper's Bazaar,* November 1961; reprinted in the retrospective *Diane Arbus: Magazine Work* (Millerton, NY: Aperture, 1984), p. 14–16.

19 A SUBLIME DEFORMITY OF NATURE: Kramer, *op. cit.,* p. 68.

21 SHE WAS SO ATTRACTED TO THE GROTESQUE: Daniel Talbot, interviewed by author, New York City, November 1990.

21 FREAKS WENT PUBLIC: Susan Sontag, *On Photography* (New York: Farrar, Straus and Giroux, 1977), p. 43.

21 AESTHETES' SUBVERSION: *Ibid.,* p. 44.

22 AS SONTAG ELABORATES: *Ibid.,* p. 40–41.

22 IT WAS RUMORED: Bosworth, *op. cit.,* p. 320.

23 A LITERATURE OF HORROR FOR BOYS: Leslie A. Fiedler, *Love and Death in the American Novel,* rev. ed. (New York: Stein and Day, 1966), p. 29.

23 ANOTHER BOOK BY FIELDER: Leslie A. Fiedler, *Freaks: Myths and Images of the Secret Self* (New York: Simon and Schuster, 1978).

Chapter One
Tod Browning's America

26	DIRT COME CRASHING DOWN: "Tod Browning's Varied Career," *Louisville Herald-Post,* February 27, 1921.

26	WAS BORN BROWNING, JR.: The exact year of Tod Browning's birth is a point of some confusion. Studio publicity materials usually gave the year as 1882, though Browning attested to 1880 when he filed a replacement birth certificate in Louisville (no original existed). 1880 seems accurate, but according to William S. Hart, Jr., a longtime friend of Browning's and part heir to his estate, Browning was actually born in 1874. "The other date was just P.R. to make him seem younger," Hart is reported to have said, and was firm about this point in at least two separate interviews, one with Alan Buster (transcript at Margaret Herrick Library, Academy of Motion Picture Arts and Sciences, Beverly Hills, California) and one with Elias Savada (unpublished transcript).

26	PETE "THE GLADIATOR" BROWNING: Biographical entry by Duane A. Smith in David L. Porter, ed., *Biographical Dictionary of American Sports* (New York / Westport, CT / London: Greenwood Press, 1987), p. 56–57.

27	A SPRIGHTLY BOY: *Louisville Herald-Post, op. cit.*

28	HE KNEW HIS PUBLIC: "Famous Mystery Pictures Are Work of Native Louisvillian," *Louisville Herald-Post,* July 18, 1928.

28	HORDES OF GYPSIES: Richard Clemensen, "Master of the Macabre," *Louisville Magazine,* June 1977, p. 22.

29	TALL AND TOWERING TODY: Dexter W. Fellows and Andrew A. Freeman, *This Way to the Big Show: The Life of Dexter Fellows* (New York: Viking, 1936).

29	TO STATE A FACT IN ORDINARY LANGUAGE: Irving Wallace, *The Fabulous Showman: The Life and Times of P. T. Barnum* (New York: Alfred A. Knopf, 1959), p. 289.

29	A THOUSAND VERSIONS OF OUR OWN FACE: Leslie A. Fiedler, *Love and Death in the American Novel,* rev. ed. (New York: Stein and Day, 1966), p. 27.

29	THE GUILLOTINE: Peter Verney, *Here Comes the Circus* (New York and London: Paddington Press Ltd., 1978), p. 225.

30	NOT A SLEAZY OPERATION: Robert Bogdan, *Freak Show: Presenting Human Oddities for Amusements and Profit* (Chicago and London: University of Chicago Press, 1988), p. 32.

30	A NATIONAL FORCE: *Ibid.,* p. 35.

31	CONFER A KIND OF LIVING DEATH: For Maxim Gorky's 1896 comments on Lumiere's Cinematograph, see *New Theatre,* March 1937, p. 11.

34	A LIKING FOR FLASHY CARS: Alanna Nash, "The man who unearthed Count Dracula—Louisville runaway Tod Browning," *The Courier-Journal* (Louisville, Kentucky), April 2, 1978.

34	SPEEDING MANIA: "The Personal Side of the Pictures," *Reel Life,* August 25, 1914.

35 WOULD PROBABLY DIE: "Film Stars in Auto Wreck; One Killed, Two Hurt," *San Francisco Chronicle,* June 17, 1915.

35 PAINFULLY CUT AND BRUISED: "Investigating Ride to Death," *Los Angeles Times,* June 17, 1915.

Chapter Two
"You Will Become Caligari":
Monsters, Mountebanks, and Modernism

38 SPECTACULAR DEMONSTRATION: "Theater Stops German Film," *Los Angeles Examiner,* May 8, 1921, p. 1.

38 WILD RIOTING: "Riot Over German Feature Picture; 'Cabinet of Caligari' Egged on Coast," *Variety,* May 13, 1921.

38 THE MOST EXTRAORDINARY PRODUCTION YET SEEN: Kenneth MacGowan, " 'Dr. Caligari,' Cubist Film, Brings up Problem of German Competition," unsourced clipping from New York paper, March 12, 1921.

38 REPRESENTS THE INEVITABLE LINE: "Noted Art Critic Praises Recent Modernist Film," *Variety,* April 15, 1921.

39 SPACE HAS BEEN GIVEN A VOICE: "Cubism on the Screen," *The New York Times,* November 28, 1920.

39 THE AGITATORS DO NOT KNOW: "Movement Started to Bar German-Made Productions," *Exhibitors Herald,* May 7, 1921.

40 FAIRLY SHRIEK: "Selling the Picture to the Public: Cubist Art Posters for Goldwyn's 'Dr. Caligari,' " *Moving Picture World,* May 28, 1921, p. 399.

42 PREGNANT FOREBODINGS: For a detailed reconstruction of Mayer's and Janowitz's contributions to *Caligari,* and the film's actual production, see Siegfried Kracauer, *From Caligari to Hitler: A Psychological History of the German Film* (Princeton, NJ: Princeton University Press, 1947), p. 61–76.

43 AN EARLIER VERSION OF THE SCREENPLAY: S. S. Prawer, in *Caligari's Children: The Film As Tale of Terror* (Oxford / New York / Toronto / Melbourne: Oxford University Press, 1980), p. 168–69, cites a typescript of the *Caligari* screenplay from the estate of actor Werner Krauss that contains the alternate framing device. Prawer suggests that this material disproves the notion that *Caligari* was intended by its authors as an antiauthoritarian parable. Given scenarist Janowitz's version of the script development, cited by Siegfried Kracauer in *From Caligari to Hitler,* it makes more sense that both alterations are producer-ordered bastardizations, the final, madhouse scenes being a compromise.

43 A REVOLUTIONARY FILM WAS THUS TURNED: *Ibid.,* p. 67.

43 DAS CABINET DES DR. CALIGARI: Many accounts give the German title as *Das Kabinett des Dr. Caligari,* although the word is spelled *Cabinet* on both the opening titles of the film itself and on original advertisements and posters. "Kabinett" is indeed the correct German spelling, but the producers, for some obscure reason, deliberately used the French / English form of the word.

43 AN IMMEDIATE COMMERCIAL HIT: For details on *Caligari*'s initial success in Germany, see Kristin Thompson, "Dr. Caligari at the Folies-Bergére," in

Mike Budd, ed., *The Cabinet of Dr. Caligari: Texts, Contexts, Histories* (New Brunswick, NJ, and London: Rutgers University Press, 1990), p. 138.

44 THE MUSICAL SETTING: Unsourced article, 1921 scrapbook of clippings for the American premiere of *The Cabinet of Dr. Caligari,* Billy Rose Theatre Collection, New York Public Library at Lincoln Center.

44 TINTS OF GREEN, BROWN, AND STEEL-BLUE: Lotte H. Eisner, *The Haunted Screen* (Berkeley and Los Angeles: University of California Press, 1973), p. 21.

44 AN EVIDENCE IN THIS PICTURE: Stanley Hochman, ed., *From Quasimodo to Scarlett O'Hara: A National Board of Review Anthology 1920–1940* (New York: Frederick Ungar Publishing Co., 1982), p. 13.

44 IT MAY CATCH THE POPULAR FANCY: *Variety,* April 8, 1921, p. 40.

44 DEGENERATE GERMAN INVENTION: Edward Weitzel, " 'Cabinet of Dr. Caligari': German Made Film Is Novel Experiment in the Weird That Will Create Great Diversity of Opinion," *Moving Picture World,* April 16, 1921, p. 755.

45 A STRANGE, WEIRD FREAK: Upton Sinclair, *They Call Me Carpenter* (Chicago: The Paine Book Co., 1922), p. 2.

45 THESE CULTURED FOREIGNERS: *Ibid.,* p. 1.

45 RISK OF STARVING FOR IT: *Ibid.,* p. 2.

45 I WALKED TOWARDS THE EXIT: *Ibid.,* p. 8.

45 A SEETHING MOB: "Theater Stops German Film," *Los Angeles Examiner, May 8, 1921, p. 1.*

46 AUTHENTIC THRILLS AND SHOCKS OF ART*: Albert Lewin, review of Caligari; Shadowland,* October 1923, p. 46.

46 ESSENTIALLY CINEMATOGRAPHIC: Ezra Pound, "Paris Letter," *The Dial,* February 1923, p. 274.

48 THE INVASION OF DEATH: Sidra Stich, *Anxious Visions: Surrealist Art* (Berkeley and New York: University Art Museum and Abbeville Press, 1990), p. 30.

48 DEDICATED OCCULTIST: Lotte H. Eisner, *Murnau* (Berkeley and Los Angeles: University of California Press, 1973), p. 109.

50 DRINKING THE BLOOD OF MILLIONS: Albin Grau, "Vampires," *Bühne und Film* No. 21 (1921), reprinted in M. Bouvier and J.-L. Leutrat, *Nosferatu* (Paris: Cahiers du Cinema / Gallimard, 1981), p. 17–20. French translation by Jean-Charles Margotton. English translation by the author.

50 A NOW-OBSCURE FILM: Alfred Krautz, ed., *International Directory of Cinematographers, Set and Costume Designers in Film: Volume 9 (Hungary)* (Munich, New York, London and Paris: K. G. Saur, 1989), p. 50.

51 AFTER DRAUGHTS OF BLOOD: Eisner, *The Haunted Screen, op. cit.,* p. 9.

53 COMPLETELY SPOILED: André Gide, journal entry, February 27, 1928, *The Journals of André Gide,* Justin O'Brien, trans. (New York: Alfred A. Knopf, 1949), p. 7–8.

54 I HAD NO IDEA WHAT I WAS: Harold Clurman, *All People Are Famous (Instead of an Autobiography)* (New York and London: Harcourt Brace Jovanovich, 1974), p. 28.

54 BY THE TIME WE REACHED HOME: Aaron Copland and Vivian Perlis, *Copland: 1900 through 1942* (New York: St. Martin's / Marek, 1984), p. 84.

54 THERE WAS A TASTE FOR THE BIZARRE: *Ibid.*

54 SHOUTED LITANIES: Steve Warren, "Surreal it hurts: Pacific Film Archive series restores the social context of surrealism," *The East Bay Guardian* (San Francisco), October 1990.

57 PRAYERS COULD STILL OCCASIONALLY BE HEARD: Mel Gordon, *Grand Guignol: Theatre of Fear and Terror* (New York: Amok Press, 1988), p. 16.

57 SNUG, EXTREMELY INTIMATE: The exact seating capacity of the Grand Guignol is something of a puzzle. Mel Gordon, in *Grand Guignol: Theatre of Fear and Terror,* gives the number as 285, and refers to other records of 230, 265, 272, and 280. François Riviere and Gabrielle Wittkop, in *Grand Guignol* (Paris: Henry Veyrier, 1979), reproduce a seating plan that includes only 175 numbered seats, five loges of four seats each, and eight screened loges. An allowance of thirty-two seats for these enclosures brings the total capacity to 227. Having recently visited the auditorium (which now employs informal, carpeted bleachers), and having considerable professional experience in small theatres, this author believes that the lowest figure is most likely the accurate one.

58 PISTOL, DAGGER AND PRIMITIVE SWORD: Gordon, *op. cit.,* p. 24.

58 ENTERING THE SMALL PLAYHOUSE: Camillo Antona-Traversi, *Histoire du Grand Guignol,* excerpted in *Le Théâtre* (Paris: Christian Bourgois Editeur), 1969, Number 2, p. 76–77. Translation by the author.

60 THINGS TOO HORRIBLE TO BE SEEN: "Grand Guignolers Thrill," *The New York Times,* October 23, 1923.

60 THOUGHT CARPENTIER COULD LICK DEMPSEY: *Variety,* October 18, 1923.

Chapter Three
Dread and Circuses

64 I KNEW HE WAS FROM KENTUCKY: Alanna Nash, "The man who unearthed Count Dracula—Louisville runaway Tod Browning," *The Courier-Journal* (Louisville, Kentucky), April 2, 1978.

64 WIFE SEPARATED FROM HIM: Eli Savada, "Tod Browning: An Annotated Filmography," *Photon* No. 23, 1973, p. 41.

64 ALL THE BAD LIQUOR IN THE WORLD: Joan Dickey, "A Maker of Mystery," *Motion Picture Classic,* April 1928, p. 80.

65 TEN BEST PICTURES: Mordaunt Hall, "Ten Best Films of 1925," *The New York Times,* January 10, 1926, p. 5.

65 A STARTLINGLY ORIGINAL ACHIEVEMENT: Mordaunt Hall, "The Screen," *The New York Times,* August 4, 1925, p. 14.

65 COLLAPSED ON THE SET: Adela Rogers St. John, "Lon Chaney," *Liberty,* May 23, 1931 (part four of five-part serial).

66 UNION DES GUEULES CASSÉES: See Alberic Cahuet, "Le Château des faces massacrés," *L'Illustration,* vol. 169, no. 2 (June 11, 1927), p. 626., as well as discussion in Sidra Stich, *Anxious Visions: Surrealist Art* (Berkeley and New York: University Art Museum and Abbeville Press, 1990), p. 26–27.

67 NO TRACES OF THE GREAT WAR LEFT: Robert E. Sherwood, *Life,* September 3, 1925, p. 24.

67 VAL-DE-GRASSE: Jacques W. Maliniak, M.D., *Sculpture in the Living: Rebuilding the Face and Form by Plastic Surgery* (New York: Romaine Pierson, 1934), p. 30.

68 BLEED LIKE HELL: Interview by Kevin Brownlow, quoted by Scott Mac-Queen, "The Phantom of the Opera—Part II," *American Cinematographer,* October 1989, p. 35.

68 PHALLAMBULIST: Roger Dadoun, "Fetishism in the Horror Film," in James Donald, ed., *Fantasy and the Cinema* (London: British Film Institute, 1989), p. 55.

70 THERE IS NOT A SCREEN PERFORMER: David Thomson, *A Biographical Dictionary of Film* (New York: William Morrow and Company, 1981), p. 93.

71 THERE IS NO LON CHANEY: Lon Chaney, "My Own Story," *Movie,* September 1925.

71 WHAT'S IT GOING TO BE, BOSS: Dickey, *op. cit.*

71 AFTER A SERIES OF MINOR HORRORS: Review of *The Unknown, New York Herald Tribune,* undated 1927 clipping.

73 BOTH TRAUMATIC AND DELIGHTFUL: Roy Newquist, *Conversations with Joan Crawford* (Secaucus, NJ: The Citadel Press, 1980), p. 69.

73 SOFT-SPOKEN: Joan Crawford, letter to Elias Savada, March 11, 1972. Courtesy of Mr. Savada.

73 THE MOST TENSE, EXCITING INDIVIDUAL: Joan Crawford, with Jean Kesner Ardmore, *A Portrait of Joan: The Autobiography of Joan Crawford* (New York: Doubleday, 1962), p. 30.

74 SELF-SOUGHT CALVARY: Alexander Walker, *Joan Crawford: The Ultimate Star* (London: Weidenfeld and Nicholson, 1983), p. 32, 34.

74 SOLDIERS WHO HAD SUFFERED GENITAL INJURIES: Kenneth S. Lynn, *Hemingway* (New York: Fawcett Columbine, 1987), p. 86.

74 ON CHRISTMAS DAY, TOO: Ernest Hemingway, "God Rest Ye Merry, Gentlemen," *The Short Stories of Ernest Hemingway* (New York: Charles Scribner's Sons, 1925), p. 396.

76 DISMEMBERED LIMBS: Sigmund Freud, "The 'Uncanny,' " in James Strachey, ed., *Complete Psychological Works,* Vol. XVII (London: The Hogarth Press, 1955), p. 244.

76 GO BITE YOURSELF: Fred Pasley, "What a Life! Directing Freaks Is a Man's Job in the 'Talkies,' " *The Evening Bulletin* (Philadelphia), February 11, 1932, p. 16.

76 KICKED BY A HORSE: Writer Elias Savada, who interviewed numerous Browning coworkers and acquaintances in Los Angeles in the early 1970s, shared this detail from his unpublished research.

76 THE AREA IN AND AROUND THE MOUTH: Frances Cooke Magregor, *Transformation and Identity: The Face and Plastic Surgery* (New York: Quadrangle / The New York Times Book Company, 1974), p. 79.

78 THE FIRST REQUIREMENT OF MENTAL HEALTH: Frederick Lewis Allen, *Only Yesterday: An Informal History of the Nineteen-Twenties* (New York and Evanston: Harper & Row, 1957), p. 99.

78 REPORTED TO BE $150,000: "Famous Mystery Pictures Are Work of Native Louisvillian," July 1928 clipping, Tennessee Artists Scrapbook, Louisville Free Public Library.

78 AN INTERNAL MEMO: Paul Kohner to Carl Laemmle, Sr., November 8, 1926; reprinted in Richard Koszarski, *An Evening's Entertainment: The Age of the Silent Feature Picture, 1915–1928* (New York: Charles Scribner's Sons, 1990), p. 212–13.

78 A SADISTIC CHARACTER: Curt Siodmak, letter to author, February 18, 1991.

79 DIANE ARBUS: Quoted in the video documentary *Masters of Photography: Diane Arbus* (Greenwich, CT: Camera Three Productions, 1989).

Chapter Four
The Monsters and Mr. Liveright

82 THE HIDEOUS PHANTASM OF A MAN: Mary Shelley, introduction to *Frankenstein* (New York: New American Library, 1978), p. x–xi.

82 I KNOW AN OLD LADY: H. P. Lovecraft, letter to Robert Barlow, December 10, 1932; Lovecraft Collection, John Hay Library, Brown University. Quoted in Raymond McNally and Radu Florescu, eds., *The Essential Dracula* (New York: Mayflower Books, 1979), p. 24.

83 HALL CAINE: *Ibid.*, p. 25.

86 FIFTY-KILO GERMAN BOMB: A photo of damage, with caption, appeared in the *Illustrated London News,* September 26, 1925.

86 I'M AWFULLY GLAD I DIDN'T WRITE IT: " 'Dracula' One Success Novel," *Los Angeles Times,* July 15, 1928.

86 WITHOUT VOMITING: Maurice Hanline, *Years of Indiscretion* (New York: The Macaulay Company, 1934), p. 13. The blurb is entertaining enough in itself to warrant quoting: "Jason Pertinax, the leading figure in this novel, dominates literary and theatrical New York in the days just before the depression as did Lorenzo the Magnificent dominate Florence. Through his amazing personality he is arbiter and patron of the seven arts and countless Pleasures; and it is a fantastic picture that the author paints of Jason's mad game of ruthless ambition and his insatiable search for the maddest and gayest things in life."

86 A REFEREE AT A SNAKE RACE: Louis Kronenberger, "Gambler in Publishing: Horace Liveright," *The Atlantic,* January 1965, p. 95.

88 TOO MANY WAR CORRESPONDENTS: "Going to the War Zone," *The Editor and Publisher,* January 30, 1915.

88 YOU SHOULD SEE HER: *Los Angeles Times, op. cit.*

89 CAME FROM TRANSYLVANIA: Robert Cremer, *Lugosi: The Man Behind the Cape* (Chicago: Henry Regnery Company, 1976), p. 101.

89 UTTERLY UNFIT: Answer for defendant, *Lugosi v. Hubert Henry Davis,* Municipal Court of the City of New York, Borough of Manhattan, Third District, May 8, 1924.

89 SOLD AT AUCTION: Notice of levy against personal property of Bela Lugosi, New York City Marshal, October 1, 1924.

91 CHEERLESS MORTICIAN: John Anderson, review of *Dracula, New York Post,* October 6, 1927.

91 THREADBARE MUSIC MASTERS: Alexander Woollcott, review of *Dracula, The World,* October 6, 1927.

91 NOCTURNAL MISCHIEF-MAKING: Percy Hammond, *New York Herald Tribune,* October 6, 1927.

91 TALK CALMLY OF THEIR MINOR VICES: Review of *Dracula, Time,* October 17, 1927.

91 THE FINAL TRIUMPHANT LOVER: Gladys Hall, "The Feminine Love of Horror," *Motion Picture Classic,* January 1931.

92 JACK OAKIE RECALLED: Jack Oakie, *Jack Oakie's Double Takes* (San Francisco: Strawberry Hill Press, 1980), p. 86–87.

92 WHEN MEN FALL IN LOVE: Adela Rogers St. John, "Clara Bow: The Playgirl of Hollywood," *Liberty,* Spring 1975 (1929 article reprint).

93 ALL I HADDA DO: David Stenn, *Clara Bow: Runnin' Wild* (New York: Penguin Books, 1990), p. 21.

93 I THINK I'LL KILL YA: *Ibid.,* p. 15.

93 BRANDISHING A BUTCHER KNIFE: *Ibid.,* p. 22.

93 UNTIL THEY BLED: *Ibid.,* p. 65–68.

94 A NOVEMBER 1929 STORY: Arthur Mefford, "Film Star's Secret Love Is Revealed," *Daily Mirror* (New York), November 5, 1929.

95 WHAT BUBBLED AND STIRRED: Kronenberger, *op. cit.,* p. 103.

95 ALMOST VISIBLE, LIKE LIGHTNING: Edith W. Stern, "A Man Who Was Unafraid," *The Saturday Review,* June 28, 1941, p. 10.

95 HBL, PUBLISHER: Search Light *(pseudonym), Time Exposures* (New York: Boni & Liveright, 1926), p. 113.

96 LOUSY LITTLE PLAY: Gilmer, *Horace Liveright: Publisher of the Twenties* (New York: David Lewis, 1970), p. 180.

97 IT IS INCONCEIVABLY CRUDE: John L. Balderston, letter to Harold Freedman, November 1928.

98 HE IS PART OF YOU: Steven Earl Forry, *Hideous Progenies: Dramatizations of Frankenstein from the Nineteenth Century to the Present* (Philadelphia: University of Pennsylvania Press, 1990), p. 96.

98 CAPTIVATED AND HAUNTED: Peggy Webling, *Peggy: the Story of One Score Years and Ten* (London: Hutchinson & Company, 1924), p. 19.

98 A COMPLETE SET OF BYRON: *Ibid.,* p. 92.

98 SOMEBODY HAD TOLD LEWIS CARROLL: *Ibid.,* p. 36–37.

99 HATED MORALS: *Ibid.,* p. 93–94.

100 MOTHER, GUIDE MY LITTLE STEPS: *Ibid.*

100 I REMEMBER WELL THE FIRST REHEARSALS: Ivan Butler, letter to author, 1990.

101 GREEN AND YELLOW VISAGE: Elizabeth Nitchie, *Mary Shelley* (New Brunswick, NJ: Rutgers University Press, 1953), p. 224.

101 ENGRAVINGS OF T. P. COOKE: For an invaluable textual and visual documentation of the early theatrical history of *Frankenstein,* see Forry, *op.cit.*

102 IT WAS VERY TAME INDEED: *Ibid.*

102 FLIMSY AS A BIRDCAGE: *The Times* (London), February 11, 1930.

104 SHE THINKS SHE'S WRITTEN A HELL OF A PLAY: John L. Balderston to Horace Liveright, February 11, 1930.

105 TWO HIGHBROW SHEETS: Balderston to Liveright, February 24, 1930.

106 HORACE LIKES DEANE ENORMOUSLY: Balderston to agent Harold Freedman, Brandt and Brandt Dramatic Department, March 24, 1930.

107 A WHOLESALE REWRITE: Balderston's version of the play is published in its entirety in Steven Earl Forry's *Hideous Progenies, op. cit.*

108 A LOOSE AND FANTASTIC BASIS: Letter from Liveright to Otto Theis, July 7, 1930; Gilmer, *op. cit.,* p. 232.

108 HE WILL MAKE A HASH OF IT: Balderston to Freedman, July 17, 1930.

109 THE MONSTER IS TO TEAR OFF AMELIA'S WEDDING GOWN: Louis Cline to Harold Freedman, October 24, 1930.

110 A NUISANCE SUIT: For a more detailed account of the *Dracula* film negotiations vis-à-vis Liveright, see David J. Skal, *Hollywood Gothic: The Tangled Web of Dracula from Novel to Stage to Screen* (New York: W. W. Norton & Company, 1990), "A Deal for the Devil: or, Hollywood Bites," p. 93–109.

110 DID NOT LACK DRAMA: Kronenberger, *op. cit.,* p. 104.

110 A SHOOTING: Lester Cohen, "Horace Liveright," *Variety,* January 10, 1962.

110 AN IDEAL SUBJECT FOR AN OPERA: *Ibid.*

Chapter Five
1931: The American Abyss

114 A BOWL OF CHERRIES: Gilbert Seldes, *The Years of the Locust* (Boston: Little, Brown and Company, 1933), p. 3.

114 VAGUE FEARS: These and other event citations are drawn from Robert H. Ferrell and John S. Bowman, eds., *The Twentieth Century: An Almanac* (New York: World Almanac Publications, 1984).

115 THE POOR WENT TO THE MOVIES: Seldes, *op. cit.*

115 SECRET MAKEUP: "Vampires, Monsters, Horrors!" *The New York Times,* March 1, 1936.

115 HUSBAND WANTED CONRAD VEIDT: Lupita Tovar Kohner, in conversation with the author, Los Angeles, California, October 1991.

116 DEVASTATING PAN: Review of *Outside the Law, Variety,* September 3, 1980.

116 CENSORSHIP ANGLES: Correspondence, E. M. Asher to Jason S. Joy, June 26, 1930. MPPDA case file on *Dracula,* Margaret Herrick Library, Special Collections, Academy of Motion Picture Arts and Sciences, Beverly Hills, California.

116 LOVE THEME FOR RELIEF: Script synopsis of *Dracula,* October 1, 1930, MPPDA case files.

116 A CONVENIENT RAILING: Universal Pictures reader's report on *Dracula* by Steve Miranda, June 15, 1927; in Philip J. Riley, ed., *MagicImage Filmbooks Presents Dracula* (Atlantic City and Hollywood: MagicImage Filmbooks, 1990), p. 30.

117 A COMPLETELY UNKNOWN ACTOR: Untitled clipping, *Los Angeles Examiner,* July 2, 1930.

117 PRODUCTION STARRING CLAIRE LUCE: Reported in *The Morning Telegraph* (New York), undated clipping, August 1930.

118 MANNERS RECALLED: David Manners, interviewed by author, March 1991, Santa Barbara, California.

118 SON OF "SCRIPT GIRL": Nicholas Webster, telephone interview with author, September 1991.

121 THAT THE SAME MAN WAS RESPONSIBLE: Review of *Dracula, Hollywood Filmograph,* April 4, 1931.

122 SIDELINE INVOLVEMENT: Kohner, *op. cit.*

124 TIGHTENED AND REEDITED: William S. Hart, Jr., interviewed by Elias Savada, April 8, 1972. Unpublished tape transcript courtesy of Mr. Savada.

125 I CANNOT SEE ONE REDEEMING FEATURE: Excerpts from complaints about *Dracula,* MPPDA case files.

125 CENSORS IN SINGAPORE: Correspondence, Jason S. Joy to Carl Laemmle, Jr., April 7, 1931.

126 THE ADDITION OF SOUND: Marguerite Tazelaar, "Director of Chaney Prefers Lighter Side of Murder," undated clipping, *New York Herald Tribune,* spring 1931.

126 DRACULA SHOULD ONLY GO FOR WOMEN: Hand-written annotation by Carl Laemmle, Jr., in shooting script of *Dracula.* See Philip J. Riley, ed., *MagicImage Filmbooks Presents Dracula,* p. 56.

126 PURPORTED INTERVIEW WITH LUGOSI: Gladys Hall, "The Feminine Love of Horror," *Motion Picture Classic,* January 1931.

128 A STOP-MOTION MONSTER: Don Shay, "Willis O'Brien: Creator of the Impossible," *Focus on Film* (Autumn 1973).

129 TANGLED MANE OF HAIR: For a detailed illustrated history of the theatrical evolution of the monster, see Steven Earl Forry, *Hideous Progenies: Dramatizations of Frankenstein from the Nineteenth Century to the Present* (Philadelphia: University of Pennsylvania Press, 1990).

129 IT WASN'T ANOTHER WAR PICTURE: See James Curtis, *James Whale* (Metuchen, NJ/London: The Scarecrow Press, 1982), p. 75.

129 PRISON CAMP: *Ibid.,* p. 3.

130 IT DOES NOT WALK LIKE A ROBOT: Garrett Fort and Francis Edwards Faragoh, screenplay for *Frankenstein* (Abescon, NJ: MagicImage Filmbooks, 1989), p. 36.

130 I SPENT TEN YEARS IN HOLLYWOOD: Margaret McManus, "Karloff Says," unsourced newspaper clipping, March 10, 1962.

130 I DIDN'T DEPEND ON MY IMAGINATION: Jack Pierce, quoted in "Oh You Beautiful Monster," *The New York Times,* January 29, 1939.

132 GROTESQUE MANNEQUINS: Cited in Jeffrey L. Meikle, *Twentieth Century Limited: Industrial Design in America, 1925–1939* (Philadelphia: Temple University Press, 1979), p. 25.

132 CURIOUS FLAT RIDGE: Fort and Faragoh, *op. cit.*

132 TELEVOX: Illustrated on cover of *Vu,* March 21, 1928.

132 DISPLACED, SUPPRESSED AND RESHAPED: Sidra Stich, *Anxious Visions: Surrealist Art* (New York: Abbeville Press; and Berkeley, CA: University Art Museum, 1990), p. 51.

133 KARLOFF'S FACE AND HEAD: Art Ronnie, "Frankenstein Remembered," *Southland Sunday* (Long Beach, California), December 5, 1971.

134 FIRST MADE ME FEEL LIKE THE MONSTER: Boris Karloff, "N.Y. Close-Up" (column), *New York Herald Tribune,* undated 1950 clipping.

134 STAGE WHISPER THE SIZE OF PASADENA: Stefan Kanfer, "Frankenstein at Sixty," *Connoisseur,* January 1991, p. 42.

135 AWFULLY STRONG STUFF: Curtis, *op. cit.,* p. 86.

135 JUST A BUNCH OF SPARKS: George E. Turner, "*Frankenstein,* the Monster Classic," in George E. Turner, ed., *The Cinema of Adventure, Romance and Terror* (Hollywood, CA: The ASC Press, 1989), p. 92.

137 NO LITTLE GIRL IS GOING TO DROWN: *Ibid.,* p. 96.

137 QUEBEC CENSORS: Correspondence, T. B. Fithian to Jason S. Joy, April 22, 1932. MPPDA case file on *Frankenstein.*

139 MORBIDITY IS NOT WITHOUT ITS CLAIM: Review of *Frankenstein, Motion Picture Herald,* February 6, 1932.

141 LITTLE ANIMAL NOISES: Tallulah Bankhead, *Tallulah: My Autobiography* (New York: Harper & Brothers, 1952), p. 80.

141 WHITE PLAINS SANITARIUM: John Kobler, *Damned in Paradise* (New York: Atheneum, 1977), p. 156.

142 SOMEBODY YOUNG: Bill Thomas, "Mamoulian on His *Dr. Jekyll and Mr. Hyde, Cinefantastique* (Summer 1971), p. 36.

142 TRANSPARENTLY NEW ENGLAND: Frank McConnell, "Rough Beasts Slouching," in Roy Huss and T. J. Ross, eds., *Focus on the Horror Film* (Englewood Cliffs, NJ: Prentice Hall, 1972), p. 26.

142 HIS FACE CAME WITH IT: Transcript of unpublished interview of Rose Hobart by Tom Weaver and Michael Brunas.

144 MUCKY WENCH: Letter from John V. Wilson to B. P. Schulberg, August 10, 1931. MPPDA case file on *Dr. Jekyll and Mr. Hyde.*

144 THEME IS TOO HARROWING: Jason S. Joy to B. P. Schulberg, December 1, 1931. MPPDA case file on *Dr. Jekyll and Mr. Hyde.*

144 LABORED ADORNMENT: Review of *Dr. Jekyll and Mr. Hyde, Variety,* January 5, 1932.

145 WAS REJECTED OUTRIGHT: MPPDA case file.

145 A BROKEN DOLL: Johnny Eck, manuscript introduction for unpublished biography, reproduced in *Pandemonium* No. 3 (1989), p. 156. My synopsis of Eck's early life and career is drawn from this material and an accompanying transcript of a 1980 interview with Mark Feldman.

145 WANTED TO BE AN ENGINEER: Matt Seiden, "What a Half-Man in Highlandtown Dreams of," *The Sun* (Baltimore), July 20, 1979.

146 PAID THE AUTHOR $8,000: Eli Savada, "The Making of *Freaks,*" *Photon* No. 23 (1973), p. 25.

147 A FAMILIAR FIGURE: "Weds Sixth Wife Again: 'Tod' Robbins, American Author, Remarries British Woman," *The New York Times,* May 6, 1934.

147 DIED IN 1949: Obituary of Clarence A. Robbins, *The New York Times,* May 13, 1949.

148 A SIDESHOW PICTURE: "Mystery Film Director," *The New York Times,* November 24, 1929.

148 ASKED FOR SOMETHING HORRIFYING: Bob Thomas, *Thalberg: Life and Legend* (Garden City, NY: Doubleday & Company, 1969), p. 187–88.

150 WASN'T AWARE AT FIRST: James Kotsilibas-Davis and Myrna Loy, *Myrna Loy: Being and Becoming* (New York: Alfred A. Knopf, 1987), p. 71.

150 TALL BLONDE WOMAN: Tod Robbins, "Spurs," *Munsey's Magazine,* February 1923.

150 VAMPS, CRUEL ONES, MAN-EATERS: John Kobal, *People Will Talk* (New York: Alfred A. Knopf, 1985), p. 45.

150 THERE WAS NOTHING WRONG WITH OLGA'S RUSSIAN: *Ibid.*

151 A CITY OF SUFFERING: Katherine Hill, "Hollywood Performers Suffer, Star Asserts," *San Francisco Chronicle,* August 21, 1932.

151 HE SAY, "I VANT TO MAKE A PICTURE": Kobal, *op. cit.,* p. 51–52.

152 MUCH TO JACKIE'S TERROR: Faith Service, "The Amazing Life Stories of the Freaks!" *Motion Picture,* April 1932, p. 100.

152 VERY, VERY DIFFICULT: Kobal, *op. cit.,* p. 53.

152 CHAINED TO HIS KEEPER: Samuel Marx, *Mayer and Thalberg: The Make-Believe Saints* (New York: Random House, 1975), p. 180.

152 COUNT DRACULA ON STAGE TEN: Budd Schulberg, *Moving Pictures: Memories of a Hollywood Prince* (New York: Stein and Day, 1981), p. 314.

153 TAYLOR RECALLED: Dwight Taylor, *Joy Ride* (New York: G. P. Putnam's Sons, 1969), p. 247–48.

153 LOUIS B. MAYER: Savada, *op. cit.*, p. 24.

153 IRVING'S RIGHT SO OFTEN: Samuel Marx, *A Gaudy Spree* (New York and Toronto: Franklin Watts, 1987), p. 132.

153 I'LL TAKE THE BLAME: Marx, *Mayer and Thalberg, op. cit.*

153 BANISHED FROM THE COMMISSARY: Savada, *op. cit.*

153 BAD ENOUGH TO SEE THEM: *Ibid.*

154 LEARNED VERY LITTLE: "Circus Oddities Are a Race Apart," *The Morning Telegraph Talking Picture Magazine* (advertising supplement to *The Morning Telegraph*, New York), January 3, 1932.

154 GIBBERISH LANGUAGE: *Ibid.*

154 CARPATHIAN MOUNTAINS: *Ibid.*

154 MONIED ARISTOCRACY: "Freak Tent Celebrities Are Rich Aristocrats of Circus," *The Morning Telegraph Talking Picture Magazine, op. cit.*

154 A JEWISH GIRL FROM SPRINGFIELD: *Ibid.*

155 RONALD COLEMAN'S SIGNATURE: *Ibid.*

155 SWIFT AND CERTAIN: *Time*, April 18, 1932, p. 17.

155 SUBHUMAN ANIMALS: *Ibid.*, p. 18.

155 PURE SENSATIONALISM: Louella O. Parsons, " 'Freaks' Picture Grotesque and Sensational," *Los Angeles Examiner*, February 13, 1932.

155 PLANNED BY METRO: *Variety*, July 12, 1932.

156 A LITTLE GEM: "The Current Cinema," *The New Yorker*, July 16, 1932.

156 AN INSULT TO ALL FREAKS EVERYWHERE: Joseph Mitchell, "Lady Olga," *McSorley's Wonderful Saloon* (New York: Duell, Sloan and Pearce, 1943), p. 95.

156 RANDIAN'S OBITUARY: "The Final Curtain," *Billboard*, December 29, 1934.

158 MAYER AND HIS AIDES: For details of the purported cover-up, see Samuel Marx and Joyce Vanderveen, *Deadly Illusions: Jean Harlow and the Murder of Paul Bern* (New York: Random House, 1990), especially chapter four, "The Creative Team," p. 36–51.

159 PENIS OF AN INFANT: Irving Shulman, *Harlow: An Intimate Biography* (New York: Bernard Geis Associates, 1964), p. 37.

159 TURN HIMSELF INTO A WOMAN: Harold Robbins, *The Carpetbaggers* (New York: Pocket Books, 1962 reprint), p. 322.

Chapter Six
Angry Villagers

162 CAVALRY BOOTS: Jack Vizzard, *See No Evil: Life inside a Hollywood Censor* (New York: Simon and Schuster, 1970), p. 39.

162 PERHAPS IT WOULD BE WISE: Jason S. Joy to Will H. Hays, December 5, 1931, MPPDA case files, Special Collections, Academy of Motion Picture Arts and Sciences Library, Beverly Hills, California.

162 WITH THE CRASH: Vizzard, *op. cit.,* p. 38–39.

162 SOMETHING EQUALLY AS EFFECTIVE: Joy to Hays, January 11, 1932, MPPDA case files.

163 SPOTTED IN A RESTAURANT: Biography of Arlene Francis in playbill for *The Doughgirls,* New York, December 30, 1942.

163 ANOTHER FACE ON THE BARROOM FLOOR: Lee Belser, "Arlene Francis Returns to Films After an Absence of 28 Years," *Los Angeles Mirror,* July 5, 1961.

163 THEY TOLD ME IT WAS A SMALL PART: Arlene Francis, interviewed by author, New York City, April 16, 1991.

164 BLUE AND WATERLOGGED: Arlene Francis with Florence Rome, *Arlene Francis: A Memoir* (New York: Simon and Schuster, 1978), p. 19–20.

166 MODERN COLLOQUIALISMS: John Huston, *An Open Book* (New York: Alfred A. Knopf, 1980), p. 58.

166 AN OCCASIONAL MODIFIED SHRIEK: Joy to Laemmle, January 8, 1932, MPPDA case files.

166 ELIMINATE ALL DISTINCT VIEWS: *What Shocked the Censors: A Complete Record of Cuts in Motion Picture Films Ordered by the New York State Censors from January, 1932 to March, 1933* (New York: The National Council on Freedom from Censorship, 1933).

167 HE SENT HER A TELEGRAM: "That Elegant Critter," *The American Weekly,* January 2, 1955.

167 A GASSER: Victor Sebastian, "The Indestructible Arlene Francis," *Family Weekly,* November 20, 1960.

168 THICKENING ATMOSPHERE OF MORBIDITY: Nelson B. Bell, "Thoughts on Horror Era," *The Washington Post,* February 21, 1932.

169 THEY DON'T MIND ABOUT OVERTIME: Katherine Hill, "Zombies Give Thrills on United Screen," *San Francisco Chronicle,* November 29, 1932.

169 LAUGHTON HATED THE PART: Charles Higham, *Charles Laughton: An Intimate Biography* (Garden City, NY: Doubleday, 1976), p. 39.

171 A PUMA, A CHEETAH: Elsa Lanchester, *Charles Laughton and I* (New York: Harcourt, Brace and Company, 1938), p. 106.

171 THOUGHT I HAD HAIR IN MY FOOD: Kurt Singer, *The Laughton Story* (Philadelphia and Toronto: The John C. Winston Company, 1954), p. 103.

171 A VISIT TO THE ZOO: Lanchester, *op. cit.*

171 SO'S MICKEY MOUSE: *Ibid.*

171 ALSO BANNED IN LATVIA: MPPDA case file on *Island of Lost Souls.*

171 DICTATED CUTS: The National Council on Freedom from Censorship, *What Shocked the Censors, op. cit.*

171 NEARLY 36 PERCENT OF ALL FILMS: *Ibid.,* p. 5.

172 TECHNIQUE OF CRIME: *Ibid.,* p. 13.

172 THE NEW YORK BOARD SEEKS TO JUSTIFY: *Ibid.,* p. 2.

172 COMPLAINED DIRECTLY TO WARNER BROTHERS: Correspondence from B. O. Skinner to A. S. Howson, Warner Brothers Pictures, February 9, 1933. MPPDA case files.

174 THE MOST NAUSEATING AND BY FAR THE WORST OF ITS TYPE: MPPDA case file on *Mystery of the Wax Museum,* April 15, 1933.

174 SUMMED UP THE MANIA NEATLY: Norman R. Jaffray, "The Spine Chillers," *The Saturday Evening Post,* April 29, 1933, p. 61.

175 COOPER'S FEELING: Orville Goldner and George E. Turner, *The Making of King Kong* (New York: Ballantine Books, 1976), p. 56.

175 VISION OF A GIANT APE: *Ibid.,* p. 37.

175 SHOT DOWN AND SEVERELY BURNED: *Ibid.,* p. 24.

175 I'LL HAVE WOMEN CRYING: *Ibid.*

177 AN ELDERLY JEWISH GENTLEMAN: Filler piece, *The New Yorker,* April 29, 1933.

177 DEFINITIVE DOCUMENTATION: Paul Mandell, "Enigma of *The Black Cat,*" in George E. Turner, ed., *The Cinema of Adventure, Romance and Terror* (Hollywood, CA: The ASC Press, 1989), p. 181–95.

178 PEOPLE WHO DEVOUR THEIR YOUNG: Breen to Zehner, February 26, 1934. MPPDA case file on *The Black Cat.*

178 DAVID MANNERS: Interviewed by the author, April 1991, Santa Barbara, California.

178 HAD BEEN A HANGMAN: Mandell, *op. cit.,* p. 194.

180 WOUNDED THREE TIMES: Robert Cremer, *Lugosi: The Man Behind the Cape* (Chicago: Henry Regnery Company, 1976), p. 56–57.

180 A PILE OF CORPSES: Undated publicity questionnaire for *Beautiful Film Stories* by Anna Bakacs (New York: Vantage Press, circa 1979).

182 IT WAS LOGISTICALLY EXPEDIENT: Ira Carmen, *Movies, Censorship and the Law* (Ann Arbor: University of Michigan Press, 1967), p. 129.

184 A "HOOT": James Curtis, *James Whale* (Metuchen, NJ, and London: Scarecrow Press, 1982), p. 116.

184 HIGHLY AMUSING: *Ibid.,* p. 115.

184 IS ENGAGED UPON A RAPE: Anne K. Mellor, *Mary Shelley: Her Life, Her Fiction, Her Monsters* (New York and London: Routledge, 1989), p. 122.

186 THEN MY EYES FELL UPON MY HANDS: Ernest Thesiger, *Practically True* (London: William Heinemann, Ltd., 1927), p. 118–19.

187 A VAULTLIKE DOOR SLAMMED SHUT: Gerald Gardner, *The Censorship Papers: Movie Censorship Letters from the Hays Office, 1934–1968* (New York: Dodd, Mead & Company, 1987), p. xix.

187 WHICH COMPARE HIM TO GOD: Joseph Breen to Universal Pictures, July 23, 1934, MPPDA case file on *Bride of Frankenstein.*

188 HEREWITH ARE THE PROPOSED CHANGES: Letter from James Whale to Joseph Breen, December 10, 1934. MPPDA case file on *Bride of Frankenstein.*

189 EXPOSED AND ACCENTUATED: Joseph Breen to Universal Pictures, March 23, 1935, MPPDA case file on *Bride of Frankenstein.*

189 AS LITTLE LIQUID AS POSSIBLE: Elsa Lanchester, *Elsa Lanchester, Elsa Lanchester Herself* (New York: St. Martin's Press, 1983), p. 135.

190 ELEVATED EVEN FURTHER: *Ibid.*

190 GRAVELY CONCERNED: Breen to Universal, March 23, 1935.

190 CONSIDERABLE DIFFICULTY: Breen to Universal, April 15, 1935.

190 VERY DRASTIC AND VERY HARMFUL: Paul Krieger to Sydney Singerman, May 7, 1935, MPPDA case file.

190 WHAT RESPONSIBILITY: Joseph Breen to Will Hays, May 8, 1935, MPPDA case file on *Bride of Frankenstein.*

190 THE DELETIONS OF THE SWEDISH CENSORS: Gardner, *op. cit.,* p. 71.

191 MAKING A FOOL OUT OF A KING: MPPDA case file on *Bride of Frankenstein.*

191 AGAINST LEAVING FINGERPRINTS: Joseph Breen to Louis B. Mayer, December 28, 1934, MPPDA case file on *Mark of the Vampire.*

192 QUITE A CHARACTER: James Wong Howe, interviewed in Charles Higham, *Hollywood Cameraman* (Bloomington, IN, and London: Indiana University Press, 1970), p. 87.

192 AT THE EXPENSE OF HER OWN GLAMOUR: Carroll Borland, interviewed by the author, Los Angeles, California, April 1989.

194 THE ACTUAL TRANSVECTION: Joseph Breen to Harry Zehner, January 15, 1935, MPPDA case file on *Werewolf of London.*

194 PEOPLE WITH HIRSUTE TENDENCIES: Robert Harris to Joseph Breen, January 30, 1935.

194 DEGRADING EFFECT: MPPDA case file on *Werewolf of London.*

194 BORIS KARLOFF'S DISFIGURING COSMETICS: MPPDA case file on *The Raven,* March 16, 1935.

195 BRANDISHING HIS SCALPEL: "Horror on the Screen: The Demon Surgeon," *The Times* (London), August 4, 1936.

196 IN THE THREE HORROR PICTURES: John L. Balderston, introductory note to screenplay treatment of *Dracula's Daughter* (Hollywood: Ad Schulberg & Charles Kenneth Feldman, 1934).

197 WE WANT LOVE AS WELL AS DRINK: *Ibid.*

197 WHY SHOULD CECIL DE MILLE HAVE A MONOPOLY: *Ibid.*

197 THE CENSORS WILL STAND THIS: *Ibid.*

198 UTTERLY IMPOSSIBLE FOR APPROVAL: MPPDA case file on *Dracula's Daughter.*

198 SIX-PAGE, SINGLE-SPACED MEMO: Joseph Breen to Harry H. Zehner, October 23, 1935.

199 WE SHALL BE HAPPY TO WORK ALONG WITH YOU: Breen to Zehner, January 15, 1936.

200 DIRECT INSPIRATION FOR NOVELIST: Katherine Ramsland, *Prism of the Night: A Biography of Anne Rice* (New York: Dutton, 1991), p. 40–41.

201 THE MARATHON DANCE WAS IN VOGUE: Budd Schulberg, *Moving Pictures: Memories of a Hollywood Prince* (New York: Stein and Day, 1981), p. 314.

201 CHARLES CHAPLIN: Mentioned by Sidney Pollack, the film's eventual director, in his preface to Robert E. Thompson's screenplay for *They Shoot Horses, Don't They?* (New York: Avon Books, 1969), p. 133.

201 NEVER ONCE SAW HIM ON THE BEACH: Letter from Maureen O'Sullivan to Browning biographer Bret Wood, quoted by Wood at a lecture / screening of *The Devil Doll,* Hoboken, New Jersey, May 1991.

201 GOT INTO HIS CAR AND DISAPPEARED: Edgar G. Ulmer, circa 1965, quoted in Elias Savada, *Tod Browning: Child of the Night* (Cinemateca Portuguesa: 1984), p. 124.

202 LOOKING WILDLY INTO THE FACES OF PEDESTRIANS: Katherine K. Vandervoort to Carl E. Milliken, Community Service Department, MPPDA, November 1938 (MPPDA case file on *Dracula*).

205 WE HAVE HAD SO MUCH TROUBLE: J. Brooke Wilkinson to Joseph Breen, November 4, 1938. MPPDA case file on *Son of Frankenstein*.

205 SENNWALD NOTED THE TREND: André Sennwald, "Gory, Gory, Hallelujah," *The New York Times,* January 12, 1936.

206 I KNEW TOD BROWNING WELL: Samuel Marx, correspondence with the author, December 15, 1990.

209 WAR SCARES OF UNSETTLED EUROPE: "*The Son of Frankenstein* Starts a New Horror Cycle," *Look,* February 28, 1939, p. 39.

Chapter Seven
"I Used to Know Your Daddy":
The Horrors of War, Part Two

211 HITLER'S FAVORITE MOVIES: Robert G. L. Waite, *The Psychopathic God: Adolf Hitler* (New York: Basic Books, 1977), p. 9.

211 FASCINATED WITH WOLVES: *Ibid.,* p. 26.

212 THE MEDIEVAL MIND: Barry Holstun Lopez, *Of Wolves and Men* (New York: Charles Scribner's Sons, 1978), p. 206.

212 A PROJECTION OF HUMAN ANXIETY: *Ibid.,* p. 242.

212 NOT SO MUCH AN ANIMAL: *Ibid.,* p. 204.

213 UNADULTERATED BY "IMPROVEMENTS": Curtis Siodmak, "Birth of the Wolf-man," in Dennis Daniels, ed., *Famous Monsters Chronicles* (FantaCo Enterprises, 1991), p. 145.

215 RATIONALIZING HIS AMERICAN ACCENT: *Ibid.*

216 EXPRESSIONS OF COURAGE AND CHEER: Paul Fussell, *Wartime: Understanding and Behavior in the Second World War,* New York / Oxford: Oxford University Press, 1989), p. 269–70.

216 BITING THEIR COMRADES' JUGULAR VEINS: *Ibid.,* p. 273.

216 GRIM IRONY: Harry Ludlam, *A Biography of Bram Stoker, Creator of Dracula* (London: New English Library, 1977; paperback reprint of 1962 edition, *A Biography of Dracula: The Life Story of Bram Stoker*), p. 169.

216 SHATTERED BOX-OFFICE RECORDS: See report of gross receipts and accompanying trade ad, *Variety,* April 1, 1942.

216 ROOSEVELT MEETS CHURCHILL: Review of *Frankenstein Meets the Wolf Man, The Hollywood Reporter,* February 19, 1943.

217 LOBBY CUTOUT: See photo in Philip J. Riley, ed., *MagicImage Filmbooks Presents Frankenstein Meets the Wolf Man,* Universal Filmscripts Series, Vol. 5 (Atlantic City and Hollywood: MagicImage Filmbooks, 1990), p. 24.

218 HORROR PICTURES HAVE PAID OFF: "Chillers Warm U Till with $10,000,000 Net," *Variety,* July 24, 1944.

218 ORIGINALLY CONCEIVED AS A CONTEMPORARY WAR STORY: For a detailed production history, see George Turner, ed., "The Exquisite Evil of *Cat People,*" *The Cinema of Adventure, Romance and Terror* (Hollywood, CA: The ASC Press, 1989), p. 233–43.

220 A $4 MILLION RETURN: *Ibid.,* p. 242.

220 THE DRINKING AT THIS POINT: Joseph Breen to William Gordon, RKO Pictures, July 13, 1942, MPPDA case file on *Cat People,* Special Collections, Margaret Herrick Library, Academy of Motion Picture Arts and Sciences, Beverly Hills, California.

221 SIZZLING BACON: John Dunning, *Tune in Yesterday: The Ultimate Encyclopedia of Old-Time Radio 1925–1976* (Englewood Cliffs, NJ: Prentice-Hall, 1976), p. 362.

222 PROPAGANDISTIC TONE: J. Fred MacDonald, *Don't Touch That Dial! Radio Programming in American Life 1920–1960* (Chicago: Nelson-Hall, 1979), p. 67–68.

222 THERE WAS THIS FEELING OF DREAD: Fritz Leiber, quoted in John Bryan, "Conjure Man," *The San Francisco Bay Guardian* literary supplement, April 1991, p. 4.

223 IN A PLACE LIKE ENGLAND: John T. McManus, "The Blitz Unearths a Vampire," *P.M. New York,* January 30, 1944.

223 HE GOT THE WARMEST WELCOME: Robert Cremer, *Lugosi: The Man Behind the Cape* (Chicago: Henry Regnery Company, 1976), p. 199.

223 SERVED AS AN AIR-RAID WARDEN: "Movie Mailbag: On Boris Karloff," *The New York Times,* March 9, 1969.

224 TO THE RIGHT OF THE DOOR: John Russell, *Francis Bacon* (New York: Thames and Hudson, 1985), p. 10.

225 THE SECOND SELF FUNCTIONS FULLY: Robert Jay Lifton, "Understanding the Traumatized Self," in John P. Wilson, Zev Harel, and Boaz Kahana, eds., *Human Adaptation to Extreme Stress: From the Holocaust to Vietnam* (New York and London: Plenum Press, 1988), p. 29.

225 DOCTORS AS A GROUP: Robert Jay Lifton, *The Nazi Doctors: Medical Killing and the Psychology of Genocide* (New York: Basic Books, 1986), p. 426–27.

226 EVA BERKSON: Mel Gordon, *The Grand Guignol: Theatre of Fear and Terror* (New York: Amok Press, 1988), p. 30–31.

226 THE REPERTORY REVERTED: *Ibid.*

227 THROW THEM THE PIECES: "Murders in the Rue Chaptal," *Time,* March 10, 1947, p. 44–46.

Chapter Eight
Drive-Ins Are a Ghoul's Best Friend:
Horror in the Fifties

230 50 MILLION COMIC BOOKS: Figures cited in Mike Benton, *The Comic Book in America: An Illustrated History* (Dallas: Taylor Publishing Company, 1989), p. 48.

230 APPROXIMATELY A QUARTER OF THE TOTAL COMICS-INDUSTRY OUTPUT: Peter Kihss, "No Harm in Horror," *The New York Times,* April 22, 1954.

231 ROTTING FLESH FALLING OFF RIBS: Russ Heath, quoted in Mike Benton, *op. cit.,* p. 52.

232 WHEN JASON COULD NO LONGER MAKE A SOUND: "Wish You Were Here," *The Haunt of Fear* #22 (New York: E.C. Publications, 1953), p. 8.

234 CHILDREN'S PLAY ON THE STREET: Fredric Wertham, *Seduction of the Innocent* (New York: Rinehart, 1954), p. 380.

234 HOW DID NIETZSCHE GET INTO THE NURSERY: *Ibid.,* p. 15.

234 SO NOW YOU KNOW, FIENDS: Original illustration reproduced in Wertham, *op. cit.*

235 MR. GAINES MAY HAVE DISAPPOINTED: "Men of Taste" (editorial), *The Hartford Courant,* April 23, 1954.

235 THE DISSENTING POSITION: Frederic M. Thrasher, "The Comics and Delinquency: Cause or Scapegoat," *The Journal of Educational Sociology,* December 1959, p. 195–205.

235 A TISSUE OF TROUBLESOME POINTS: Reuel Denney, "The Dark Fantastic," *The New Republic,* May 3, 1954, p. 18–19.

236 DR. WERTHAM'S ARGUMENT: *Ibid.*

236 DR. WERTHAM'S PICTURE OF SOCIETY: Robert Warshow, "Paul, the Horror Comics, and Dr. Wertham," *Commentary,* June 1954, p. 596–604.

237 RESTRICTIVE CODE: "No More Werewolves," *Newsweek,* November 8, 1954.

240 MAKEUP AND COSTUME: Maila Nurmi, interviewed by author, April 11, 1991, Hollywood, California.

241 EXAGGERATED PHYSICAL DIMENSIONS: "Physical Impossibility?", *Newsweek,* June 14, 1954, p. 6.

241 MANY ANGELENOS: "Vampire," *Newsweek,* May 24, 1954, p. 84.

242 SWEDISH MEATBALLS: : Nurmi interview, *op. cit.*

242 ONLY GUY IN HOLLYWOOD: Warren Newton Beath, *The Death of James Dean* (New York: Grove Press, 1986), p. 21.

242 BOY WHO HANGS HIMSELF: Although Nurmi remembered this story as the work of Ray Bradbury in a pulp magazine or paperback book, Bradbury himself has no recollection of ever having written it.

243 AN OPERA HE WANTED TO PRODUCE: Nurmi interview, *op. cit.*

243 DARKLY IMAGINATIVE RAMBLINGS: Beath, *op. cit.,* p. 23.

243 GOON WITH THE WIND David Dalton, *James Dean: The Mutant King* (New York: St. Martin's Press, 1983), p. 42.

244 ROSARY BEAD FOR ADOLESCENTS: Nurmi interview, *op. cit.*

244 EVERY NIGHT AT MIDNIGHT: *Ibid.*

244 DATING CARTOONS: Dalton, *op. cit.,* p. 190.

245 THE NIGHT OF JUNE 20, 1955: " 'Vampira' Meets 'The Vamp,' " *New York Mirror,* June 21, 1955.

245 WEARING THE GHASTLY ATTIRE: *Ibid.*

245 LIBERACE ASKED: Nurmi interview, *op. cit.*

246 NECROPHILIACS: John Calendo, "Vampira and the Ghost of James Dean," *Interview,* October 1975, p. 23.

246 SMASHED HIS PORSCHE: *Ibid.*

246 A MILLION DOLLARS DOWN THE TOILET: Maila Nurmi, "The One—the Only— Vampira," *Fangoria,* October 1983, p. 27.

251 NOT EXACTLY A FAMILY PICTURE: Transcript of 1953 PTA reports on *Invaders from Mars,* Billy Rose Theatre Collection, New York Public Library for the Performing Arts at Lincoln Center.

253 ONLY IF BORIS KARLOFF WOULD APPEAR: Gregory Mank, *Karloff and Lugosi: The Story of a Haunting Collaboration* (West Jefferson, NC,: McFarland & Company, 1988), p. 252.

254 YOU'RE NOT GOING TO LIKE THIS, PAUL: Paul Marco, interviewed in Tom Weaver, *Interviews with B and Science Fiction and Horror Movie Makers* (Jefferson, NC, and London: McFarland & Company, 1990), p. 285.

254 THEY WEAR MAKEUP AND HANG AROUND FUNERAL PARLORS: Hope Lugosi, interviewed by the *National Enquirer,* November 17, 1957.

255 TWELVE-TO-TWENTY-FIVE AGE BRACKET: "Quotes Psychiatrist: 'Horror' Aids Kids Shed Their Primitive Fears," *Variety,* June 4, 1958.

256 SELF ADMINISTERED PSYCHIATRIC THERAPY: *Ibid.*

256 WET HIS PANTS: William Castle, *Step Right Up . . . I'm Gonna Scare the Pants Off America* (New York: G. P. Putnam's Sons, 1976), p. 10.

256 WHEN I WAS THIRTEEN: *Ibid.,* p. 13.

256 "NAZI" VANDALISM: John Kobler, "Master of Movie Horror," *The Saturday Evening Post,* March 19, 1960, p. 100.

257 LLOYD'S OF LONDON: "Blood Runs High But Ideas Low," *Variety,* July 23, 1958.

257 10 MILLION MARK: *Ibid.*

259 ABSOLUTE PANDEMONIUM: Tom Weaver, "An Outspoken Conversation with Robb White," *Filmfax* No. 18, p. 94.

259 AUDIENCE WOULD TASTE THE FOG: Kobler, *op. cit.*

260 HORROR IS NOW ONE OF THE BASIC AMERICAN COMMODITIES: Hollis Alpert and Charles Beaumont, "The Horror of It All," *Playboy,* March 1959, p. 74.

261 THANK GOD FOR THE HORROR PICTURES: *Ibid.,* p. 86.

Chapter Nine
The Graveyard Bash

264 "SICK" WAS THE MAGIC WORD: Albert Goldman, from the journalism of Lawrence Schiller, *Ladies and Gentlemen, Lenny Bruce!!* (New York: Random House, 1974), p. 214–15.

264 WHEN SICK HUMOR ERUPTED: Albert Goldman, *Freakshow: The Rocksoulbluesjazzsickjewblackhumorsexpoppsych Gig and Other Scenes from the Counter Culture* (New York: Atheneum, 1971), p. 223.

264 SHUT UP AND DR-R-RINK: John Cohen, ed., *The Essential Lenny Bruce* (London: Open Gate Books, 1973), p. 107–08.

265 COUNT CONDU: Jack Kerouac, *Dr. Sax* (New York: Grove Weidenfeld, 1987; reprint of 1959 edition), p. 106.

265 JACK WAS DRINKING SO HEAVILY: Daniel Talbot, interviewed by author, New York City, November 1990.

265 ONE OF PHILADELPHIA'S MAINLINE DOWAGERS: Roul Tunley, "TV's Midnight Madness," *The Saturday Evening Post,* August 16, 1958.

266 JOHN ZACHERLE: Interviewed by author, New York City, November 27, 1991.

267 I BELONGED TO HIS FAN CLUB: Cynthia Heimel, "Interview with an Ex-Vampire," *New York,* April 24, 1978, p. 56–58.

267 "DINNER WITH DRAC": Dick Clark and Richard Robinson, *Rock, Roll & Remember* (New York: Popular Library, 1978), p. 196–200.

267 DICK CLARK: *Ibid.*

268 MAKING FACES AT THE CAMERA: Zacherle interview, *op. cit.*

268 IMPROBABILIA: Forrest J Ackerman, interviewed by author, Los Angeles, California, April 1991.

268 HYMIE TAUBMAN: Bill Warren, *Keep Watching the Skies!* (Jefferson, NC: McFarland & Company, 1988), p. 321.

269 A GREAT OPERATOR: April Smith, "Citizen Pain: The Publisher Who Built a Vampire Empire," *Rolling Stone,* April 25, 1974.

271 THE FATHER WHO HAD DESERTED HIM: Stephen King, interview in *Playboy* magazine, reprinted in Tim Underwood and Chuck Miller, eds., *Bare Bones: Conversations on Terror with Stephen King* (New York: McGraw-Hill, 1988), p. 35–36.

271 THE "LOST FATHER" MOTIF: For a detailed discussion, see Joseph Reino, *Stephen King: The First Decade* (Boston: Twayne Publishers, 1988).

271 SPIELBERG'S MOTHER: Fred A. Bernstein, *The Jewish Mothers Hall of Fame* (Garden City, NY: Doubleday & Company, 1986), p. 2.

272 SPIELBERG HIMSELF RECALLED: Stephen Spielberg, introduction to catalog, *Science-Fiction, Fantasy, Horror: the World of Forrest J. Ackerman at Auction* (New York: Gurnsey's, December 12–13, 1987).

272 JOE DANTE: Interviewed by author, Burbank, California, April 1991.

275 JUST LIKE THE PLASTIC JESUS: Stephen King, *'Salem's Lot* (New York: Signet Books / New American Library, 1976), p. 137.

275 INITITATION RITES: Walter Evans, "Monster Movies and Rites of Initiation," *Journal of Popular Film,* Vol. IV, No. 2 (1975), p. 137.

277 MASTURBATION AND MENSTRUATION: Walter Evans, "Monster Movies: A Sexual Theory," *Journal of Popular Film,* January 1973, p. 356.

278 INTENSIFIED THEIR CHILDREN'S ANXIETIES: David S. Greenwald and Steven J. Zeitlin, *No Reason to Talk About It: Families Confront the Nuclear Taboo* (New York: W. W. Norton & Company, 1987).

278 PERHAPS EVEN INSANE: Robert K. Musil, "Growing up nuclear," *The Bulletin of the Atomic Scientists,* Vol. 38, No. 1 (January 1982), p. 19.

278 PICTURES OF THEIR GIRLFRIENDS: Bobby Pickett, interviewed by author, Boston, Massachusetts, March 1991.

279 "MONSTER TWIST": Fred Bronson, *The Billboard Book of Number One Hits,* revised edition (New York: Billboard Publications, 1988), p. 118.

282 WHAT IS LEFT UNSAID: Review of "The Addams Family," *Variety,* September 23, 1963.

282 SIMILARLY SKEPTICAL: Review of "The Addams Family," *Daily News* (New York), September 19, 1964.

282 HAVE A SEX LIFE: John Astin, foreword to Stephen Cox's *The Addams Chronicles* (New York: Harper Perennial, 1991), p. xii.

284 TOGETHER IN THE SAME BED: *Ibid.,* p. 150.

284 STORY LINES WERE OFTEN REMARKABLY SIMILAR: *Ibid.,* p. 151.

284 REMCO INDUSTRIES: Philip Shabecoff, "Advertising: Monster Market Creeping Up," *The New York Times,* August 30, 1964.

284 TOYLAND '64 LOOKS LIKE A CHARNEL HOUSE: "The Return of the Monsters," *Look,* September 8, 1964, p. 47.

285 ARBUS PHOTO: Smith, *op. cit.*

Chapter Ten
It's Alive, I'm Afraid

287 LISTEN, HENRY FRANKENSTEIN: Screenplay by William Hurlburt and John L. Balderston, in Philip J. Riley, ed., *The Bride of Frankenstein,* Universal Filmscripts Series (Abescon, NJ: MagicImage Filmbooks, 1989).

288 THE PILL WAS RUSHED: For a discussion of chemical contraception from a feminist standpoint, see Flora Davis, *Moving the Mountain: The Women's*

Movement in America Since 1960 (New York: Simon and Schuster, 1991), p. 236–37.

289 COST ONLY $300,000: Jay Robert Nash and Stanley Ralph Ross, *The Motion Picture Guide,* Vol. VII (Chicago: Cinebooks, 1987), p. 3687.

289 HE HAD A DEFORMED AND SHORTENED ARM: The Insight Team of *The Sunday Times* of London, *Suffer the Children: The Story of Thalidomide* (New York: The Viking Press, 1979), p. 112.

290 THEY HADN'T SEEN ANY SKIN: David F. Friedman, *A Youth in Babylon: Confessions of a Trash Film King* (Buffalo, NY: Prometheus Books, 1990), p. 63.

291 THROAT CANCER: I am indebted to both Elias Savada and Bret Wood for granting me access to their unpublished research material regarding Browning's final days.

291 A HEALTHY RUN: "1932 'Freaks' Draws Street People, '72," *Variety,* July 19, 1972.

291 FREAKS ARE PEOPLE, INDIVIDUALS: Montague Addison, letter to *Films in Review,* June–July 1971.

293 LEVIN TOLD: Interview profile of Ira Levin, *Publishers Weekly,* May 22, 1967, p. 19.

293 PLOTTED THE BOOK BACKWARDS: Marthe MacGregor, "This Week in Books," *New York Post,* September 30, 1967.

293 TOO GIMMICKY: *Publishers Weekly, op. cit.*

293 "CONDEMNED" RATING: " 'Rosemary's Baby' Given a 'C' Rating by Catholic Office," *The New York Times,* June 21, 1968.

294 HATE MAIL: William Castle, *Step Right Up . . . I'm Gonna Scare the Pants Off America* (New York: G. P. Putnam's Sons, 1976), p. 28.

295 FIVE HUNDRED CHILD ACTRESSES: Pauline Kael, *Reeling* (Boston and Toronto: Atlantic Monthly Press / Little, Brown and Company, 1976), p. 251.

295 LINDA BLAIR: Greta Blackburn, "The Star: Linda Blair," *Fangoria* (January 1987), p. 20–21.

297 TABOO IDEAS AND SUBJECTS: Alan Dundes: *Cracking Jokes: Studies of Sick Humor Cycles and Stereotypes* (Berkeley, CA: Ten Speed Press, 1987), p. vii.

300 A LONG AND LOVING CLOSEUP: David Cronenberg, discussing *The Brood*; *Cinefantastique,* Vol. 10, No. 4, Spring 1981.

300 ACTIVENESS AND RAGE: Robin Wood, "Cronenberg: A Dissenting View," in Piers Handling, ed., *The Shape of Rage: The Films of David Cronenberg* (Toronto / New York: General Publishing Co., Limited / New York Zoetrope, 1983), p. 131.

300 A CRAZY HOUSEWIFE: Philip French, review of *The Brood; Observer* (London), March 9, 1980.

305 TRADE HUMOR: F. Paul Wilson, "Foet," in Thomas F. Monteleone, ed., *Borderlands 2* (New York: Avon Books, 1991), p. 11.

Chapter Eleven
Scar Wars

307 I HAD CHOSEN THE PHOTOGRAPHY SCHOOL: Bob Martin, "Tom Savini: A man of Many Parts," *Fangoria* #6, p. 50.

308 I SAW A LOT OF BLOODSHED: James Verniere, "An Interview with Tom Savini," *The Aquarian,* November 24–December 1, 1982.

308 DRILL SERGEANT: Tom Savini, *Bizarro* [original title: *Grande Illusions*] (New York: Harmony Books, 1983), p. 11.

308 A HUMAN ARM: *Ibid.,* p. 12.

308 MY MARRIAGE WENT INSTANTLY INTO THE TOILET: *Ibid.*

308 I WAS PLAYING THE PART OF RENFIELD: *Ibid.*

311 WHAT I HAD SEEN FOR REAL IN VIETNAM: Martin, *op. cit.*

311 WE BUILT A SPECIAL TILED FLOOR: Saul Bass, interviewed by Tony Crawley in *Hammer's House of Horror,* March 1978, p. 37.

315 AMPLE OPPORTUNITY TO RUN AWAY: Joe Dante, interviewed by author, Burbank, California, March 1991.

315 38.5 MILLION COPIES: J. Randy Taraborelli, *Michael Jackson: The Magic and the Madness* (New York: Birch Lane Press, 1991), p. 322.

316 HEAVILY FINANCED: Taraborelli, *op. cit.,* p. 325.

316 RICK BAKER RECALLED: R. H. Martin, "Zombies A-Go Go" (sidebar to "Rick Baker: The Wonder Years, Part One"), *Fangoria,* March 1984, p. 44.

317 JEHOVAH'S WITNESS: Taraborelli, *op. cit.,* p. 327–28.

318 AN ODD LITTLE CLEFT: Stephen Holden, "The Dark Side of Peter Pan," *The New York Times,* September 13, 1987.

320 A CLOSED, SELF-SUFFICIENT SYSTEM: Constance Penley, "Feminism, Film Theory and the Bachelor Machines," *The Future of an Illusion: Film, Feminism, and Psychoanalysis* (Minneapolis: University of Minnesota Press, 1989), p. 57.

321 NINE FRENCH WOMEN DIED: Naomi Wolf, *The Beauty Myth: How Images of Beauty Are Used Against Women* (New York: William Morrow and Company, 1991), p. 236–37.

321 THE MEDICAL CODE OF NUREMBERG: *Ibid.,* p. 236.

323 ALMOST UNIVERSAL FEELING OF POWERLESSNESS: V. Vale and Andrea Juno, eds., *Modern Primitives* (San Francisco: Re / Search Publications, 1989), p. 4.

324 IT WOULD BE REASSURING: Robert Robertson Ross and Hugh Bryan McCay, *Self Mutilation* (Lexington, MA, and Toronto: Lexington Books, 1979), p. 11.

324 DISMEMBERED PRIMAL BEINGS: Armando R. Favazza, *Bodies Under Siege* (Baltimore: Johns Hopkins University Press, 1987), p. 1.

325 GREG NICOTERO: Interviewed by author, Chatsworth, California, March 14, 1991.

328 PEOPLE READING ON THE SUBWAY: Dante interview *op. cit.*

328 ABSOLUTELY APPALLING: Anthony Timpone, "Elegy: A Nightmare on 10 Downing Street," *Fangoria* (March 1988), p. 6.

328 A BATCH OF HORROR COMICS: "Churchill Plans to Read Horror Comics to See Whether They Should Be Banned," *The New York Times,* November 12, 1954.

328 CURRENT EDITOR: Anthony Timpone, interviewed by author, New York City, November 1991.

328 CAT-AND-MOUSE GAMES: Ken Sanders, "MPAA War Story," *Fangoria,* August 1990, p. 52–55.

Chapter Twelve
"Rotten Blood"

344 A REASON TO TALK ABOUT BODILY FUNCTIONS: Jack Rems, interviewed by the author, Berkeley, California, October 1991.

345 PARANOID POISON FANTASIES: Lloyd deMause, *Reagan's America* (New York: Creative Roots, 1984), p. 119.

345 MIRACULOUS ALLEGORY: *Ibid.,* p. 118.

345 I JUST COULDN'T STAND TO WATCH: *Ibid.,* p. 41.

345 SPEAKING DIRECTLY TO POWERFUL FANTASIES: Robert Kastenbaum, " 'Safe Death' in the Postmodern World," in Anne Gilmore and Stan Gilmore, eds., *A Safer Death: Multidisciplinary Aspects of Terminal Care* (New York and London: Plenum Press, 1988), p. 12.

345 BLOOD-STEALING CATASTROPHE: Robert Kastenbaum and Beatrice Kastenbaum, *Encyclopedia of Death* (Phoenix, AZ: Oryx Press, 1989), p. 284.

346 THE HOMOSEXUAL IS EATING LIFE: Anita Bryant, quoted in *Time,* June 13, 1977, p. 20.

346 LIKE THE SAINTS: Katherine Ramsland, *Prism of the Night: A Biography of Anne Rice* (New York: Dutton, 1991), p. 115.

347 SUGGEST THE VESTMENTS OF A CATHOLIC PRIEST: Joyce Carol Oates, "Dracula," in David Rosenberg, ed., *The Movie That Changed My Life* (New York: Viking, 1991), p. 63.

348 THE BLOOD RAN IN TINY RIVULETS: Anne Rice, *The Queen of the Damned* (New York: Ballantine Books, 1989 reprint), p. 222.

348 THE VAMPIRE LESTAT WAS GOD: *Ibid.,* p. 230.

349 OUR OWN NEGLECT AND DENIAL: Jack Anderson, "Of the Vampire Within," *The New York Times,* December 8, 1991.

349 PERSUASIVE JUSTIFICATION: Susan Sontag, *Illness As Metaphor and AIDS and Its Metaphors* (New York: Anchor Books, 1990), p. 182.

350 SKEWING BASIC RESEARCH: See Bruce Nussbaum, *Good Intentions: How Big Business and the Medical Establishment Are Corrupting the Fight Against AIDS* (New York: Atlantic Monthly Press, 1990).

350 DISSENTING OPINIONS ON THE ROLE OF HIV: The first mainstream book challenging the HIV hypothesis was Jad Adams' *AIDS: The HIV Myth* (New York: St. Martin's Press, 1989).

350 YOU CAN MAKE UP SOME GREAT MYSTERIES: Celia Farber, "Fatal Distraction," *Spin,* June 1992, p. 84.

350 THE AIDS PROBLEM HAS ALREADY BEEN SOLVED: Barbara Ehrenreich, "Phallic Science," *The Worst Years of Our Lives* (New York: Pantheon, 1990), pp. 258–59.

Chapter Thirteen
The Dance of Dearth

354 ONE OF THEM IS THE BIBLE: Clive Barker, "On Censorship," in Stephen Jones, ed., *Clive Barker's Shadows in Eden* (Lancaster, PA: Underwood-Miller, 1991), p. 402.

355 THE BIGGEST AND BEST-EDUCATED GROUP: Landon Y. Jones, *Great Expectations: America and the Baby Boom Generation* (New York: Ballatine Books, 1981), p. 189.

355 A VERY PECULIAR GIRL: Charles L. Grant, "Stephen King: 'I Like to Go For the Jugular,' " *Rod Serling's Twilight Zone,* April 1981, p. 18.

356 HUNG HERSELF ONE SUMMER: *Ibid.*

357 THINK OF THE BILLS: Stephen King, *Danse Macabre* (New York: Berkley Books, 1982), p. 144.

357 UNHAPPY AND DIFFERENT: Stephen King, "The *Playboy* Interview" (1983) in George Beahm, ed., *The Stephen King Companion* (Kansas City and New York: Andrews and McMeel, 1989), p. 27.

358 WE LIVED IN A TRAILER: Tabitha King, introduction to *Carrie: The Stephen King Collector's Edition* (New York: Plume, 1991), p. ix.

358 XEROXES OF THE MANUSCRIPT: Harlan Ellison, "Harlan Ellison's Watching: In Which We Discover Why the Parents Don't Look Like Their Children," in George Beahm, ed., *The Stephen King Companion, op. cit.*

358 INFUSES A TASTE FOR LETTERS: Alexis de Tocqueville, *Democracy in America* (New York: Alfred A. Knopf, 1945), Vol. 2, p. 64.

360 FIRST HARDCOVER PRINTINGS: Figures are drawn from sidebar to Bill Goldstein's article "King of Horror," *Publishers Weekly,* January 24, 1991, p. 7.

360 AFFORD TO BUY HARDCOVERS: Stephen King, "My Say," *Publishers Weekly,* November 15, 1985.

360 HIS FAN MAIL: David Sherman, "The Stephen King Interview," *Fangoria* No. 35 (1984), p. 40.

361 WORST POSSIBLE MORAL UNIVERSE: Lloyd Rose, "The Triumph of the Nerds," *The Atlantic,* September 1986, p. 103.

364 A STRANGE CIRCUS ATMOSPHERE: STEPHEN KING, STEPHEN KING'S DANSE MACABRE, P. 23.

364 SEARS ROEBUCK CATALOG: Ron Burnett, review of *It, The Christian Science Monitor,* September 19, 1986, p. 21.

364 EVOKES CHILDHOOD IN THE 1950s: David Gates, review of *It, Newsweek,* September 1, 1986.

365 DEPRESSED ME FOR WEEKS: Sherman, *op. cit.*

365 IF YOU VALUE WIT: Walter Kendrick, "Stephen King Gets Eminent," *The Village Voice,* April 29, 1981.

367 CYNICALLY PIOUS: Victoria Raidin, *New Statesman,* March 3, 1988.

367 LIMITED PARTNERS: Backers list for *Carrie, Show Business,* August 24, 1988.

367 THERE ISN'T A CHANCE IN HELL: Ken Mandelbaum, *Not Since Carrie: 40 Years of Broadway Musical Flops* (New York: St. Martin's Press, 1991), p. 351.

367 A CAUTIONARY FAIRY TALE: Nicholas de Jongh, *The Guardian,* February 20, 1988.

370 STUPENDOUSLY, FABULOUSLY TERRIBLE: Linda Winer, " 'Carrie': Staging a Horror on Broadway," *Newsday,* May 13, 1988.

370 LESS CAUSTIC THAN USUAL: John Simon, "Blood and No Guts," *New York,* May 23, 1988, p. 60.

370 CURSES AND SLAPS HER POOR DAUGHTER: Jack Kroll, "Shakespeare to Stephen King: The Sins of 'Carrie,' " *Newsweek,* May 23, 1988, p. 74–76.

370 BALLETOPORN: Mimi Kramer, "Bloody Awful," *The New Yorker,* May 23, 1988, p. 85.

370 AS THE AUDIENCE FILES OUT: Mandelbaum, *op. cit.,* p. 9.

371 SEARS, NOT SAKS: Joe Queenan, "And Us Without Our Spoons," *The New York Times Book Review,* September 29, 1991, p. 13.

371 GREY POUPON: Bret Easton Ellis, *American Psycho* (New York: Vintage Books, 1991), p. 328.

372 WOULD KIDS BE LIKE VEAL?: Bill Watterson, "Calvin and Hobbes," undated cartoon clipping, Universal Press Syndicate, 1990.

373 THAT THE EIGHTIES WERE SPIRITUALLY DISGUSTING: Norman Mailer, "Children of the Pied Piper," *Vanity Fair,* March 1991, p. 159.

373 DUMB AS HELL: Alfred Kazin, " 'American Psycho': Horror Show of Monotony, Heavy-Handedness," *The New York Observer,* April 1, 1991.

373 BLOODY CLOTHES: Ellis, *op. cit.,* p. 81.

373 BLACK COMEDY: Phoebe Hoban, " 'Psycho' Drama," *New York,* December 17, 1990, p. 35.

375 PUBLISHED AND BOMBED: *Ibid.*

Chapter Fourteen
The Monster Millennium

383 PROBLEMS OVER WHICH THEY HAD LITTLE CONTROL: Kim Foltz, "Consumer Pessimism Rises, A Report by Grey Indicates," *The New York Times,* March 25, 1991.

384 BEING DEPLOYED OUT HERE: Letter from serviceman to *Fangoria* magazine, March 30, 1991. Files of Starlog Publications, New York City.

384 "TALES FROM THE CRYPT": John J. O'Connor, " 'Tales from the Crypt' Raises Ratings for HBO," *The New York Times,* June 26, 1991.

384 TRADITIONAL TRAVELING SIDESHOW: Ann Japenga, "Over the Edge?" *Los Angeles Times,* September 1, 1992. Also see Gina Arnold, "Lollapalooza: The Greatest McTour on Earth," *LA Weekly,* September 4–10, 1992.

385 GROSSED $25 MILLION: Bernard Weinraub, "Addamses Startle at Box Office, Too," *The New York Times,* November 25, 1991.

385 THESE ARE WEIRD TIMES: *Ibid.*

385 SECRET CRAVING FOR DIONYSIAN TRUTHS: Camille Paglia, *Sexual Personae: Art and Decadence from Nefertiti to Emily Dickinson* (New York: Vintage Books, 1991), p. 268.

386 INCANTATIONS THAT COUNT: Leonard Wolf, "In Horror Movies, Some Things Are Sacred," *The New York Times,* April 4, 1976.

386 THE PUBLISHED SCRIPT: Bruce Joel Rubin, *Jacob's Ladder* (New York: Applause Theatre Book Publishers, 1990), p. 181–84.

387 RATHER LIKE A HAUNTING: David Manners, interviewed by author, April 1991, Santa Barbara, California.

INDEX

Page numbers in *italics* refer to illustrations.

Abbott and Costello Meet Frankenstein, 218, 247
abortion, 290
  horror-movie metaphors for, 297–98, 302–5
Academy Awards:
  of Giger, 301
  of March, 145
  for *Silence of the Lambs,* 382
Ackerman, Forrest J, 268–71, *269,* 273–74, 315, 326, 387
Addams, Charles, 239, 240, 281, 282
Addams Family, The, 385
"Addams Family, The," 281–84, *283*
Addison, Montague, 291
After Hours, 268–69
AIDS, 333–34, 383, 388
  blood fetishists and, 342
  vampire fears and, 345–51, *332, 347*
AIDS and Its Metaphors (Sontag), 349–50
Aldrich, Robert, 311
Alfred A. Knopf, 371, 373, 376
Alien, 300–301, *302*
Alien 3, 301–2
Allan, Elizabeth, 191, 192
Allan, Frederick Lewis, 78
Allen, Debbie, 367, 370
All Quiet on the Western Front, 118, 128, 136
Amazing Colossal Man, The, 250
"American Bandstand," 267
American International Pictures (AIP), 256
American Museum, 30
American Psycho (Ellis), 371–76, *374*
American Vampires (Dresser), 343
American Werewolf in London, An, 315, *316,* 317
Amityville Horror, The, 357

animal-men, 216
animation, stop-motion, 175
Ankers, Evelyn, *214*
anorexia nervosa, 351
Antona-Traversi, Camillo, 58–60
Anxious Visions (Stich), 48
Ape Man, The, 218
Arbus, Diane, 15–23, *17,* 285, 387
  Freaks and, *14,* 15–17
  at Hubert's Museum, 17–18, *17*
  identity as defined by, 79
  Jack Dracula and, 18–19
  Mae West and, 21
  Sontag on, 21–22
  suicide of, 22
Arlen, Richard, *170*
Art Deco, 132
Art Institute of Pittsburgh, 331
Art Moderne, 132
Asher, E. M., 116, 178, 199
Associated Press, 195
Astin, John, 282
Astley, Philip, 29
Atherton, Gertrude, 96
Atlantic, 361
atomic-bomb metaphors, 247–48, *249,* 278
Attack of the Crab Monsters, The, 250
Attack of the Fifty-Foot Woman, 250
Atwill, Lionel, *173, 208,* 174, 206, 209
Auerbach, L., 39–40
Aurora Plastics, 263, 274, 277
Ayers, Lew, 118

"bachelor machine," 320–21
Baclanova, Olga, 16, 22, *149,* 150–52, *151,* 155, 172
Bacon, Francis, 224–25, *224,* 313, 386
Bakacs, Anna, 180

Baker, Rick, 315, 316–17, *316, 326*
Balderston, John L., *87,* 181
  and *Bride of Frankenstein,* 182, 183–84
  and *Dracula's Daughter,* 196–98
  and stage production of *Dracula,* 86–89,
    104–9
  and stage production of *Frankenstein,* 97,
    98, 104–10, 128
  World War II involvement championed
    by, 222
Bankhead, Tallulah, 141
Bara, Theda, 89, 94, 240
Barber, Ellis, 245
Barker, Clive, 330, 354, 375, 376, 384
Barnum, P. T., 30
Barry, Julian, 265
Barrymore, John, 139, 140–41
Barrymore, Lionel, 191
Bartel, Paul, 372
Bartlett, Elise, 110
Bat, The (Rinehart and Hopwood), 84
Batchelor, C. D., *219, 222*
Bates, Kathy, 326
Bathory, Elizabeth, 312
Bauhaus, 130, *131, 179*
Baum, Vicki, 150
Beaser, Herbert W., 235
Beast from 20,000 Fathoms, The, 250
Beast with a Million Eyes, The, 253
Beath, Warren Newton, 243
Beauty Myth, The (Wolf), 321
Beginning of the End, The, 248
Bell, Nelson B., 168
Bellmer, Hans, *188*
B.E.M.s, 253
Ben, 315
Ben Hur, 142
Beranger, Clara S., 140
Berger, Howard, 325
Berkeley, Busby, 174
Berkson, Eva, 226–27
Bern, Paul, 158–59
berserkers, 212, 386
Biltmore Theatre, 92
Binet, Alfred, 57, 60
Biograph, 32
birth-control pill, 288
birth-process metaphors, 287–305
Bixby, Jerome, 361
Bizarre, 240
Blackbird, The, 71, 75
Black Cat, The, 118, 177–81, *179, 180,*
    268, 387
  censorship of, 178, 180
  World War I and, 177–78, 181
"Black Cat, The" (Poe), 177
Black Dahlia, The (Ellroy), 376
Black Dragons, 223
Black Oxen (Atherton), 96
blacks, 356
  censorship and, 201
Blacula, 356

Blechman, L. G., 182
Blind Bargain, A, 66
Blood Feast, 312
blooc fetishists, 334–43
Blood of Dracula, 256
Blood Salvage, 328–30
Blue Jay, The (Webling), 100
Boasberg, Al, 148
Bodies Under Siege (Favazza), 324
Body Snatcher, The, 221
Bogdan, Robert, 30
Bonfils, Frederick G., 30
Boni & Liveright, 108
Booth, Elmer, 34–35
Booth, Margaret, 34*n*
Borland, Carroll, 192, *193*
Bosworth, Patricia, 17
Bottin, Robb, 313, *314,* 315
Bow, Clara, 96
  Lugosi's affair with, 92–95, *93*
Bradbury, Ray, 25, 29, 364
Brain from Planet Arous, The, 251–52
Bram Stoker's Dracula, 386
Breen, Joseph, 166*n,* 171, 178, 187–
    90, 191, 194, 198–200, 205,
    220
Bride of Frankenstein, 182–91, *187, 188,*
    205, 317, 320, 381
  censorship of, *160,* 186–91
  psychosexual aspects of, 184–85, 189,
    287–88, 294
  writing of, 182–85
Bride of Re-Animator, 325
Bride of the Monster, 253
British Board of Film Censors, 195, 205
British Film Institute, 137
Brodie, Deacon, 139
*Bronx, New York, 1964: Meeting the Famous
    Monsters,* 285
Brood, The, 298–300, *299*
Browning, Pete "The Gladiator," 26–27,
    27
Browning, Tod, 16, 23, *24,* 25–35, *27, 32,
    33, 62, 75,* 116, 178, 264, 357, 364
  alcoholism of, 33–34, 64, 124
  automobile accident of, 34–35, 63
  background of, 26–28
  carnival career of, 25–26, 28–31
  castration fear and symbolism in movies
    of, 74–79, 126, 345
  Chaney and, 64, 65, 71, 77, 78, 79, 115,
    116, 147
  character of, 33–34, 35, 73, 78, 120–21,
    152, 201
  collapse of career of, 156–58, 200, 206
  dance marathons and, 201
  death of, 18, 78, 291
  Dracula directed by, 115, 117, 120, 121–
    28, 148, 191
  early movie career of, 32, 63–64
  Freaks directed by, *14,* 145–59, *151, 157,*
    290, 387

Mark of the Vampire directed by, 191–92, *193*, 200
  MGM salary of, 78
  stagey directing technique of, 192
  working-class appeal of, 78
Bruce, Lenny, 264–65, 266, 282
Bryant, Anita, 346
Bucket of Blood, A, 256
Buckley, Betty, *369*
Burne-Jones, Philip, 55, 88
Busch, Charles, 348
Butler, Ivan, 100–101, 102, 104
Byron, George Gordon, Lord, 82, 98, 137, 184, 186

Cabbage Patch dolls, 304
Cabinet of Dr. Caligari, The, 36, 37–48, *42,* 54, 55, 58, 115, 132, 134, 138, 164, 178, 206, 222, 251, 318, 364
  anti-German sentiment and, 37–38, 39, 44–46
  Berlin premiere of, 43
  cast of, 41
  expressionist style of, 39, 40, 43
  New York premiere of, 38, 40
  original musical accompaniment to, 43–44
  plot of, 40–41
  as political allegory, 41, 43, 168
  reviews of, 38–39, 44, 46–47
  tinting of, 44
Caine, Hall, 83
"Calvin and Hobbes," 372
"camp" sensibility, 184–85
cannibalism, 371–72, 382, 385
Capizzi, Leonard, 279
Carew, Edwin, 125
Carewe, Arthur Edmund, 117, 125
Carmilla (Le Fanu), 200
Carpenter, John, 313, *314*
Carpetbaggers, The (Robbins), 159
Carradine, John, 217
Carrie (movie), *352,* 366
Carrie (musical), 366–68, *369*
Carrie (novel) (King), 277, 355–58, 366
Carroll, Lewis, 98–99
Carroll, Virginia, 30
Castle, William, 256–57, 259, 294, 312
Castle of Frankenstein, 19
castration fear and symbolism, 74–79, 126, 345
Cat and the Canary, The (Willard), 85, 115
Cat Creeps, The (*El Voluntad del Muerto*), 122
Catholic Church, 137, 182, 293–94, 347–48
Cat People, 218–21, *219*
Cat's Eye, 366
censorship, 109, 161–63, *165*
  of *The Black Cat,* 178, 180
  of *Bride of Frankenstein, 160,* 186–91
  of *The Brood,* 300

of *Cat People,* 220–21
  of *Dr. Jekyll and Mr. Hyde,* 144, 145
  of *Dracula,* 125–26, 162
  of *Dracula's Daughter,* 198–200
  of *Frankenstein,* 137–38
  of *Freaks,* 150, 155, 171, 172
  of *Island of Lost Souls,* 171
  of *Mark of the Vampire,* 191
  MPAA ratings and, 328–30
  of *Murders in the Rue Morgue,* 166, 171
  political organization of, 182, 312
  standards in, 171–74
  of *The Witch of Timbuctoo,* 201
  see also Production Code
Censorship Papers, The (Gardner), 187
Chandler, Helen, 113, *121,* 124, 126, 191
Chandu the Magician, 226
Chaney, Lon, 29, *62,* 65–74, *66, 67, 69, 70,* 77, 85, 113, 126, 142, 173, 206, 307, 318, 326, 361, 364
  background of, 65
  Browning and, 64, 65, 71, 77, 78, 79, 115, 116, 147
  character of, 73, 78
  death of, 115, 116, 291
  Dracula and, 115, 117
  star persona of, 70–71
  torturous physical disguises used by, 65–74
  working-class appeal of, 78
Chaney, Lon, Jr., 78, *214,* 215, 218, 313–14
Chaplin, Charles, 201
child abuse, 361–62
  blood fetishists and, 335–38, 343
Children of the Corn, 303
Child's Play, 303, *304*
Choisy, Camille, 58, 226–27
Chong, Ping, 348–49
Christian Science Monitor, 364
Churchill, Winston, 328
Cinderella legend, 356–57
CinemaScope, 259
Cinerama, 259
circus sideshows, 28–30, 65
Citizen Kane, 39, 206
Clark, Dick, 267
Clarke, Mae, 129, 133
Cline, Louis, 109, 134
Clive, Colin, 129, 137, 181, 186
Clurman, Harold, 53–54
Cohen, Herman, 255–56
Cohen, Lawrence, 366
Cold War metaphors, 247–48, 250–51
collodion, 308
Columbia Pictures, 218, 222, 256
"comeback" performances, 312
comic books, *see* horror comics
Comics Code Authority, 237
Comics Magazine Association of America, 237
Conjure Wife (Leiber), 222

Connelly, Joseph, 281
Conreid, Hans, 237
Conway, Jack, 153
Conway, Tom, 220
Cook, Barbara, 366, 367, 368
Cook, The Thief, His Wife and Her Lover, The, 372
Cooke, Thomas Potter, 101
Cooper, Merian C., 175
Cooper, Wyllis, 221
Copland, Aaron, 53–54
Coppola, Francis Ford, 386
Corman, Roger, 242, 256
cosmetic surgery, 167–68, 318–22
Count Dracula Fan Club, 343
Count Yorga, Vampire, 339
Courtenay, William, 117
Cox, Stephen, 282
Craig, Johnny, 232
Crawford, Joan, 73–74, 312
Crawling Eye, The, 253
"Crazy Sunday" (Fitzgerald), 153
Creation, 175
Creature from the Black Lagoon, 247, 364
Cremer, Robert, 223
Crime in the Madhouse, A (de Lorde and Binet), 58
Crime SuspenStories, 235
Criminal Code, The, 134
Cronenberg, David, 298–300
Cry of the Werewolf, 218
Cry to Heaven (Rice), 339–40
Cuban missile crisis, 277–78, 279
cubism, 40, 55, 71, 130, 132
Cummings, Constance, 163
Curse of Frankenstein, The, 311
Curse of the Cat People, The, 221
Cyclops, The, 253

Dadoun, Roger, 68
Dagover, Lil, *36*
Dahmer, Jeffrey, 382
Dalí, Salvador, 114, 313, *329*
dance marathons, 201
Dance of Death, 230–31
Danse Macabre (King), 364, 365
Dante, Joe, 274–75, 297, 315, 328, 361
Dante's Inferno, 205
Dark Half, The (King), 360
Davis, Bette, 164*n,* 312
Davis, Flora, 288
Davis, Hubert Henry, 89
Davis, Jack, 232
Davis, Marjorie Ross, 125
Dawn of the Dead, 309–11, *309,* 325, 376, 377
DC Comics, 230–31
dead-baby jokes, 296–97
Deadly Mantis, The, 248
Dead Ringers, 298
Dead Zone, The (King), 360, 366

Dean, James, 242–44, *243,* 246
Dean, Priscilla, 64
Deane, Hamilton, *103, 105,* 110
　Dracula staged by, 86, 88, *88,* 102, 106, 107
　Frankenstein staged by, 97–105, *101, 103*
Deathdream, 308
Death of James Dean, The (Beath), 243
DeCarlo, Yvonne, 281
"Deep Sea Divers, The," 31
de Jongh, Nicholas, 367–68
de Lorde, André, 57, *59,* 60
deMause, Lloyd, 344–45
Democracy in America (Tocqueville), 353, 358
De Palma, Brain, *352,* 366
Devil Doll, The, 201
Diane Arbus (Bosworth), 17
Dickey, Joan, 64
"Dinner with Drac," 267, 315
Dinosaur and the Missing Link, The, 175
Dr. Jekyll and Mr. Hyde (1920), 139, 140–41
Dr. Jekyll and Mr. Hyde (1931), 141–45, *143,* 162, 194, 226
　casting of, 142
　censorship of, 144, 145
　political metaphor in, 159
　psychosexual aspects of, 144
　transformation scenes in, 142
Dr. Sax (Kerouac), 265
Dr. Warren and Mr. O'Connor, 140
Do-It-Yourself Monster Make-Up Handbook (Smith), 307, 326–27, *327*
Doll, The, 188
Donovan's Brain, 251
doppelganger:
　as basis of monster images, 76
　day-care workers as, 361–62
　Dorian Gray as, 139, 140
　Dracula as, 83, *123,* 139
　Frankenstein's monster as, 83, 97–98
　in *Invasion of the Body Snatchers,* 250
　Jekyll/Hyde duality as, 139
　Nazi medical atrocities and, 225–26
　sexual, 323
"doubling," 225–26, 361
Dracula:
　AIDS and, *332,* 347
　evolution in image of, 83, 91, 217–18, 264–65, 348–49, 386
　Frankenstein's monster compared with, 81–82, 83–84, 100, 311, 351
　origin of, 82, 386
　as outmoded horror icon, 247, 253–55
　Peter Pan as variation on, 320
　as primary horror icon, 19, 145, 159
　religious image of, 278, 347
　as werewolf, 212–13
Dracula (1931 film), 16, 109, 110, 113–28, *117, 119, 121,* 138, 142, 144, 145,

146, 148, 158, 166, 177, 181, 197, 278, 335, 382, 388
addiction metaphor in, 124
Browning vs. Freund as director of, 121–22, 126, 191
casting of, 115–18
censorship of, 125–26, 162
as formula for other movies, 168–69, 191–92
Frankenstein on double-bill with, 202–5, *203, 204*
negative reactions to, 125–26
political metaphor in, 159
psychological effects of, 127–28
psychosexual aspects of, 126–27, 159
soundtrack of, 126
Spanish-language version of, 122, *123,* 127
studio cuts in, 124–25
Dracula (Stoker novel), 55, 139, 140, 216, 220*n*, 294, 335
authorship of, 82–83
film rights to, 84, 110
Frankenstein compared with, 83
Liveright's stage production of, *80,* 84, 86–92, *88, 90, 93,* 96, 106*n*, 256
Nosferatu as unauthorized adaptation of, 50–51, 86
Dracula's Daughter, 195–200, *200*
censorship of, 198–200
copyright dispute over, 196, 198
psychosexual aspects of, 197–200
Dracula, Jack, 18–19
"Dracula's Guest" (Stoker), 196, 198
Drake, Francis, *183*
Drakula, 50
Dresser, Norine, 343
drug addiction, 253–54, 349
Duchamp, Marcel, 320
Dunn, Nora, *332*

Earles, Daisy, 152, 153, 156
Earles, Harry, 65, 147–48, *149,* 152, 153
Earth vs. the Spider, 248
Eating Raoul, 372
E.C. Comics, *see* Entertaining Comics Group
Eckhardt, John, 145–46, *146, 152,* 156, 387
Eckhardt, Robert, 145–46
Edison, Thomas, 97, 128
Editor and Publisher, 88
Eggar, Samantha, *299*
Ehrenreich, Barbara, 350
Eisner, Lotte H., 48, 51
Elephant Man, 225, 298, 319–20
Elephant Man, The, 298, 317
Ellis, Bret Easton, 371–78, *374*
Ellroy, James, 376
"Emergo," 257
Endore, Guy, 181, 191
Englund, Robert, *306,* 330

Entertaining Comics Group (E.C. Comics), 230, *231,* 232, 233, 234, 235, 263–64, *271,* 358, 364, 383
Eraserhead, 298
Erdmann, Hans, 51
Ernst, Max, 132
Evans, Walter, 275–77
Evil Dead II, The, 325
Exorcist, The, 294–95, 324, 326
Exposition Internationale des Arts Décoratifs et Industriels Modernes (1925), 130–32
expressionism, 40, 51, 55, 130, 164, 166, 177, 181, 209

"Fall of the House of Usher, The" (Poe), 177
Famous Monsters of Filmland, 19, 269–74, *269, 270,* 315, 326, 358
Famous Players-Lasky, 139
Fangoria, 328–31, *329,* 360, 383–84
Faragoh, Francis Ford, 129
Farrell, Nancy, 223–24
Farrow, Mia, *286,* 293
Favazza, Armando R., 324
"Feminine Love of Horror, The," 126–27
Fiedler, Leslie, 23, 364
Fiend Without a Face, 252
Films in Review, 291
First National, 128
Fithian, T. B., 137
Fitzgerald, F. Scott, 153
Fitzgerald, Zelda, 153
5,000 Fingers of Dr. T., The, 237
Florescu, Radu, 83
Florey, Robert, 128–29, 130, 164, 213, 320
Flowers in the Attic (Andrews), 303
Fly II, The, 330
"Flying Purple People Eater," 267
"Foet" (Wilson), 305
Forbidden Planet, 124
Fort, Garrett, 129, 199
Fortune, 132
14th Street Museum, 156
Fox, 117, 218, 330
Fox, Sidney, 164*n*
Francis, Arlene, 163–67, *165*
Frankenheimer, John, 302
Frankenstein (1931 film), 16, 108, 110, 128–39, *133, 134,* 144, 145, 148, 162, 163, 182, 197, 226, 278, 382
audience reactions to, 135
casting of, 129–30, 164
censorship of, 137–38
design of, 130–32
Dracula on double-bill with, 202–5, *203, 204*
drowning scene in, 136–37
exploitation stunts and, 138–39
place and time of, 135–36
political metaphor in, 159
sources of, 134

Frankenstein: An Adventure in the Macabre
    (Webling), 97–98
Frankenstein; or, the Modern Prometheus
    (Shelley), 82, 83, 134, 294
    early film adaptations of, 97, 128
    feminist subtext of, 184
    film rights to, 128
    stage productions of, 95, 97–110, *101,*
        103, 105, 107
Frankenstein; or, the Vampire's Victim, 84
Frankenstein Meets the Wolf Man, 216–17,
    217
Frankenstein's monster, *101, 103, 105,*
        107, 131, 218
    as Christ, 189
    Dracula compared with, 81–82, 83–84,
        100, 311, 351
    Karloff as, *112,* 130, 132–37, 206–9
    machine aesthetic and, 132–33
    origin of, 82
    as primary horror icon, 19, 145, 159
    psychosexuality of, 184
    as vampire, 83–84
Freaks, 14, 15–17, 18, 21, 75, 145–59, *146,*
        149, 151, 154, 162, 168, 200, 206,
        345, 387
    casting of, 145–46, 150–52
    censorship of, 150, 155, 171, 172
    exploitation in, 153–55, 291
    as financial disaster, 158
    negative reactions to, 16, 153, 155–56,
        158
    political metaphor in, 159
    psychosexual aspects of, 158–59
    revival of, 290–92
    short story source of, 146–48
    story of, 16, 148–50
freak shows, 17–18, 19, 30
Freedman, Harold, 97, 128
Freeman, 39
Freud, Sigmund, 76
Freudianism, 77, 79, 91–92
Freund, Karl, 121–22, 166, 168, 181
Friedkin, William, 295
Friedman, David F., 290, 312
Frolic Theatre, 60
From Beyond, 313
Fromm, Erich, 250
Frye, Dwight, 134
Fulton (Helen Hayes) Theatre, 91
Fussell, Paul, 215–16

Gacy, John Wayne, 363
Gaines, William, 234–35
Galás, Diamanda, 342
Galeen, Henrik, 51
Gance, Abel, 205–6
Garbage Pail Kids, 303–4
Gardner, Gerald, 187
Garton, Ray, 344
Gasser, Lajos, 50
geeks, 28, 127

Gerald's Game (King), 379
Ghost of Frankenstein, 216
Ghoul, The, 204
Giant Claw, The, 248
Gide, André, 51–53
Giger, H. R., 301
Gilda Stories, The (Gomez), 348
"God Rest Ye Merry, Gentlemen" (Hem-
    ingway), 74
Godzilla, 248, *249,* 278
Goering, Hermann, 226–27
Goldbeck, Willis, 148
Goldman, Albert, 264
Goldwyn Company, 40, 43
Golem, The, 51, *52,* 134, 177
Gomez, Jewelle, 348
Googie's, 242, 244
Gordon, Leon, 148
Gordon, Mel, 58, 226
Gordon, Stuart, 313
Gore, Michael, 366
Gorky, Maxim, 31
Grand Guignol, 55–60, *56, 59,* 102, *183,*
    226–27
Grand Hotel, 150
Grau, Albin, 48–50
Gray, Nan, 200, *200*
Great Britain:
    horror movies banned in, 195, 205,
        218
    movie censorship in, 171, 174, 201
Great Depression, 114, *119,* 145, 162, 168–
    69
*Great Expectations: America and the Baby
    Boom Generation* (Jones), 354–
    55
Great Train Robbery, The, 32
Green, Betty, 154–55
Greenaway, Peter, 372
Greenwald, David S., 278
Gremlins, 272, 297
Gremlins 2: The New Batch, 326
Griffith, D. W., 32, 34*n,* 35, 64
Grogh, 54
Gross Anatomy, 325
Grosz, Karoly, 132
guillotines, as sideshow attraction, 29
Gwynne, Fred, 281
gypsies, 28

Hall, Mordaunt, 65
Hallatt, Henry, *101,* 104, 105
Hamilton, R. F. "Tody," 29
Hamilton Deane Company, 100
Hammer Films, 311, 339
Hammond, Percy, 91
Hampton, Benjamin, 46
Hanline, Maurice, 86
Harding, Lyn, 106–7, *107*
Harlow, Jean, 150, 158
Harlow: An Intimate Biography (Shulman),
    158

Harper's Bazaar, 19
Harris, Richard, 324
Harris, Robert, 194
Harris, Thomas, 372, 382
Harrison, Michael, 189*n*
Hart, William S., Jr., 124
Hartford Courant, 235
Hateley, Linzi, 368, *369*
Haunted Screen, The (Eisner), 51
Haunt of Fear, 230, 232
Hays, Will, 162, 190
Hays Office, 162, 171
   see also Production Code
Hayworth, Rita, 192
Haze, Jonathan, 242
Hearst newspapers, 39, 44
Heath, Russ, 230
Hellraiser series, 384
Hell's Angels, 129
Hemingway, Ernest, 74
Hilton, Daisy and Violet, 152, 153
Hitchcock, Alfred, 57, 311
Hitler, Adolf, 211–12
Hobart, Rose, 142
Hobson, Valerie, 187
Holden, Gloria, 199, *200*
Hollywood, Calif., as "city of suffering,"
   151
Hollywood Filmograph, 121
Hollywood Gothic (Skal), 50*n*
Hollywood Reporter, 201, 216–17
homosexuality, 178, 184–85, 200, *200,*
   234, 346, 348
Hoover, Herbert, 161
Hopkins, Anthony, 382, *383*
Hopkins, Miriam, 144
Hopper, Hedda, 244
Hopwood, Avery, 84
horror comics, 229–37, *231,* 335–36, *336*
   controversy over, 233–37
   Dance of Death as formula in, 230–31
   popularity of, 230
horror movies:
   Americanization of European settings in,
      136, 142, 213–15
   American literature and, 29, 200, 265; *see*
      also King, Stephen
   economic and class warfare metaphors
      in, 159
   end of first cycle of, 206, 218
   European, 60–61
   formulas followed in making of, 168,
      181, 218, 248, 255
   four primary icons of, 19, *20,* 145, 159
   modern art movements and, 55, 71, 114,
      130–32, 313
   1950s trends in, 247–48
   numbers of, 260
   physical deformation and mutilation in,
      19, 55–60, 65–74, 194–95, 206, 331
   political metaphors in, 41, 43, 168, 222–
      23, 247–48, 250–51

profitability of, 218, 220, 260
promotional gimmicks for, 257–59
protests against, 192, 195, 201–4, 251,
   293–94; *see also* censorship
psychology in, 180, 181, 191, 199, 255–
   56
psychosexual aspects of, 68, 73, 74–79,
   126–27, 140–41, 144, 158–59, 175,
   177, 184–85, 189, 191, 197–200,
   220, 277, 287–305, 320–24
revivals of, 202–4, 278, 335, 382
social commentary in, 257, 259
spoofs of, 174
as term, 144
see also movies
Horror of Dracula, 311
Horror of the Black Museum, 256
House, 386
House of Dracula, 217
House of Frankenstein, 217
House of Wax, 247
House on Haunted Hill, 257, *258*
Howard, Leslie, 129
Howe, James Wong, 192
Howling, The, 272, 315, 325
Hubert's Museum, 17–18, *17*
Hughes, Hatcher, 172
Hughes, Howard, 129
Hugo, Victor, 130
Humanoids from the Deep, 295
Hume, Cyril, 124
humor, horror and, 263–65, 296–97
Hunchback of Notre Dame, The, 66–67,
   69
Hunt, Martita, 185
Huntley, Raymond, *88,* 89
Hurlbut, William, 182, 184
Hush . . . Hush, Sweet Charlotte, 311–12
Huston, John, 138, 166
Hyams, Leila, *170*
Hyde, Buddy, 223

Incredible Shrinking Man, The, 250
Ingels, "Ghastly" Graham, 232
initiation rites, 356
   horror movies as metaphors for, 275–
      77, 278, 297, 331
Interview with the Vampire (Rice), 340, 344,
   346
Intolerance, 64
Invaders from Mars, 250–51
Invasion of the Body Snatchers, 250
Invasion of the Saucer Men, 252–53, *252*
Invisible Man, The, 182
Iron John (Bly), 356
Island of Lost Souls, 169–71, *170,* 194, 226
Island of the Alive, 298
It (King), 360, 362–64, *363,* 366, 375
It Came from Beneath the Sea, 248
It Lives Again, 297
"It's A Good Life" (Bixby), 361
It's Alive, 296, 297

I Walked with a Zombie, 221
I Was a Teenage Frankenstein, 255
I Was a Teenage Werewolf, 228, 255–56

J'Accuse, 205–6, 207
Jackson, Michael, 315–20, *317, 319,* 361
Jacob's Ladder, 386
Jaffray, Norman R., 174
Janowitz, Hans, 41–43
Januskopf, Der (The Head of Janus), 51
Japan:
    AIDS awareness in, *347*
    horror movies produced in, 248
    movie censorship in, 190–91
Jekyll/Hyde duality:
    as doppelganger, 139
    as primary horror icon, 19, 145, 159
    see also Dr. Jekyll and Mr. Hyde (1920);
        Dr. Jekyll and Mr. Hyde (1931);
        *Strange Case of Dr. Jekyll and Mr.
        Hyde, The*
JFK, 250
Jim Bludso, 64
Johann, Zita, 168
Johnny Got His Gun (Trumbo), 221
Jones, Carolyn, 282
Jones, Ernest, 191
Jones, Landon Y., 354–55
Journey's End, 129
Joy, Jason S., 116–17, 144, 161–63, 166,
    171
Joyce, James, 162
Jukes, Bernard, 88–89

KABC-TV, 239, 240, 244
Kael, Pauline, 295
Kanfer, Stefan, 134
Karloff, Boris, 134, 168, 204, 213, 279
    in *The Black Cat,* 177, 178, *179,* 180, 181
    in *The Body Snatcher,* 221
    in *Frankenstein, 112,* 128, 130, 132–37,
        160, 278
    Lugosi compared with, 169, 253
    Lugosi teamed with, 177, *179,* 194, 209,
        268
    in *Son of Frankenstein,* 206–9, *208*
    as World War II air-raid warden, 223–24
Kastenbaum, Robert, 345
Kazanjian, Aram, 167
Kefauver, Estes, 234–35
Kendrick, Walter, 365–66
Kennedy family, 281
Kerouac, Jack, 265
"Killers, The" (King), 271
King, Stephen, 277, 354–79, *359, 363*
    analysis of novels of, 355–57, 362–64
    background of, 271, 358
    critics' responses to, 364–66, 371
    Ellis compared with, 371, 375–78
    film versions of novels of, 366
    sales figures for books of, 358–60
    as transformation myth, 361

King Kong, 128, 171, 175–77, *176,* 204,
    211, 248
King's Row, 345
K.N.B. EFX Group, 325, 326
Kobal, John, 150–51
Koerner, Charles, 218
Kohner, Lupita Tovar, 116, 122
Kohner, Paul, *68,* 115, 122, 177
Korean War, 229, 251, 383
Kracauer, Siegfried, 43
Kramer, Hilton, 19–20
Kramer, Mimi, 370
Krieger, Paul, 190
Kroll, Jack, 370
Kronenberger, Louis, 95, 110
Kruger, Barbara, 305
Kruger, Otto, 199
Kubin, Alfred, 42–43
Kubrick, Stanley, 293*n,* 366
Kurtzman, Robert, 325

Ladies and Gentlemen, Lenny Bruce!! (Gold-
    man), 264
Laemmle, Carl, Jr., 109, 113, 116, 122,
    126, 128, 129, 164*n,* 166, 198
Laemmle, Carl, Sr., 67, *68,* 113, 115, 116,
    118, 137, 139, 268
Lajthay, Karoly, 50
Lanchester, Elsa, 171, 186, *188,* 189–
    90
Landau, Arthur, 158
Landis, John, 315, *316,* 317, 318
Landon, Michael, *228,* 255
latex foam, 312–13
Laughton, Charles, 169–71
Lee, Christopher, 311, 339
Le Fanu, J. Sheridan, 200
Legion of Decency, 182, 293
Leiber, Fritz, 222
Leni, Paul, 115–16, 122, 177
Lenny (Barry), 265
Leopard Man, The, 221
Leroux, Gaston, 63, 68
lesbianism, 200, *200*
    see also homosexuality
Levin, Ira, 292, 293
Levy, José, 86, 102
Lewis, Al, 281
Lewis, David, 130, 135
Lewis, Herschell Gordon, 312
Lewton, Val, 218, 220, 221
Life, 67, 241
Life Without Soul, 128
Lifton, Robert Jay, 225–26
"Lights Out," 221–22
liposuction, 321
Little Shop of Horrors, The, 242, 256
Little Theatre, 86, 102, 104, 106, 169
Live Girls (Garton), 344
Liveright, Horace, *111,* 134–35
    background of, 84, *85*

Dracula staged by, *80,* 84, 86, 88, *90,* 92, *93,* 96, 106*n*
   Frankenstein and, 95, 104–10, *107*
   later career of, 110–11
Lloyd Webber, Andrew, 367
London After Midnight, 77–78, *77,* 191
Look, 209, 284
Lopez, Berry Holstun, 212
Lorre, Peter, 181, *183,* 209
Lost Boys, The, 320
Lost World, The, 128, 175
Love and Death in the American Novel (Fiedler), 23
Love at First Bite, 339
Lovecraft, H. P., 82–83, 96–97, 313
Loy, Myrna, 150
Luce, Clare, 117
Ludlam, Harry, 216
Lugosi, Bela, 51, *123,* 140, 171, 199, 218, 226, 242, 245, *255,* 317
   in *The Black Cat,* 177, 178, *179,* 181
   Bow's affair with, 92–95, *93*
   character of, 89, 118, 164, 178
   in *Dracula,* 117–18, *117, 119,* 121, *121,* 124, 126–27, 197, 256, 278, 335
   Dracula delusions of, 118, 120
   final years of, 253–54
   in first stage production of *Dracula, 80,* 89–92
   Karloff compared with, 169, 253
   Karloff teamed with, 177, *179,* 194, 209, 268
   in *Mark of the Vampire,* 191, *193*
   in *Murders in the Rue Morgue,* 163, 164, 166, 333, 345
   in *The Return of the Vampire,* 222–23
   roller-skating by, 240
   in *Son of Frankenstein,* 209
   in test shooting of *Frankenstein,* 129
   3-D *Dracula* remake sought by, 247
   voice of, 89
   Weeks's three-day marriage to, 94–95
   in World War I, 178–80
   in World War II moral programs, 223
Lugosi, Hope Lininger, 254
Luxury, 117–18
lycanthropy, *see* werewolves
Lynch, David, 298
Lyne, Adrian, 386
Lynn, Jennie, 152
Lynn, Kenneth S., 74

Macabre, 256–57
McConnell, Frank, 142
McCoy, Horace, 201
MacDonald, Philip, 182
MacGowan, Kenneth, 38
Macgregor, Frances Cooke, 76–77
McKay, Hugh Bryan, 324
McLaglen, Victor, 65, 150
McMahan, Jeffrey N., 348

McNally, Raymond, 83
Mad, 235, 328
Mad Love, 181, *183,* 195, 205
Mailer, Norman, 373
Maliniak, Jacques W., 67
Mamoulian, Rouben, 141–42, 144
Man Called Horse, A, 324
Mandelbaum, Ken, 370
Mandell, Paul, 177
Manners, David, 118, 121–24, *121,* 168, 178, 180, *180,* 387–88
"Man or Machine," 41–42, 132
Mansfield, Richard, 139, 141
Man Who Laughs, The, 130, 151
Mapplethorpe, Robert, 18
March, Fredric, 142, *143,* 145
Mark of the Vampire, 191–92, *193,* 200, 205
Martin, 309
Marx, Samuel, 158, 206
Mary Shelley: Her Life, Her Fiction, Her Monsters (Mellor), 184
Mask of Fu Manchu, The, 171
"Masque of the Red Death, The" (Poe), 333–34
masturbation, 277
Maurey, Max, 57
Maw, The (Kubin), 42
Mayer, Carl, 41–43
Mayer, Louis B., 153, 158, 159, 191, 196
Mayfair Theatre, 166–67
MCA, 137
Melford, George, 122
Méliès, Georges, 31, 175
Mellor, Anne K., 184
Mengele, Josef, 195, 226, 321
menstruation, 277, 355
Menzies, William Cameron, 250
Merrick, John, 225, 298, 319–20
Méténier, Oscar, 55, 57
Metro-Goldwyn-Mayer (MGM), 34*n,* 64, 78, 115, 116, 181, 200, 206
   Freaks and, 16, 145–46, 148, 150, 153, 163, 290
   Mark of the Vampire and, 191–92
   Universal's legal disputes with, 191–92, 196, 198
microcephaly, 152
Miracle Man, The, 65
Miracles for Sale, 75, 206
Misery, 326
Model, Lisette, 18
Modern Primitives (Vale and Juno), 323
Money Changers, The, 46
"Monkey's Paw, The" (Jacobs), 232, 308, 362
Monogram, 152, 218
Monroe, Marilyn, 93
Monster, The (Wilbur), 84–85, 256
Monster Culture, 263–85, 328–31
"Monster Mash," 279, *280,* 281, 315, 378
"Monster Movies: A Sexual Theory" (Evans), 277

"Monster Movies and Rites of Initiation"
    (Evans), 275–77
Monster Walks, The, 171
Montagnier, Luc, 350
Mora, 191
Morris, Chester, 117
Mosher, Bob, 281
Motion Picture Association of America
    (MPAA), 328–30
Motion Picture Classic, 126–27
Motion Picture Herald, 139, 155
Motion Picture Producers and Distributors
    Associaton (MPPDA), 125, 137,
    144, 163, 171, 178, 182, 194
movies:
    auteur theory of, 291–92
    as Depression-era escape, 115, 168
    early history of, 31-32
    MPAA ratings of, 328–30
    silent vs. sound, 126
    television as competition for, 247, 259
    3-D, 247, 259
    see also horror movies
Moving Pictures (Schulberg), 201
Moving Picture World, 40, 44
Moving the Mountain (Davis), 288
Mullis, Kary, 350
Mummy, The, 168, 197
Munsey's Magazine, 146
"Munsters, The," 281–84, *283*
Murders in the Rue Morgue, 163–68, *165,*
    177, 226, 320, 333, 345
    casting of, 163–64
    censorship of, 166, 171
    expressionist style of, 164–66
    reactions to, 168
Murders in the Zoo, 171
Murnau, F. W., 48, 50–51, 68, 122, 140
music, in Monster Culture, 267, 315–18
Musil, Robert K., 278
mutation metaphors, 247–50
Mystery of the Wax Museum, 171, 172–74,
    173, 226
Mystic, The, 75

Nathan, George Jean, 81, 172
National Catholic Office for Motion Pic-
    tures, 293–94
National Council on Freedom from Cen-
    sorship, 171–72
National Organization for Women, 373
Naughton, David, 315, *316*
Nazi Doctors, The (Lifton), 225–26
NBC radio network, 221
NBC-TV, 349
necrophilia, 174
Needful Things (King), 371
Newsweek, 241, 370, 383
New York, 267, 370
New York, N.Y., 204
    The Cabinet of Dr. Caligari premiere in,
        38, 40

Dr. Jekyll and Mr. Hyde premiere in, 144
Dracula stage premiere in, 91
Frankenstein Meets the Wolf Man premiere
    in, 217
Freaks premiere in, *154,* 155
    Théâtre du Grand Guignol in, 60
New Yorker, 156, 175–77, 239, 281, 295,
    370
New York Herald Tribune, 71–73, 91
New York Post, 91, 303
New York State Censor Board, 155, 166,
    171–72
New York Times, 39, 60, 65, 115, 130, 147,
    192, 205, 220, 223–24, 250, 281,
    284, 318, 349, 383, 384
Nicotero, Greg, 325, 326
Nightmare on Elm Street series, *306,* 330,
    331, 362
Night of the Living Dead, 307–8, 309, 357
No Reason to Talk About It (Greenwald and
    Zeitlin), 278
Nosferatu, 48–53, *49,* 68, 86, 122, 141, 142,
    222, 265, 318, 348–49
*Not Since Carrie: 40 Years of Broadway Mu-
    sical Flops* (Mandelbaum), 370
Nurmi, Maila:
    attempted murder of, 245
    Dean's relationship with, 242–44, 246
    as Vampira, *238,* 239–42, 244, 245, 247,
        266, 337, 338

Oakie, Jack, 92
Oates, Joyce Carol, 347
Oboler, Arch, 221
O'Brien, Willis, 128, 175
Occhiogrosso, Peter, 267
O'Connor, John J., 384
Of Wolves and Men (Lopez), 212
Old Dark House, The, 182
O'Neill, Eugene, 96, 172
Only Yesterday, 78
On the Nightmare (Jones), 191
Open Book, An (Huston), 166
Orlac Händes (The Hands of Orlac), 51, *53,*
    181
O'Sullivan, Maureen, 201
Otis, James, 29
Ouspenskaya, Maria, 215, 217
Outside the Law, 64, 116

Packer, Al, 30
Paglia, Camille, 385
Paramount Pictures, 169, 385
    Dr. Jekyll and Mr. Hyde and, 141–42,
        144, 162
Paramount Publix Corporation, 108, 109
Parsons, Louella, 155
Patrick, Dora Mary, *105*
Patrick, Robert, 385
Peggy: The Story of One Score Years and Ten
    (Webling), 98
Penalty, The, 65, *66, 67,* 73

Penley, Constance, 320
"Percepto," 257–59
Perkins, Maxwell, 172
Persian Gulf War, 383–84
Persistence of Memory, The (Dalí), 114
Peter Pan, 320
Peterson, Dorothy, *80*
Petiot, Marcel, 227
Pet Sematary (King), 362, 366
"phallambulism," 68
Phantom of the Opera, The, 66–68, *70, 72,* 173, 177
Phantom of the Opera, The (Leroux), 63, 68
Philbin, Mary, *70*
Pichel, Irving, 142
Pickett, Bobby "Boris," 278–81, *280,* 315
Picture of Dorian Gray, The (Wilde), 139, 140
Pierce, Jack P., 130, 132, 189–90, 215, 326
pinheads, 15, 16, 152
Pinocchio, 216
"Pit and the Pendulum, The" (Poe), 195
Plan Nine from Outer Space, 247
plastic surgery, 167–68, 318–22
Playboy, 260, 268, 320, 328, 357–58
Plymouth Theatre, 141
Poe, Edgar Allan, 51, 57, 60, 163, 164, 166, 177, 189, 195, 333
Polanski, Roman, 288, 292
Pommer, Erich, 43
Porter, Edwin S., 32
posttraumatic stress syndrome, 311
Pound, Ezra, 46–47
"poverty row" thrillers, 218, 240
Presumption; or the Fate of Frankenstein, 101
Price, Vincent, 257, *258,* 315
Production Code, 116, 117, 161, 162
  see also censorship
Production Code Administration, 182, 186, 187, 189
Prophecy, 302
Psycho, 301, *310,* 311, 323, 378, 382
"psychoanalysis," origin of term, 55
"Purloined Letter, The" (Poe), 189

Queen of the Damned, The (Rice), 344, 348

Rabe, David, 308
Radio City Music Hall, 175, 211
radio horror and mystery shows, 221–22
Rakowitz, Daniel, 372
Randian, Prince, 152, 156
Randolph, Jane, 220
Rapf, Harry, 153
Rathbone, Basil, 209
Raven, The, 194, 195, 205
Raymond, Janice G., 323
Reagan, Ronald, 344, 345, 349, 353, 354, 372
Reagan's America (deMause), 344–45
Re-Animator, 313
Red Dragon (Harris), 372

Reed, Tom, 184
Reel Life, 34
Reinhardt, Max, 177
Reiss, Lionel, 40
religious organizations, censorship and, 162, 182, 293–94
Remco Industries, 284
Repulsion, 288
Return of the Ape Man, 218
Return of the Vampire, The, 222–23
Revenger's Tragedy, The (Tourneur), 263
rhinoplasty, 167
Rice, Anne, 200, 339–40, 344, 346, 348
Riesner, Dean, 239, 246–47
Right to Dream, The, 89
Rinehart, Mary Roberts, 84
RKO, 175, 218, 221
Road to Mandalay, The, 71
Robbins, Clarence Aaron "Tod," 64, 146, 147, 150
Robbins, Harold, 159
Robbins, Tim, 386
Robertson, John S., 140
Robinson, Edward G., 116
Robinson, George, 122
Robinson, William J., 192
Rocky Horror Picture Show, The, 54, 323
Rodan, 248
Roland (John Zacherle), 266–68
Romero, George, 307, 308, 309, 311, 357, *377*
Rose, Lloyd, 361
Rosemary's Baby, 292–94, *286*
Ross, Robert Robertson, 324
Rossitto, Angelo, 152, 387
Rothafel, S. L. "Roxy," 40, 43
Rubin, Bruce Joel, 386
Ruric, Peter, 178
Ruskin, John, 98
Russell, G. Malcolm, *101*
Rymer, James Malcolm, 83

St. John, Adela Rogers, 92
Salem's Lot (King), 274–75, 358–60, 365, 366
Sanders, Ken, 328–30
Saturday Evening Post, 174, 265
"Saturday Night Live," *332*
Savage, Robert, 93–94
Savini, Tom, 307–11, *309,* 325, 331, 384
Sayles, John, 315
Scheffauer, George, 39
Schildkraut, Joseph, 110
Schlitze, 152
Schoedsack, Ernest B., 175
Schreck, Max, *49, 50,* 141, 142
Schulberg, B. P., 144
Schulberg, Budd, 152, 200–201
Schumacher, Joel, 320
Schwarzenegger, Arnold, *380,* 384–85
science-fiction themes, in 1950s horror movies, 251–53

Scott, Ridley, 300
Seduction of the Innocent (Wertham), 234–36
See No Evil (Vizzard), 162
Seigmann, George A., 34, 35
Seldes, Gilbert, 114, 115
self-multilation, 323–24
Sells-Floto Circus, 30
Selznick, David O., 196, 198, 199, 218
Senate, U.S., horror comics hearings in, 234–35
Sennwald, André, 205
Shadowland, 46
Shaw, George Bernard, 86
Shearer, Norma, 153
Shelley, Mary, 82, 83, 135, 137, 184, 186
Shelley, Percy Bysshe, 82, 137
Sherriff, Robert C., 129, 198, 199
Sherwood, Robert Emmet, 129
"Shindig," 279
Shining, The (King), 360, 366
"Shock Theatre," 265–66, 364
Shortt, Edward, 195
Show, The, 75, *75*
Shulman, Irving, 158
Siamese twins, 148–49, 152, 153
sideshows, 29–30, 65
Siegel, Don, 250
Silence of the Lambs, The, 382–83, *383*
Silence of the Lambs, The (Harris), 372, 382
Simmons, Jack, 242, 244
Simon and Schuster, 371, 373, 376
Sinclair, Upton, 44–45, 46
Singerman, Sydney, 190
Siodmak, Curt, 78, 213, 215
Skinner, B. O., 172, 190
slasher movies, 297
Smell-o-Vision, 259
Smith, Dick, 307, 326, *327*
Snow, Elvira, 152
Snow White and the Seven Dwarfs, 211, 240
Something Wicked This Way Comes (Bradbury), 25
somnambulism, 168–69, 251
Sondheim, Stephen, 372
Son of Frankenstein, 206–9, *208*
Sontag, Susan, 21–22, 349–50
Spacek, Sissy, *352*, 366
Sparks, Robert, 138
special effects, 307–15, 325–27
Spielberg, Steven, 271–72, 274–75
"Spine Chillers, The" (Jaffray), 174
splatter films, 312, 326, 334
"Spurs" (Robbins), 146–48
Stand by Me, 366
Starlight, 139
Steinem, Gloria, 269–70
Stenn, David, 93
Stern, Edith, 95
Stevenson, Robert Louis, 51, 139
Stich, Sidra, 132
Sticks and Bones, 308–9
Stoker, Bram, 50, 82–83, 196, 217

Stoker, Florence, 50, 51, 84, 86, 87, 88–89, 110, 196, 198
Stone, Oliver, 250
stop-motion animation, 175
stop-motion lap dissolves, 314
Stork Woman (Betty Green), 154–55
Strait-Jacket, 312
Strange, Glenn, 218
Strange Case of Dr. Jekyll and Mr. Hyde, The (Stevenson):
  real-life inspiration for, 139
  silent-film versions of, 51, 139–41
  stage versions of, 141
  see also Dr. Jekyll and Mr. Hyde (1931); Jekyll/Hyde duality
Strickfaden, Kenneth, 135
Stromberg, Hunt, Jr., 240
Struss, Karl, 142
Student von Prag, Der (*The Student of Prague*), 51, 226
Suffer the Children, 289–90
Sullivan, Thomas Russell, 139
Sun Also Rises, The (Hemingway), 74
surrealism, 47, 48, 54–55, 71, 114
Sweeney Todd: The Demon Barber of Fleet Street, 372

Talbot, Dan, 21, 265
Tales from the Crypt, 230
"Tales from the Crypt," 384
Tammen, Harry H., 30
Tarantula, 248
Tartikoff, Brandon, 385
Taylor, Dwight, 153
Technicolor, 173
teenagers, as targeted market, 255
television:
  blandness of, 239
  as competition for movies, 247, 259
  late-night horror movies on, 240, 265–68, 291
  monster-based series on, 281–84
Terminator, The, 384–85
Terminator 2: Judgment Day, *380*, 384–85
Thalberg, Irving, 64, 148, 150, 153
thalidomide, 290–91, 386
Théâtre du Grand Guignol, 55–60, *56*, *59*, *183*, 226–27
Théâtre-Libre, 55
Them, 248
Thesiger, Ernest, 185–86, 381
They Call Me Carpenter (Sinclair), 44–45
They Shoot Horses, Don't They? (McCoy), 201
Thing, The, 313, *314*
This Island Earth, 251
Thomson, David, 70
Thorndike, Sibyl, 86*n*, 102
3-D movies, 247, 259
Three Studies for Figures at the Base of a Crucifixion (Bacon), 224–25, *224*, 313

"Thriller," 315–18, *317*
Time, 91, 155, 227, 365
Times (London), 102–4, 195
Timpone, Anthony, 328, 331
Tingler, The, 257–59, *260*
Toby Tyler, or Ten Weeks with the Circus
    (Otis), 29
Tourneur, Cyril, 263
Tourneur, Jacques, 218
Tovar, Lupita, 116, 122
toys, as horror movie spin-offs, 263, 274–
    75, 284
Transsexual Empire, The (Raymond), 323
transsexuals, 322–23
transvestites, 152, 227
Treasure Island (Stevenson), 139
Tree, Dorothy, 167
Trumbo, Dalton, 221
Turner, George E., 135
Twentieth Century Fox, 117, 218, 330
"Twilight Zone," 361, 364
Twilight Zone: The Movie, 361
2001: A Space Odyssey, 39, 293*n*

Ulmer, Edgar G., 177–81, 201
Ulmer, Shirley, 177, 178
Ulysses (Joyce), 162
" 'Uncanny,' The" (Freud), 76
Undying Monster, The, 218
Unholy Three, The, 64–65, 71, 116, 147,
    201
Union des Gueules Cassées, 66, 206
Universal Pictures, 64, 67, 151, 205, 217,
    265, 281
    The Black Cat and, 177, 178, 181
    Bride of Frankenstein and, 182, 189, 190
    Dracula and, 16, 109–10, 113, 115, 117,
        122, 124–27, 146, 148, 162, 335
    Dracula's Daughter and, 195–200
    Frankenstein and, 16, 128, 129, 132, 134,
        137–38, 148, 162
    horror movie profits of, 218
    horror movies dominated by, 181
    MGM's legal disputes with, 191–92,
        196, 198
    Murders in the Rue Morgue and, 163–66
    toys based on monster characters of, 274
    Werewolf of London and, 194
    The Wolf Man and, 213
Unknown, The, 62, 71–73, 75, 76, 345

vagina dentata, 78
Valentino, Rudolph, 64
Vampira, *see* Nurmi, Maila
Vampire, The (Burne-Jones), 55
Vampire Lesbians of Sodom, 348
vampires, 237, *336*
    American literature and, 340, 343–44,
        346, 348
    blood fetishists and, 334–43
    Browning's first use of, 78
    Catholic Church and, 347–48

female, 196–200, 294, 335
first movie appearance of, 48–51
Frankenstein's monster as, 83–84
Gide's view of, 51–53
incest guilt and, 191
invitations required by, 113
as primary horror icon, 19, 48
as psychological compulsion, 199
werewolves and, 212–13
see also specific movies
Vampires Anonymous (McMahon), 348
"vamps," 89, 93
Vampyre, The (Polidori), 82, 83
Vandervoort, Katherine K., 202–4
Van Enger, Charles, 68
Van Sloan, Edward, 106, *121,* 138, 168
Variety, 38, 44, 60, 110, 116, 144, 155–56,
    204, 282
Varney the Vampyre (Rymer), 83
Vault of Horror, 229, 230, 335
Veidt, Conrad, *36,* 41, 51, *53,* 115–16,
    130, 132, 151, 164, 181
Verney, Peter, 29
Vietnam War, 215, 291, 295, 307–8, 311,
    386
Village of the Damned, 288–89, *289*
Villarias, Carlos, *123*
Virgin of Stamboul, The, 64
Visaroff, Michael, 191
Vizzard, Jack, 162
voodoo, 201

Wagner, Sam, 156
Waite, Robert G. L., 211–12
Walker, Alexander, 74*n*
Walsh, Raoul, 34, 64
Walt Disney, 216, 240
Warhol, Andy, 21–22
Warner Brothers, 172, 174
War of the Colossal Beast, 250
Warren, James, 268–71, *270,* 285, 326
Warshow, Robert, 236
Wartime (Fussell), 215–16
Washington Post, 168
Waterloo Bridge, 129
Watterson, Bill, 372
Webling, Lucy, *99*
Webling, Peggy:
    background of, 98–100, *99*
    and first stage adaptation of *Frankenstein,*
        97–98, 100–101, 102, 104, 106, 108,
        128
Webster, Aileen "Webby," 118, 120
Webster, Nicholas, 118–21
Weeks, Beatrice, 94–95
Wegener, Paul, 51, *52*
Weird Tales, 96, *210,* 222
Wells, H. G., 169
Wells, Jacqueline, 180, *180*
Werewolf of London, 194, 205, 213
werewolves, *213, 237*

werewolves (*continued*)
  vampires and, 212–13
Wertham, Fredric, 233–37, 243, 244, 335, 373
West, Mae, 21, 242
West, Nathanael, 15, 158
West of Zanzibar, 75
Whale, James, *185,* 199
  Bride of Frankenstein directed by, 182–89, 320
  "camp" sensibility of, 184–85
  Frankenstein directed by, 129, 130, 132, 135, 137
"Whirl of Mirth, The," 31
White, Ed, 266
White, Robb, 259
White Zombie, 168–69
Wicked Darling, The, 64
Wiene, Robert, 43, 51
Wilbur, Crane, 84, 256
Wilde, Oscar, 140
"Wild Man of Borneo," 28
Wilkinson, J. Brooke, 205
Willard, John, 85
Willard & King Company, 31
"William Wilson" (Poe), 51
Wilson, Alice, 64
Wilson, F. Paul, 305
Winer, Linda, 370
Winfrey, Oprah, 384
"Wish You Were Here" (Ingels), 232–33
"Witch Doctor," 267
Witch of Timbuctoo, The, 201
Wizard of Oz, The, 148
Wolf, Leonard, 385–86
Wolf, Naomi, 321
Wolf Man, The, 213–15, *214,* 218, 313–14
Wolfson, P. J., 181
wolves:
  Hitler's fascination with, 211–12
  in symbolism and mythology, 212
  see also werewolves

women's clubs, 236
  censorship and, 162
Wood, Edward D., Jr., 247, 253
Wood, Robin, 300
Woods, James, *332*
Woolf, Edgar Allan, 148
Woollcott, Alexander, 91
World War I, 318, 386, 388
  artists and writers as affected by, 47–48, 58
  The Black Cat and, 177–78, 181
  Lugosi in, 178–80
  maimed veterans of, 65–66, 127, 185–86, 205–6
World War II, 386, 388
  atrocities in, 225–26, 227, 229
  morale programs in, 223
  propaganda in, 221–22
  sanitization of brutality in, 215–16
  U.S. entry into, 222
  vampirism in, 216
WOR-TV, 267
WPLJ-TV, 266
Wrangell, Basil, 153
Wray, Fay, 167, *173*
Wright, Willard Huntington, 38–39
Wyatt, Jane, 199
Wyman, Jane, 345

Yarbro, Chelsea Quinn, 344
Years of Indiscretion (Hanline), 86
Years of the Locust, The (Seldes), 114
Youngson, Jeanne, 343
Yuzna, Brian, 313, 325

Zacherle, John (Roland/Zacherley), *262,* 266–68, 279n, 315
Zehner, Harry H., 198
Zeitlin, Steven J., 278
Zola, Émile, 55
zombies, 168–69